TOWARD ECONOMIC COOPERATION IN ASIA

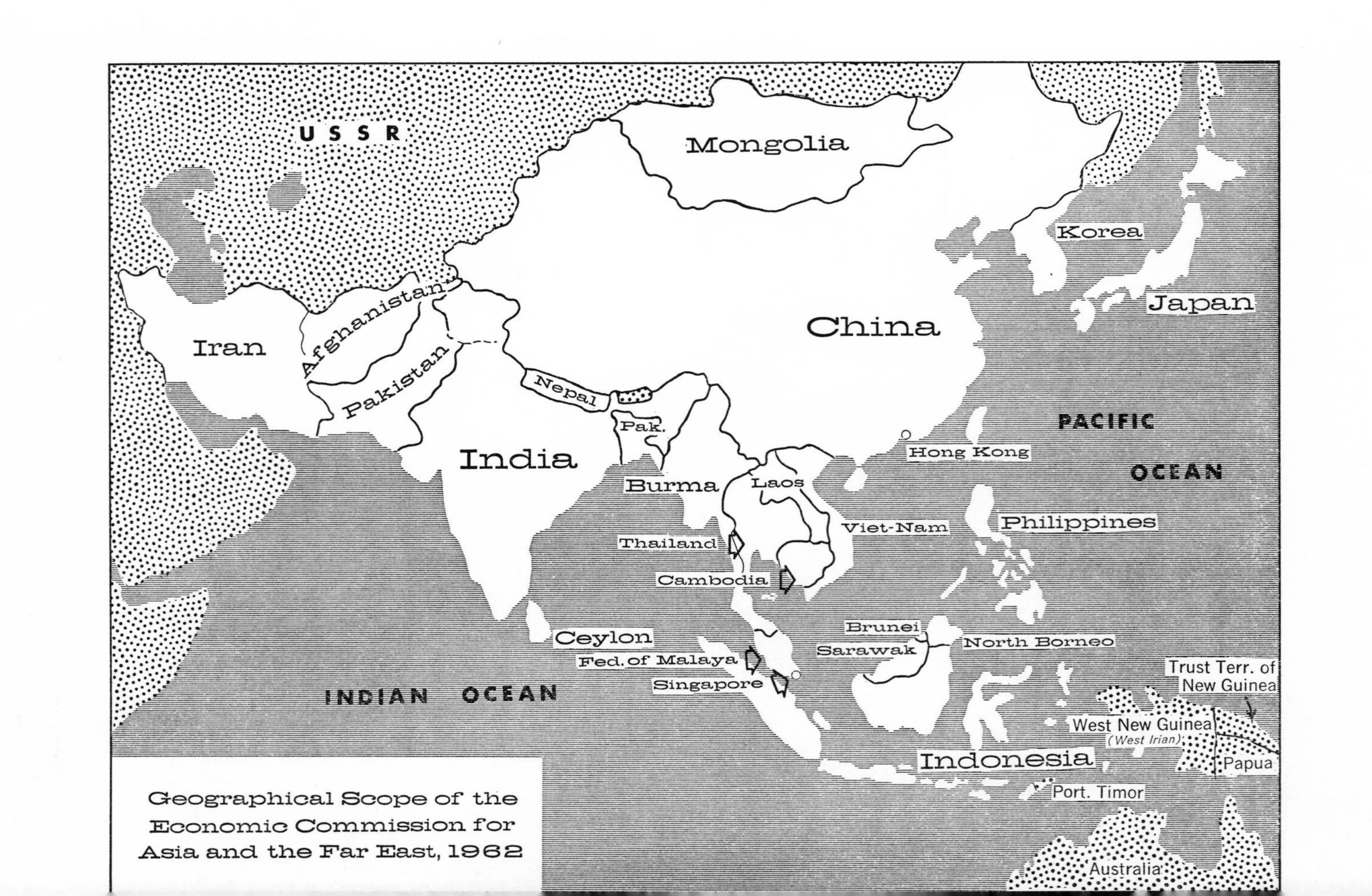

Geographical Scope of the Economic Commission for Asia and the Far East, 1962

Toward Economic Cooperation in Asia

The United Nations Economic Commission for Asia and the Far East

by DAVID WIGHTMAN

Published for the Carnegie Endowment for International Peace

New Haven and London, Yale University Press

1963

Designed by John O. C. McCrillis,
set in Linotype Baskerville type,
and printed in the United States of America by
Vail-Ballou Press, Inc., Binghamton, N.Y.

Library of Congress catalog card number: 63-10890

Preface

In the autumn of 1958 the Carnegie Endowment for International Peace commissioned me to write an historical appraisal of the United Nations Economic Commission for Asia and the Far East (ECAFE). The assignment had its origin in a resolution passed by the Commission at its tenth anniversary session in 1957 requesting the Executive Secretary "to arrange for the early publication of a history of the first decade of the Commission." The Secretariat had not proceeded far with the preparation of an official history when, on the suggestion of Mr. W. R. Malinowski of the United Nations Department of Economic and Social Affairs, Mr. C. V. Narasimhan, the then Executive Secretary of ECAFE, decided that a completely independent history of the Commission would be more useful. The Carnegie Endowment agreed to sponsor the study and the Ford Foundation generously provided the financial support that made it possible. The duties of a university teacher and the limitations of an author approaching Asia as a complete stranger have made it a lengthier undertaking than was originally expected. One compensation, perhaps, is that the study now covers the first fifteen years of ECAFE and not simply its first decade. The opinions expressed and conclusions reached are those that seemed valid on the basis of the information available up to the middle of 1962.

The book makes no pretense to be a critique of the approaches to economic development commonly propounded and accepted in the region by economic theorists and practitioners. But as the writing progressed, I began seriously to doubt the applicability of some of the concepts their analysis has frequently employed. Concepts such as savings and employment or underemployment rest on assumptions about human conditions, attitudes, responses, types of behavior and ways of organizing it, which approximate well enough to the social realities of the economically advanced countries of the West out of which they were born, but do not appear to correspond in the same way to much of the social realities of Asia. Distinctions between consumption and savings, for instance, have been drawn with a courage that is little short of astonishing. It does not, however, lie within the scope of this study or the competence of the author to attempt a searching scientific examination of the extent to which the noneconomic assumptions underlying the tools of economic analysis fashioned in Western societies fit the social conditions of Asian societies. That is a task that must be left to other and greater minds. If words like savings and underemployment appear at various places in this book, it is only because it seemed safer to follow the terminology of the economist than to flounder about in the deep waters of methodology.

The proceedings and activities of the United Nations are frequently misunderstood or misinterpreted, and not always unintentionally, by those who inform and influence public opinion in its member countries. A good deal of criticism has recently been directed against the United Nations in Western countries, for instance, because it is being used in ways they never intended or expected. In part this reflects a failure to grasp that the membership produced by the liquidation of colonial power has inevitably brought into the United Nations a whole range of diplomatic concerns that were not the predominant ones of its founder members. The appointment of U Thant to succeed Dag Hammarskjold as Secretary-General was an important *signum temporis*. Another and earlier symptom of the same trend was the creation of regional economic commissions for Asia and the Far East, Latin America, and then Africa. Largely through these organizations the United Nations has pioneered the path of economic development through international cooperation. Perhaps I may be permitted to hope, therefore, that this study will not only illuminate the historical significance of ECAFE and its sister regional commissions, particularly the one for Africa, but also help in a modest way to develop and strengthen their functions.

The study is by no means based solely on publicly available sources of information. During the course of lengthy field trips in 1959 and 1961, I visited and interviewed innumerable government and United Nations officials in Afghanistan, Burma, Ceylon, India, Indonesia, Japan, Malaya, Pakistan, the Philippines, South Viet-Nam, Taiwan, Thailand; Washington, New York, and London. Delegates from these and other countries were also interviewed at the annual sessions of the Commission in 1959 and 1961 and, in the latter year, at some meetings of its subsidiary bodies as well. Many of those most directly concerned with the past and present fortunes of ECAFE have, in fact, collectively contributed a great deal to the writing of this history. Among a host of useful contributions, those of Dr. P. S. Lokanathan, the first Executive Secretary of ECAFE, Professor Gunnar Myrdal, Mr. P. J. Stent, Mr. David K. Owen, and Mr. Harold E. Caustin were particularly appreciated. I should also like to express my gratitude to Mr. C. V. Narasimhan, and the Secretariat of ECAFE, especially U Nyun, its present Executive Secretary, and Mr. V. M. Bhatt, as well as to Mr. C. Hart Schaaf, the Executive Agent of the Committee for Co-ordination of Investigations of the Lower Mekong, and Mr. Walter Hecht of the United Nations Department of Economic and Social Affairs, for the facilities they granted and for their many valuable insights into the subject matter of the book. Above all, I owe a singularly large debt to the inspiration, unflagging interest, and wise counsel of Mr. Malinowski. The Carnegie Endowment and Miss Anne Winslow, its Editor-in-Chief, provided sundry helpful services including the editing and indexing of the manuscript and were very forbearing of missed deadlines. My wife and family endured with heartening understanding the long and unsettling experience of never being quite sure whether I really belonged to them.

It only remains to emphasize that the author alone is responsible for the views expressed and errors made.

DAVID WIGHTMAN

University of Birmingham
July 1962

Contents

PART FOUR

PERSPECTIVE VIEW

Abbreviations

AFETC	Asia and Far East Travel Commission
ASA	Association of Southeast Asia
BTAO	Bureau of Technical Assistance Operations
CAFEA	Commission on Asian and Far Eastern Affairs
ECA	Economic Commission for Africa
ECAFE	Economic Commission for Asia and the Far East
ECE	Economic Commission for Europe
ECLA	Economic Commission for Latin America
ECOSOC	Economic and Social Council
EEC	European Economic Community
EFTA	European Free Trade Association
EPTA	Expanded Programme of Technical Assistance
EPU	European Payments Union
ERP	European Recovery Program
FAO	Food and Agriculture Organization
GATT	General Agreement on Tariffs and Trade
IAEA	International Atomic Energy Agency
IBRD	International Bank for Reconstruction and Development
ICAO	International Civil Aviation Organization
ICC	International Chamber of Commerce
ICS	Indian Civil Service
ILO	International Labour Organisation
IMF	International Monetary Fund
ITU	International Telecommunication Union
IUOTO	International Union of Official Travel Organizations
NATO	North Atlantic Treaty Organization
NGO'S	Nongovernmental organizations
NSGT	Non-Self-Governing Territories
OPA	Asian Productivity Organization

OEEC Organization for European Economic Co-operation

SCAP Supreme Commander of the Allied Powers in Japan
SEATO South East Asia Treaty Organization
SITC Standard International Trade Classification

TAA Technical Assistance Administration
TAB Technical Assistance Board
TAC Technical Assistance Committee
TARS Technical Assistance Recruitment Services

UNESCO United Nations Educational, Scientific and Cultural Organization
UNRRA United Nations Relief and Rehabilitation Administration

WFTU World Free Trade Unions
WHO World Health Organization
WMO World Meteorological Organization

Note: All documents and resolutions cited in the footnotes throughout this book are documents of various United Nations bodies, unless otherwise stated. The Official Records of the General Assembly and of ECOSOC are cited as GAOR and ECOSOC,OR, respectively.

PART ONE

PRELUDE TO COOPERATION

CHAPTER 1

Introducing the Regional Setting

The most striking geographical fact about the region covered by ECAFE is its vast expanse. Stretching from Iran through Indonesia to Japan and including mainland China and Taiwan,[1] its boundaries encompass from one-sixth to one-seventh of the world's land surface. Its physical features have also been cast in heroic mold. Great mountain chains, plateaus, river basins, and seas divide up the region and control its climate. Thus the Himalayas protect India from the cold winds that blow outward from central Asia in winter. But where this air passes into the region over water, it becomes moisture-laden and brings snow or rain to central and southern China, Japan, the Philippines, and Ceylon. Apart from these areas and those lying close to the Equator, the region is practically rainless in the winter half of the year. Its rainy period is the summer when the winds blow inward from the ocean and the monsoon bursts suddenly and violently. Where the monsoon comes into contact with high mountain ranges near the coast, the resulting rainfall is very heavy indeed.

India, the Indo-China Peninsula, and south China have a typically monsoon climate with cool and hot dry seasons followed by a rainy season. The summer rainfall of central and northern China and Japan is due to similar causes but their winters are cooler

1. Throughout this book China, Nationalist China, or Taiwan will be the names used for the Republic of China, and Communist China, mainland China, or Peking the names used for the Chinese People's Republic (CPR). UN publications refer to the two countries as China:Taiwan, and China:mainland. Since Communist China is not represented in ECAFE, although it does lie within its geographical region, it is virtually excluded from the scope of this study.

and less dry than in the tropical monsoon areas. Indonesia, Malaya, and, in modified degree, Ceylon, have uniformly high temperatures all the year round and no typically dry season. Only in the western part of the region, cut off from the oceans by distance and mountains, are the rainfall low and the temperatures extreme. The climate of Asia and the rhythm of the monsoon in particular profoundly affect the daily and secular life, the work and rituals of its peoples. Such is their dependence on the monsoon, for instance, that any uncertainty in its timing or incidence may spell for millions of them the difference between food and famine.

Within this physical setting live over half the world's population. Its distribution, however, is very uneven. India, with about 430,000,000 people, and mainland China with probably around 700,000,000 people, together account for over 70 per cent of the region's total population. Indonesia, Japan, and Pakistan each have between 90,000,000 and 100,000,000 people; Burma, Iran, the Philippines, South Korea, and Thailand between 20,000,000 and 30,000,000 and Afghanistan, Ceylon, South Viet-Nam, and Taiwan between 10,000,000 and 15,000,000.[2] All other ECAFE countries have each under 10,000,000 people. Roughly speaking the crude birth rate of the region, not counting Japan, is about double and the crude death rate about the same as the typical rates for Western countries. In no other region of the world is population pressure so great. Rates of population growth of 3 per cent or more per annum are experienced in several Asian countries. Assuming no major changes in existing fertility and mortality rates, the total population of the region, including Communist China, will double in about twenty years and thus equal by then the total population of the world today. The prospect is alarming in the extreme. At best, it means that Asians will have to devote a large part of their current development efforts to defending, rather than raising, their living standards. At worst, it

2. Henceforth, for simplicity, the following countries will be known as:
 a. South Korea (for the Republic of Korea).
 b. Thailand (for Siam). (In June 1939 Siam changed its name to Thailand and, after the invasion of Japan, declared war on the Allies. During the peace negotiations in September 1945, to avoid a minor point of irritation with Britain, which never recognized the new name, Thailand became Siam once more. In August 1948 the country was again renamed Thailand.)
 c. South Viet-Nam (for the Republic of Viet-Nam).

is not inconceivable that drastic Malthusian checks will begin to operate within a generation.

The population of the region is distributed unevenly not only between but within countries. Apart from the dense concentrations of people to be found in many Asian cities, the most congested areas are the alluvial plains where climate and soil favor the cultivation of land by age-old techniques. Judged by the ratio of rural population to arable land it is, in fact, the most densely populated region of the world. But there are anomalies. Burma, Thailand, and the Indo-China Peninsula are relatively empty compared with India and Pakistan. It is no coincidence that these areas have drawn people from India and China in the past and include the region's principal food-exporting countries. Again, the congestion of Java stands out in sharp contrast to the rest of the Indonesian Archipelago. From the standpoint of Asian economic development, however, population density in itself means little. What matters is the capacity of economic activity to support increasing numbers of people.

Agriculture is the dominant economic activity of the region. It accounts in most ECAFE countries for more than 40 per cent of the national output and 60 per cent of the gainfully occupied population; in some cases the proportions exceed 50 per cent of the national output and 70 per cent of the gainfully occupied population. As industry is a rather small sector of the economies of all Asian countries, except Japan, it is the level of agricultural productivity that mainly determines the standard of living of their peoples. No simple relationship exists, however, between dependence on agriculture and living standards. Thailand, for instance, has a larger proportion of its gainfully occupied population in agriculture but a higher living standard than India and Pakistan. The governing factor is the kind of agriculture that geography and history have determined. Thus plantation agriculture, which has many of the characteristics of modern forms of economic organization, provides Ceylon and Malaya with higher per capita incomes than most ECAFE countries.

To attempt to give Asian living standards a quantitative meaning, however, would be a highly suspect statistical exercise. Even if reliable figures were available, serious conceptual difficulties would remain. For one thing the composition of their national production and consumption is very different from that of economically advanced countries. It is enough to emphasize that by comparison with the latter, they are all, with the exception of Japan [3] and Malaya, very poor indeed. Furthermore, because their income distribution is believed to be more unequal than that of the developed countries and may be getting more unequal still, it seems probable that the bulk of Asian peoples enjoy an income well below the already very low national averages calculated for these countries. The generally accepted prescription for this problem is to shift resources out of agriculture into industry. But their very poverty makes it difficult for ECAFE countries to devote a larger proportion of their national resources to building up industrial capacity. This vicious circle of low productivity and poverty is further aggravated by the one-sided dependence of their economies on the production and export of a narrow range of primary products.

The ECAFE region exports predominantly primary products in return for a large part of its requirements of consumer goods and most of the equipment and raw materials needed for its industrial development. About two-thirds of its international trade is with countries outside the region. It is a major supplier of the rice, rubber, tea, jute, and jute products entering international trade and a substantial contributor to world trade in oils and oil seeds, cotton, sugar, pepper, hides, and skins. As individual ECAFE countries depend on a narrow range of these commodities for the bulk of their export income, fluctuations in world prices and in their terms of trade are of vital concern to them. It has not been uncommon in the post-World War II period for their export proceeds to rise or fall by 15 per cent from one year to the next and in extreme cases by 30 to 45 per cent. Raw material exporters have suffered more than food exporters. Furthermore, because import prices have in general varied less than export prices, the terms of trade of ECAFE countries have tended to fluctuate in line with the unit value of their exports. In other words, their capacity to import from export earnings has also fluctuated substantially. Indeed, through the working of world market forces they have lost very much more foreign exchange than they have gained

3. For other obvious reasons also, Japan does not fit most of the broad generalizations made about the ECAFE region in this brief introduction.

through foreign aid. The long-run answer to the problem is for them to diversify production and trade. But although most Asian countries have set their sights on industrial development, the progress made in this direction during the past ten years has been very limited.

Before World War II Japan was the only country in the region with a well-developed industrial base. China and India had some industry but all other Asian countries had to start their postwar industrial development virtually from scratch. At the end of the last decade the region's industrial output was only about one-sixteenth of the world's output of manufactured goods and Japan alone accounted for almost 50 per cent of the region's output. The share of industry in national output and employment in most ECAFE countries is much less than the share of agriculture. In Burma, India, Pakistan, the Philippines, Taiwan, and Thailand the contribution of manufacturing to total output ranges from 12 to 18 per cent only. Outside Japan and possibly the Philippines and Taiwan as well, the proportion of the gainfully occupied population in manufacturing nowhere exceeds 11 per cent. Apart from Japan and mainland China, only India has enough known coal and iron ore resources at present to permit any concentration on the development of heavy industry. Otherwise manufacturing in the region largely means the production of consumer goods. Textiles and food processing are the two main industrial activities. The former predominates, for instance, in India and Pakistan and the latter in the Philippines and Taiwan. Both activities account in most ECAFE countries for between 45 and 75 per cent of total manufacturing employment and for at least 60 per cent of value added by manufacturing. They also explain why small-scale rural industries dominate the pattern of their manufacturing output and employment.

Nearly all ECAFE countries are pursuing the objectives of economic development through a considerable amount of government activity, direction, and planning. The completeness, intensity, and effectiveness of this effort, however, have varied widely. So have the results. Apart from Japan and Taiwan, which achieved much better performances, aggregate income in the region has grown at an annual average rate of between 3 and 5 per cent during the last decade. This compares favorably, it is true, with recent growth rates in many developed countries. But when allowance is made for population increase, per capita income in most ECAFE countries has grown only at about or below 2 per cent per annum. Consumption per head has also grown very slowly or negligibly. Agricultural production seems to have increased rather less than aggregate income. It would appear that the extremely low productivity of Asian agriculture has not risen markedly during the last decade. On the evidence available for a few countries industrial production has risen much more impressively, but then it started from a very small base. Judged by the rather greater proportion of their planned expenditures devoted to transport, communications, and power than to manufactures and mining, most ECAFE countries are still primarily concerned with building up the infrastructure, the basic facilities and services that industrial development requires.

It is admittedly difficult to select meaningful indicators of economic growth. Moreover, some of the important results of development efforts—for instance, creating new attitudes and institutions or more rational behavior patterns—are not susceptible to measurement. Even so, it is difficult to escape the impression that, despite the lavish attention it has received, economic progress in the region during the last decade has been far from impressive. It has certainly been below expectations. Only Hong Kong, the Philippines, and Taiwan, as well as Japan, have made significant economic strides. But this hardly outweighs the fact that three of the region's most populous countries, India, Indonesia, and Pakistan, have recorded, respectively, a slow rate of growth, a declining rate of growth, and economic stagnation.

Among the major impulses to economic development in the region since World War II has been the achievement of political independence by one Asian country after another. Before the war a vast area from Baluchistan to the South China Sea, except for Thailand, lay under direct European control or, as in the case of the Philippines, United States tutelage. The present ECAFE region then contained only six sovereign states: Afghanistan, China, Iran, Japan, Nepal, and Thailand. In the postwar period not far short of 600,000,000 people in the region have been liberated from colonial rule and the number of sovereign states has risen to seventeen.[4] The Philippines gained its independence in 1946, India and Pakistan in 1947, and Burma and Ceylon in 1948. In the latter year the Republic of Korea was established. Indonesia achieved complete sovereignty at the end of 1949 and Cambodia, Laos, and South Viet-Nam at the end of 1954. Finally in 1957 Malaya became fully independent.

The achievement of political independence was a traumatic experience which confronted the new governments with immense problems and prospects. In the case of India and Pakistan, independence was accompanied by the terrible disorders, bloodshed, and forced migrations that followed the partitioning of British India. Colonial rule was liquidated hectically in Burma and violently in Indonesia and Viet-Nam. Civil disturbances in these three countries have continued to plague their political stability. Internal rebellion also followed independence in the Philippines and delayed it in Malaya. The body politic of Laos has been torn apart by warring factions and Cold War politics. These internal splits and tensions and the upsurge of centrifugal forces in the newly independent countries have tended to weaken the authority of the state. The legacy of resistance and disobedience to authority, especially where independence was actively fought for, has made "direct action" a continuing part of political activity. In some cases the ethnic minorities left behind in the retreat of colonial rule have complicated the struggle for internal cohesion. Political concepts borrowed from the West are having to be adapted to Asian conditions. In several countries the process has entailed the replacement of outwardly democratic forms of government by authoritarian regimes. But whether democratic or dictatorial, a strong impression remains that in none of the newly independent countries is the authority of the state powerfully exercised to enforce the social reforms and disciplines modernization necessitates. Some have had to build up new armies, police forces, and administrations virtually from scratch. In other more fortunate cases such as India, the tasks of economic development and the demands of national security have considerably expanded them. It is hardly surprising, therefore, that public administration and defense have absorbed an increasing share of

4. Excluding the governments of North Viet-Nam and North Korea.

the national incomes of ECAFE countries. What is more remarkable is that most of the new states have not fallen apart at the seams.

In addition to the problems of asserting the authority of the state over their territorial inheritance, the new governments had to begin to weld their peoples into national communities. In some countries, Ceylon and the Philippines for instance, a strong sense of national unity was manifest from the outset; in others, such as Burma and Indonesia, it was palpably weak. The notion of a Pakistan state gained its appeal from religious solidarity. In India the powerful and well-organized political movement of the Indian National Congress has been an important unifying element. But in all cases the most potent consolidating force has been the appeal of nationalism. This involves more than the recognition of national personality or pride in the cultural heritage. Its content also includes a commitment to the ideas of economic progress, social welfare, and modernization. It thus represents in a projected and enlarged form the desires and strivings of countless individual Asians. All the same, with few exceptions, no ECAFE country has yet attained anything like the degree of national cohesion and social discipline manifested in Western societies on the eve of their industrial revolutions.

Looked at closely in terms of the extent and capacity for modernization, the ECAFE region presents a bewildering kaleidoscope in which the individual pieces are ill assorted in size, shape, and substance. The ethnic, language, cultural, and behavior patterns appear to emphasize variety, not uniformity. But in a wider perspective the similarities stand out and differences of detail fade into the background. All belong to ancient civilizations which, by comparison with the West since the Renaissance, have a pronounced nonsecular cast. Regarded not in a philosophical sense but as a body of learned and sanctioned beliefs, attitudes, and modes of behavior, this common religiosity conflicts with the search for the rationality that economic progress demands. As far as Asia is concerned there seems to be more than a grain of truth in the Marxist dictum that religion is the "opium of the people." Most of the region is in the realm of the monsoon and its peoples live and die in much the same manner. Nearly all ECAFE countries are desperately poor and seek economic advancement and more equal opportunity through deliberate state initiative. Most of them are struggling for national cohesion against fissiparous elements in their body politics. Generations of alien rule and interference have given them a common political background and heritage. In many cases their political boundaries, concepts, and even their sense of nationhood form part of the legacy of colonialism. This common experience has also left a legacy of bitter resentment against colonialism and, what is often connected with it, racialism. From the self-conscious, self-regarding emotions engendered by the impact of European domination emerged their sense of identity with one another.

The point is perhaps best summed up in the words of a distinguished Asian writer. "All the Asian countries," K. M. Panikkar has written, "have had to go through the same suffering, fight the same battles and meet the same enemy. The evolution towards political freedom has been, generally speaking, on parallel lines. The racial arrogance of the Europeans, their assumed attitude of intellectual and moral superiority, and even the religious propaganda to which all Asian countries were subjected, gave rise to a common political outlook in the Asia of the twentieth century." [5] The struggle and compulsions to translate this community of outlook into practically relevant economic cooperation is the principal theme of this study.

5. K. M. Panikkar, *Asia and Western Dominance* (New York, Day, 1954), p. 494.

CHAPTER 2

The Roots of Cooperation

The formal origins of ECAFE can be traced back to the Temporary Sub-Commission on the Economic Reconstruction of Devastated Areas which the United Nations Economic and Social Council (ECOSOC) established in June 1946. The Sub-Commission was authorized "to make enquiries with the consent of the government concerned in countries which have been occupied or devastated by the war, except Germany and Japan, with a view to making a preliminary report not later than September 2, 1946, on the problems of economic reconstruction in the countries visited, bearing in mind the special claims of countries members of the United Nations." Its terms of reference also directed it to advise the Council on "the measures of international co-operation by which reconstruction in those countries might be effectively facilitated and accelerated." [1] To enable the facts of physical devastation to be collected and collated in as complete a picture as possible, the Sub-Commission established two working groups, one for Europe and Africa, the other for Asia and the Far East.

The Working Group for Europe organized its field teams quickly, gathered a great deal of information, and was drafting its findings and recommendations before the Asian Group had even settled the methods and scope of its own investigations. The preliminary report the Sub-Commission presented to ECOSOC in September 1946 [2] could, therefore, cover only European problems.

1. ECOSOC Res. 2/6, June 21, 1946.
2. Doc. A/147, Oct. 26, 1946.

It did, however, include an important proposal for the creation of an economic commission for Europe.[3] The Working Group for Asia and the Far East was much slower off the mark partly because most members of the Sub-Commission[4] felt that the economic reconstruction problems of Europe were more urgent than those of Asia.[5] Apart from this, the great dearth of essential economic data about Asia, its vast distances, and distempered political conditions were bound to make the Sub-Commission's task more difficult there than in Europe. China and India, supported by France, nevertheless pressed for a report to be completed by the first session of ECOSOC in 1947 for otherwise, they feared, Asia would be left behind Europe in any scheme of United Nations assistance for economic reconstruction. Australia, Britain, Canada, and New Zealand, on the other hand, opposed any commitment to speed at the expense of thorough inquiry.[6]

On October 3, 1946, ECOSOC directed the Secretary-General to prepare background material on the reconstruction problems and needs of Asia, to organize a field survey of the countries concerned, and to reconvene the Asian Working Group at Nanking in time for it to prepare a preliminary report for the Council's next session in March 1947.[7] But owing to the Secretariat's heavy involvement with the second session of the General Assembly later that year, no field survey or meeting in Nanking could, in fact, be arranged. It was decided, instead, that the Working Group should reconvene the following February at Lake Success, New York, to prepare a report on the basis of material assembled by the Secretariat.

3. For the mixture of ideas and hopes underlying this proposal, see: David Wightman, *Economic Co-operation in Europe* (New York, Praeger, 1956), chap. 1.

4. The Sub-Commission consisted of Australia, Belgium, Canada, China, Czechoslovakia, Ethiopia, France, Greece, India, the Netherlands, New Zealand, Norway, Peru, the Philippines, Poland, the Soviet Union, the Ukrainian Soviet Socialist Republic, the United Kingdom, the United States, and Yugoslavia.

5. The UN Acting Secretary-General appeared to support this view, for he wrote on July 4, 1946, that "in view of the great volume of work before the Sub-Commission in connexion with Europe, it was decided that the Working Group for Asia and the Far East should confine itself at this stage to a preliminary discussion of the manner in which its enquiries could best be conducted." Doc. E/EMP/Sub.1/WGFE/2, 1946.

6. Doc. E/EMP/Sub.1/WGFE/5, 1946.

7. ECOSOC,OR: 1st Yr., 3rd Sess., Suppl. No. 9, Annex 34.

Meanwhile, in November 1946, the preliminary report of the Temporary Sub-Commission came before the Second Committee of the General Assembly. Of the fifty-four countries represented on the Committee, three were recognizably Asian—China, India, and the Philippines—nineteen were Latin American, and about ten others could also be said to represent underdeveloped regions. In other words, by contrast to their position in ECOSOC, the underdeveloped countries commanded a majority of the votes. The ensuing debate was largely conducted by the Europeans and North Americans on one side and the Latin Americans and Asians on the other. While some of the European delegates, especially those from war-devastated countries, pressed for an immediate decision on the creation of an economic commission for Europe,[8] the Latin Americans argued that any commission set up to deal with economic reconstruction should not be limited to Europe or to war-devastated areas. The Philippines, after mentioning the need in Asia for an agency to replace the United Nations Relief and Rehabilitation Administration (UNRRA), plumped for the creation of an economic commission for Asia and the Far East along the same lines as the one for Europe.[9] It was, however, the personal diplomacy of P. C. Chang, the leader of the Chinese delegation, that linked these two proposals together.

At a time of considerable improvisation within the United Nations all kinds of personal initiatives were possible without formal instructions from governments. Chang had no brief from his Foreign Office on an economic commission for Asia and the Far East; nor did he even consult the Chinese representative on the Security Council about the proposal. He simply felt that its great power status entitled China to as much consideration from the United Nations as Europe. But he spoke for Asia also in arguing that so vast a proportion of the world's population could not go unrepresented and unassisted in any United Nations effort to deal with postwar economic reconstruction. The impending demise of UNRRA lent urgency to his plea as far as China was con-

8. In September 1946 ECOSOC had failed to endorse this particular recommendation of its Temporary Sub-Commission on the Economic Reconstruction of Devastated Areas. Wightman, pp. 5–6.

9. GAOR: 1st Sess., 2nd Part., 2nd Cmtte., 20th–23rd Mtgs., Nov. 20–30, 1946.

cerned. The United States and British governments had already made it plain that they would not contribute to the financing of its operations after the end of 1946. As these two countries had accounted for about 90 per cent of UNRRA's resources, their resolve amounted to a death blow for the organization and its principle of multilateral assistance for relief and rehabilitation on the basis of need. Yet by common consent it was recognized that its tasks were by no means completed. This was nowhere more apparent than in China, the largest single recipient of UNRRA assistance, which, on its termination, faced widespread starvation and a deepening economic, political, and military crisis. The wounds of eight years of war in China could not be healed by only two years of intensive relief and rehabilitation. The Philippines and Korea had also received UNRRA assistance, though to a very limited extent.[10]

Western delegates in general were, nevertheless, distinctly cool to the idea of an economic commission for Asia and the Far East. Some felt it looked too much like an imitation of the Economic Commission for Europe (ECE) without the special European conditions that made this particular idea feasible. All the same, it was difficult for them openly to resist the argument that if the United Nations responded to the needs of Europe it could hardly overlook those of Asia. That this did not happen was largely due to the support Chang received from the Latin Americans. The fact that he was also the Chinese Ambassador to Chile, knew well Hernán Santa Cruz, the prominent Chilean representative to ECOSOC, and sided with the Latin Americans on many issues no doubt helped his diplomacy. What kind of an understanding he reached with them is not known. But it may not be without significance that when, in August 1947, Santa Cruz surprised ECOSOC by moving that an economic commission for Latin America be established, China was among those countries selected to draft its terms of reference. At any rate, Latin American support was decisive in securing from the Second Committee a unanimous recommendation "that, in order to give effective aid to the countries devastated by war, the Economic and Social Council, at its

10. *UNRRA: The History of the United Nations Relief and Rehabilitation Administration*, ed. George Woodbridge (New York, Columbia University Press, 1950).

next session, give prompt and favourable consideration to the establishment of an Economic Commission for Europe and an Economic Commission for Asia and the Far East." It was little more than a formality for the General Assembly in plenary session to endorse this recommendation and to do it, once more, unanimously.[11]

The United Nations was thus committed to the creation of an Economic Commission for Asia and the Far East (ECAFE) before the Temporary Sub-Commission on the Economic Reconstruction of Devastated Areas had advised ECOSOC on "the measures of international cooperation by which reconstruction" in war-devastated Asian countries "might be effectively facilitated and accelerated." In January 1947, the Economic and Employment Commission of ECOSOC formulated guiding principles for the terms of reference of ECE, but thought that those of ECAFE should be considered separately since ECOSOC had not received a report on the economic reconstruction needs of Asia and the problems facing the two commissions might not be the same.[12]

The Working Group for Asia and the Far East, under Chang's chairmanship, reconvened at New York in February 1947, as arranged, to consider a Secretariat draft of its report to ECOSOC. With few reliable figures available, the report had inevitably to be largely descriptive of general conditions and needs; it was far from comprehensive and, from the standpoint of economic analysis, of very limited value. The inventory of misery and destruction revealed was nonetheless formidable. With an eloquent sympathy for the new spirit and expectations abroad in the region, the report recognized that reconstruction in Asia could not be construed in the narrow sense of restoring prewar conditions; this could be only a first step in a long-term process of economic development. "We who belong to Asia," the Indian representative reminded the first session of ECAFE in June 1947, "are not looking for palliatives and short-term remedies, for our problem is not one created by war, but one of longer standing." [13] New machinery was needed, the Working Group thought, to promote and co-

11. General Assembly Res. 46(I), Dec. 11, 1946.

12. Doc. E/CN.1/SR.5–6, Jan. 23–24, 1947 (Economic and Employment Commission).

13. Doc. E/CN.11/AC.1/5, July 10, 1947. For the Philippine statement to the Working Group for Asia and the Far East, Aug. 9, 1946, see Doc. E/EMP/SUB.1/WGFE/4, Aug. 9, 1946.

ordinate reconstruction in this broader sense and to bring all international aid activities in the region "into a common focus so that they may supplement and re-enforce each other." This would be an essential task of ECAFE.[14]

The Indian delegate to the Working Group stressed that the devastated areas of Asia were just as much in need of provisions, raw materials, technicians, shipping and industrial equipment as Europe. "It was for the proposed Economic Commission for Asia and the Far East," he maintained, "to decide and arrange actual assistance. . . . Countries needing assistance should be invited to submit applications supported by facts and figures which would then be investigated by the Commission." [15] In addition, China wanted it to furnish actual technical assistance and "be empowered to invite experts." The guiding principles the Working Group formulated for ECAFE's terms of reference, which were much the same as those drafted for ECE, merely suggested, however, that the Commission might make recommendations regarding technical assistance to United Nations organs and the specialized agencies.[16]

Acting on the General Assembly's instructions, ECOSOC in March 1947 unanimously established ECE and ECAFE.[17] While the mandates given the organizations were very similar, the Council was unable to complete final and comprehensive terms of reference for ECAFE.[18] It wanted the Commission's guidance in particular on the problem of associating the non-self-governing territories of

14. ECOSOC, OR: 2nd Yr., 4th Sess., Suppl. No. 10, 1947.

15. Docs. E/CN.1/Sub.1/C.2/SR.2, Feb. 20, 1947; SR.3, Feb. 17, 1947. On this last point the statement that the United States delegate, Isador Lubin, made to the Economic and Employment Commission a few days after George C. Marshall's historic speech at Harvard University on June 5, 1947, was also revealing. The short-run problem of economic stability in the countries devastated by war, Lubin argued, was largely a problem of overcoming shortages of food, fuel, raw materials, transport facilities, and productive equipment. He suggested that ECE and ECAFE be requested to make an inventory of those deficiencies to ascertain the minimum requirements of these countries and the extent to which they could be met from indigenous production or out of existing resources of foreign exchange. The other aspect of the problem, he continued, was the available supply of goods as measured by that demand and in this connection he drew the attention of the Economic and Employment Commission to the "Marshall Offer." Doc. E/CN.1/SR.29, June 12, 1947.

16. A draft submitted by China provided the basis of the Working Group's suggested terms of reference for ECAFE. See Doc. E/CN.1/Sub.1/C.2/W.17, Feb. 27, 1947.

17. ECOSOC Res. 36 and 37(IV), Mar. 28, 1947.

18. See Doc. E/366, Mar. 22, 1947.

Asia with its activities. Nor did it decide there and then to give ECAFE the all-important authority to recommend directly to member governments and set up subsidiary bodies. What had been immediately created was, in effect, a purely research organization of very limited Asian membership. The Council accordingly instructed the Commission to appoint at its first session a committee of the whole to consider and make recommendations on its membership and geographical scope and on any other changes or additions to its terms of reference.

The timing of the decision to create ECAFE was thus largely dictated by the determination of a few Asian countries, above all China, to secure from the United Nations a tangible recognition that the economic problems of Asia were no less important and urgent than those of Europe. With the support of the Latin Americans they carried the day. The significance of its creation, however, is not explained by these political maneuvers in the General Assembly. The real roots of ECAFE are to be found in the ferment of ideas and movements which marked the political awakening of Asia after generations of colonial rule and foreign domination.

During World War II thoughtful persons, especially in North America, China, and Oceania, saw that the application, to postwar Asia, of the declared war aims of the Grand Alliance and the principles of the Atlantic Charter of 1941 would call for new forms of international economic collaboration and regional organization. "The Charter assures to the peoples of South Eastern Asia and the South-West Pacific," Herbert V. Evatt declared in 1942, "that they shall be able to live out their lives in freedom from want as well as freedom from fear. These peoples cannot be excluded from the system of economic collaboration which the United Nations have envisaged." [19] Others pointed out, moreover, that even "though the world were ready for a powerful federation of all states, the peculiar and complex problems of the Far Eastern area would require regional machinery decentralised and adapted to this particular environment. Remote control without strong institutions constantly active on the spot, would be handicapped

19. Quoted in Julius Stone, "The Atlantic Charter and the Problems of S. E. Asia and the Pacific," a paper presented to the Eighth Conference of the Institute of Pacific Relations, Mont Tremblant, Quebec, Dec. 1942.

by distance and unfamiliarity."[20] Furthermore, this same stream of informed opinion was in favor of organizing the postwar recovery of Asia through the United Nations.[21]

It was, however, a burgeoning Asian political consciousness as demonstrated, for example, at the Asian Relations Conference held at New Delhi during March and April 1947 that provided the real impetus to regional organization. The idea of this conference, Jawaharlal Nehru said, arose simultaneously in many minds and in many Asian countries because there was a "widespread urge and an awareness that the time had come for us, peoples of Asia, to meet together, to hold together and to advance together." As European domination recedes, so "the walls that surrounded us fall down and we look at one another again and meet as old friends long parted."[22] After the war, Asians began to discover one another as neighbors just as Africans have recently been doing. It was literally true at the Asian Relations Conference that some delegates saw for the first time what the faces of other Asian nationalities looked like. This sense of enforced separation in the past enhanced in their eyes the significance of reunion. Representing more than a score of nations, cultures, and languages, they met to affirm the common bond uniting them: that they were Asians determined to assert Asia's place in the world community.[23] This event, Nehru thought, "may well stand out as a land-mark which divides the past of Asia from the future."

It was clear from the Asian Relations Conference that sooner or later, even without United Nations action, the Asian countries

20. Percy E. Corbett, *Post-War Worlds* (n.p., Institute of Pacific Relations, 1942), p. 78. On the need for postwar regional organization in the Far East, see also, e.g., J. B. Condliffe, *Agenda for a Post-War World* (London, Allen and Unwin, 1943), pp. 73–77; and the proceedings of the Eighth Conference of the Institute of Pacific Relations. For an indication of the early wartime output of writing on the aims and consequences of the war in the Pacific, see: W. L. Holland, "War Aims and Peace Aims in the Pacific," *Pacific Affairs, 15* (Dec., 1942).

21. E.g.: "it is better that recovery should be organised through the machinery of the United Nations rather than be the concern of one or two nations." *Problems of Economic Reconstruction in the Far East,* Report of the Tenth Conference of the Institute of Pacific Relations, Sept. 1947.

22. Jawaharlal Nehru, *Independence and After* (Toronto, Longmans, 1950). A collection of the more important speeches from Sept. 1946 to May 1949.

23. For a useful eyewitness account of the Conference, see Nicholas Mansergh, "The Asian Conference," *International Affairs* (London) *23* (July 1947). This and subsequent Asian conferences are further discussed in Chap. 16.

themselves would have set up their own regional organization. On almost the same day that Nehru inaugurated the Conference, ECOSOC passed the resolution establishing ECAFE. This represented the first important admission of the United Nations that the world included Asia in its own right and not simply as a responsibility of a few colonial powers. It was a tangible recognition of the political renaissance of Asia.[24]

24. The name ECAFE is in itself a curious legacy of an era when Europe was the center and arbitrator of world affairs, for where else is the "Far East" supposed to be far from? Significantly, Chang was against the term "Far East" as China, he said, regarded itself as being the center of the earth's surface. See ECOSOC,OR: 4th Sess., 72nd Mtg., Mar. 18, 1947, para. 40.

CHAPTER 3

Settling the Membership

When the first session of ECAFE opened in June 1947, its membership consisted of four Asian[1] and six non-Asian countries.[2] A regional economic commission for Asia in which Asians were in a minority was a strange creation indeed. To give it a more Asian complexion meant finding a formula to permit those territories that fell within its geographical scope but were non-self-governing or not yet member states of the United Nations to participate in its activities.[3] It was chiefly to answer this most important question that the Commission, as directed by ECOSOC, immediately set up a Committee of the Whole.[4]

To benefit from the guidance of the United Nations Legal Department, the Committee of the Whole met at New York in July 1947. The venue did not please India and the Soviet Union, whose delegates argued that all questions affecting ECAFE should be discussed in Asia; if legal advice or other assistance from Headquarters were needed, it should be made available at the seat of the Commission. Four different proposals regarding membership were presented to the Committee.

1. China, India, the Philippines, and Thailand.

2. Australia, France, the Netherlands, the Soviet Union, the United Kingdom, and the United States.

3. These were initially: Burma, Ceylon, Indo-China, Hong Kong, Malaya, the Netherlands Indies, Singapore, British North Borneo, Brunei, and Sarawak.

4. A committee of the whole is much the same as a Commission session, except that it is confined to considering an agenda "as specified and determined by the Commission at its previous ordinary sessions." See P. S. Lokanathan, "ECAFE–The Economic Parliament of Asia," *Indian Yearbook of International Affairs,* 2 (1953).

The United Kingdom restated a suggestion made earlier to ECOSOC that non-self-governing territories should be eligible to become associate members without voting rights. This category of membership had first been adopted by the World Health Organization (WHO).[5] India wanted countries of the ECAFE region to be represented by nominees of their own national governments with full rights and privileges. It felt strongly that Asian representatives should have a clear majority in the Commission. The Soviet Union thought that nonmember countries of the United Nations might be admitted to the Commission in a consultative capacity on questions of particular concern to them. This proposal accorded with the provisions of paragraph 8 of ECE's terms of reference but did not explicitly cover non-self-governing territories. The Philippines proposed that any territory within ECAFE's geographical scope should be admitted to membership "upon election by the Economic and Social Council on the Commission's recommendation"; any territory not elected should be invited by the Commission to participate in its work in a consultative capacity.

The United Nations Legal Department pointed out that "while there was no explicit provision in the Charter on the subject, the Charter in spirit and in principle envisages a clear difference between members and non-members and that this difference rested upon the fundamental principle that rights of membership should not be granted unless the obligations of membership were also assumed." Full membership for non-self-governing territories, the Department advised, would be contrary to the Charter and only in very exceptional circumstances should it be granted in a subordinate United Nations organ to a nonmember state of the United Nations.

When it came to a vote, the Committee adopted the British proposal. But could the application for associate membership be made by the territory itself, as India then demanded, or only, as Britain insisted, by the power responsible for its international relations? The Committee again adopted the British view and the territories eligible for associate membership were listed.[6]

5. Article 8 of its Constitution dated July 1946.

6. North Borneo, Brunei, and Sarawak; Burma; Ceylon; the Indo-Chinese Federation; Hong Kong; the Malayan Union and Singapore; and the Netherlands Indies.

Britain, France, and the Netherlands did something to allay Asian anxieties by promptly announcing their intention to sponsor their Asian colonies for such membership. They would have found it difficult not to submit these applications, especially as associate membership came to be regarded as an indication of fitness for statehood.

India, supported by the Philippines and Thailand, also wished to grant full membership to Asian states not members of the United Nations. But China, France, the Netherlands, the Soviet Union, and the United States opposed this idea. The Committee recommended, instead, that these states be admitted to associate membership on presenting their own application; when they became members of the United Nations they would automatically become full members of ECAFE. The Committee agreed, however, that associate members should "participate as fully as possible in the work of the Commission" and enjoy all the rights and privileges of membership except that of voting and holding office in the Commission itself or a committee of the whole. It also proposed that any territory that was not an associate member could, with the agreement of the power responsible for its international relations, be invited to participate in the discussion of any question of particular concern to it.

The Committee of the Whole made no formal recommendation to change the geographical scope of ECAFE. Thailand thought it should comprise all countries east of Iran, and the Soviet Union appeared to favor a membership which implied an extension of its geographical scope to all the Middle Eastern countries except Turkey, which was already a member of ECE. The Russians repeated this suggestion to ECOSOC in August 1947 and to the General Assembly the following November but it was rejected each time. The proposal would certainly have removed the predominance of the Western powers in ECAFE, but only by giving Middle Eastern countries a clear majority over the Asian countries explicitly included within ECAFE's geographical scope. Spokesmen for the Middle East, such as Egypt, Iraq, and Lebanon, did not support it, however, because they wanted their own regional economic commission—an economic commission for the Middle East. The Committee, in conclusion, suggested that to ECAFE's original terms of reference be added the power to recommend directly to its member governments and the specialized agencies, to establish subsidiary bodies, and to consult the Supreme Commander for the Allied Powers in Japan (SCAP) and the control authorities in Korea. This brought ECAFE into line with the mandate given to ECE.[7]

In August 1947, ECOSOC completed ECAFE's terms of reference by accepting all the recommendations of the Committee of the Whole.[8] India still felt strongly that the colonial powers should not be able to dictate the composition of ECAFE. To ensure that Asian peoples were represented by delegates of their own choice, non-self-governing territories should be permitted to present their own applications for membership. Although India did not this time press its views to another vote, its tenacious championing of Asian aspirations left no doubt that it interpreted the disagreements on membership in terms of colonial rights versus equal rights and self-determination. Asian views had been voted down because the Commission was not fully representative of Asian opinion. The Western powers had by no means heard the last word on this subject.

The first major change in the membership of the Commission occurred at its second session in November 1947. Having entered the United Nations the previous September, Pakistan took its seat for the first time and the colonial powers presented the applications of their Asian territories for associate membership. Burma, Ceylon, Hong Kong, Malaya, and British Borneo[9] were readily accepted, though the Soviet Union abstained from voting for them on the ground that non-self-governing territories should present their own applications and be admitted only in an advisory capacity on problems directly concerning them. France proposed Cambodia and Laos, which were admitted, but not Viet-Nam at this stage because of the difficulty of forming a representative government there. The Soviet Union doubted the representative character of the Cambodian and Laotian governments as well and abstained from voting for them. The representation of Thailand proved a little troublesome since the Thai

7. For discussions of the Committee of the Whole, see Docs. E/CN.11/AC./SR.1–10, July 1947, and for its report: Doc. E/491, July 23, 1947. ECAFE's mandate is further commented upon in Chap. 5.

8. Doc. E/512, Aug. 5, 1947 and ECOSOC Res. 69(V), Aug. 5, 1947.

9. Malaya and British Borneo comprised five territories: the former, the Malayan Union and Singapore; the latter, North Borneo, Brunei, and Sarawak.

government had been forcibly overthrown and a number of member states had not yet recognized its successor. After a lengthy debate it was agreed to admit the Thai delegation with full rights on the understanding that this did not imply any diplomatic recognition of the new government. But by this time the Thai delegation had departed in a pique and could not be induced to return. The episode was only mildly difficult, however, compared with the case of Indonesia.

At this same session in November 1947, the Netherlands proposed associate membership for the Netherlands Indies. The Republic of Indonesia, a government in active rebellion against the Netherlands, also applied for admission. The formal question thus presented to the Commission was whether or not the Republic was a fully sovereign state responsible for its own international relations. India, which had recognized the de facto authority of the Republican government, was against taking a strictly legal view of the problem and again argued that ECAFE should properly represent the collective will of Asian peoples. As the Security Council had the conflict in Indonesia on its agenda, the Commission accepted, against the votes of India, Pakistan, the Philippines, and the Soviet Union, a Chinese proposal to postpone further consideration of both applications until its next session.[10] The Security Council, however, could not help ECAFE decide the legal status of the Republican government since it was concerned not with this question but with bringing about a cease-fire and political settlement in Indonesia. In any case, ECAFE was fully entitled by its terms of reference to decide the issue itself.[11] The motion of China amounted to an abstention on its part because, owing to the harsh treatment the Chinese in Indonesia received from both sides, it had become the most directly affected third party in the conflict.[12]

10. Docs. E/CN.11/SR.21–25, Nov. 28–Dec. 3, 1947 and E/CN.11/58, Dec. 5, 1947.

11. This was reaffirmed by ECOSOC Res. 144B (VII), Aug. 16, 1948.

12. "The Indonesian Republicans have shown almost as much antagonism to the Chinese as to the Dutch. . . . Local Chinese organizations have appealed to the Chinese Government for protection, but though China is at the moment too weak to take any drastic action, the attitude of China in the United Nations is by no means so favourable as that of India towards the claims of the Indonesian Republic." G. F. Hudson, "Chinese in Southeast Asia," *Eastern World* (Oct. 1947), quoted in Victor W. Purcell, *The Chinese in Southeast Asia* (Toronto, Oxford, 1951), p. 565.

In March 1948, ECOSOC acted on an earlier recommendation of the Commission and admitted New Zealand into ECAFE.[13] On its entry into the United Nations the following month, Burma also became a full member. That made six Asian and seven non-Asian countries with the right to vote when the third session of the Commission opened in India in June 1948. In his welcoming speech, Prime Minister Nehru hoped the Republic of Indonesia would be represented as well. The Netherlands delegation argued that since the Republic controlled only part of the territory of Indonesia while the Netherlands was responsible for the international relations of the whole country, only it could present the Indonesian application for associate membership. If this was acceptable, it was prepared to select two advisers from the Republican government to serve on the delegation. India replied that, since the Republic, at the express invitation of ECOSOC,[14] had attended the United Nations Conference on Trade and Employment from November 1947 to March 1948 and had signed its final act, the Havana Charter, it was, in fact, responsible for its own international relations. Burma, Ceylon, Pakistan, and the Soviet Union supported the Indian view. They might have added that several states, including Australia, Britain, and the United States, had already accorded the Republic de facto recognition.

However, Britain, France, and the United States disagreed that control over commercial relations meant the same thing as responsibility for international relations. Until full sovereignty was transferred to the Republic, the United States delegate maintained, ECAFE could not constitutionally take a decision on its application. Britain and France were also naturally sensitive to any precedent which encouraged independence movements in their own colonial territories to seek United Nations recognition. Australia and New Zealand hovered between the opposing arguments by suggesting that, if the Netherlands agreed, the Republic might be granted provisional associate membership. China tried to mediate but failed when the Netherlands refused to accept its compromise suggestion that the Republic and the Netherlands Indies should both be admitted as associate members. The Nether-

13. ECOSOC Res. 105(VI), Mar. 8, 1948.

14. ECOSOC Res. 62(V), Aug. 1, 1947. It was an Indian initiative in the Council that led to this invitation.

lands apparently strove for an outright political victory which, as events were to prove, they would almost certainly not have won had a final vote been taken. Their obduracy embarrassed the United Kingdom, for instance, partly because the issue advertised a large split in the Commonwealth and partly because it put the United Kingdom in the position of appearing to oppose the aspiration of Asian colonies for self-government. It was the Philippines this time that rescued the Netherlands by proposing a further postponement of the question to the next Commission session. This was carried by 6 votes to 5 with China and Thailand abstaining.[15]

The showdown came at the fourth session of the Commission in December 1948. Britain, the Netherlands, the United States, and, this time, Australia also wanted to delay a decision once more so as not to upset current negotiations between the Netherlands and Republican governments. The case for further postponement collapsed, however, when the press reported a breakdown in these negotiations. New Zealand thereupon proposed that both the Republic of Indonesia and the "Rest of Indonesia" [16] be admitted to associate membership. The Netherlands, no doubt sensing defeat in the air, indicated it would walk out if the Republic were admitted. The proposal was nevertheless carried by 8 votes to 2 with Britain, France, and Thailand abstaining. The Chinese delegation was also instructed to abstain but ignored its brief and voted in favor. The Soviet Union supported the resolution, it declared, only on the understanding that it was voting for the Republic and against the Netherlands Indies. The real anomaly of including the "Rest of Indonesia," however, was the fact, as France pointed out, that no application on its behalf had been made. Only the United States joined the Netherlands in voting against the resolution.[17] The delegate of the Republican govern-

15. Britain, France, the Netherlands, New Zealand, the Philippines, and the United States voted in favor and Australia, Burma, India, Pakistan, and the Soviet Union against. See: DOCS. E/CN.11/SR.32–33, June 2, 1948; E/CN.11/SR.37–38, June 28, 1948; E/CN.11/102, June 10, 1948.

16. An expression used in ECAFE documents to denote that part of Indonesia not controlled by the Republic of Indonesia. This territory did not include West New Guinea, which was not within the geographical scope of ECAFE.

17. The United States vote, which Indonesia did not quickly forget, is hard to explain, especially when, on the launching of another Dutch "police action" in Indonesia in December 1948, the United States suspended the Indonesian com-

ment, who had sat among the public during the long debate, took his seat at the table and the Netherlands delegation withdrew from all further participation in the proceedings.[18] The Netherlands reappeared, however, at the Commission session the next year.

The supporters of the New Zealand resolution contended that they were not pronouncing upon or attempting to prejudice a political settlement of the dispute in Indonesia. But the Commission, in admitting the Republic of Indonesia, had said in effect that it was responsible for its own international relations. The United Nations had lent the prestige of its own recognition to the Republican cause. That was a political decision, the first of its kind on this issue in any United Nations body and one which the Republican government greatly welcomed. No sooner had it been taken, however, than the Netherlands launched another "police action" in Indonesia, put the Republican leaders in prison, and a government of the Republic of Indonesia ceased in practice to exist. Full sovereignty, except over West New Guinea, was finally transferred to Indonesia in December 1949. Accordingly, the Commission, in May 1950, united the divided membership of the country into one associate membership [19] and on its entry into the United Nations the following September Indonesia automatically became a full member of ECAFE. West New Guinea, or West Irian as the Indonesians called it, continued, however, to poison Indonesia's relations with the Netherlands. On one occasion it led Indonesia to question openly the basis of continued Netherlands membership in ECAFE.[20]

Although the Indonesian case proved to be the most contentious, it was by no means the only controversial question of membership

---

ponent of Marshall Plan aid and threatened to suspend direct aid to the Netherlands as well. See Charles Wolf, *Foreign Aid: Theory and Practice in Southern Asia* (Princeton, Princeton University Press, 1960).

18. Docs. E/CN.11/SR.45, Dec. 1, 1948; SR.46, Dec. 2, 1948; SR.53, Dec. 8, 1948; SR. 54, Dec. 9, 1948; SR.55, Dec. 10, 1948; E/CN.11/166, Dec. 8, 1948.

19. Doc. E/CN.11/249, May 17, 1950. China, meaning now Taiwan, abstained on this resolution because Indonesia had recognized and favored the seating of Communist China.

20. See: *ECAFE Annual Report to ECOSOC, 19 February 1954–7 April 1955,* Doc. E/CN.11/407, Apr. 19, 1955, paras, 203–04. The Netherlands could not and did not explicitly justify its continued membership by virtue of its responsibility for West New Guinea since, according to the terms of reference, the territory is not within the geographical scope of ECAFE.

the Commission decided. In 1948 the Soviet Union wanted membership for Viet-Nam discussed but the chairman ruled that no proper application had been received. In October 1949, however, the Commission was faced with applications for associate membership from the Ho Chi Minh government of the Democratic Republic of Viet-Nam and the Bao Dai government of the State of Viet-Nam.[21] Both applications claimed to represent the same territory. The Soviet Union supported the first and France sponsored the second. In the interests of liquidating colonialism, India, as in the Indonesian case, supported the admission of both governments. The Commission voted, however, for the French candidate and against the Russian proposal. Burma, the Philippines, and Thailand abstained and Pakistan was absent from the voting.[22] Similarly, and by a larger margin, the Commission rejected a Russian-supported application from the Democratic People's Republic of Korea [23] and accepted a United States proposal to admit the Republic of Korea as an associate member.[24] India again voted for both applications. Asian delegates were noticeably more hesitant about Viet-Nam than Korea. They apparently felt misgivings about the Bao Dai government and believed that Ho Chi Minh really did control most of the country. The Republic of Korea, on the other hand, had been endorsed by the General Assembly on December 12, 1948, as the only lawful government in Korea. Both decisions were as much political as the admission of Indonesia.

Nepal was the first noncolonial territory to be admitted as an associate member of ECAFE. This was unanimously agreed in November 1948 after ECOSOC had approved an earlier Commission recommendation to include Nepal within its geographical scope.[25] The question of representation, however, which most obviously cut across the usual line of debate between the anticolonial sentiments of Asian delegates and the formal or legalistic

21. Now known as North Viet-Nam and South Viet-Nam, respectively.

22. Docs. E/CN.11/SR.62, Oct. 21, 1949; E/CN.11/232/Rev.1, Nov. 11, 1949.

23. Henceforth called North Korea.

24. Docs. E/CN.11/SR.63, Oct. 23, 1949; E/CN.11/233/Rev.1, Nov. 11, 1949. ECOSOC Res. 187(VIII), Mar. 10, 1949, had already included Korea within the geographical scope of ECAFE.

25. Docs. E/CN.11/103, June 10, 1948; E/CN.11/152, Nov. 30, 1948; ECOSOC Res. 144(VII), Aug. 2, 1948.

views of the West was that of Communist China. Technically this was, and still is, a question of credentials, not membership.

A Chinese People's Republic (CPR) was formally established in China on October 1, 1949, and recognized the next day by the Soviet Union. When the first session of ECAFE's Industry and Trade Committee opened on October 12, the Russian delegation met and voted with representatives of the Nationalist Chinese government which had fled to Formosa, or Taiwan. Nor did it challenge the Chinese delegation's credentials when the fifth session of the Commission opened at Singapore on October 20. At the Industry and Trade Committee's second session in May 1950, however, the Russians demanded the exclusion of the Taiwan delegation and the seating of representatives from Communist China; otherwise the Soviet Union would withdraw from the proceedings and not recognize the legality of any decisions taken in its absence.[26] Britain and Taiwan, backed by France and Thailand, contested the propriety of the Russian motion. It would be quite wrong, they argued, for associate members which had no vote in the Commission and were not members of the United Nations, to pronounce upon the credentials of a United Nations member. The Executive Secretary, as acting chairman, on being pressed for a ruling said it was a procedural question which could not be ruled out of order.[27] His decision was then challenged and defeated on a vote. Only Burma and India supported his ruling. Other Asian countries were not represented or, as in the case of Pakistan and the Philippines, their delegates had not yet arrived. The Soviet Union refused to vote on the ground that its motion was substantive, not procedural.[28]

A few days later the Russians presented the same motion to the Commission and repeated their threat to walk out if it was not accepted. The Soviet Union evidently expected defeat for it sent

26. In January 1950, Communist China's Premier and Foreign Minister, Chou En-lai had urged the UN to expel "the illegitimate delegates of the Chinese Kuomintang reactionary clique." When the Security Council refused to do so, the Soviet Union withdrew from the Council from January to August 1950.

27. The Executive Secretary was technically correct since, by adopting the rules of procedure of the Commission, the Committee was subject to rules 11 and 12 which provide for the consideration of the credentials of representatives. See Appendix II.

28. Docs. E/CN.11/I&T/SR.9–16, May 15–30, 1950.

no delegates from Moscow to this session. Senior officials at United Nations Headquarters, meanwhile, had been calculating the chances of ECAFE seating a delegation from Peking. By May 1950, after all, six of the thirteen voting members of the Commission had already recognized Communist China.[29] Depending on whether and, if so, which countries abstained, a favorable vote was not unthinkable at that stage. In the absence of any instructions to the contrary from a superior body, there was no legal objection to ECAFE taking such a decision. In the event, most of the opponents of the Russian motion did not contest the competence of the Commission to judge the question but thought it should be decided by a higher United Nations body. When a Thai amendment to this effect was carried by 8 votes to 3, the Russian delegation withdrew from the session.[30]

The Soviet Union reappeared at the 1951 Commission session and again introduced the same proposal. This time Thailand, supported by the United States, argued that as the General Assembly had the question under consideration[31] it was no longer within the competence of ECAFE. The acting chairman, a Burmese, declined, however, to rule the Russian motion out of order. "If the subject were postponed," the British delegate stated, "the representative of the Nationalist Government would be sitting at the meeting when his Government could not apply the recommendations of the Commission." The chairman's decision was, nevertheless, challenged and overruled by 8 votes to 5, with Indonesia abstaining. On this occasion Britain and Pakistan joined Burma, India, and the Soviet Union in voting against the challenge. That was the nearest Communist China came to being admitted into ECAFE. By now the Russians also wished to unseat the delegations of South Korea and South Viet-Nam but, by 7 votes to 5, with Britain and France abstaining, the Commission again

29. Burma, India, the Netherlands, Pakistan, the Soviet Union, and the United Kingdom. Two associate members without a vote in the Commission—Ceylon and Indonesia—had also recognized Communist China.

30. Doc. E/CN.11/247, May 17, 1950. Burma, India, and the Soviet Union voted against the Thai amendment and Britain and Pakistan abstained.

31. Under its Res. 396(V), Dec. 14, 1950, the General Assembly recommended that, in the interests of uniformity, whenever more than one government claimed to represent a member state and the question became the subject of controversy in the UN, it should be considered by the General Assembly or by the Interim Committee if the General Assembly was not in session.

ruled their motion out of order.[32] That Burma, India, Indonesia, and Pakistan voted for it clearly showed, however, the extent of Asian antipathy toward the Syngman Rhee and Bao Dai regimes.

Formal Russian motions to seat Communist China were introduced at nearly every Commission session down to 1957 and on each occasion the opponents successfully moved the adjournment of the debate on the ground that the General Assembly had cognizance of the problem. In subsidiary bodies it was more usual for them to be ruled out of order. Only Burma, India, and Indonesia consistently supported the Russian position. From 1957 onward, the Soviet Union refrained from introducing formal motions in the Commission and merely regretted the absence of Communist China. But the very mention of the subject still provoked some sharp rejoinders, especially from the Philippines, South Korea, and Taiwan. Similarly, the Russians ceased, from 1955 onward, to move the exclusion of the delegations from South Korea and South Viet-Nam.

Although the General Assembly removed the possibility of autonomous ECAFE action on the seating of a delegation from Peking, any matter relating to Communist China continued to excite and divide the Commission. At its 1955 session, for instance, the Philippines, South Korea, Taiwan, and the United States vigorously protested against the circulation of a statement from the World Federation of Trade Unions (WFTU) which they branded as Chinese propaganda. That six out of the eight WFTU delegates actually came from Peking heightened their resentment, for this looked like the presence of Communist China in disguise.[33] The following year Communist China's Ambassador to India sent a memorandum to the Executive Secretary on the economic achievements of his country. This was made available, but not circulated, to members of the Commission. A Taiwan version of the economic situation there was circulated, however, since the government was still formally recognized by the United Nations. So sensitive were Taiwan and the United States on the whole subject that they tried hard to stifle even the Secretariat's

32. Doc. E/CN.11/SR.79, Mar. 8, 1951.

33. Doc. E/CN.11/408, May 24, 1955. This proportion of WFTU delegates from Peking had increased from none in 1952, to 6 out of 10 in 1953, and 6 out of 9 in 1954.

efforts to cover mainland China in its current economic reporting.[34]

Meanwhile, the years since these great political debates have seen a gradual extension in the geographical scope and membership of ECAFE. Shortly after the signing of a Japanese Peace Treaty in September 1951, Japan intimated to the Executive Secretary that it wished to send observers to the next Commission session and become a member or associate member. Hitherto Japanese experts had participated in ECAFE activities only as advisers to the delegations from SCAP. On receiving the Japanese message, the Executive Secretary wanted to invite Japanese observers to all meetings in addition to the Commission session. The United Nations Legal Department saw no objection to this, though Headquarters was anxious to avoid any action that would expose the Secretariat to the charge of making a political judgment and therefore thought the invitation should come from the Commission itself. Through a misinterpretation of cables, however, the Executive Secretary himself did, in fact, invite Japanese observers to a number of ECAFE meetings. At the Commission session in January 1952, Pakistan proposed the inclusion of Japan within the geographical scope of ECAFE and its immediate admission to associate membership as soon as ECOSOC approved this recommendation. The Philippines thought the second part of the proposal premature, since until Japan and a majority of the signatory powers actually ratified the Peace Treaty, Japan would not be responsible for its own international relations. But the Commission was in no mood for legal niceties and readily accepted the Pakistan resolution.[35] So did ECOSOC.[36] In 1953 Afghanistan was admitted to ECAFE [37] and attended the Commission the following year. Through an oversight of the Secretariat and the ignorance of the Afghan government it was not at the time of admission included within the geographical scope of ECAFE. But this omission ECOSOC rectified one year later.[38]

34. See pp. 89–91.

35. Doc. E/CN.11/344, Apr. 21, 1952.

36. ECOSOC Res. 419(XIV), June 10, 1953.

37. ECOSOC Res. 465(XV), Apr. 24, 1953. Had an economic commission for the Middle East been established, Afghanistan would almost certainly have not become a member of ECAFE.

38. ECOSOC Res. 516B(XVII), Apr. 20, 1954. If a member country is not included

The representative character of ECAFE was also strengthened when its associate members became full members. This process would have happened more quickly had a deadlock not prevailed in the Security Council between the West and the Soviet Union over their respective candidates for admission to the United Nations. On the initiative of Cambodia and Pakistan, the Commission actually recommended to ECOSOC in 1953 that it "admit to membership those associate members who are responsible for their own international relations and who apply to the Commission for such membership." [39] The Soviet Union immediately saw this as an attempt to bypass the Security Council and accused the West of inspiring the move so as to give regimes like the Bao Dai government full rights in the Commission. Others agreed with the aim but not the method of the proposal. They wanted the decision on admission to full membership left to ECOSOC, not ECAFE, for otherwise, as the Russian statement indicated, the Commission would get embroiled in highly political judgments about which governments were truly responsible for their own international relations. An amendment to this effect twice resulted in a tied vote, however, and so was rejected.

When this recommendation came before ECOSOC in April 1953, France and the United States jointly proposed the admission of Cambodia, Ceylon, Japan, Laos, Nepal, South Korea, and South Viet-Nam to full membership in ECAFE. But about half the Council opposed the idea on the general ground that, having refused full membership in ECE to certain European states that were not members of the United Nations, ECOSOC could not take a different decision regarding Asian countries in the same position. In addition some delegations, India and the Philippines included, doubted whether the constituent states of Indo-China were really responsible for their own international relations. To India and the Soviet Union it was quite unrealistic to admit these smaller Asian states and exclude Communist China. On the initiative of

---

within the geographical scope of ECAFE, its economic problems are not subject to ECAFE inquiry. This is the technical justification for referring to Australia, France, the Netherlands, New Zealand, the United Kingdom, the Soviet Union, and the United States as the "outside powers."

39. Doc. E/CN.11/370, Feb. 14, 1953. This proposal was considered to be a logical extension of the rights accorded to associate members in 1951 by a statement of the Commission known as the "Lahore Agreement." See p. 51.

India, ECOSOC decided by a very close vote to adjourn its debate on the proposal.[40] But after the Commission had again requested a favorable response to its wishes,[41] the Council, noting "that the General Assembly had determined that Cambodia, Ceylon, the Republic of Korea, Japan, Laos, Nepal and Viet-Nam were eligible for membership in the United Nations," agreed the next year to their admission as full members of ECAFE.[42]

On achieving its political independence in 1957 Malaya was elected to the United Nations [43] and thereby became a full member of ECAFE. As a result the designation of the associate membership of "Malaya and British Borneo" was changed in 1958 to that of Singapore and British Borneo. In view of the measure of self-government subsequently accorded to Singapore and Brunei, these two territories were each made associate members in 1960, leaving North Borneo and Sarawak with the joint associate membership.

In 1958 Iran applied for inclusion within the scope and membership of ECAFE.[44] Although this was unanimously recommended by the Commission and approved by ECOSOC, several members were not happy about Iran's application. India, for instance, feared it would strengthen Moslem influence and the pro-Western group within the Commission. Others felt the scope of ECAFE was being unduly extended. It was, nevertheless, difficult openly to oppose membership for Iran when Afghanistan had been admitted. Those opposed to Iran's application wrote their misgivings into the Commission's report, instead, by stating that "any further extension of the geographical scope of the Commission would require most careful consideration, having regard to the need for efficiency in the work of the Commission and other

40. ECOSOC,OR: 15th Sess., 699th–701st Mtgs., Apr. 24–27, 1953.

41. Doc. E/CN.11/387, Feb. 18, 1954.

42. ECOSOC Res. 517A(XVII), Apr. 22, 1954. Not the least of the complications involved was the question of a contribution to the UN budget of nonmember countries elected to full membership in a UN body. ECOSOC, therefore, requested the Secretary-General to "undertake such consultations and further steps as may be required to obtain the agreement of the above non-member States and the General Assembly to appropriate contributions by these States to the United Nations budget."

43. General Assembly Res. 1134(XII), Sept. 17, 1957.

44. Again, had an economic commission for the Middle East been established, Iran would not have applied to ECAFE.

criteria."[45] If this meant anything at all, it gave warning of their likely opposition to any further proposal for extending ECAFE's domain.

Finally, in December 1961, ECOSOC admitted the Mongolian People's Republic as a full member of ECAFE. This was first proposed by the Soviet Union in 1956 when the Executive Secretary received a cabled application from the Mongolian government. After a lengthy procedural discussion which was, in reality, a political debate,[46] on whether the application should be considered, the Commission agreed to forward it to ECOSOC without any recommendation, together with a record of its debate.[47] When the Soviet Union tried again the following year to have the application considered, the Commission decided that it was now within the competence of ECOSOC rather than ECAFE. Mongolia had thus to wait six years before being admitted.[48]

45. *ECAFE Annual Report to ECOSOC, 29 March 1957–15 March 1958,* Doc. E/CN.11/482, n.d., para. 260.

46. E.g., as Mongolia had diplomatic relations outside the Communist bloc only with India, its application was regarded by the Philippines, South Korea, South Viet-Nam, and Taiwan as a Communist attempt to infiltrate the Commission. See Doc. E/CN.11/451, Mar. 18, 1957.

47. *ECAFE Annual Report to ECOSOC, 8 April 1955–14 February 1956,* Doc. E/CN.11/430, Mar. 1956, para. 201.

48. For a summary of the present membership of ECAFE, see Chap. 5.

CHAPTER 4

Defining the Tasks

Like its sister commission for Europe, ECAFE was directed to "initiate and participate in measures for facilitating concerted action for the economic reconstruction of Asia and the Far East and for maintaining and strengthening the economic relations of these areas both among themselves and with other countries of the world." If the objectives of ECAFE for Asia and the Far East were the same as those of ECE for Europe, the starting line was different. ECE gained immediate impetus by absorbing the activities of three emergency economic organizations in Europe.[1] In Asia there were no "going concerns" ECAFE could absorb, no activities it could take over and continue. It had to build a work program out of virtually nothing. With little advance preparation, a makeshift home, and a skeleton staff, the Commission began its first meeting at Shanghai in June 1947.

One thing only was generally agreed beforehand: the report of the Working Group for Asia and the Far East was incomplete and not altogether accurate. Much more information was required on the economic conditions, problems, and needs of the region before ECAFE could begin to define and undertake specific reconstruction tasks. In welcoming the delegations the Assistant Secretary-General in charge of the Department of Economic Affairs, David K. Owen, advised the Commission to select priorities and not spread its net too widely. Britain thought it might begin by investigating short-term reconstruction needs in the fields of trans-

1. Wightman, *Economic Co-operation.*

port, fuel, and trained personnel. The United States stressed the importance of removing obstacles to trade.

To other delegations, however, these suggestions implied a rather narrow view of the functions of ECAFE. India and the Soviet Union, for instance, wanted a comprehensive investigation, a full budget, of Asian needs and resources. Both countries evidently sought to get away from the notion of war devastation underlying the setting up of ECAFE and treat it as an instrument for Asian economic development. This did not please China. Australia was close to India in thinking that the industrialization of the region could be assisted through ECAFE. In its view the Commission provided an opportunity to work out a new basis of cooperation between Asia and the West. Some delegates suggested individual country investigations; others favored a regional approach. The Soviet Union proposed large field teams of government representatives with unspecified functions. The majority thought the initial inquiries could be left to the Secretariat. Britain and the United States were nevertheless concerned that no large tasks should be placed on so small a staff. India replied that it was the duty of the United Nations to provide the staff necessary for whatever work program the Commission decided. The Philippines was mainly interested in a quick appeal for material assistance and therefore wished to dispense with investigations where adequate information on reconstruction needs was already available. It sought from ECAFE, in other words, an endorsement of its claim for financial aid.

What finally emerged from this somewhat confusing debate [2] was a compromise resolution embodying most of the suggestions made.[3] This directed the Secretariat to investigate the short-term reconstruction requirements of ECAFE countries [4] for food, seed, fertilizers, textiles, raw materials, coal and other fuels, and agricultural, mining, and transport equipment. It should indicate how and to what extent these demands could be met from national, regional, or outside sources. The Secretariat should also study and make proposals on ways of increasing the supply of trained

2. Docs. E/CN.11/SR.1–14, June 16–28, 1947, E/CN.11/AC.2/SR.1–2, June 19–20, 1947.

3. Doc. E/CN.11/26, June 25, 1947.

4. ECAFE countries in this study mean Asian countries within the geographical scope of ECAFE.

personnel and of getting outside technical assistance. If it thought field teams were desirable for any part of these investigations it should make suggestions on their character, scope, and functions to the next session of the Commission. As this was fixed for the following November, the Secretariat was left little time in which to complete its tasks.

By the opening of the second session at Baguio in the Philippines, the Executive Secretary, P. S. Lokanathan,[5] was ready with his own ideas. In addition to the work already begun he suggested the Commission might examine the relevance of the Japanese economy to the reconstruction problems and needs of the region; the economic significance for ECAFE countries of the growth of substitutes; the lessons of UNRRA in the field of agricultural rehabilitation; and, with the International Monetary Fund (IMF), the extent, causes, and remedies of foreign exchange shortages. He envisaged the creation of committees on industry and materials, transport, fuel and power, technical training and recruitment, and, jointly with the Food and Agriculture Organization (FAO), one on food and agricultural production. The information these committees would need could probably best be assembled through working parties. Some of these subsidiary bodies might be made responsible for allocating scarce commodities such as food, fertilizers, fuel, and raw cotton. While it would be premature, Lokanathan admitted, to establish immediately a full panel of committees on all aspects of economic reconstruction, the Commission might begin with one or two of the ones he suggested as, for instance, a joint ECAFE/FAO committee on food and agricultural production. He proposed, in any case, to convene an early conference of senior government officials engaged in the planning and administration of reconstruction and development programs within the region. Initiating and coordinating the activities of the specialized agencies, he thought, might prove another fruitful line for ECAFE

5. P. S. Lokanathan. Born 1894. Educated Bangalore, Madras University, and London School of Economics. Later professor of economics at Madras University. President of the Economic Association of India, editor of the *Hindustani Times*, and then of the *Eastern Economist*. Also served on Consultative Committee of Economists to the Indian government and Labour Advisory Board of the Madras government. Indian delegate to World Business Conference 1944, Pacific Relations Conference 1945, and UN Conference on Trade and Employment 1947. Publications include works on industrial welfare and industrial organization in India.

to follow. Finally, the Secretariat would collect and evaluate statistical and other data and publish an annual economic survey of Asia and the Far East.[6]

These ideas bore a striking resemblance to the functions and structure of ECE at that time. Both bodies, it is true, were set up with similar mandates and the same emphasis on immediate postwar reconstruction. But the principal activities of ECE, not least its allocation functions, were derived from the emergency economic organizations it absorbed. In Asia the allocation of food, fuel, and edible oils was organized through the Office of the United Kingdom Special Commissioner in South East Asia.[7] Unless ECAFE took over this work it had small hope of building up its own allocation machinery. A few Asian countries, the Philippines especially, wanted ECAFE to allocate rice and agricultural equipment but the Special Commissioner felt the Commission was not well enough equipped and organized to assume this responsibility. There was also some expansive talk about ECAFE coordinating national reconstruction and development programs and the activities of the specialized agencies. India suggested it should fix national production targets and then ensure they were reached.

All Asian delegates, at any rate, appeared to hope the Commission would act as a begetter and channel of aid from the West. Whatever the motives behind aid to Europe, President Manuel Roxas declared in his opening speech, they applied equally to Asia and the Far East. All this boiled down to a demand, not yet explicitly stated, for a program of aid and reconstruction on the scale being planned for Europe at that time by the incipient Or-

6. Docs. E/CN.11/37–41, Oct. 23, 1947.

7. The United Kingdom Special Commissioner in South East Asia was appointed in March 1946 and took over the economic coordination work of the Supreme Commander for the Allied Powers in the area. The economic organization of the Special Commissioner prepared rice shipping programs, recommended allocations of coal and edible oils, made a general review of the food situation and the supply of consumers goods, collected statistical and other economic information, and convened occasional conferences on food, nutrition, fisheries, social problems, and statistics. Only representatives of British territories and the Allied Forces attended its meetings at first; but from August 1946, Thailand, the Netherlands Indies, and Indo-China also participated, and China, the Philippines, and the United States were represented by unofficial observers. The economic organization of the Special Commissioner and SCAP were the only two effective reconstruction agencies in the region. For an outline of the activities of the former, see Docs. E/CN.11/36, Nov. 20, 1947; E/CN.11/88, May 7, 1948.

ganization for European Economic Co-operation (OEEC). The United States, on the other hand, deprecated the "undue prominence" given to external financial assistance in the debate. Dependence on foreign aid over a protracted period, the United States delegate said, "may be definitely harmful through discouraging national initiative, trade and other prerequisites to a realisation of a healthy independent economy. It will be in the interests of all to create as expeditiously as possible self-supporting economic conditions deriving from greatly augmented production and a revitalised and expanding foreign trade." To this end Asian countries should strive to achieve a sound currency, an effective mobilization and use of domestic financial resources, and a reduction of trade barriers.[8]

The Western powers, particularly Britain, were no less deflating about the other functions Asian members and the Executive Secretary had in mind for ECAFE. The two main dangers before the Commission, the British delegate argued, were attempting too much at one time and usurping the functions of other international bodies. Principal decisions at this session certainly reflected this caution. A working party of not more than four experts was set up to report upon the industrial development plans of individual countries "with due attention to extractive industries and transport, and the relations of these plans to the industrial progress of the area as a whole." It should pay special attention to the need for technical skill and capital equipment and consider how much and in what form these requirements could be met from local sources or with outside assistance. ECAFE countries were urged "to exchange views on their plans for industrial development and, as far as possible, to co-ordinate their efforts so that the maximum and most efficient use may be made of the resources available, bearing in mind the urgent need for a balanced industrial development of the area as a whole."[9] The Commission directed the Executive Secretary to consult FAO and the International Labour Organisation (ILO) about joint action with ECAFE in the field of agriculture and technical training respectively and to establish close liaison with the United Kingdom

8. Docs. E/CN.11/SR.15–29, Nov. 25–27, 1947, E/CN.11/AC.3/SR.1–9, Nov. 29–Dec. 6, 1947; E/CN.11/AC.4/SR.1–6, Dec. 1–3, 1947.

9. Doc. E/CN.11/62, Dec. 8, 1947.

Special Commissioner in South East Asia. The Secretariat should also establish a trade promotion section, formulate a program of work in the field of statistics, and publish an annual *Economic Survey of Asia and the Far East.*[10] The British delegation had gained all its main objectives. ECAFE had avoided unilateral action in the fields of other bodies, premature decisions on standing committees, allocation or other operational functions, and an over-ambitious work program.

Little further progress toward developing its functions and structure was made by the Commission at its third session in June 1948. Most delegations seemed poorly prepared, some of the documents had evidently been written in a hurry, and the general debate was superficial. The Working Party on Industrial Development in particular had not managed to complete its task in time and presented only an interim report.[11] The lack of reliable and comparative data made it difficult to collate the economic programs of ECAFE countries. It concentrated instead on showing how their immediate rehabilitation requirements depended on the import of materials and equipment from advanced industrial nations. The Commission directed it to complete the report and to co-opt additional experts to prepare detailed studies on fuel and power; transport and transport equipment in relation to industry; fertilizers and agricultural requisites; basic materials, including ores and metals; textiles; cottage and small-scale industry; and heavy engineering industries. The Working Party in addition should estimate the immediate and long-term capital requirements of ECAFE countries and how they might be met from local and foreign sources.[12] Most Asian delegates talked vaguely about the desirability of devising international arrangements for this purpose without explicitly demanding anything so definite as the Asian equivalent of the European Recovery Program (ERP). The Western powers said nothing, however, to encourage their hopes. On the contrary the United States delegation pointed out that its country was already carrying heavy foreign assistance burdens and emphasized the importance of attracting foreign capital by offering adequate security and a reasonable return.

10. ECOSOC,OR: 6th Sess., 1948, Suppl. No. 8.
11. Doc. E/CN.11/82, May 6, 1948, and Corr. 1, June 4, 1948.
12. Doc. E/CN.11/114, June 14, 1948.

Another subject the Commission asked the Working Party on Industrial Development to report on was the difficulties hampering a full use of Japanese resources for the benefit of the region. The specter of increased Japanese trade competition this conjured up did not please Britain. On the larger problem of foreign exchange shortages IMF was requested to examine whether, and if so, to what extent, a multilateral clearing system would help to overcome the payments problem and facilitate the trade of the ECAFE region. The chances of IMF producing a favorable verdict seemed rather remote, however, since both Britain and the United States strongly opposed the idea. On the side of organization the Commission approved the creation of a joint ECAFE/FAO Working Party on Agricultural Requisites and a Secretariat section on technical training. A Russian proposal for a full committee on labor was defeated on the grounds that this would obviously duplicate the functions of ILO.[13]

When the Commission met again in November and December 1948 the hitherto implicit desire of Asian countries to use ECAFE as a lever to prize from the United States an Asian Recovery Program finally came into the open. It certainly lay behind much of the thinking that went into the completed report of the Working Party on Industrial Development. This roughly calculated the cost of various national economic development programs in the region over an average period of five years at $14 billion, of which about half constituted the foreign exchange requirement.[14] "It is indeed obvious," the Executive Secretary remarked, "that, however much the plans of these countries may be reduced in their content, scope and duration they cannot be put through without substantial external aid, physical and financial."

China and India quite simply demanded a Marshall Plan for Asia. The United States answered with an uncompromising refusal. It was prepared to assist them as much as it could, but only through private investment and government loans. ECAFE countries, the United States delegation advised, should seek through expanding exports and political stability to create the conditions necessary to attract such assistance. It warned them against the

13. Docs. E/CN.11/SR.30–43, June 23, 1948–June 14, 1948. (Meetings of June 2–29, 1948.)

14. Doc. E/CN.11/131, Oct. 31, 1948.

creation of industries dependent on a high degree of protection for their survival. Heavy industry in particular was not essential to improve living standards; nor was the integration of national economic programs. As to the possibility of direct ECAFE assistance to individual countries, the United States delegation maintained that the mandate of the Commission did not permit it to assume operational responsibilities. Britain agreed with the United States that there were few spheres of industrial development where international action could usefully be taken.

Asian countries did not cease after this to remind the West of their need for assistance or to contrast what they were receiving with what was being done for Europe under the Marshall Plan.[15] But the rude shock given to their hopes of ECAFE at this session momentarily subdued their interest in the Commission. They wanted help and got sermons. At any rate, on the discussion of the report of the Working Party on Industrial Development they had no firm proposals to make. The Working Party recommended that the Commission establish a committee on industrial development. Executive Secretary Lokanathan publicly pressed and privately lobbied for the proposal and for the setting up of standing committees on trade and technical training and one jointly with FAO on agriculture.[16] Permanent committees, he believed, were now required for implementing effectively the Commission's recommendations. Burma, Cambodia, China, India, Nepal, the Philippines, the Soviet Union, and Thailand favored a committee on industrial development. But the Western powers, with Britain once more their chief spokesman, preferred that studies and recommendations should continue to be made by expert groups rather than by representative bodies. Britain insisted that the proper way to proceed was first to isolate and define problems, decide what should be done about them, and then consider the machinery needed to tackle them. Senior officials at

15. "The countries in South and South-East Asia are no doubt appreciative of the efforts which are being made in several places to give them technical training and knowledge, but it is often asked," the Pakistan Prime Minister Liaquat Ali Khan told the Commission in 1951, "whether in the great oceans of misery and suffering which comprise Asia and the Far East, the loan of a few technicians, the grant of a few scholarships and a periodic compilation of economic data, do in fact constitute effectual measures to remove poverty and suffering so rampant in these areas." Doc. E/CN.11/SR.78, Mar. 8, 1951.

16. Doc. E/CN.11/138, Oct. 18, 1948.

Headquarters also criticized Lokanathan for stressing organization rather than problems. At their suggestion the British delegation proposed that, as the report of the Working Party on Industrial Development contained numerous recommendations and had been received late, it should be submitted to a committee of the whole in about three months' time.

Lokanathan urged the Commission then and there to devise "an instrument appropriate to the real needs in the field of accomplishment, otherwise . . . the work of the Commission itself might suffer." Intergovernmental cooperation could not be pursued through expert groups which did not actually represent or speak for governments.[17] Nothing would be lost if a committee on industry was set up immediately. The Executive Secretary's suggestion, the United Kingdom delegate bluntly rejoined, was "entirely premature and inappropriate and had little chance of acceptance by the Economic and Social Council." With this, France, the Netherlands, and the United States agreed. While most Asian delegates supported Lokanathan's position in principle, they were obviously not ready to formulate specific proposals or problems for a standing committee to tackle and so fell in with the British motion to refer the Working Party's report to a committee of the whole. The idea of a committee on technical training was a nonstarter when ILO informed the Commission of its intention to establish a tripartite manpower committee for Asia and to open an Asian field office. But at least ECAFE could take some credit for galvanizing ILO into action in Asia. As for Lokanathan's suggestion of a joint ECAFE/FAO committee, the Commission decided, again largely on British insistence, that any such initiative must come from FAO.[18]

At the summer session of ECOSOC in 1948, the Soviet Union compared the methods of ECAFE unfavorably with those of ECE. While the latter created representative committees, the former created Secretariat services or expert groups. It therefore advocated ECAFE committees on trade, industrial development, and agriculture.

17. On the report of the joint ECAFE/FAO Working Party on Agricultural Requisites, the Indian delegate also argued that effective action "called for a body which would make specialised recommendations having at least some degree of assurance that they would be accepted by the governments concerned." Doc. E/CN.11/SR.50, Dec. 3, 1948.

18. Docs. E/CN.11/SR.44–58, Nov. 30–Dec. 13, 1948.

Other members of the Council pointed out that it was up to the Commission to decide what subsidiary bodies it wished to establish.[19] All the same, ECOSOC recommended that ECAFE "consider and keep under review . . . the establishment . . . and the terms of reference, of appropriate bodies, including committees, that could promote the successful accomplishment of its tasks." [20] In short, the Council expected some action from ECAFE.

When the Committee of the Whole met in March 1949, Lokanathan recommended that it create a single Committee on industry and trade.[21] Senior officials at Headquarters still felt he had not produced a convincing case in terms of the problems to be tackled by such a committee. In their view, he continued to emphasize objectives that presumed and depended upon the provision of substantial external financial assistance. Lokanathan's proposal nevertheless received overwhelming Asian support. In the face of this solid backing, the Western powers realized it was no longer practical politics to oppose all standing committees. The British, Indian, and United States delegations accordingly drafted, and the Committee of the Whole accepted, a composite resolution setting up a Committee on Industry and Trade.

The new Committee was empowered to establish subsidiary bodies and to provide expert advice to governments on specific projects or aspects of industrial development. It would pay special attention, however, to projects or programs which promised early results and were of special importance to the region. The Russians voted against the resolution because they thought the Industry and Trade Committee should make its recommendations and reports only to the Commission and not directly to the member governments. Its powers, in their view, constituted a threat to the internal affairs of member countries. At the following ECOSOC session, the United States disagreed with the decision to give the Committee authority to set up subsidiary bodies. It would only approve the resolution on the understanding that this did not constitute a blank check for the creation of an indefinite number of subsidiary bodies under the full Committee and that

19. ECOSOC,OR: 7th Sess., 186th–188th, 190th–192nd, 196th, 200th, 204th–206th Mtgs., July 30–Aug. 19, 1948.

20. ECOSOC Res. 144C(VII), Aug. 18, 1948.

21. Doc. E/CN.11/183, Mar. 4, 1949.

ECOSOC would be informed of all such proposals where they entailed financial implications.[22]

The Committee of the Whole also set up a subcommittee on iron and steel and an ad hoc subcommittee to consider and recommend improvements in travel facilities. In conclusion the Secretariat was directed to study a number of special problems such as coal resources, chemical fertilizers, the mobilization of domestic capital, and trade with Japan.[23] At the Commission session the following October, several Asian delegates wished to add an inland transport committee to the ECAFE structure. On the insistence of the Western powers, however, the question was postponed until a conference, or ad hoc committee, of transport experts which ECAFE expected to convene in 1950[24] had first reported on the scope for international cooperation in this field.

By now Asian thinking about the functions of ECAFE had shifted completely away from reconstruction to economic development. The Industry and Trade Committee and the Iron and Steel Subcommittee were the first extensions of its functions to emerge from their aspiration for industrial development. While this was clearly recognized to be something to be achieved primarily by national efforts, they wanted ECAFE to assist governments to formulate and implement specific projects, by channeling technical guidance, surveying natural resources and the best methods of utilizing them, collecting and collating the data required for shaping national economic policies, and analyzing the factors affecting economic growth. Lokanathan and some Asian members, notably India and Pakistan, hoped it could also help governments to prepare schemes for financial support from the International Bank for Reconstruction and Development (IBRD). But Britain and the United States dismissed the idea as a matter not for ECAFE but for direct dealings between governments and the Bank itself. Nor in their view should ECAFE attempt to advise the Bank on the conditions, character, and priorities of its lending.[25]

The inauguration of the United Nations Expanded Programme of Technical Assistance (EPTA) in 1949 provided a further op-

22. ECOSOC,OR: 9th Sess., 297th Mtg., July 15, 1949.
23. Docs. E/CN.11/AC.11/SR.1–6, Mar. 28–Apr. 5, 1949.
24. See p. 206.
25. Doc. E/CN.11/I&T/SR.1–8, Oct. 12–18, 1949.

portunity to enhance the value of ECAFE to its Asian members. Lokanathan certainly saw it that way. To the Commission, in October 1949, he suggested that ECAFE should receive and channel technical assistance requests, including applications for fellowships, and arrange for their provision directly or through Headquarters.[26] This clearly implied that ECAFE should actually have some technical assistance funds to allocate. It was to have an operational role in EPTA. The Director of the United Nations Department of Economic Affairs gave no encouragement to these suggestions. On the contrary, he emphasized to the Commission that responsibility for administering and implementing EPTA was given explicitly to the Secretary-General. Centralized operations were necessary and desirable, he added, if only because technical assistance funds had to be allocated between different regions. In plain truth, Headquarters disapproved of the role Lokanathan envisaged for ECAFE. Nor did the Commission endorse his ideas. At the same time it evidently expected ECAFE to play a substantive part in EPTA. It directed the Secretariat to help governments prepare their technical assistance schemes and asked ECOSOC to "consider in what ways the Commission and its Secretariat may with advantage participate in the specific aspects of the technical assistance programme under the administration of the Secretary-General." [27]

The declared policy of the Secretary-General on the subject was "that the secretariats of the regional economic commissions shall play a full and active role in the development of the programme and should have an important part in stimulating and developing its implementation." [28] Actually, their role amounted to very little. First, the regional secretariats were to help governments understand how to make and formulate precisely their requests for assistance, but were not to stimulate requests. Second, they should assist Headquarters to evaluate these applications and suggest how they might be granted. Third, they were to identify and promote possible regional technical assistance projects such as seminars, training courses, and study tours. In addition, it was always open to the commissions to make recom-

26. Doc. E/CN.11/200, Sept. 6, 1949, and Corr. 1, Oct. 17, 1949.
27. Doc. E/CN.11/231, Oct. 29, 1949.
28. Doc. E/CN.11/AC.12/2, Oct. 26, 1949.

mendations to ECOSOC on policy matters affecting EPTA. Full administrative, financial, and operational control over the United Nations part of the program was centralized at Headquarters. In July 1950, a new department, the Technical Assistance Administration (TAA), was established there for this purpose under a Director General who reported direct to the Secretary-General. The executive secretaries of the regional commissions offered to act as the regional arm of TAA; but the latter refused to delegate any of its responsibilities. The Western powers that donated the bulk of the funds also favored this high degree of centralization. Despite the assurance of a "full and active role," the regional commissions were given no significant tasks. The aims of ECAFE and those of United Nations technical assistance operations were to be pursued apart, rather than support and complement one another.[29]

Thus even tangible assistance from the United Nations itself was steered clear of ECAFE. Its activities would have to be very largely self-help exercises. By 1949 the foundations of this kind of cooperation were beginning to be laid. In that year ECAFE's Bureau of Flood Control came into operation,[30] and its Industry and Trade Committee and Iron and Steel Subcommittee held their first sessions. Ad hoc conferences on travel facilities and inland transport problems were also convened. "There had perhaps been some tendency in the past," the Commission reported to ECOSOC in 1951, "to instruct the secretariat to make studies which, while of broad economic interest, did not bear immediate relation to the actual plans of the countries concerned. There seems now to be a growing realization of the need for relating regional studies to national plans." [31]

At the same time Asian governments were growing administratively stronger and beginning to define their national economic objectives. Their delegates gradually became better informed, more experienced in international conference techniques, and more possessive toward ECAFE. A new assertiveness crept into their speeches. They grew noticeably more resentful of the im-

29. For further comment, see Chap. 15.

30. See p. 174.

31. *ECAFE Report to ECOSOC, 6 April 1949–20 May 1950*, Doc. E/CN.11/241/Rev.1, May 23, 1950, Part VI, p. 48.

perious attitude of the Western powers toward ECAFE and of the time wasted on purely political propaganda between the West and the Soviet Union. Asian views and concerns, they felt, should carry more weight in the deliberations and decisions of the Commission.

The dominating role of the Western powers might have been more tolerable to Asian delegates if it had been more constructive. In fact it was essentially negative. They consistently opposed proposals for extending ECAFE's functions beyond those of collecting information and publishing studies. Only very reluctantly did they capitulate to the Asian demand for a committee on industry and trade. They poured cold water on all ideas for facilitating an expansion of intraregional trade. They opposed the development of heavy industry in Asia on the ground that iron and steel supplies were becoming more plentiful and cheaper in Europe and the United States. Indeed, so equivocal did their approach to Asian industrialization seem that the Philippines urged the Commission in 1950 to put itself on record as clearly favoring the region's industrial development.[32] In Asian eyes their outlook mocked the purpose of ECAFE as an instrument of Asian aspirations. Furthermore, the Western powers used their superior voting strength to ensure that their own views prevailed. But when Britain, at a subsidiary body meeting in 1950, went to the length of actually casting two votes, one for itself and the other for Malaya and British Borneo which its delegate also represented,[33] Lokanathan and the Asian members decided the time had come for the position of the outside powers in the Commission to be seriously reviewed.

The Executive Secretary felt strongly that the outside powers should not participate on an equal basis with Asian members. One way to ensure this limitation would be to deny them voting rights. But the Assistant Secretary-General in charge of the Department of Economic Affairs, David K. Owen, thought it would be preferable to encourage them to practice restraint in expressing views and using votes contrary to Asian wishes, than to attempt formally to change ECAFE's terms of reference. With

32. Doc. E/CN.11/SR.75, May 30, 1950.

33. For this episode, see p. 207. Associate members, it should be remembered, have the right to vote in subsidiary bodies.

Owen's approval, Lokanathan presented a memorandum along these lines to the 1951 session of the Commission at Lahore. "It has been argued, in my view not unreasonably," the memorandum stated, "that when the Commission collectively reaches a decision by vote, especially on matters not directly involving countries outside the region, such a decision should in fact reflect the view of the members of the region or the majority thereof; and that a Commission decision reached because the votes of non-regional members outweighs the votes of regional members, or most of them, is anomalous and inappropriate. Yet such decisions have from time to time in fact been taken. While it may not be desirable to make any formal change in the membership of the Commission, member governments might nevertheless wish to employ devices, formal or informal, to ensure that decisions of this regional Commission accurately reflect the views of its regional members. Such devices might include abstention of non-regional members or at any rate the exercise of restraint in voting, especially on matters predominantly concerning the region." [34]

The memorandum was discussed at a private meeting of the heads of delegations. The British delegate fought hard against the sentiments it expressed; but in the face of strong Asian support for them, not least from Pakistan, he conceded defeat. More than that, he agreed to join the delegates of Burma, India, and Pakistan in distilling the general consensus of the meeting and became the chairman of their drafting group. Interestingly enough all four delegates were former members of the Indian Civil Service (ICS). As a result of their drafting, the Commission wrote into its annual report to ECOSOC a statement of principle on the question raised by Lokanathan which became known as the Lahore Agreement or Convention. "Member governments feel," the Commission declared, "that the time has come when clearer recognition should be given to the principle that member countries belonging to the region should take their own decisions in the Commission on their own economic problems; and that in doing so they should take full account of the views of the associate members in the region, to be ascertained when not known by referring any specific resolution to a committee. In pursuance of this principle the member countries of the Commission not in the region

34. Doc. E/CN.11/278, Jan. 18, 1951.

would be willing, as a general rule, to refrain from using their votes in opposition to economic proposals predominantly concerning the region which had the support of a majority of the countries of the region." [35]

Two points are worth noting about this Agreement. First, it did not limit the freedom of action of the outside powers on political issues or on economic questions that did not predominantly concern the region. Second, it advanced the status of associate members in the Commission by treating their views as if they were votes. But what mattered most was the spirit of the Agreement. It affirmed that ECAFE existed primarily to serve the interests of its Asian members. What this meant in terms of the scope and methods of cooperation subsequently pursued through ECAFE, the rest of this study seeks to examine.

35. *ECAFE Report to ECOSOC, 28 February 1951–7 March 1951*, Doc. E/CN.11/306, Apr. 16, 1951, para. 341.

PART TWO

THE MACHINERY OF COOPERATION

CHAPTER 5

The Commission

The essential purpose and character of the Commission are set out in the first paragraph of its terms of reference. This directs it to "initiate and participate in measures for facilitating concerted action for the economic reconstruction and development of Asia and the Far East, for raising the level of economic activity in Asia and the Far East and for maintaining and strengthening the economic relations of these areas both among themselves and with other countries of the world." Two points need to be noted about this wording. First, the word "development" was not included in the original terms of reference ECOSOC drafted in 1947; it was added in 1951,[1] at the suggestion of the Executive Secretary, to put greater emphasis on economic development in the declared objectives of the Commission. Second, the inclusion of the word "measures" underlines the fact that ECAFE was designed to carry out practical tasks. In addition, it is empowered to "make or sponsor such investigations and studies of economic and technological problems and developments within territories of Asia and the Far East" and to "undertake or sponsor the collection, evaluation and dissemination of such economic, technological and statistical information" as it deems appropriate.

Two further responsibilities were also added in 1951. Within its available resources the Secretariat may "perform such advisory services . . . as the countries of the region may desire, provided that such services do not overlap with those rendered by the specialised agencies or the United Nations Technical Assistance Ad-

1. Doc. E/CN.11/304, Mar. 7, 1951.

ministration." Second, the Commission shall "assist the Economic and Social Council at its request in discharging its functions within the region in connexion with any economic problems, including problems in the field of technical assistance." [2] Following the inclusion of the social aspects of economic development in the mandate of the Economic Commission for Africa (ECA) which ECOSOC established in 1958, ECAFE was also empowered to "deal as appropriate with the social aspects of economic development and the inter-relationship of the economic and social factors." [3] This marked no new departure in the scope of its activities; it merely formalized an existing situation.[4] Similarly, when the African Commission was mandated to establish appropriate liaison and cooperation with the other regional commissions, ECAFE's terms of reference were altered to include the same provision.[5] This again merely gave legislative sanction to well-established practices.

The Commission may make recommendations on any matter within its competence directly to its member governments and to the specialized agencies concerned with its activities, provided it takes no action in respect of any country without the agreement of the government of that country. The only proposals which must have the prior approval of ECOSOC are those that "would have important effects on the economy of the world as a whole." After consulting any specialized agency functioning in the same general field and with the approval of the Council, the Commission may set up such subsidiary bodies as it deems appropriate. It is also empowered under the terms of reference to draft its own rules of procedure.

By virtue of this mandate ECAFE, like its sister regional commissions, has enjoyed a considerable measure of autonomy. It is subject to the policy directives of ECOSOC and the General Assembly,

2. The responsibilities of ECLA with regard to UN technical assistance activities were defined in more far-reaching terms. Thus the equivalent part of its mandate directs it to "assist the Economic and Social Council and its Technical Assistance Committee in discharging their functions with respect to the United Nations technical assistance programme, in particular by assisting in their appraisal of these activities in the Latin-American region." See *ECLA Annual Report to ECOSOC, 17 June 1951–14 February 1952,* p. 1. For the further evolution of ECAFE's mandate see pp. 336–39.

3. ECOSOC Res. 723(XXVIII), July 17, 1959.

4. See pp. 263–64.

5. ECOSOC Res. 723 (XXVIII), July 17, 1959.

but these are invariably couched in flexible language. Usually these directives take the form of guiding principles on matters of concern to ECAFE insofar as they directly refer to the regional commissions, or appear to be relevant to their functions and activities, or envisage action on a regional basis. The Soviet Union showed some tendency in the early years of ECOSOC to introduce resolutions giving detailed directives to the regional commissions but these found no support among other members. The United States evinced a marked inclination in the past to judge the merits of various proposals concerning or emanating from the regional commissions by whether they strengthened or weakened the authority of the parent body. This point of view was shared also by Britain and other Western nations. In the face of strong currents of regional political consciousness, however, ECOSOC dared not hold the regional commissions on a tight rein, especially as its own membership became steadily less representative of the growing voting power of the African-Asian bloc in the General Assembly. It is now, in fact, the General Assembly more than ECOSOC which shapes the policies that vitally affect the regional commissions.[6]

The Council requires the Commission to submit an annual report on its activities and plans.[7] The discussion of this report is the main occasion on which the parent body appraises the work of ECAFE as a whole. In the earlier years of ECAFE the report to ECOSOC was prepared and issued by the Secretariat on its own responsibility, but from 1951 onward, it has been formally adopted and issued by the Commission itself. It is also worth noting that ECAFE and its sister commissions in Europe and Latin America were created as an experiment; it was not taken for granted that they would necessarily become permanent organs of the United Nations. Their permanent status was only confirmed by ECOSOC in 1951 [8] after a searching review of all three commissions. But in theory the Council could at any time abolish them just as it

6. Significantly, it was a General Assembly directive to ECOSOC and not an ECOSOC recommendation to the General Assembly which in each case initiated the creation of regional commissions for Asia, Latin America, and Africa.

7. ECAFE's original terms of reference required it to submit interim reports to each regular session of ECOSOC in addition to a full report once a year. But in 1949 the Council waived this obligation and left the submission of any interim reports to the discretion of the Commission.

8. ECOSOC Res. 414(XIII), Sept. 18–20, 1951.

created them. Their strength rests on a *de facto* rather than a *de jure* status. It stems from their representative character within their respective regions, the degree of regional solidarity they embody, the practical nature of their activities, and the degree of self-discipline imposed by the sense that they also form part of a wider framework of agreed purposes, the United Nations itself.

At present eighteen Asian [9] and seven non-Asian countries [10] have full membership in ECAFE and four Asian territories [11] have associate membership. While the geographical scope of ECAFE is entirely the responsibility of ECOSOC, admission to associate membership is entirely within the power of the Commission. As already indicated, associate members have all the privileges of full membership except the right to vote and hold office at sessions of the Commission or in a committee of the whole.[12] They may, in other words, vote and hold office in any of its subsidiary bodies, including any ad hoc committees established during sessions of the Commission itself. One small discrimination they suffered originally was removed in 1953 when, on the initiative of Cambodia, the Commission amended its rules of procedure to give them the right, hitherto not formally sanctioned, of proposing items for inclusion in the Commission's agenda.[13]

Under its terms of reference ECAFE is obliged to invite, at their request, United Nations member countries not members of the Commission to participate in meetings of concern to them in a consultative capacity.[14] The first participation of this sort was at the regional trade promotion conferences convened by ECAFE in 1951 and 1953. Indeed, for the second of these two conferences

9. Afghanistan, Burma, Cambodia, Ceylon, China, India, Indonesia, Iran, Japan, Laos, Malaya, Mongolia, Nepal, Pakistan, the Philippines, South Korea, South Viet-Nam, and Thailand.

10. Australia, France, the Netherlands, New Zealand, the Soviet Union, the United Kingdom, and the United States.

11. Brunei, Hong Kong, North Borneo and Sarawak, and Singapore.

12. In 1954 the Commission asked ECOSOC to allow it to elect a chairman or vice chairman from the delegations of associate member countries but the Council ignored the recommendation.

13. Doc. E/CN.11/367, 1953.

14. Paragraph 9 of the terms of reference states: "The Commission shall invite any Member of the United Nations not a member of the Commission to participate in a consultative capacity in its consideration of any matter of particular concern to that non-member." For a legal interpretation, see p. 59 n. 18.

ECOSOC passed a special resolution [15] authorizing ECAFE to invite three countries that were members of ECE but not of the United Nations.[16] No United Nations member country attended the Commission itself in a consultative capacity until 1952. Since about 1955 the number has grown rapidly and at the 1960 and 1961 sessions, for example, fourteen countries, the bulk of them European, attended in this capacity.[17] On one occasion the exercise of this right seriously embarrassed ECAFE's relations with one of its most important Asian members. The episode is worth recounting in some detail for it raised an important point of principle for the United Nations.

In 1960 the Commission was due to meet in Karachi. But on the last-minute instructions of the Secretary-General the venue was switched to Bangkok because Pakistan refused to give an assurance that it would grant a visa to the Ambassador of Israel in Bangkok to enable him to represent his country in a consultative capacity. In taking this decision the Secretary-General was upholding a fundamental principle, namely, the absolute right of access of United Nations members to United Nations meetings. In the opinion of the United Nations Legal Division, paragraph 9 of ECAFE's terms of reference gives the Commission and the Secretariat no discretion whatsoever; ECOSOC had, in effect, given a standing invitation to any United Nations member to attend the Commission session.[18]

15. ECOSOC Res. 459(XIV), Dec. 19, 1952.

16. See p. 241.

17. They included West Germany which, although not a member of the UN, is permitted to participate under ECOSOC Res. 617(XXII) of July 20, 1956, "on a basis similar to that provided in paragraph 9 of the terms of reference of the Commission."

18. The position regarding its subsidiary bodies is more complex. In the opinion of the UN Legal Division they are obliged to invite UN member countries to participate in a consultative capacity only if they have adopted by decision or in practice the rules of procedure of the Commission. This is because rule 3 of the Commission is identical with paragraph 9 of its terms of reference. But as its subsidiary bodies are free to adopt their own rules of procedure they are normally in a position to decide the question themselves. Where the participants at ECAFE meetings act in their own personal capacity and not as government representatives, no UN member country, indeed not even a full member of the Commission, has the right to participate, for such meetings are of a nongovernmental nature even though the experts may be selected by the governments. The reports of ECAFE subsidiary bodies have not always been accurate, therefore, in referring to the participation of

Pakistan's refusal to grant the usual facilities to a representative of Israel was an emotional and political decision designed to improve its standing with the Arab bloc. It succeeded in doing so at the expense of its obligations under the United Nations Charter and its relations with ECAFE. The Pakistan government was nevertheless offended by the Secretary-General's action. Its officials in Karachi maintained that Pakistan's position in the matter had long been made clear, yet only after preparations for receiving the Commission were well advanced and the invitations issued did the Secretariat decide to make it an issue of principle. On the other hand, Pakistan could have pointed out to the Arab bloc that it was merely acting as host to a United Nations conference and not itself sponsoring the conference.[19] By this time, however, the matter had become, under the rules of procedure, the responsibility of the Secretary-General and was being dealt with through the Permanent Pakistan Mission at United Nations Headquarters. While awaiting a reply to the request for the usual facilities to be granted to the representative of Israel, Headquarters had to proceed on the assumption that Pakistan would, in fact, honor its obligations under the Charter. In these circumstances there was no way of preventing it issuing invitations to the Commission session in Karachi. Only at the last minute, when no reply had been received, did the Secretary-General feel compelled to move the session to Bangkok.

The Commission is also obliged by its terms of reference to invite the specialized agencies[20] to participate in a consultative capacity. They have, in fact, been most punctilious in their attendance at the Commission and have collaborated as well in

---

a UN member country in a consultative capacity under paragraph 9 of the Commission's terms of reference.

19. It is relevant to note in this connection that trainees from Taiwan have participated in the Lahore Training Centre for Railway Operating and Signalling Officials (see p. 210) though Pakistan does not recognize Taiwan. On one occasion ECAFE had to make extraordinary arrangements when Cambodia and Thailand broke off diplomatic relations, to enable the Cambodian delegate to attend a meeting in Bangkok of the Committee for Co-ordination of Investigations of the Lower Mekong. (See p. 202). In other words, it should not have been beyond the wit of the Pakistan government to devise a similar formula in this case. The writer learned in Karachi that the Pakistan Foreign Minister favored some such solution but was overruled by his colleagues and senior officials.

20. E.g., FAO, IMF, ILO, UNESCO, the World Bank.

many of the substantive activities of its subsidiary bodies. The United Nations Technical Assistance Board (TAB) and the Special Fund are also usually represented at the Commission session. As regards intergovernmental organizations outside the United Nations, the terms of reference permit the Commission to invite them in a consultative capacity, but naturally do not make it mandatory. In fact, this kind of invitation has been confined almost exclusively to the Colombo Plan Bureau and the Interim Commission of the International Trade Organization/General Agreement on Tariffs and Trade (GATT). In 1961 it was extended to the League of Arab States and in 1962 to the Asian Productivity Organization (OPA) as well.[21]

The terms of reference and rules of procedure of the Commission contained no reference at first to nongovernmental organizations (NGO's). The omission was quickly pointed out by ECOSOC and, in June 1948, the Commission broadly defined the conditions under which NGO's could attend its meetings and be consulted by it on matters in which they had special competence or knowledge.[22] These are very similar to the arrangements made by ECOSOC.[23] Further clarifications were made by ECOSOC in 1951 [24] and 1952,[25] the most important of which required NGO's to consult the Executive Secretary on the form and content of their written statements before submitting them to the Commission. This was done on the recommendation of ECOSOC in an attempt to ensure that NGO's obeyed the injunction against attacking governments in their statements.

The NGO's that have participated in the Commission and its subsidiary bodies fall into two main categories: those representing important segments of the community [26] and those with spe-

21. The Commission and its Committee on Trade also recently invited the European Economic Community (EEC) to participate in their debates on trade problems.

22. Doc. E/CN.11/100/Rev.1, June 8, 1948.

23. For details of these arrangements, see *Non-Governmental Organisation,* Background Paper No. 76, New York, UNDPI, Research Division, April 1953.

24. Doc. E/CN.11/299, Mar. 6, 1951.

25. Doc. E/CN.11/339/Rev.1, Feb. 6, 1952.

26. E.g., International Chamber of Commerce; the International Confederation of Free Trade Unions; the World Federation of Trade Unions; the Inter-Parliamentary Union; and the World Federation of United Nations Associations. These are known under ECOSOC arrangements as Category A organizations.

cialized skills.[27] The ECAFE Secretariat in turn has been represented at some NGO conferences. But with few exceptions NGO's have not been closely associated with the substantive activities of ECAFE. The lack of well-developed NGO's in the region with specialized skills has in fact hampered the Commission, for inevitably the Secretariat has been burdened with tasks its sister commission in Europe, for example, has left to such organizations.

The present working site of ECAFE is Bangkok. When ECOSOC established regional commissions for Europe and Asia it was generally felt that their headquarters should be located at the regional offices of the United Nations. In the case of Europe that meant Geneva. But no similar office existed in Asia and none has been established. It is doubtful if one would ever have been opened in Europe if the Palais des Nations at Geneva had not already been taken over from the League of Nations. Pending the opening of a United Nations regional office for Asia, ECOSOC declared Shanghai to be the temporary home of ECAFE. It agreed to consider the question again in 1948 after hearing the Commission's own views.[28] At the Commission's second session in the Philippines in 1947 that country suggested Baguio as the headquarters of ECAFE. China reacted sharply and at once proposed it should remain in Shanghai. Britain felt the question could be deferred until the following session but that as the Secretariat and its records were already at Baguio, they might as well remain there until a new site was chosen. The United States, however, was most anxious not to offend China and persuaded Britain to withdraw the second part of its proposal. A simple motion postponing the issue was thereupon carried.[29]

In June 1948 the Commission received further invitations. The Indian delegation offered its own country but did not press the invitation for fear of prejudicing India's claim to the United Nations regional office for Asia. The Philippines repeated its offer. Malaya, supported by Britain, suggested Singapore. China still wanted ECAFE to remain in Shanghai. France and Pakistan agreed that this was the best temporary solution though the latter put

27. E.g., International Organization for Standardization; World Power Conference; and the International Geological Congress. These are known under ECOSOC arrangements as Category B organizations.

28. ECOSOC Res. 37(IV), Mar. 28, 1947.

29. Doc. E/CN.11/SR.28, Dec. 8, 1947 and Doc. E/CN.11/68, Dec. 8, 1947.

in a word for Karachi as the permanent home. When the Executive Secretary also thought ECAFE should remain temporarily in Shanghai the Commission fell in with this view.[30]

The stay in Shanghai was short and uncomfortable. In the first place, owing to the high and fluctuating cost of living, it proved to be a very costly home. The official rate at which salaries and office expenditure had to be exchanged was considerably less than the market value of the United States dollar so that, by the end of 1947 for instance, the Chinese government pocketed fifty-five cents for every dollar ECAFE spent. No satisfactory agreement over a fair rate of exchange was reached with China and the gap between the official rate and the market rate continued to widen. Constantly rising prices and the uncertain political outlook caused hardship to the Secretariat and militated against the recruitment of competent staff. Chinese Communist military victories put an end to this situation. In December 1948 the Secretariat was compelled to move to Singapore for about two weeks and then, early in 1949, with the consent of Thailand, it settled in Bangkok. When ECOSOC in 1951 made ECAFE a permanent body it confirmed Bangkok as its working site "until such time as the site of the office of the United Nations in Asia and the Far East shall be determined." [31]

That was not, however, the end of the story. At sessions of ECOSOC in 1951 and the Commission in 1952, the Philippines offered to house ECAFE in Manila but suggested that its headquarters should rotate every three or four years between different countries of the region. This would have been a costly habit. Ceylon declared it was equally anxious to act as host to ECAFE. The Commission thereupon decided to postpone further discussion of the question until its next session.[32] The following year the Philippines repeated its offer and Burma, India, and Pakistan came forth with new invitations. But none was prepared to press for a decision on its offer without some strong indication of a possible acceptance. Thailand indicated that ECAFE was most welcome to stay in Bangkok.[33] The Commission avoided an embar-

30. Doc. E/CN.11/120, June 11, 1948.

31. ECOSOC Res. 414(XIII), Sept. 18–20, 1951.

32. Doc. E/CN.11/344 and *ECAFE Annual Report to ECOSOC, 29 January 1952–8 February 1952,* paras. 176–77, Doc. E/CN.11/342, Mar. 19, 1952.

33. "So far as the rival claims of would-be hosts for regional offices are concerned . . . the governments of under-developed countries tend to regard such

rassing decison by leaving it to the Secretary-General to investigate the various sites offered, including Bangkok, and make the final choice.[34]

Many factors had to be carefully weighed in the selection of a suitable site: local operating costs [35] and diplomatic representation; office, hotel, and conference facilities; international communications; climate; the welfare of the staff in terms of housing, health, and educational amenities; and the political status of the would-be host country. Two senior members of the Secretariat, one from Headquarters and one from ECAFE, visited Karachi, Lahore, Hyderabad, Bangalore, Colombo, Rangoon, and Bangkok. On the basis of their report the Secretary-General decided ECAFE should remain in Bangkok. What, in fact, most determined this decision was not the relative merits of Bangkok over other possible sites but the political situation in Indo-China at that time. With civil war raging there and the possibility of Chinese Communist intervention, many senior United Nations officials as well as Western diplomats felt that any departure by ECAFE from Bangkok might well be interpreted as a United Nations retreat in the face of Communist expansion in South-east Asia. ECAFE in Bangkok was an important symbol of United Nations presence and interest in the welfare of the peoples of that area. The decision that it should stay there was actually taken before other possible sites had been investigated.

From a number of standpoints Bangkok is a good working site. It has well-developed air communication, adequate hotel accommodations, wide diplomatic representation, and houses the offices of other international agencies.[36] Among tinkling temples and the

---

offices as symbols of prestige." They also provide the host country with dollars and other useful benefits. See Walter R. Sharp, *Field Administration in the United Nations System* (New York, Praeger, 1961), p. 93.

34. For statement to the Commission of the Assistant Secretary-General in charge of the Departments of Economic Affairs and Social Affairs, see *ECAFE Annual Report to ECOSOC, 9 February 1952–14 February 1953,* Doc. E/CN.11/372, Mar. 2, 1953.

35. E.g., in 1952 Thailand, in an anti-inflationary move, appreciated its currency. The Assistant Secretary-General expected this to add over $250,000 in 1953 to the operating costs of ECAFE in Bangkok. In fact, its total actual expenditure between 1952 and 1953 rose by less than half this amount.

36. E.g., the following have regional field offices there: the Food and Agriculture Organization; the International Civil Aviation Organization; United Nations Chil-

amiable, gentle effervescence of Thai life, ECAFE has been able to function in a setting of comparative dignity and tranquillity. On the other hand, Bangkok has a very debilitating climate, a high cost of living, and is not an intellectually exhilarating city. Over the last decade, however, the working and living conditions of the Secretariat have improved greatly, not least because of air conditioning. Compared with other international agencies in Bangkok, ECAFE was slow to reach a satisfactory agreement with the Thai government on privileges, immunities, and facilities.[37] The fault lay partly at least in the somewhat peremptory manner of Lokanathan's dealings with the Thai government. Housed in an old palace, the office accommodation of the Secretariat left much to be desired. Its working conditions improved enormously in 1953 when the Thai government moved ECAFE into an entirely new building.[38] There it has remained ever since. Whatever the disadvantages of Bangkok as a working site it is not easy to suggest an obviously better alternative.

The total actual expenditure of ECAFE in 1960 was roughly $1,800,000 as compared with approximately $250,000 during its first year of operation. In addition, the United Nations Bureau of Technical Assistance Operations (BTAO) [39] made available about $200,000 from technical assistance funds for the regional projects ECAFE sponsored that year. The cost of established posts in the Secretariat accounts for over 80 per cent of ECAFE's total expenditure.[40] Thus, the steepest rises in the budget, notably from 1950 to 1951 and from 1956 to 1957, have corresponded with relatively big jumps in the number of professional staff.

The Commission itself holds an annual public session [41] lasting about two weeks and in a different place each year. Indeed, only

---

dren's Fund; and the Technical Assistance Board; while the World Health Organization has an area office there. Bangkok is also the home of the South East Asia Treaty Organization (SEATO).

37. Sharp, *Field Administration,* p. 110.

38. This was actually built to accommodate delegates at a time when there was a severe shortage of hotel rooms in Bangkok. The Thai government converted the building into offices for the Secretariat, added a conference hall and committee rooms, and presented it to the UN rent free. Part of it is occupied also by ICAO.

39. BTAO superseded TAA in 1958 as the entity within the Department of Economic and Social Affairs responsible for UN technical assistance operations.

40. See Appendix III.

41. Until the end of 1949 it met twice a year.

three of its eighteen sessions have been held in Bangkok. It has met three times in India, twice each in Australia and Japan, and once each in Burma, Ceylon, China, Indonesia, Malaya, Pakistan, the Philippines, and Singapore. It will be noticed that one of the countries the Commission has twice visited, Australia, lies outside its geographical scope. It has also met twice as a committee of the whole, at Lake Success in 1947 and at Bangkok in 1949.

The idea of holding its session at different places was agreed by the Commission at its very first session in June 1947.[42] The practice has a number of advantages. First, it enables the host government to demonstrate its regard for ECAFE. There is, indeed, an element of friendly rivalry and national prestige in the nature and scale of the hospitality proffered. An impending Commission session stimulated some governments into building a special conference hall, a facility that subsequently enabled them to act as host to other international gatherings. Second, other members of the Commission can get to know the host country better, especially as visits and tours are usually arranged during the session. Finally, it helps arouse the interest of the people of the host country in the United Nations. Sometimes, however, hotel and conference facilities or climatic considerations have dictated a location well away from the principal centers of radio and press coverage where the Commission might hope to arouse the greatest local interest.

Although the financial organs of the United Nations, particularly the Advisory Committee on Administrative and Budgetary Questions, at one time criticized the practice of holding Commission sessions outside Bangkok, the extra cost involved is only a very small percentage of ECAFE's total expenditure. For example, the Tokyo session of 1955 cost ECAFE nearly $31,000 and was the most expensive ever held; yet this sum amounted to only 2.7 per cent of its total expenditure that year. The second most expensive session was held at Broadbeach, Australia, in 1959 and cost ECAFE practically $29,000; but this was only 1.6 per cent of its total expenditure that year.[43] The cost to the host country is probably greater. But a point not overlooked by the treasuries of would-be host governments is that such international conferences bring in

42. *ECAFE Report to ECOSOC on its First and Second Sessions,* Doc. E/606 and Corr.1, Jan. 8, 1948, chap. 8, p. 8.

43. See Appendix III.

valuable foreign exchange to an amount exceeding perhaps their own local currency costs. More serious is the extra burden on the Secretariat arising from servicing meetings away from Bangkok since many facilities and requirements have then to be arranged on an ad hoc basis.

When weighing up the pros and cons of what might be called a roving Commission session, it should never be forgotten that because of the nature of the region it serves, ECAFE must do all it can to publicize its actions and promote its purposes. For instance, ceremonial openings by distinguished public figures are an essential ritual of its meetings. It is compelled of necessity to be deeply involved with promotional activities that help to foster regional consciousness.

The official working languages of the Commission are English and French. At its first session in 1947 a United States proposal that English should be the sole working language was actually carried on a vote. The Secretariat pointed out, however, that this would be contrary to United Nations language practice and suggested French as well. Russian interpretation is also provided by the Secretariat. Simultaneous translation was first introduced into the proceedings of the Commission in 1955. Its absence in earlier years must have aggravated the atmosphere of sessions already polluted with the gunsmoke of political acrimony and procedural wrangles. A number of meeting places in the region—for example, Bangkok, Bangalore, New Delhi, Karachi, Kuala Lumpur, and Tokyo—have been equipped to provide simultaneous translation. The choice of venue is not limited on this account, however, as ECAFE has its own portable equipment.

Since 1950 it has been the practice of the Commission and its subsidiary bodies to elect the leader of the host delegation chairman of the session.[44] Until 1955 only one vice-chairman was elected. But deepening political divisions in the region made it advisable to provide for two vice-chairmen[45] so that if one was elected from a member or close friend of the South East Asia Treaty Organization (SEATO), the other could be selected from one of the politically nonaligned Asian countries. This has been

44. This was not possible from 1947 to 1949 as the Commission then met twice a year, while under the rules of procedure the chairman is elected for the whole year.

45. *ECAFE Annual Report to ECOSOC, 19 February 1954–7 April 1955,* Doc. E/CN.11/407, Apr. 19, 1955, para. 215.

the pattern invariably followed since. Voting in ECAFE is by a simple majority of those present. The Soviet Union originally wanted a two-thirds majority of those present on all "important questions" but won no support. All meetings of the Commission are public except when heads of delegations are informally called together, usually to decide some potentially controversial issue or procedural matter.[46]

The Commission is in theory ECAFE's top policy-making body. Its most important single task each year is to review the work of its subsidiary bodies, redirect their activities, instituting new ones or terminating old ones. But in practice appraising the work program as a whole is one of the functions the Commission performs least well. On the other hand, major policy issues have arisen from time to time which only it could decide. This is especially true of deadlocks that developed in the committees because the delegates were not in a position to commit their governments to actions with large political implications or overtones. In recent years the level of representation at the Commission has been comparatively high with a sprinkling always of delegates of ministerial rank. While ministers are not necessarily better informed than their senior officials, usually the contrary, it is useful to ECAFE for delegates of cabinet rank to learn of its activities and purposes at first hand. Moreover, as already mentioned, delegates of this importance may be required to deal with situations which officials have insufficient authority to unscramble.

Since 1953 the Commission has also held every year a full dress debate on the economic situation of the region. Gradually over the years it has evolved, in fact, a fairly standardized agenda; a few items may change from one session to the next but the bulk do not. It is thus a little misleading to label it the "Economic Parliament of Asia." [47] Colorful images of this kind, however, are a necessary ingredient of the propaganda by which international

46. Calling the heads of delegations together has been established by practice, for the rules of procedure do not envisage such informal meetings.

47. This phrase was used by the Indonesian Prime Minister in opening the 1952 session of the Commission and has often been repeated since. But some years previously a one-time staff member wrote: "ECAFE, though it has no legislative powers is, in a real way, the first Parliament of Asia." Victor Purcell, "The Economic Commission for Asia and the Far East," *International Affairs* (London) *24* (April 1948).

organizations must project themselves to governments and the wider public, not least in underdeveloped regions. On the other hand, ECAFE, over the last fifteen years, has schooled many Asian delegates in international conference techniques and parliamentary procedures at the international level. This has been an important function since neither experience has been part of the political tradition of Asian countries. Early Commission sessions were somewhat confusedly organized; but now they compare well with international conferences in other parts of the world, including those organized at United Nations Headquarters. As the biggest public occasion of ECAFE to receive press attention, the annual Commission session also helps to stimulate thinking about Asian problems in their regional setting and, last but not least, about the United Nations itself.

CHAPTER 6

Subsidiary Bodies

In 1949 ECAFE established its first permanent and representative subsidiary body, the Industry and Trade Committee. But what was formed turned out to be more like a holding company. Within two years its lengthening agenda embraced industrial development and planning, technical training and assistance, iron and steel, electric power, minerals, cottage and small-scale industries, housing and building materials, the financial aspects of economic development, trade and travel promotion, and international financial and trade problems. The list could easily be extended. It is hard to believe that such an omnibus body could have worked well and efficiently. Its agenda was clearly overloaded and the delegations rarely had enough people competent to deal with so wide a range of technical matters. What gradually helped to lighten the load was the creation of further subsidiary bodies. This ensured a proper consideration of specialized problems by expert government representatives and helped to increase government responsibility for acting upon the recommendations reached. The trend also shifted the center of ECAFE activity further away from general studies and discussions toward practical action and operational responsibilities.

Subcommittees were set up for iron and steel in 1949, electric power in 1951, minerals in 1954, and trade the same year. An Inland Transport Committee with separate subcommittees on railways, highways, and waterways was established in 1951. In 1957 the Industry and Trade Committee was transformed into the Industry and Natural Resources Committee and the Subcommittee on

Trade raised to the status of a full committee. A Bureau of Flood Control was created in 1949, a joint ECAFE/FAO Agricultural Division in 1952, and a Social Affairs Division in 1956. Permanent working parties were formed for cottage and small-scale industries in 1951, economic development and planning in 1955, housing and building materials in 1958, and senior geologists the following year. In 1957 a Committee for Coordination of Investigations of the Lower Mekong was established. In addition, regular regional conferences have been organized in the fields of statistics and water resources development. A variety of ad hoc conferences, working parties, study groups, and seminars have been convened from time to time on a host of other specialized subjects.

In the creation of permanent subsidiary bodies the Commission has moved cautiously. Only after the need was clearly felt and lengthily debated, and not usually without some experience first with an ad hoc status, was any subsidiary body made permanent. What constituted need, however, was often a matter of dispute. Even the omnibus Industry and Trade Committee was not created until after a Working Party on Industrial Development and a Secretariat Section on Trade Promotion had been in existence for two years. Not until after the experience of two regional trade promotion conferences and three years with subcommittee status was a full committee in the field of trade established. Again, working parties were invariably made permanent only after they had first been tried out on an ad hoc basis or, as in the case of housing and building materials, at secretariat level.

The essential difference between a working party and a subcommittee or full committee is that whereas the former usually functions as a group of individual experts with no authority to commit governments, the latter consists of official government representatives. Thus, while the recommendations of a subcommittee would normally require only formal endorsement by the parent body, those of a working party might well have to be considered in more detail. The committees and subcommittees of the Commission are free to draft their own rules of procedure, though they usually adopt formally [1] or in practice those of the Commission. They may also make recommendations directly to governments participating in their activities; consequently gov-

1. E.g., the Subcommittees on Electric Power, Highways, and Waterways.

ernments can act straightway on the decisions reached. This has the effect of giving these bodies a *de facto* authority which they do not possess or seek to possess *de jure*. But like the Commission they cannot take any action with respect to a country without the consent of the government of that country. The specialized agencies have taken part in many of their meetings and a number of United Nations members not members of ECAFE have also been represented on some of them.

All subsidiary body meetings are ordinarily open to the public. But whereas the proceedings of the committees are formal and summary records are kept, those of other subsidiary bodies are usually less formal and no summary records are kept. In the case of ECAFE's trade promotion talks [2] and the Committee for Coordination of Investigations of the Lower Mekong, however, the proceedings are not public. These exceptions are significant. They indicate that as ECAFE moved on to the plane of facilitating actual government negotiations, promotional activity and publicity had to bow before the demands of quiet diplomacy.

Until 1957 the Industry and Trade Committee met just prior to the annual Commission session and in the same place. The Industry and Natural Resources Committee followed suit for one year but since 1959 it has always met at Bangkok. The Trade Committee has always, and the Transport Committee nearly always, been convened at Bangkok. While these three committees hold annual sessions, subcommittees, working parties, and regional conferences normally meet at rather longer intervals. Many of these meetings have been held outside Bangkok so that their discussions can be complemented by visual demonstrations, visits to sites, installations, structures, and exhibitions.[3] In this way countries can learn from one another in a most practical fashion. It also provides a further opportunity for the host country to

2. See pp. 254–57.

3. In 1953 a meeting of the Railway Subcommittee was actually held at Paris. Headquarters deeply disapproved of the idea, however, and the example was not repeated because, apart from the expense, it weakens the case for a specifically regional examination of regional problems. In 1955 the Soviet delegation issued a general invitation to the Commission to hold one of its future sessions in the Soviet Union, "conditions permitting," but this has never been seriously entertained.

demonstrate its regard for ECAFE and for ECAFE to make an impact on the host country. Again, the meetings of subsidiary bodies follow the Commission's ritual in having some important public figure perform a ceremonial opening. Finally, the fact of being able to organize a successful international meeting, however modest in scale, helps to enhance the self-confidence and assurance of the smaller and more underdeveloped countries of the region.

A government offer to act as host country is not, however, in itself a sufficient reason for meeting elsewhere. The greater the number of meetings held outside Bangkok the greater the burden on the ECAFE budget and the Secretariat workload. For this reason the Secretariat's policy is to convene as many as possible at ECAFE headquarters. Although the financial saving to be gained by holding meetings in Bangkok cannot be very much, since only once during the last decade has the total cost of all subsidiary body meetings risen over one per cent of ECAFE's total expenditure,[4] the reduction of the servicing burden on the Secretariat could well be considerable. But what matters most is not where meetings are held but the total number the Secretariat is involved in helping to organize or service.

The Secretariat claims to have stabilized this total in recent years at about an average of eighteen meetings a year. But if all those mentioned in ECAFE's annual report are meetings the Secretariat has helped to organize, whether or not ECAFE was the principal sponsor, there was in fact a substantial increase in the workload of the Secretariat from this cause between 1957 and 1960. The biggest increases took place in 1959 and 1960. Over this same four-year period roughly 30 per cent of all the meetings listed took place outside Bangkok. But in 1959 and 1960 again the proportion was rather larger. From this evidence it would appear that the burden on the Secretariat from servicing or contributing to meetings has increased sharply in recent years. The number of professional staff, it should be added, has not grown in proportion. Nor must it be forgotten that the number and length of meetings convened by international agencies and de-

4. See Appendix III. It will be noticed that this cost is considerably smaller than that of holding the Commission session outside Bangkok.

manding the presence of government representatives and experts place a burden on national administrations as well. It is not therefore surprising that ECOSOC and the General Assembly should have directed their subsidiary organs in recent years to pay careful regard to this aspect of the problem.

CHAPTER 7

The Secretariat

From the standpoint of United Nations administration the ECAFE Secretariat forms part of the Department of Economic and Social Affairs and undertakes the duties of that department in regard to Asia and the Far East.[1] These duties, broadly speaking, entail the Secretariat to play the dual role of an institution for research and a service to assist government. In practice the two functions are closely linked, for the purpose of the research is to provide a basis for government discussions and actions.

At the end of 1960 there were 208 established posts in the Secretariat,[2] about 40 per cent being in professional grades and the remainder in general service grades, comprising secretaries, clerks, computers, messengers, and drivers. Ten years previously the total number of posts was 75, of which over half were in professional grades. The biggest jump in numbers during the decade occurred between 1956 and 1957 when the total establishment increased from 154 to 201 and the professional staff from 57 to 79. For the last four or five years, however, the total establishment has been more or less stabilized. Roughly 40 per cent of the professional staff may be called the hard core of the Secretariat, the

1. Paragraph 17 of the Commission's terms of reference reads: "The Secretary-General of the United Nations shall appoint the staff of the Commission, which shall form part of the Secretariat of the United Nations." The ECAFE Executive Secretary has the status of an undersecretary and though in theory he acts for and is responsible to the Secretary-General, in fact he reports to the Undersecretary for Economic and Social Affairs at Headquarters.

2. Excluding two professional posts in the joint ECAFE/FAO Agricultural Division which were on the FAO payroll.

rest being on rotation or short service contracts. As the general service staff are locally recruited about 80 per cent of them are Thai nationals.

Some 23 nationalities were represented in the Secretariat, only about half being Asian. However, over 80 per cent of all professional posts and an even larger proportion of the more senior posts were held by Asians.[3] ECAFE countries have understandably attached much importance to the region being well represented at all levels of the Secretariat. Indians formed the largest single group, followed by Chinese, Japanese, and Thais. These four nationalities accounted in fact for over half the professional staff, and the first three shared about half the senior posts. The relatively large representation of India and China dates back to the beginnings of ECAFE when they were among the very few Asian countries from which staff could be recruited.[4] Thus of the 19 staff members who had served more than five years in the Secretariat by the beginning of 1961, 12 were Chinese or Indian. Relative to its wealth of professional skill, Japan was not especially well represented. Two factors hampered a larger recruitment from this source. First, Japan did not become a member of the United Nations until 1956 and before then ECAFE could only recruit Japanese with the special permission of the Secretary-General in each case. Second, not many Japanese seem able to master a sufficient command of the English language. Relative to their number in the Secretariat, however, the Japanese held a good share of the more senior posts. It is rather surprising to note in this connection that not one single Thai was to be found among the senior staff.

Some caution must be exercised in drawing detailed conclusions from data on the Secretariat at any one moment of time for they are, in fact, constantly changing. The over-all picture, however, seems rather stable. From this it is clear that on the staff side ECAFE has become a thoroughly Asian organization. This is just as its Asian member countries wished. It has provided ECAFE with professional specialists familiar with the region's needs and

3. If French translators and English editorial writers are excluded, non-Asians held less than 20 per cent of the substantive posts and less than 10 per cent of the senior positions.

4. In 1950 Chinese, Indians, and Thais formed about 40 per cent of the professional staff; this proportion had not altered ten years later.

problems at first hand. But it did, and still does, pose some difficult recruiting problems.

In the first place the ECAFE countries best placed to supply well-qualified staff have either, like India, already more than filled their over-all United Nations quota or, like China, are beyond the recruiting pale for political reasons. For the reason already given it is not easy to recruit Japanese. Pakistan has tended in the past to feel underrepresented, not least in the senior positions and especially by comparison with India. Indeed, Pakistan government officials have regarded ECAFE as an Indian-dominated organization. The first two Executive Secretaries were Indian. The first, Lokanathan, it is fair to note, recruited heavily from India and showed some preference for his home state, Madras.[5] But, as already indicated, in getting together a staff quickly he had few Asian sources to choose from and naturally used the contacts he already knew. His successor, C. V. Narasimhan,[6] also from Madras incidentally, filled a few senior positions from India. It is also true, however, that when Lokanathan retired in June 1956, the Indian government made it clear to the Secretary-General that India was not in competition for this post. The appointment of another Indian as Executive Secretary was very much the Secretary-General's deliberate choice.[7] Though government officials in Karachi believe otherwise, there is really no evidence that Pakistanis have been discriminated against in the matter of staff appointments and promotions. At the beginning of 1961, for instance, two of the three Pakistanis in the Secretariat held posts at director level.

A further complication limiting the sources from which senior

5. A prominent Pakistan official once quipped that Lokanathan had set up a branch of the Madras government at Bangkok!

6. C. V. Narasimhan. Born 1915. Educated: Trichinopoly, Madras, and Oxford. Entered Indian Civil Service 1936 as District Officer Madras state; later in Madras Secretariat. Joined Union government 1950 as Deputy Secretary, Ministry of Agriculture. From 1953 to 1956 coordinator of foreign assistance, Ministry of Finance. Represented India, Colombo Plan Consultative Committee meetings, 1950, 1953; led the Indian delegation to the 1954 and 1955 meetings. Responsible for preparing India's "country programme" 1956–57 for EPTA. Appointed ECAFE Executive Secretary September 1, 1956.

7. This was not a foregone conclusion; an eminent Indonesian economist was first approached but declined. Some Asian governments submitted official candidates; for personal or general political reasons they were not accepted.

staff may be recruited is that throughout the United Nations the choice of nationality for these positions is heavily circumscribed by political considerations. Governments are not slow to stake a claim to a vacant senior post for one of their own nationals. Thus, after two Indian Executive Secretaries, it was virtually impossible politically to appoint the third from India.[8] Government officials in smaller Asian countries as well as in Pakistan have at times remarked unfavorably on the weight of Indians in the Secretariat.[9] Their feelings were well considered when, on Narasimhan's transfer to Headquarters in 1959, a Burmese, U Nyun,[10] the then Deputy Executive Secretary,[11] was appointed his successor. From the standpoint of good public relations it is unfortunate that no sufficiently well-qualified Thai seems available to fill another senior position.[12] The smaller Asian countries, on the other hand, can least afford to spare able men. It is a nice point whether the removal of desperately scarce talent from a small underdeveloped country is a price worth paying for a greater national or regional share of United Nations posts. A further difficulty with recruiting from small countries is that a man qualified for, say, a middling grade post in the Secretariat, may occupy or be offered a senior position in his own government. ECAFE and Bangkok cannot compete against that sort of advancement.

Two principal means have been used to ease the acute staffing

8. Burma allegedly threatened to withdraw from ECAFE when the second one was appointed.

9. Government officials and the local press in Bangkok have been known to refer satirically to "ICAFE," the Indian Commission for Asia and the Far East.

10. U Nyun. Born 1911. Educated Rangoon University, London School of Economics and Political Science, and London School of Oriental Studies, entered Indian Civil Service 1931. Became Undersecretary and Permanent Secretary, Ministry of Commerce and Industry, Burma government; leader of various Burmese trade missions; and Burmese representative at a number of international economic conferences, including 1950 session ECAFE Industry and Trade Committee. Joined ECAFE Secretariat 1951 as Chief of Industry and Trade Division; appointed Deputy Executive Secretary 1957 and Executive Secretary 1959.

11. It is relevant to point out that before U Nyun was appointed to this position in 1957, all the Deputy Executive Secretaries of ECAFE had been British, United States, or French nationals. Perhaps this was why in 1957 the Soviet Union expressed an interest in having a Soviet national in this post; it could hardly complain, however, when a Burmese was appointed instead.

12. Acidly critical articles on the treatment of Thai nationals in ECAFE appeared in the local Bangkok press in March, October, and November 1954. They showed such a surprisingly detailed knowledge of the Secretariat, however, as to arouse the suspicion that they originated from within the organization.

problems of the Secretariat: the temporary secondment of staff from Headquarters and ECE and the short-term employment of consultants on specific assignments. There would seem to be a good case for intensifying these ameliorations by promoting a greater interchange of staff between Bangkok and New York or Geneva [13] and by increasing ECAFE's consultant funds.[14] Consultants are a particularly useful relief as they permit greater flexibility in the work program than would be possible if all ECAFE's staff funds were locked up in highly specialized types of regular appointments. This is all the more important in periods of relatively rapid change in the character and scope of the Secretariat's activities.

Broadly speaking the Secretariat is organized into the Office of the Executive Secretary, the Research and Planning Division, the Technical Divisions, and the Division of Administration.

The Office of the Executive Secretary maintains over-all control of the Secretariat as a whole, keeps an eye on the political implications of its work program, and notes points which might otherwise be overlooked. By means of regular senior staff meetings, as well as through the normal work of his Office, the Executive Secretary is kept informed of what is happening in every part of the organization. He must also undertake the most important diplomatic activities of the Secretariat and is ultimately responsible for maintaining good relations with the member governments and other international agencies. His Office may also be said to include the information,[15] editorial, and language services of the Secretariat. On this reckoning there were 11 professional posts in this Office at the beginning of 1961, including the Executive Secretary and his Deputy.

The Research and Planning Division, with 21 professional posts at that time,[16] was the largest single division in the Secretariat. For administrative purposes it is divided up into a Survey Branch, an Economic Development Branch, and sections on economic studies, statistical compilation, and statistical develop-

13. For further comment, see Chap. 15.

14. Less than 2 per cent of ECAFE's total expenditure in 1960 was for consultants. This was a smaller proportion than ten years previously, for while total expenditure had risen that for consultants had not. See Appendix III.

15. The information service of ECAFE acts also as an information center for the Office of Public Information at Headquarters.

16. Excluding language, editorial, information, and administrative service posts, roughly one-third of ECAFE's professional staff are economists and statisticians.

ment.[17] In addition to its own economic and statistical work, the Division has collaborated extensively on a host of studies produced by the Technical Divisions. Its most conspicuous responsibility and achievement, however, is the annual *Economic Survey for Asia and the Far East.* It also services the Working Party on Economic Development and Planning, the Conferences of Asian Statisticians and a few ad hoc expert meetings.

The Technical, or substantive, Divisions consist of separate Divisions for Industry, Transport, Agriculture,[18] and Social Affairs, a Trade Branch, and a Bureau of Flood Control and Water Resources Development. At the beginning of 1961 they shared between them 35 professional posts, the largest number, 16, being in the Industry Division. The latter, in turn, is divided into sections on metals and engineering, small industries, mineral development, housing and building materials, electric power, and industrial studies. The Transport Division is organized into sections on highways and highway transport, inland waterways, railways, and a general section. The Technical Divisions service ECAFE's three standing committees and the overwhelming bulk of its other subsidiary bodies. While the Agricultural and Social Affairs Divisions have no regular forums to service, they have been involved in quite a number of ad hoc meetings.

The Division of Administration is primarily responsible, as its name implies, for the administrative management of the Secretariat and for ensuring it conforms to the standard practices and procedures laid down by Headquarters. This covers such matters as finance, personnel administration, conference and travel arrangements, document reproduction, printing and distribution, procurement of supplies, and maintenance of property. The chief of this Division and its chief finance and personnel officers are usually posted to ECAFE for two or three years from Headquarters. At the beginning of 1961 it had seven professional posts.

Finally, special mention should be made of the ECAFE Library. At the very outset the Commission requested its member governments to supply the Secretariat regularly with all their economic and statistical publications. It was around this nucleus that the

17. A branch is a Secretariat unit of a standing higher than a section, but lower than a division.

18. Partly staffed by FAO.

Library grew. By the middle of 1961 it housed over 22,000 volumes and received currently more than 800 periodicals and serials. As an economic research library for the region it is unequaled. Its services have been extended to many outside the Secretariat, such as government officials, technical assistance experts, and scholars.[19] A request for help from the Ford Foundation to enable it to meet the growing demands being made upon it was answered in 1955 with a grant of $25,000.[20] This markedly improved its resources. What it now requires is more suitable accommodation; the need may well become urgent if, as the Secretariat hopes, an Asian Institute of Economic Development is founded in Bangkok.[21]

In general, the organization of the ECAFE Secretariat is "characterized by horizontal strength, [but] is at many points weak in depth." [22] For instance, its sections on electric power, metals and engineering, mineral development, housing and building materials, railways, highways, and highway transport each contained only two professional posts at the beginning of 1961. This point must be borne in mind when evaluating the progress and achievements of ECAFE's substantive activities.

19. In addition to special bibliographies and reading lists prepared from time to time in response to specific requests, the Library distributes a semiannual list of its accessions under the title *Asian Bibliography* to over thirty countries.

20. Up until then it had to rely on an annual budget of $4,000.

21. See p. 108.

22. Doc. A/3041, Nov. 23, 1955, p. 10. This observation, although seven years old, is still true.

PART THREE

COOPERATION IN PRACTICE

CHAPTER 8

Economic Research, Statistics, and Planning

Economic Surveys

At the time ECAFE was created an economic profile of its region could barely be drawn. Outside the data gathered by the imperial powers on economic conditions in their colonial territories, much of it reflecting the rather limited functions of colonial administrations, there was little exchange of information within the region or between it and the rest of the world. A fair amount, it is true, was known about larger countries like China, India, and Japan and about internationally traded commodities such as rubber, tin, and tea. But from the standpoint of basic economic and statistical data, most of South-east Asia was still uncharted territory.

In 1947 the Commission approved the Executive Secretary's intention to produce an annual economic survey of Asia and the Far East.[1] This was a formidable task. The paucity of essential, reliable, and up-to-date statistics, the changing political boundaries to which available data had to be adjusted, the distempered state of many government administrations, the vast distances and slow communications in the region, the lack of an adequate library, research staff, and travel funds, were among the more frustrating handicaps confronting the Secretariat. Nevertheless, with the help

1. See Doc. E/CN.11/63, Dec. 8, 1947. It is worth noting that in the case of ECE the decision to produce an annual *Economic Survey of Europe* was taken solely by the Secretariat without any prior approval, much less a directive, from the Commission.

of four correspondents and two consultants, a regional *Economic Survey for 1947*, the first of its kind, was issued the following year. That it was of rather poor quality is hardly surprising; the remarkable thing is that it was produced at all in the time available. Since then the feat has been repeated annually and in recent years the quality of the *Survey* has become widely respected.[2]

Since 1950 the Secretariat has also produced a quarterly *Economic Bulletin for Asia and the Far East*.[3] This allowed the economic situation in the region to be kept under review in the intervals between the production of the *Survey*. Considering the scarcity of essential data and Secretariat resources, however, it is questionable whether ECAFE should have followed quite so closely on the heels of ECE in this regard. Significantly, the Economic Commission for Latin America (ECLA) started its *Bulletin* much later. In 1953 the quarterly coverage of the ECAFE *Bulletin* was changed to half-yearly and in 1960 the attempt to provide meaningful continuity was abandoned altogether. The *Bulletin* has fully justified itself, however, as an outlet for economic statistics, research articles, special notes, and the reports of expert meetings.

The *Surveys* covering the years 1947 to 1952 examined large subjects such as production, international trade and payments, monetary and fiscal developments on a regional basis. A short summary of the current economic situation for the whole region appeared in all subsequent *Surveys* but from 1953 to 1956, at the express wish of the governments, their main focus became a review of developments in each Asian member country separately. The change of emphasis doubtless created a greater government interest in the *Survey*, particularly among the smaller countries which liked to see some space specifically devoted to them. The Secretariat felt as well that these country chapters helped to build up the essential data required for a more penetrating analysis of regional problems. This phase of the *Survey's* evolution ended in 1957 when country reviews were eliminated in favor of a larger examination of economic development problems on a re-

2. The year used in the title of all ECAFE *Economic Surveys* refers to the period covered, not the year of issue. The *Survey* for 1947 was published in Madras, those for 1948–51 in New York, and subsequent editions in Hong Kong.

3. Hereafter referred to as the *Economic Bulletin*. This was also produced in response to a Commission resolution. See Doc. E/CN.11/222, Oct. 28, 1949.

gional basis once more. The postwar development of Asian economies of contrasting types was appraised in 1957, industrialization in 1958, long-term foreign trade trends in 1959, public finance in 1960, and economic growth in 1961.

Although the abandonment of country chapters was disliked by some ECAFE countries, there were timely reasons for the decision. In the first place, this kind of annual review of national economic developments was being increasingly produced by central banks or other official agencies in Asian countries. Moreover, as the *Survey* became from 1953 onward the basis for a regular debate in the Commission on the economic situation in the region, it had to be produced before complete data were available for the year it covered. To try to draw significant conclusions from known trends in the first six months of the year and some sketchy statistics for the third quarter, especially when the details invariably changed little in any case, was a singularly unrewarding exercise. Apart from the limitations this new production timetable inevitably imposed, the country chapters were heavily descriptive and statistical rather than analytical. In the early years of ECAFE the governments assumed the *Survey* would be a factual report and actually doubted whether the Secretariat should arrive at any conclusions, much less recommendations.[4] Certainly this was the safer course for the Secretariat to follow, especially as national economic problems were often burning domestic political issues.[5] By 1955, however, several countries, Asian and non-Asian, were urging it to be bolder and produce a more searching and critical appraisal of the economic performance and policies of individual countries.[6] Whether the Secretariat could or should have been more critical in the *Survey* at that time is a question not easily answered.

In the first place, apart from countries outside the region, the demand for greater boldness came from those like India, Japan,

4. For the discussion of the Secretariat's plan for the 1949 *Survey* at the fourth session of the Commission, see Doc. E/CN.11/146, Nov. 28, 1949.

5. "The Secretariat," said Lokanathan to the Commission in 1955, "had had to exercise a 'calculated courage' and use sometimes involved sentences in order to state facts while being sure no adverse effects would be produced upon the position of the country concerned." Doc. E/CN.11/408, May 24, 1955.

6. For debate on the *Economic Survey* at the eleventh session of the Commission, see Doc. E/CN.11/408, May 24, 1955.

and Pakistan which had some tradition of vigorous economic debate. Smaller Asian countries tended to be rather more sensitive to possible criticism; to have wounded their pride for the sake of boldness would not have been an obvious gain to ECAFE. How much, if any, criticism a government is prepared to take from the *Survey* depends also on how well it respects the quality of the Secretariat's research work and the stature of the Executive Secretary. In some cases there is a greater readiness to swallow plain speaking from an organization like the World Bank simply because it has badly needed funds to offer. Finally, while some Asian government officials wished to see national developments and policies more critically appraised by the *Survey,* others feared this might strengthen the power of political oppositions, unofficial and official, to create political mischief.

The most important inhibition on the Secretariat's critical faculties arose, however, from its own practice of sending drafts of the country chapters to the governments concerned for their comment before the *Survey* was issued. Yet, it should be pointed out that the resolution passed by the Commission in 1947 instructing the Secretariat to publish an annual *Survey* did not mean it had first to be submitted to the governments for their approval. As the Executive Secretary rightly reminded the Commission when governments chose to ignore the fact, the *Survey* was published on the sole responsibility of the Secretariat. Why then did the Secretariat follow a practice which seemed inconsistent with this principle and was certainly against the advice and policy of United Nations Headquarters? Country chapters, it maintained, were sent to the governments merely to have the facts verified and, if possible, supplemented. On one occasion, however, Lokanathan publicly admitted that government comments had also modified the Secretariat's interpretation of the facts.[7] It would be a remarkable government official who did not take the opportunity to see that the draft presented his own country in the

7. "When the draft had been mailed to governments," Lokanathan said to the Commission in 1954, "they had been requested to send their observations especially concerning factual statements, though comment on interpretation was also welcome. A series of comments had been received from many of the governments; the facts in the *Survey,* and to a certain extent, the interpretation of facts, had been modified accordingly in the printed text distributed to delegates." Doc. E/CN.11/389, Mar. 25, 1954.

best possible light; and sometimes more than the facts had to be altered to achieve this result.[8] The plain truth is that because of the scarcity of reliable data and adequate research staff, the Secretariat was in a weak position; it was better to catch as many errors as possible before the *Survey* was issued than risk an avalanche of corrections at the Commission session. The elimination of the country chapters, which was foreshadowed by Lokanathan and accepted by his successor, Narasimhan, thus represented the decision of a stronger, more confident Secretariat.

The quality of the *Survey* has advanced a long way since the early editions, when help was sought from a variety of sources, including the specialized agencies, and gifted young economists at Headquarters could show their mettle by savagely mauling its first draft. The invitation to certain humiliation which the Secretariat courted by sending Headquarters a first draft was also withdrawn in 1957. The *Survey* was subsequently issued in mimeographed form and governments were expected to make any factual corrections at the Commission session. The Secretariat then considered these before a final version was printed and put on sale. Judging from the very few corrections that are now in fact made, the time would seem ripe for the Secretariat to follow the practice of ECE and issue only a printed edition of the *Survey* to the governments. This would demonstrate beyond all doubt the right of the Secretariat to publish on its own responsibility.

The most striking illustration of government pressure to dictate the contents of the *Survey* arose from the publication in the quarterly *Economic Bulletin* for November 1953 of an article reviewing economic developments in Communist China. The Executive Secretary could defend this decision by referring to the thin thread of declared interest the Commission had shown in having a more thorough coverage of mainland China.[9] It was, nevertheless, harshly condemned by Taiwan and the United States at the following Commission session and for this reason

8. There was an element of absurdity about a situation where, at the Commission session in 1955, for example, the Pakistan delegation urged the Secretariat to express itself more boldly in the *Survey;* yet that very delegation included an official who admitted to the writer that his amendments to the Secretariat's draft of the Pakistan chapter regularly went beyond the merely factual.

9. See: *ECAFE Report to ECOSOC, 29 January 1952–8 February 1952,* Doc. E/CN.11/342, Mar. 19, 1952, para. 155.

Lokanathan decided to consult Asian governments, but not the outside powers, on whether the Secretariat should continue to cover the subject. As only Cambodia, South Korea, South Viet-Nam, and Taiwan objected, all the *Surveys* from 1954 to 1957 included a separate treatment of developments in mainland China as well as in Taiwan. On each occasion, the Philippines, South Korea, Taiwan, and the United States strenuously opposed the inclusion on the ground that the Secretariat, despite its general warnings about the difficulties of verification, too readily accepted Communist claims at their face value and did not stress the totalitarian nature of the regime in mainland China and the social costs it exacted in terms of human dignity and freedom. In addition, they privately disliked the impression the *Survey* gave of the existence of two Chinas.

The sharp reaction of the United States has to be seen against the background of the dark shadow cast by Senator McCarthy over the Washington scene in the early years of the Eisenhower Administration. United States officials also felt that if a proper evaluation of Communist data was a difficult enough task for the large United States Consulate General in Hong Kong and the Central Intelligence Agency, it was quite beyond the slender resources of the Secretariat. Publicly and privately, Taiwan and the United States therefore pressed the Secretariat to eliminate all coverage of economic developments in mainland China, or if they had to be mentioned, to seek government clearance for the draft before the *Survey* was issued.[10]

At the Commission in 1956, the Philippines, backed by South Korea and Taiwan, actually threatened to introduce a resolution formally requesting the exclusion of mainland China from the *Survey,* but stayed their hand on the assurance of the Executive Secretary that he would fully consider the question. Not surprisingly, Burma, India, and the Soviet Union opposed any intention to exclude the subject.[11] The following year the Philippines appeared to argue that the *Survey* should not cover mainland China because its Communist regime lay outside the terms of

10. In 1956 and 1957 Taiwan actually circulated to the Commission its own version of the economic situation in Communist China. See Docs. ECAFE/L.102, Jan. 27, 1956 and L.123, Mar. 16, 1957.

11. Doc. E/CN.11/451, Mar. 18, 1957.

reference of ECAFE.[12] This was completely muddled thinking. It is a geographical entity called China, not a particular political regime, that is named in the terms of reference and is thus within the scope of the Secretariat's research work.

All the same, it is a moot point whether, despite understandable difficulties such as the impossibility of official contacts and field trips to Communist China, the Secretariat has made a sufficient effort to analyze and evaluate the official claims of its government.[13] It may plead in defense that the research staff available for this purpose is too limited; but that is precisely why its critics have urged it to drop the subject. On this score the Secretariat is still open to political attack. If the voice of protest has been muted recently it is because the changing character of the *Survey* no longer made it appropriate to single out Communist China for separate treatment.

Since 1954 the *Survey* has shown a greater readiness to commit itself on controversial policy questions, though still perhaps in a general way rather than by naming countries. It has no rival as the standard reference work on the economic situation and problems of the region as a whole and the Secretariat needs fear no longer any invidious comparison with the standards set by similar publications from other international organizations. A Japanese version has been produced since 1950, at first by the Central Bank but more recently by a Japan ECAFE Association,[14] and some other Asian governments have translated the *Survey* in whole or in part for the benefit of their own ministries and agencies.[15] Outside government circles, newspapers in the region of the caliber of the *Far Eastern Economic Review,* for example, give it a good deal of notice, while many of the best known departments of economics in Asian universities use it for teaching purposes. Reliable figures for the circulation of the *Survey* within the region are not, however, easy to obtain. For instance, around 2,000 copies of the *Survey for 1957,* or roughly a third of the total number printed, were distributed within the region, but the free or

12. Doc. E/CN.11/453, May 22, 1957.

13. It should not be assumed in this respect that only official information from Communist China, and not from any other government in the region, is unreliable.

14. See p. 319.

15. French editions were published for the years 1949–52 and 1954–59.

official distribution greatly exceeded the number sold. The reverse was true for copies distributed outside the region. The readership in Asia may well be limited by inadequately developed distribution outlets and by a uniform pricing policy for United Nations publications which inevitably makes them relatively more expensive in the poorer countries of the world.

Although the Commission in its early years would appoint an ad hoc committee to examine the Secretariat's outline plan for the *Survey,* it never actually discussed the finished product until its 1953 session. The Soviet Union had wanted to discuss it from the start but was opposed, notably by Britain, on the ground that the *Survey* was a Secretariat document for which the Commission had no responsibility. Nevertheless, that did not prevent the Russians from finding an opportunity to castigate it as a thoroughly tendentious and reactionary document because it did not attack colonial exploitation by Western monopolies or the survival of feudal relationships and resurrected the "cannibalistic" theories of Malthus.[16] In 1952, however, the Commission accepted a United States suggestion that its future sessions open with a general debate on the economic situation of the region on the basis of the *Survey*. This has since become the most discussed item on the Commission's agenda.

Because the Commission session is the greatest public occasion on which its member countries can review their economic experiences, policies, hopes and fears, or make important announcements, this debate inevitably takes the form less of a dialogue than of a series of carefully composed statements. In this respect ECAFE shares the general disease of United Nations bodies in having an excess of parliamentarianism with too little of its substance. Some observers have remarked that this occasion has not been notable for the readiness of Asian countries to address themselves to regional problems, especially those highlighted by the *Survey,* as opposed to purely national stock-taking. On the other hand regional and national concerns are often identical. Repeatedly expressed anxieties, for instance, about fluctuations in primary commodity prices, the lack of capital, and the need for more aid have been themes common to most Asian speeches.

16. For British and Soviet statements to the 1949 session of the Commission, see Doc. E/CN.11/146, Nov. 28, 1949.

What the *Surveys* and these annual debates have thus helped to fashion is a greater sense of regional economic consciousness.

Statistics

To say that statistics are indispensable to rational policy-making for economic and social development and therefore to all ECAFE activities may be a trite observation; but it has tremendous implications. This was early recognized by the Commission when in 1947 it directed the Secretariat to collect, collate, analyze, and compare statistical data and assist ECAFE countries to strengthen the organization and functioning of their statistical services.[17] In 1949 a small Statistics Section was established in the Secretariat for this purpose and given wide responsibilities. These included the maintenance of basic statistical series, the study of problems of methodology and comparability, the location of gaps in published series, the review of national statistical services, and the organization, as soon as possible, of a regional conference of statisticians in collaboration with the specialized agencies and the United Nations Statistical Office.[18]

The Secretariat immediately set to work to build up comprehensive files of basic statistical series for all ECAFE countries. Its *Economic Bulletin* became partly a quarterly statistical bulletin and, since the 1952 edition, regular statistical series have appeared in the *Survey*. The marked improvement over the years in the coverage and quality of Asian economic statistics is mirrored in these publications and in 1956, after much labor, the Secretariat was able to issue a comprehensive *Guide to Asian Economic Statistics*. The skill accumulated by the Secretariat in the handling and evaluating of statistical material from all Asian countries has given ECAFE the only unit of its kind capable of compiling at reasonably short notice all the empirical data available for research on regional economic problems. From a national or regional standpoint its statistical files are by now fairly complete.

During the course of short field trips the Secretariat has also advised countries on the development of their statistical services. Its influence has probably been more pervasively exerted, however, through the regional statistical conferences it has convened

17. Doc. E/CN.11/63, Dec. 8, 1947.
18. Doc. E/CN.11/233/Rev.1, Nov. 11, 1949.

in collaboration with the specialized agencies and the United Nations Statistical Office. The first of these, organized jointly with the International Monetary Fund (IMF) in 1951, discussed foreign trade and balance of payments statistics. On its recommendation a working party was convened the following year by ECAFE and the United Nations Statistical Office to formulate guiding principles for adapting the Standard International Trade Classification (SITC) of commodities to the ECAFE region as a basis for reporting trade statistics on a comparable basis.[19] Of the fifteen Asian countries that now apply SITC, five adopted it following this Working Party. Four of the twelve Asian countries publishing balance of payments data began to do so only after the first regional statistical conference.

The second regional conference held jointly with FAO dealt with price and production, including agricultural production statistics; and the third, in 1954, with problems of national income accounting. The development of these latter statistics has been quicker than for most other series. For instance, at the request of the Commission in 1950 a considerable body of work was done on methods used in ECAFE countries to calculate national income and capital formation.[20] The fourth and fifth regional conferences in 1956 and 1957 concentrated their attention on the plans and problems of countries proposing to participate in the World Census of Population and World Census of Agriculture during or close to 1960.

Another earlier achievement of ECAFE in this field which deserves special mention was its pioneering work, in collaboration with the Fiscal and Financial Branch at Headquarters, on the reclassification of Asian budgets. The expanding role governments came to play in promoting economic and social development made it ever more necessary for policy-makers to have a clear picture of how the economy was affected by the ways in which governments spent money, raised revenue, borrowed or repayed debts. This was all the more essential for those Asian governments that had not completed a full set of national income ac-

19. For report, see Doc. E/CN.11/317, Jan. 11, 1952.

20. E.g., "Problems of National Income Estimates in ECAFE Countries," *Economic Bulletin for Asia and the Far East, 2*, No. 1 (1951); and "Analysis of National Income in Selected Asian Countries," ibid., *3*, Nos. 1–2 (1952).

counts. The economic function, purpose, and impact of government transactions could not, however, be clearly seen from the kinds of classifications customarily used in the accounts of public bodies. The Secretariat therefore reclassified the budgets of several countries according to economic and functional categories into what might be described as "policy accounts" and published its findings in the *Economic Bulletin*.[21] Following up this work an expert workshop on problems of budget reclassification in the ECAFE region was convened in 1955, and again in 1957 and 1960,[22] to consider the problem in detail. As a result Burma, Ceylon, India, Japan, Malaya, the Philippines, Singapore, South Korea, South Viet-Nam, Taiwan, and Thailand have all published budgetary figures in reclassified form according to the functional and economic categories recommended.

In 1957 the Commission resolved to transform the periodic regional conferences of statisticians into a permanent body, to be called the Conference of Asian Statisticians, under the general guidance of ECAFE and the United Nations Statistical Commission.[23] This new organization was to serve as a forum for those at the level of directors of central statistical offices and help them plan their work on a continuing basis, especially as regards the statistics required for economic planning and development policies, rather than confine its attention, as the earlier regional conferences had done, to one or two specific subjects. A separate Statistics Development Section, staffed by the United Nations Statistical Office as well as ECAFE, and under a chief who was also the United Nations Regional Statistician, was set up in the Secretariat to service the Conference.

The statistical collections needed by economic planners and policy-makers have to be patiently and systematically built up over a period of time. The Conference of Asian Statisticians accordingly recommended that governments draw up long-range programs for the development of statistical data[24] and also provided advice on how to carry them out. From time to time the

21. *I*, No. 3 (1951).

22. For reports, see Docs. ST/TAA/SER.C/25, May 1956, and 30; n.d., 1958; and ST/TAO/SER.C/48, 1961.

23. *ECAFE Annual Report to ECOSOC, 15 February 1956–28 March 1957*, Doc. E/CN.11/454, May 8, 1957.

24. Doc. E/CN.11/456, May 27, 1957.

Conference has set up small expert groups to investigate specialized problems more thoroughly than its own plenary meetings allowed. Recognizing, for example, that a complete enumeration is often difficult and costly, the Asian statisticians agreed that much of the data the planners required could be obtained by sampling methods, thereby saving considerably on time, money, and manpower. As the 1960 Censuses on Population and Agriculture gave considerable scope for sampling experiments, a working group of experts was convened in 1959 to provide practical guidance on the scientific formulation and efficient application of sample surveys.[25] Two months later a similar group met to consider the special problems of estimating capital formation in ECAFE countries.[26]

One of the important standing items on the agenda of the Conference has been the supply and training of statisticians. The Secretariat has reviewed the training facilities available in the region[27] and is expected to report on statistical manpower in the region in the light of probable future demand. It is the intermediate supervisory staff and statistical operators who appear to be in shortest supply. Another expert working group in 1960 thoroughly examined this particular aspect of the problem and made detailed recommendations on the content, methods, and organization of the training needed to fill the gap.[28]

In connection with the earlier promotional work of the Conference to persuade countries to participate in the World Censuses of Population and Agriculture, Asian countries were urged to take advantage of the United Nations FAO Census Training Centre established at Tokyo in 1958 with the help of funds from the Ford Foundation and EPTA.[29] Many, in fact, have done so. In addition, a team of census advisers, financed by the United States/FAO Program of Census Technical Assistance and under the direction of the United Nations Regional Statistician in ECAFE, has given much direct advice to Asian countries. The existence of this service, it is worth noting, is a good example of the decentralization

25. For report, see Doc. E/CN.11/517, Dec. 31, 1959.

26. For report, see Doc. E/CN.11/518, Dec. 31, 1959.

27. See, e.g., Doc. E/CN.11/ASTAT/CONF.3/L.10.7, 1960.

28. For report, see Doc. E/CN.11/545, Dec. 28, 1960.

29. The creation of such a center was recommended by the first Conference of Asian Statisticians in 1958.

of United Nations technical assistance operations. Preparations are now being made for the World Program of Industrial Inquiries which the United Nations proposes to launch in 1963. As a first step ECAFE organized a seminar in 1961 to discuss the industrial statistics that will be needed in connection with the World Program.[30]

Sometimes the problems considered by the Asian statisticians as, for example, agricultural producer prices, mineral and transport statistics, have been referred to them by other ECAFE meetings. The division of function between the technical statistician and the policy-maker, which this practice illustrates, involves the danger that because each may be working in ignorance of the needs and problems of the other, statistical resources will be seriously wasted. The statistician does not always know precisely for what purpose the statistics are required; the policy-maker does not always appreciate what kind and amount of statistics would adequately serve his purpose. Collecting statistics is a real cost which could be further economized by Asian governments if their administrators became more statistically minded and their statisticians had more experience of economic policy-making.

ECAFE's work in this field has thus been concerned with correct compilation and analysis of the statistics required for current policy-making, including reclassification to provide additional information, the strengthening of national statistical services, and long-term work on the development of statistical data. In all of this activity it has acted primarily as a catalytic agent. To ensure that the results maximized international comparability, its program has been dovetailed with the world-wide one of the United Nations Statistical Office and Statistical Commission. As already indicated this was achieved by placing the Conference of Asian Statisticians under the joint guidance of the United Nations Statistical Commission and ECAFE and by making the chief of the Secretariat's Statistical Development Section the United Nations Regional Statistician.

These pioneering efforts to map out the statistical contours of the ECAFE region may not be the kind of activity that makes the headlines; but it is the sort of work international organizations are eminently fitted to carry out and governments strongly sup-

30. For report, see Doc. E/CN.11/ASTAT/CONF.4/L.2.

port. As good statistics, moreover, are an essential ingredient of all ECAFE investigations, it would be fair to accord the claims for extra statistical staff a particularly high priority in any future expansion of the Secretariat.

Planning for Economic Development

Soon after World War II, government planning became widely adopted in the ECAFE region as an indispensable means of guiding and accelerating economic development. The words "plan" and "planning" are very flexible, however, and encompass a variety of policies, ranging from a centrally directed distribution of most resources and the output they produce, as in Communist China, to the coaxing of economic activities by monetary and fiscal policies in the direction established by long-term projections, as in the case of Japan. The first plans Asian countries prepared were almost invariably no more than an agglomeration of individual projects in the public sector of the economy, many of which had already been started. They were formulated without regard to any consistency or balance between their separate parts, or a realistic assessment of available resources.[31] Not all of them were officially adopted or carried out. Considering the dearth of essential statistical data and qualified planners and the conditions of inflation and political instability under which postwar rehabilitation was tackled, more ambitious economic planning was hardly feasible.

After 1949 these first plans were greatly revised. The early blighting of Asian hopes for the equivalent of a Marshall Plan, continuing internal unrest, the lending operations of the World Bank, and the launching of the Colombo Plan and EPTA compelled Asian governments to work out their priorities more systematically. The beginnings of comprehensive economic planning in the ECAFE region may fairly be dated from the early part of the last decade.[32] For various reasons, however, ECAFE did not

31. "The development plans of some of the countries," said the Burmese delegate to the ECAFE Committee of the Whole, "were only an indication of their spirit of independence and of self-reliance." Doc. E/CN.11/AC.11/SR.3, Mar. 30, 1949.

32. For useful summaries of the progress of economic planning in the ECAFE region, see the reports on Industrial Development and Planning, Docs. E/CN.11/I&T/15, Mar. 31, 1950 and I&T/29, Dec. 9, 1950 and its *Economic Surveys* for 1949, 1950, 1955, and 1956.

begin to mount a major analytical attack on the problems involved until 1955. In the first place, it had to give priority to urgent rehabilitation tasks in specific fields such as flood control, transport, basic industries, and natural resources. Second, adequate statistical data had to be collected. Third, Asian governments for some years were far from agreed on what role ECAFE should play in the field of economic planning, while some of the outside powers seriously doubted whether it should encourage the process at all. The question tended to produce a dialogue between the apostles of extreme viewpoints.

There were some governments like France, the Philippines, and Taiwan which thought ECAFE should coordinate national reconstruction and development programs.[33] Burma and Thailand, both large rice exporters, supported this view as regards agriculture because traditionally big food importers such as India were bent on pursuing self-sufficiency in staple agricultural products.[34] The Commission, to begin with, urged countries to exchange views on their plans and as far as possible coordinate their efforts "so that the maximum and most efficient use may be made of the resources available bearing in mind the urgent need for a balanced industrial development of the area as a whole." [35] But it did not indicate how this should be done. The Secretariat seemed of two minds about whether such cooperation was needed just yet.[36] Pakistan, which was to prove the most out-

33. For the Philippines statement to the Commission, see Docs. E/CN.11/SR.24, Dec. 3, 1947, and SR.220, Mar. 12, 1960, and to the Industry and Trade Committee, see Doc. E/CN.11/I&T/SR.17–32, Feb. 20–Mar. 3, 1951. For Taiwan's viewpoint, see UN Sales No.:1952.II.F.2 and for French statement to Commission's Second Session, see Doc. E/CN.11/SR.26, Dec. 3, 1947.

34. For statements of Burma and Thailand to the Industry and Trade Committee, see Doc. E/CN.11/I&T/SR.9–16, May 15–30, 1950. But to the same committee the following year the Thai delegate argued that there could be no regional planning without a regional government. Meanwhile, free trade would ensure a proper division of labor between countries.

35. Doc. E/CN.11/62, Dec. 8, 1947.

36. "Though many of the problems involved are national ones," the *Economic Survey* for 1949 declared, "none of the countries of the region can hope to function satisfactorily as a closed, self-contained economy. The national plans need to be co-ordinated to take full advantage of the possibilities of trade, of exchange of services and knowledge, and of technical assistance co-operatively organised. By comparing their projects, furnishing assistance to each other and taking account of each country's comparative advantages, the countries of the region can make more rapid progress both in using their own resources and in persuading foreign lenders

spoken critic of all notions that appeared to threaten the sovereign status of national plans, declared it was too industrially backward to worry about a coordinated development of the region as a whole.[37]

Opinions on how ECAFE might assist the national planning process were no less divided. India suggested at first that it should help countries to fix their production targets and then make periodic surveys to ensure that plans were being carried out within the period specified.[38] Indonesia and Pakistan, however, wanted only direct practical advice on specific projects.[39] Burma argued that ECAFE "should attach the same degree of importance to assisting some countries in the formulation of economic plans as assisting others in carrying them out." [40] Britain did not agree that over-all national plans were the concern of ECAFE and doubted the value of the direct advisory services it could render. To the United States all economic planning was ideologically suspect. Apart from the fear that it might involve legislative action against United States firms, much of the talk about it in United Nations bodies seemed dangerous nonsense to United States officials, for without a properly developed apparatus, planning could only mean regimentation. On the other hand, when in the early years of the Eisenhower Administration the baleful influence of Senator McCarthy seemed all pervasive, the United States delegates were as dogmatic on the subject as the Russians. Indeed, many of the earlier discussions within the United Nations about economic planning took the form of broad-based preaching rather than dispassionate analysis of the problems involved.

---

that their projects will succeed." Here was the germ of the case for regional economic integration. On the other hand, in a report issued in 1951 on Industrial Development and Planning, the Secretariat thought that "as development is still in an early stage, it would appear premature to visualize any larger concept of interdependence by which appropriate industrial plans could be so co-ordinated as to obtain large-scale economies of manufacture in one country for supply to some of the others in the region." Doc. E/CN.11/I&T/29, Dec. 9, 1950.

37. For the Pakistan statement to the Industry and Trade Committee, see Doc. E/CN.11/I&T/SR.9–16, May 15–30, 1950.

38. For the Indian statement to the Commission in Nov. 1947, see Doc. E/CN.11/SR.27, Dec. 5, 1947 and to the Committee of the Whole, see Doc. E/CN.11/AC.11/SR.5, Apr. 5, 1949.

39. Statements to Industry and Trade Committee, Doc. E/CN.11/I&T/SR.9–16, May 15–30, 1950.

40. Statement to Committee of the Whole, Doc. E/CN.11/AC.11/SR.3, Mar. 30, 1949.

The final consideration delaying ECAFE's entry into the field of economic planning proper was the financial approach which dominated earlier thinking on the subject. For some years it was widely believed that once the technical feasibility of a project had been established, the planning process merely entailed finding the money; the real problem was how to mobilize and allocate financial resources. Through its Working Party on Industrial Development ECAFE first tried to estimate the financial cost, especially the foreign exchange cost, of the economic development programs of various Asian governments.[41] But on the initiative of the United States, which had been exhorting them to practice the virtues of self-help rather than rely unduly on foreign aid, the emphasis switched to an examination of ways to improve the mobilization of domestic capital.[42]

All rough and ready calculations showed a tremendous gap between the capital investment Asian countries needed to maintain a reasonable rate of economic growth and their capacity to mobilize domestic savings. Most of them lacked well-organized capital markets and joint stock forms of economic organization. Where modern financial institutions existed, they were invariably in the hands of foreigners and did not cater to the large mass of Asian peoples. In the past, the fiscal operations of colonial administrations were confined almost exclusively to raising revenue and few attempts were made to encourage savings and investment. In these circumstances and because of low levels of income, Asian governments had to try to mobilize small per capita savings from large populations.

In collaboration with IMF the Secretariat made a country-by-country survey of existing institutions for mobilizing savings,[43] on the basis of which a working party of experts met in 1951 and 1952 to examine the problems in detail and make specific recommendations.[44] The experts concentrated on promotional techniques to mobilize financial resources by encouraging government bond sales, life insurance, provident fund schemes, building

41. See, e.g., Doc. E/CN.11/131, Annex G, Nov. 8, 1948.

42. Committee of the Whole, Doc. E/CN.11/AC.11/1, Apr. 5, 1949.

43. *Mobilization of Domestic Capital in Certain Countries of Asia and the Far East*, UN Sales No.: 1951.II.F.3. See also article in *Economic Bulletin, I*, No. 1 (1950).

44. *Mobilization of Domestic Capital: Report and Documents of the First and Second Working Party of Experts*, UN Sales No.: 1953.II.F.2; and UN Sales No.: 1953.II.F.4.

and loan societies, post office savings, and new investment bodies such as development corporations.[45]

The prospect of closing the gap between savings and investment was too distant for most Asian governments, however, and they resorted to budget deficits to finance a substantial part of their development expenditures. But could such a policy increase the rate of capital formation without causing serious price inflation? Faced with a choice, they generally took the view that it "may be better to have inflation and a larger national output, than to have stable prices and economic stagnation." [46] But what were the safe limits to budget deficit financing? And considering the small proportion of the national income collected by their revenue systems, could not Asian governments do more to raise tax yields? ECAFE decided to examine these questions thoroughly and accordingly renamed its expert Working Party on the Mobilization of Domestic Capital, the Working Party on the Financial Aspects of Economic Development. At meetings held in 1953 and 1954 [47] the experts indicated the lines along which governments should overhaul their tax systems and considered the concept of a budget deficit.[48] As the safety limits of deficit financing are set by a host of interrelated factors, it was not sensible to condemn the policy out of hand. ECAFE nevertheless thought it should only be adopted, especially by weaker governments, with extreme caution.

As actual planning experience developed, it became clearer

45. See also, *Foreign Investment Laws and Regulations in Countries of Asia and the Far East,* UN Sales No.:1951.II.F.1. It is believed that a few Asian countries used this report to help them revise their laws and regulations affecting the foreign investor. This study was brought up to date with some expansion in coverage in Doc. ECAFE/L.122, of which the introduction was published in the *Economic Bulletin, 3,* No. 1 (1957).

46. "Some Financial Aspects of Development Programmes in Asian Countries," *Economic Bulletin, 3,* Nos. 1–2 (1952). See also: "Inflation and the Mobilization of Domestic Capital in Underdeveloped Countries of Asia," ibid., *2,* No. 3 (1950); "Taxation and Economic Development in Asian Countries," ibid., *4,* No. 3 (1953); "Deficit Financing for Economic Development with Special Reference to ECAFE Countries," ibid., *5,* No. 3 (1954); "Economic Concepts of Budget Deficits," ibid., *7,* No. 1 (1956).

47. For reports, see Docs. ECAFE/I&T/FED./2, Sept. 12, 1953, and E/CN.11/I&T/106, Nov. 16, 1954. Papers for these meetings were prepared by the staff of IMF, the World Bank, and the UN Fiscal and Financial Branch, as well as by the ECAFE Secretariat and government experts.

48. ECAFE's work on budget reclassification followed logically from this first examination of budget deficit financing. See pp. 94–95.

that the mobilization of domestic financial resources was only one aspect of promoting long-term economic growth. It continues to occupy an important place in ECAFE's economic research program, especially as the progress made by Asian countries in mobilizing domestic savings has been rather disappointing. For instance, the Secretariat recently began in collaboration with Asian central banks a series of intensive country studies on the sources and methods for raising domestic savings.[49] But if economic growth was to be accelerated all other limiting factors had also to be tackled.

The Secretariat had kept the progress of industrial development and planning under review from the outset[50] and in 1950 the Executive Secretary suggested that senior planners should meet, with a few experts drawn from outside the region, to appraise the adequacy of existing machinery and methods of such planning in Asian countries. He thought they might also consider the idea of creating a regional institute, similar to the Lahore Training Centre for Railway Operating and Signalling Officials,[51] specifically for training economic planners. Australia, Britain, France, and India felt that senior officials would not be available to attend a conference of this kind and the Industry and Trade Committee deferred the idea.[52] Four years later it accepted the Secretariat's suggestion for a Working Party on Economic Development and Planning to be convened in 1955.[53]

Toward the end of 1954 the Executive Secretary decided the moment was opportune for a major leap forward in this and other fields of ECAFE activity. Asian countries appeared to be viewing their record of economic progress with some concern. Most of them seemed unable to achieve any significant degree of industrialization and remained dangerously exposed to the vicis-

49. For the first fruits of this research, see "Savings in the Economic Growth of Post-war Japan," *Economic Bulletin, 11,* No. 2 (1960).

50. See, e.g., Docs. E/CN.11/I&T/15, Mar. 31, 1950, and I&T/29, Dec. 9, 1950.

51. See p. 210.

52. Doc. E/CN.11/I&T/SR.9–16, May 15–30, 1950.

53. For this particular Committee meeting the Secretariat had prepared a report on the Techniques of Material Resources Budgeting. Doc. E/CN.11/I&T/97, Dec. 21, 1953. The Commission that year rather surprisingly included the new Working Party on the work program without mentioning it in the body of its report to ECOSOC. See *ECAFE Annual Report to ECOSOC, 15 February 1953–18 February 1954,* Doc. E/CN.11/378, Mar. 1954.

situdes of world markets. They faced a number of fundamental problems of economic growth for which there were as yet no clear answers. They needed a well-founded body of techniques for appraising their past record and shaping their future policies. In an Aide Mémoire to the heads of delegations attending the Commission in 1955 Executive Secretary Lokanathan set down his ideas on how ECAFE might help them.[54] This program contained three principal features.

First, the Secretariat proposed to establish an economic development section which would make an analytical survey of economic development in ECAFE countries, formulate a body of economic programing techniques, and study fundamental questions of economic growth and policy including methods of making long-range economic projections. Second, ECAFE would help governments examine their plans in a regional context, for it had become evident that "some measure of co-ordination of development plans among countries of the region will be necessary if they are to avoid uneconomical use of resources and difficulties in marketing." The emergence of surpluses in rice, textiles, and some minerals were the chief dangers Lokanathan had in mind. Difficulties might also arise for some industries, the heavier branches of engineering for instance, where economies of scale were necessary but internal demand too limited. Lokanathan suggested that the Secretariat's new economic development section review existing plans and the implications of their fulfillment as a preliminary step to their subsequent examination at a meeting of government experts, reinforced, if necessary, by international experts, which ECAFE would convene. The report of the experts would be submitted to the governments and in "due course the actual process of co-ordination and adjustment of plans on a reciprocal basis might be undertaken at a high level by a meeting of the Ministers of Economic Affairs, Commerce and Industry of a group or groups of countries of the region." In addition, ECAFE could help Asian countries reach agreement on the production of certain commodities for the use of other countries also. By thus broadening its available market the industry in question could obtain the economies of large-scale production.

54. These were not the only considerations that prompted the Executive Secretary's initiative and his Aide Mémoire contained suggestions for an intensification of cooperation through ECAFE in other fields as well. See p. 292.

Finally, Lokanathan suggested a strengthening of ECAFE's advisory services in the field of economic planning. A team of senior staff members, headed by the Executive Secretary, might visit one or two Asian countries during 1955, preferably the smaller ones, which had not yet formulated or were in the process of formulating their economic development plans, to advise them on the problems involved.

Lokanathan's program has been mentioned at length because it signposted the road along which regional cooperation in ECAFE was destined to travel.[55] All the most important subsequent developments in its work program can be found in this Aide Mémoire. At the time, however, the governments were unwilling to accept the whole of it at one swallow. After some argument and misgivings they agreed to an intensification of the Secretariat's research work on economic planning and development problems and the proposed strengthening of its advisory services. They also agreed that the Secretariat "was now in a position to offer, if so requested, its services to the countries of the region to assist governments in examining their economic development programmes in a regional context" [56] and should, in any case, continue to act as a clearing-house of information on existing plans and their implications.

But delegates refused to commit themselves to any degree of coordination of national development plans, much less to accept the particular steps Lokanathan had suggested for bringing this about. Some delegates professed to be without instructions on this fundamental question; it is more likely, however, that they dared not confess their preference for highly nationalistic economic policies in a body dedicated to regional cooperation.[57] Pakistan, which had just begun its First Five Year Plan, felt no such inhibition. It was not for ECAFE, the Pakistan delegate declared, to sit in judgment on national economic development plans.[58] In any case, he

55. Public confirmation of the program can be found in the Executive Secretary's opening statement to the Commission; see Doc. E/CN.11/408, May 24, 1955.

56. *ECAFE Annual Report to ECOSOC, 19 February 1954–7 April 1955*, Doc. E/CN.11/407, Apr. 19, 1955, paras. 220–24.

57. Which perhaps explains why the heads of delegations were against submitting Lokanathan's Aide Mémoire to the full Commission, for this would have virtually compelled them to declare their positions publicly.

58. For Pakistan's statement to the Commission regarding its work program in the field of economic development and planning, see Doc. E/CN.11/408, May 24, 1955. According to one of the leading Pakistan delegates to the Commission that year, his government feared that regional economic planning meant, for instance,

added, a great deal more actual development was needed before serious marketing or regional coordination problems would arise. Ceylon, Hong Kong, Japan, the Philippines, Taiwan, and Thailand shared Pakistan's skepticism of regional planning. India thought the question might be further considered at a later date. In plain truth, the idea was not accepted because Asian governments did not have sufficient political trust and confidence in one another. The Secretariat had to be content with a more extensive research program and the new Working Party on Economic Development and Planning which the Industry and Trade Committee had approved the previous year.

The first and second sessions of this Working Party in 1955 and 1956 discussed the major determinants of economic growth, the methods, including programing techniques, of formulating economic plans, the objectives to reconcile, and the means of achieving them.[59] Subsequent meetings have concentrated on particular economic sectors in relation to the planning effort and economy as a whole. Thus the agricultural sector was discussed in 1957 at a session held jointly with FAO, industrialization in 1958, the social aspects of economic development planning in 1959, and transport in 1960.[60]

The deliberations and reports of the Working Party on Economic Development and Planning have a distinctly academic flavor about them. The delegates have not been senior planning officials, but those for the most part in the middle ranks of government administration. Even then, many of them did not hold positions at the center of the planning process. There is no reason to question the educational value they derived from the papers and proceedings of the Working Party; but it is much less clear whether the same view can be taken of the final report. Despite the fact that the delegates participated as experts and not as of-

---

that Pakistan would continue to sell jute to Indian jute mills and not develop its own mills. That political mistrust of India dominated its thinking also helps to explain why, at this same Commission session, Pakistan doubted the value at that stage of a study of international highways and gave the Secretariat a clear hint not to extend its work on flood control and water resources development to the Indus basin.

59. For reports, see *Economic Bulletin, 6,* No. 3 (1955) and *7,* No. 3 (1956).

60. For reports, see: ibid. *8,* No. 3 (1957); *9,* No. 3 (1958); *10,* No. 3 (1959); and *11,* No. 3 (1960).

ficial representatives who could commit their governments to the conclusions reached or recommendations made, the Secretariat has steadfastly insisted that an agreed report must be issued. The attempt to distill a common denominator out of many diverse opinions, however, too often left a residue of commonplace conclusions. The report on industrialization, for example, which ought perhaps to have been the most valuable, is singularly vague and lacking in coherence. The Secretariat may attach more importance to the working papers and discussion than to the final report.[61] But for those who do not participate in the Working Party it would seem more useful to publish its proceedings and papers in full as has been done in the case of some other ECAFE meetings.[62]

A working group of this nature, with a wide range of general questions on its agenda and a fairly large number of participants, could obviously not delve deeply into some of the more technical problems of economic planning. In 1959 and 1961 the Secretariat, with the financial help of BTAO, accordingly convened small expert groups to study and provide practical guidance on various aspects of programing technique. The first group issued a general guide to programing techniques which countries can apply at various stages in the development of their national plans and statistical resources; [63] the second concentrated on workable techniques for industrial planning and the statistical information available and required in Asian countries for this purpose.[64] The previous year a joint ECAFE/FAO expert group had met to examine selected aspects of agricultural planning.[65]

A dilemma inherent in programing techniques is that a model that is statistically possible to apply may be too simple to yield

61. The papers contributed by the governments have sometimes given the Secretariat useful information. For instance, the chapter on "Salient Features of Economic Development Plans" in the *Survey* for 1956 was partly based on the papers governments submitted to the first and second sessions of the Working Party. It is also true that the principal Secretariat paper is usually published in the *Economic Bulletin*.

62. E.g., Proceedings of the Regional Technical Conferences on Water Resources Development and of the Symposium on the Development of Petroleum Resources of Asia and the Far East.

63. *Programming Techniques for Economic Development*, UN Sales No.:60.II.F.3.

64. *Formulating Industrial Development Programmes*, UN Sales No.:61.II.F.7.

65. For report, see Doc. E/CN.11/L.91, Jan. 13, 1961.

significant results, while a more elaborate model may be impossible to apply because the statistical data are not available. Nor are they much use without personnel trained to apply them. Existing training facilities for this purpose are extremely limited, however, and almost exclusively outside the region. "Even where courses relating to economic development are provided they are seldom oriented towards the particular needs of practical planners." [66] In 1960 six junior government economists and statisticians from six Asian countries were awarded BTAO fellowships to attend a nine-month in-service training course which the Secretariat provided in economic development analysis and policy. A similar course for another seven trainees was organized in 1961. But the Secretariat's own work program sets strict limits on the number of trainees it can properly supervise and the range of problems they can study. A better solution, which is now being explored, is to convert this in-service training program into a properly organized Asian Institute of Economic Development with full-time staff.[67] In March 1962, the Commission approved the Executive Secretary's conception of such an institute and recommended that an ad hoc committee of interested governments prepare and submit an application for financial support from the United Nations Special Fund. Over a five-year period the total cost of the project is expected to amount to more than $3,500,000, of which about $2,500,000 may be required from the Special Fund. It is hoped that the Institute will be open for training in January 1964. The Secretariat is also proposing to revive Lokanathan's idea of strengthening its advisory services by organizing, in collaboration with BTAO, a small panel of experts, a regional advisory group, to help governments, especially in the smaller countries, formulate and implement their economic de-

66. *Programming Techniques for Economic Development,* p. 76. The World Bank's Economic Development Institute, for example, does not meet this need and is in any case fairly expensive for Asian governments.

67. See Doc. E/CN.11/L.105, 1962. General Assembly Res. 1708(XVI), Jan. 8, 1962, had called for "the establishment of economic development and planning institutes which will be closely linked to the respective regional economic commissions." A Latin American Institute for Economic and Social Planning was formally established in June 1962. Very much the same idea had been suggested by Lokanathan and accepted by the Industry and Trade Committee. See Doc. E/CN.11/267, Feb. 25, 1951.

velopment programs. It is hoped to make this service available from the beginning of 1963.

As already indicated, the Working Party on Economic Development and Planning did not attract high-level planners; nor did it provide a forum for the exchange of actual experiences or case histories of practical planning problems and the solutions attempted. For this purpose the Secretariat suggested to the Commission in 1959 that every three years the Working Party become a conference of Asian planners. This would be attended by ministers and top officials responsible for economic planning and be held, if practicable, shortly before the Commission session.[68] The proposal was not enthusiastically received by the governments. They feared that such a conference might overshadow the standing of the Commission and disliked the idea of a body of ministers reporting to a body in which many governments were represented by lesser officials. The Commission, therefore, agreed to the proposal on condition that the conference would consist of top officials only and meet at a time well away from the Commission session.[69]

The first Conference of Asian Planners met at New Delhi in 1961. Not all the principal participants were the top-level planners or policy-makers they were supposed to be. Its first business was to evaluate the development efforts of Asian countries during the last decade, including their machinery for formulating and carrying out economic plans, and indicate lessons for the future. From the standpoint of regional cooperation, however, this was not the most significant part of its proceedings. The previous year the Commission had given the Secretariat a broad mandate to explore all ways of promoting the economic growth of Asian countries through a greater measure of regional economic integration.[70] Cooperation of this nature is bound, however, to entail some kind of mutual adjustment or coordination of national development plans. The Working Party on Economic Development and Planning agreed that a fuller exchange of information and

68. See Doc. E/CN.11/L.65, Jan. 19, 1959.

69. For its terms of reference, see *ECAFE Annual Report to ECOSOC, 16 March 1958–19 March 1959,* Doc. E/CN.11/506, n.d.

70. See pp. 299–300.

"other suitable arrangements" were needed "to enable each country to take into account the industrialisation plans of other countries within the region." [71] Several delegations expressed a similar opinion to the Commission in 1959.[72] But were Asian governments really prepared to accept the notion of what OEEC termed a "confrontation" of national plans and work to bring about some degree of adjustment among them in the interests of a better regional specialization? This was the big question which lent special interest to the Conference of Asian Planners.

The Secretariat felt it was up to the governments now to dictate the running and put forward no precise proposals of its own on what should be done. Some countries still thought the question was not especially urgent; Ceylon and Pakistan, for example, emphasized that national economic development must come first. The delegates of more independent standing on the other hand, such as P. C. Mahalonobis and Lokanathan in the Indian contingent, and Jan Tinbergen, the chief Netherlands representative, stressed what they called integrated planning at the regional level, including for this purpose the need to make long-range projections of the economic growth of the ECAFE region. The general consensus, as expressed in the report of the Conference,[73] picked its way cautiously between these two standpoints.

Recognizing that national plans would need adjusting as they progressed, the Conference thought it would be to the mutual advantage of Asian countries if this process were viewed against a larger perspective of growth and in a regional setting. In a number of cases the small size of the national market restricted the development of industries requiring large-scale economies for efficient operation and the scope for import substitution as a means to industrialization. These limitations, the planners agreed, underlined the need for international cooperation to enlarge na-

71. "Some countries," the Working Party continued, "had found after they had formulated and sometimes started, their industrialisation plans, that other countries in the region were making similar plans. This could have serious effects if each of the countries making such plans had been intending to export part of the output of the new industries. The wastage of resources might have been avoided if there had been some institutional exchange of information and co-ordination." *Economic Bulletin, 9,* No. 3 (1958), p. 63.

72. E.g., Ceylon, Japan, South Korea, and South Viet-Nam. Doc E/CN.11/508, May 11, 1959.

73. Doc. E/CN.11/571, Oct. 12, 1961, and *Economic Bulletin, 12,* No. 3 (1961).

tional markets, which, as countries like Burma, Malaya, the Philippines, and Thailand rightly emphasized, might be more feasible to begin with among a few countries than on a full-scale regional basis. At any rate "the significance of the plans for other countries could be considered more fully than in the past both by the countries concerned and, on a broader basis, by the ECAFE Secretariat." Moreover "since coordination between plans of economic development . . . must be conceived in terms of accelerated economic growth," the Secretariat should project the course of economic development of Asian countries and the region as a whole over the next ten to fifteen years. Finally, the Conference discreetly "noted that there would be need for a suitable machinery or forum to assist the planning agencies of individual countries in promoting regional co-operation, in formulating and reviewing national development plans and in considering possibilities of economic development in the region as a whole." It requested Asian governments "to consider steps for achieving greater regional co-ordination in plans for economic development."

The achievements of this Conference, it is fair to say, were not momentous. The governments seemed more ready to load the Secretariat with further studies than commit themselves to clear-cut courses of action. No revolutionary decisions were made; but none was expected. Its significance has to be judged against the long uphill struggle in ECAFE to make the economic planning of Asian countries more regionally conscious. This aim, once so deeply suspect, has now become respectable in the eyes of most Asian governments; they are less inclined to feel a threat to their national sovereignty when regional cooperation in economic development planning is discussed. In short, they have moved closer to accepting the imperatives enunciated in the program Executive Secretary Lokanathan put before them in 1955.

CHAPTER 9

Industrialization

Metals and Engineering

Few constants stood out more clearly from the uncertain and fumbling beginnings of ECAFE than the insistence of the Asian members that it must help them to industrialize. Against the prevaricating tactics of the Western powers they won their first important victory for this viewpoint with the setting up in 1949 of an Industry and Trade Committee. They tended, however, to equate industrialization with heavy industry. The traditional capitalist pattern of development, building up consumer goods industries first, then gradually following with the capital goods to support them, did not appeal to the Asian appetite for rapid economic growth.[1] They believed, in other words, that modern technology made it possible to skip some of the stages of industrialization historically experienced in the West. Burma, Ceylon, Indo-China, Indonesia, Pakistan, and the Philippines were all considering specific projects for developing an iron and steel industry; India's existing three large steel companies were proposing to expand their productive capacity.[2] It was in response to these aspirations that ECAFE established an Iron and Steel Subcommittee, its first specialized subsidiary body, at the same time as its Industry and Trade Committee. But a more immediate Asian predicament also lay behind its creation.

1. The Indian Second and Third Five Year Plans are perhaps the most outstanding examples in the region of programs for economic development based on the premise that heavy industry is fundamental to rapid growth.

2. Docs. E/CN.11/I&S/2, Aug. 1, 1949 and I&S/11, Mar. 8, 1950.

Heavy industry in the ECAFE region was concentrated mostly in Japan with some small production in China and India. In the pre-World War II period the region produced only 5 to 6 per cent of the world's output of iron and steel. As a result of the contraction in Japanese production, its share fell to barely over 2.5 per cent in 1949, and an acute shortage of iron and steel and capital goods, particularly for rehabilitating transport facilities and industrial plants, was felt throughout the region. The Working Party on Industrial Development reported that the planned production targets for the industry in ECAFE countries would not meet their requirements.[3] Long delivery dates and foreign exchange shortages made it unlikely that the gap could be filled by imports from Europe and North America.

The Western powers were, nevertheless, opposed to the creation of heavy industry in Asia. They argued that it was not necessary for economic development.[4] In any case, they warned, with the great expansion in iron and steel production capacity in Western Europe and the United States, supplies were rapidly improving, prices would probably fall, and this would create difficulties for those ECAFE countries wishing to establish the industry.[5] ECE lent verisimilitude[6] to their fear that the world's steel-producing capacity was being overexpanded. The Soviet Union, on the other hand, preached at length to the Asians on the importance of developing heavy industry as the only sure basis for real economic independence.[7] To the cautious, if not restrictionist, note sounded by the West, India replied that Asian countries could not expect to wait five or six years to see what supplies would be available at what prices. Many things could happen to upset expectations

3. Doc. E/CN.11/131, Oct. 31, 1948.

4. For the United States, Netherlands, and French statements to the fourth and fifth sessions of the Commission, see Docs. E/CN.11/SR.48, Dec. 2, 1948, SR.64, Oct. 24, 1949, and SR.65, Oct. 26, 1949.

5. For British statement to the Industry and Trade Committee in 1949, see Docs. E/CN.11/I&T/SR.1–8, Oct. 12–18, 1949. Japan later on also cautioned Asian countries against an excessive preference for heavy industry. See, e.g., Japanese statements to the Commission, Docs. E/CN.11/408, May 24, 1955, and 451, Mar. 18, 1957.

6. See ECE, *European Steel Trends in the Setting of the World Market*, 1950. Also, Wightman, *Economic Co-operation*, pp. 96–97.

7. For Soviet statement to the Commission's fifth session, see Doc. E/CN.11/SR.64, Oct. 24, 1949.

and leave Asia again at the end of the queue.[8] This prophecy came true all too quickly. The outbreak of the Korean war in 1950 and the consequent Western rearmament left Asian countries once more deeply worried that the lengthening delivery dates for capital goods would seriously disrupt their economic development plans. It is against this background, as well as in terms of their conception of industrialization, that the enthusiasm of Asian countries for heavy industry must be understood.

The work of ECAFE's Iron and Steel Subcommittee proceeded from the conviction that Europe's great lead over Asia in this industry was based less on the extent of its natural resources—no European country outside the Soviet Union was self-sufficient in both the key materials of iron ore and coking coal—than on its ability to use them more effectively. ECAFE's survey of mineral resources in the region[9] showed that many Asian countries had abundant raw materials for iron and steel making provided they were scientifically prepared and treated. The Iron and Steel Subcommittee set out to show them how. Its first task, however, was to survey the plans and intentions for the industry in each country to determine the principal obstacles hampering their fulfillment. A general review of plans and problems became, in fact, a standing item on its agenda. ECAFE could do nothing about the lack of domestic financial resources and foreign exchange for developing this industry; its function has largely been to organize and provide the technical information Asian countries require.

At the time the Subcommittee was set up a number of Asian countries, notably Burma, Ceylon, Indonesia, and the Philippines, were planning to manufacture steel out of their considerable stocks of war scrap.[10] India and Pakistan were short of scrap while Indo-China had a large surplus. The Secretariat examined the latest techniques of scrap collecting in Western Europe and North America and advised the Subcommittee accordingly.[11] It also com-

8. For Indian statement to the Industry and Trade Committee, see Docs. E/CN.11/I&T/SR.1–8, Oct. 12–18, 1949.

9. See p. 151.

10. Ceylon, for example, informed the Industry and Trade Committee in 1953 that it imported each year a tonnage of agricultural implements equivalent to the scrap it exported; it therefore wished to turn this scrap into agricultural implements; see Doc. E/CN.11/I&T/78, July 9, 1953. Burma and Indonesia were believed to have large enough scrap reserves to support a small steel industry for 20–30 years; see Doc. E/CN.11/I&S/44, Sept. 10, 1953.

11. Doc. E/CN.11/I&S/21, Dec. 10, 1950 and Corr.1, Jan. 2, 1951.

piled a simplified standard classification system for scrap so as to hasten deliveries, lessen the chances of error, and lower grading and sorting costs. The Subcommittee thought countries might try out the system and in the light of their experience see what changes were necessary.[12] Little progress in applying it, however, has actually been made.

Where the development of iron and steel production was not immediately feasible, the Subcommittee advised governments to consider the technical and economic possibilities of having some steel rolling mill capacity.[13] As early as 1948, Burma, for example, determined to set up a rerolling mill to use steel produced from remelted scrap. The Secretariat and Subcommittee have therefore studied many features of the latest rerolling mill practice, including quality control, layout, and equipment, and formulated guidance for modernizing old mills or establishing new ones.[14]

From scrap and rerolling mills it was a logical next step to consider methods of making steel itself. For producing steel in rather small quantities, provided plenty of scrap and reasonably priced electric power is available, the Subcommittee favored the installation of electric arc furnaces. If liquid pig iron and scrap could be used, then open-hearth furnaces should be built; with only liquid iron, top-blown oxygen converters were recommended.[15] These last two methods, however, pointed to one of the most serious obstacles to the growth of heavy industry in Asia, namely, the lack of a plentiful supply of coking coal for pig iron production. Apart from Communist China and India, no country in the region has a substantial reserve of good quality coking coal and many of them have none at all. There has consequently been a widespread and strong desire to produce iron and steel without it.[16]

Great strides have been made since the war in techniques of making iron without metallurgical coal by using, to name only a few examples, electric smelting, low-shaft electric furnaces, and

12. Doc. E/CN.11/I&T/118, Sept. 23, 1955.

13. Doc. E/CN.11/I&T/18, Apr. 17, 1950.

14. Docs. E/CN.11/I&S/30, Nov. 6, 1951; ECAFE/I&T/Sub.2/3, 1955; and E/CN.11/I&NR/Sub.2/L.4, 1957.

15. Docs. E/CN.11/I&S/34, 1952; ECAFE/I&T/Sub.2/2, June 22, 1955; and Doc. E/CN.11/I&NR/30.

16. E.g., in Burma, Ceylon, Indonesia, Malaya, Pakistan, the Philippines, South Korea, and Thailand.

sponge iron processes. The Secretariat and Subcommittee have been examining the relative merits and disadvantages of various methods and their practical relevance to the ECAFE region.[17] For instance, abundant hydro-power might point to electric smelting and ample forest resources to charcoal blast furnaces.[18] The Subcommittee stressed the importance of investigating the chemical and physical properties of the raw materials in each case before a final choice of process, or combination of processes, was made. It also reminded governments that the economics of making iron without coking coal needed careful examination.[19] At this time Burma, Indonesia, the Philippines, and Thailand were all reported to be actively considering the inclusion of some project of this kind in their development plans. By the end of 1961, however, although a number of Asian countries had begun to implement their projects, India was the only country in the region actually making pig iron without coking coal and then only in a pilot plant. Apparently not even the Japanese consider it a commercial proposition.

In 1952 ECAFE and TAA arranged for a group of Asian iron and steel experts to visit Japan, and virtually the whole of the following session of the Iron and Steel Subcommittee was devoted to discussing their report.[20] Many of the operating techniques they observed were thought to be applicable in other Asian countries.[21] It is worth noting that Japan invited this Study Tour before it actually became a member of ECAFE. A further Study Tour, this time to Western Europe, was organized in 1957 with the help of TAA and ECE during which some especially interesting examples of new processes for using noncoking coals in pig iron manufac-

17. See, e.g., Docs. ECAFE/I&T/Sub.2/4, July 5, 1955, and E/CN.11/I&NR/Sub.2/L.6, May 8, 1957.

18. E.g., Malaya informed the Industry and Trade Committee in 1958 that it was interested in producing iron without coking coal by electric smelting but had not yet fully explored the economics of iron smelting; see Doc. E/CN.11/I&NR/8, June 4, 1958. It was reported in 1958 that wood charcoal from rubber timber might be used in Ceylon by 1962 for a pig iron plant using local ores; see Doc. E/CN.11/I&NR/12, Nov. 26, 1958. Surprisingly enough, Ceylon did not participate in the work of the Iron and Steel Subcommittee until 1958 and Malaya until 1960.

19. Doc. E/CN.11/I&NR/1, June 19, 1957.

20. Doc. ST/TAA/SER/C.5, 1953.

21. E.g., Burma informed the Industry and Trade Committee in 1953 that a definite decision on the size and type of its proposed steel mill became possible as a result of the Study Tour; see Doc. E/CN.11/I&T/78, July 9, 1953.

ture were seen in the Lorraine basin and West Germany.[22] In addition to this much-studied subject, the Subcommittee has examined other highly technical problems such as blending and benefication techniques for making inferior coal and iron ore usable in iron and steel production, continuous casting processes,[23] and foundry practices.[24] The Secretariat prepared a directory of laboratories in the region[25] and has helped Asian countries with few or no such testing facilities to have their raw materials investigated by laboratories in other countries inside and outside the region.[26]

Disseminating technical information has been one of ECAFE's continuing functions. Since 1957 ECAFE has periodically issued an *Iron and Steel Bulletin* containing statistics and information on current developments and modern techniques in the industry. The Secretariat has rendered direct advisory services to Burma, Ceylon, Indonesia, and Thailand and participated in a United Nations Industrial Survey Mission and Steel Mission to Singapore in 1960 and 1961. Finally, the Subcommittee has publicized the advantages of simplifying the specifications of iron and steel products.[27] Uniform standard specifications help to reduce the costs not only of steel production but also of the steel consuming industries. The Indian "steel economy" program, for example, showed that with certain modifications in specifications and designs it was possible to reduce the steel consumption of some transforming industries by 20 to 25 per cent. The Subcommittee agreed that as the domestic steel market of many ECAFE countries had common features it would be useful to evolve regional standard specifications for selected types and shapes of steel. It suggested in 1958 that an ad hoc working party be convened to consider the problem, but no date for this has yet been fixed.[28]

22. For report, see Doc. E/CN.11/I&NR/Sub.2/L.11, Sept. 4, 1958.

23. Doc. E/CN.11/I&NR/Sub.2/L.7, May 7, 1957, and Doc. E/CN.11/I&NR/1, June 19, 1957.

24. Doc. E/CN.11/I&NR/Sub.2/L.24, 1960.

25. Doc. E/CN.11/I&S/29, Nov. 8, 1951.

26. See p. 155.

27. See Docs. E/CN.11/I&NR/Sub.2/L.5, May 6, 1957, and I&NR/Sub.2/L.17, Aug. 17, 1958; also Docs. E/CN.11/I&NR/1, June 19, 1957, and I&NR/12, Nov. 26, 1958.

28. *Review of the Iron and Steel Industry in the ECAFE Region*, Doc. E/CN.11/I&NR/Sub.2/L.21, 1960.

Among the more fundamental obstacles to the development of iron and steel production in the ECAFE region is the shortage of skilled personnel. Steel makers of high caliber can be produced only through long practical experience. Burma's steel rolling mill, for example, which was eventually opened in 1957, soon ran into trouble because it lacked suitable technical and managerial staff, including cost accountants, to run it efficiently.[29] The Subcommittee reviewed the whole problem of training and requested the Secretariat to examine the chances of establishing a regional training institute for the industry.[30] This idea appears to have been too ambitious, however, for the present directive to the Secretariat merely asks it to explore the possibility of organizing regional training courses in India and Japan.

After a decade of hoping, planning, and investigating, what could ECAFE countries show by way of progress in developing an iron and steel industry? In 1960 mainland China, India, and Japan accounted for 99 per cent of the region's total crude steel output of 32,000,000 ingot tons. The output of all other ECAFE countries together was rather less than 1,000,000 tons. Pakistan, the Philippines, South Korea, and Taiwan have made good beginnings; Ceylon, Indonesia, and Malaya have started to construct iron and steel plants with foreign assistance; Thailand proposes to expand its present very small capacity; Singapore plans to establish a steel plant; Hong Kong has some steel furnaces and rolling mills; South Viet-Nam has rolling mills and Cambodia aspires to have a modest plant. The region's per capita consumption of steel was only about fifteen kilograms as against, for instance, 200 kilograms in Europe.[31]

One important limitation on the development of the industry in South-east Asian countries has been the size of their markets for iron and steel products. This was insufficiently appreciated by the Iron and Steel Subcommittee in the earlier years because

29. India and Pakistan came to the rescue by sending skilled personnel to help operate the plant and by arranging for Burmese technicians to be trained in their own plants.

30. Docs. E/CN.11/I&NR/Sub.2/L.8, May 7, 1957, and I&NR/Sub.2/L.14, Aug. 27, 1958; also Docs. E/CN.11/I&NR/1, June 19, 1957, and I&NR/12, Nov. 26, 1958.

31. *Progress and Problems of Industrialisation in the ECAFE Region, 1961*. Doc. E/CN.11/I&NR/L.24, 1961; and *Review of the Iron and Steel Industry in the ECAFE Region*, Doc. E/CN.11/I&NR/Sub.2/L.21, 1960.

it had been far more concerned with primary technological processes than with the economics of the industry. The one piece of economic advice the Subcommittee gave Asian countries during this early period was not well received by its parent Committee. It felt that Asian countries, instead of trying to establish uneconomic iron and steel plants, might consider "methods of obtaining assured supplies of necessary products at assured prices, including such methods as long term import agreements and stockpiling." [32] This statement came under heavy fire in the Industry and Trade Committee, notably from Burma, on the grounds that there were noneconomic considerations such as national self-sufficiency, prestige, or defense, which governments must consider when deciding whether or not to establish or expand iron and steel plants. Furthermore, it was not always possible to tell from blueprints whether an industrial project would prove to be economical, at any rate in the long run.[33] The Subcommittee accepted the rebuke at its next session.[34] All the same, the ultimate consequences of the most defensible departures from a strict economic criterion are so unpredictable that the onus is always on those who want to adopt some other criterion to prove their case. At least they should be aware of the real economic cost of launching projects for essentially noneconomic reasons. Poor countries can ill afford the muddles that may otherwise result. It was therefore unwise of the Industry and Trade Committee to rule that the Secretariat "should not undertake a general study of economic aspects" of iron and steel plans "as a separate project." [35]

Some reference to costs, it is true, was made in various technical papers of the Secretariat. But on the whole, the Subcommittee continued to proceed on the assumption that a thorough investigation of costs, benefits, the economic optimum scale of operations and the foreign exchange implications of investment decisions or consumption trends, could safely be left to the countries themselves. In fact, there is no reason to assume that governments, particularly in smaller countries, did not need as much guidance

32. Doc. E/CN.11/I&T/18, Apr. 17, 1950.

33. Docs. E/CN.11/I&T/SR.9–16, May 15–30, 1950.

34. Doc. E/CN.11/I&T/34, Feb. 16, 1951.

35. *ECAFE Annual Report to ECOSOC, 6 April 1949–20 May 1950,* Doc. E/CN.11/241/Rev.1, May 23, 1950.

from ECAFE on these matters as on the technology of iron and steel making.[36]

One of the first things a steel manufacturer in nineteenth-century Europe or the United States asked himself before installing, modernizing or extending an iron and steel plant was how far there was likely to be a market for the increased output. The failure to assess properly the pattern of domestic demand was one reason why part of Burma's steel mill was closed down in 1959 so as to concentrate production on more profitable items. It was not, however, until 1957 that the Subcommittee considered methods of estimating the future demand for steel in ECAFE countries. By adopting methods earlier used by ECE, the Secretariat prepared a report on Asian steel consumption trends and future demand.[37] It was found that calculations by "end-use," that is, projecting figures of past consumption group by group into the future, were the most realistic and reliable for the ECAFE region. In spite of their inherent defects, long-term projections do highlight the magnitude of the task facing economic planners. Thus it has been estimated that the ECAFE region's total steel consumption[38] will rise from about 20,000,000 tons in 1957 to 73,000,000 tons during 1972–75, when it will then exceed its total production by over 8,000,000 tons.[39]

By 1957 the Subcommittee was beginning to flavor its technical guidance with economic prudence; it became more conscious of the need to ensure that what was technologically possible was also economically feasible. It thought, for example, that a study should be made of steel production costs and prices in various ECAFE countries;[40] but this has not yet been done. By this time, in plain truth, much of the effectiveness of its one-sided concentration on highly technical studies had evaporated. In recogni-

36. E.g., at the 1956 session of the Industry and Trade Committee, the Philippines expressed an interest in basic data on investment, costs of production, and efficiency for iron and steel plants; while Pakistan stated it regretted that no consideration had been given to the commercial aspects of the industry in the Subcommittee's reports and wished to know more about them; see Doc. E/CN.11/I&T/124, June 18, 1956.

37. See Docs. E/CN.11/I&NR/Sub.2/L.3, Apr. 29, 1957, and I&NR/Sub.2/L.15, Aug. 26, 1958.

38. Excluding Communist China and North Korea.

39. ECE, *Long Term Trends and Problems of the European Steel Industry, 1959.*

40. Doc. E/CN.11/I&NR/1, June 19, 1957.

tion of this fact and of the importance of market demand, the scope of the Subcommittee was broadened in 1959 to include selected steel-consuming industries, other metals, and the foundry industry, and its name was changed to the Subcommittee on Metals and Engineering.

Smaller countries were now encouraged to develop heavy industry by working backward from simple fabrication to the primary processes of steel and pig iron production. Because their demand was principally for light merchant sections, the subcommittee recommended that they begin by establishing small rolling mills on the basis of imported billets. As their market expanded, so larger mills could be set up to produce, for example, rails and light structural steel.[41] This is a good approach provided the cost of imported billets makes it economically feasible. Much depends in practice on the price charged by Japanese steel manufacturers, since, owing to the heavy freight charges from Europe and North America, they practically monopolize the supply of raw steel to the region.[42] Similarly, countries with no well-established manufacturing industries to support a foundry industry, supplying spare parts and replacements, could at least establish small foundries for supplying certain types of consumer goods such as cast-iron pipes and builders' hardware.[43] This, nevertheless, presupposes that the shortage of pig iron, as well as of trained personnel and capital, which has held back foundry production in most ECAFE countries, can also be overcome.

In addition to a general review of engineering industries in the region,[44] the Secretariat has made a preliminary survey of the problems and potentialities of developing machine tools,[45] in-

41. Doc. E/CN.11/I&NR/30, Jan. 17, 1961. The Secretariat made much the same suggestion regarding the way Asian countries could begin to meet their own demand for aluminum products; if they have no bauxite resources or aluminum production, they might start by fabricating imported billets. See *Development of Aluminum Production and Fabrication Industries in the ECAFE Region,* Doc. E/CN.11/I&NR/Sub.2/L.23, 1960. The argument would have been strengthened had this paper included information on the present and prospective demand of ECAFE countries for aluminum products.

42. The writer was informed in Taiwan that Japanese steel-makers fix the export price at a level which barely makes it profitable to import steel for fabrication.

43. Doc. E/CN.11/I&NR/Sub.2/L.24, 1960.

44. Docs. E/CN.11/I&NR/Sub.2/L.2, May 2, 1957, and I&NR/Sub.2/L.26, 1960.

45. Docs. E/CN.11/I&NR/L.9, Oct. 28, 1959, and I&NR/Sub.2/L.20, 1960.

dustrial machinery manufactures,[46] and shipbuilding and ship repair industries[47] in ECAFE countries. Apart from mainland China, India, and Japan, the growth of engineering industries in the region has been greatly hampered by the lack of sizable domestic markets and iron and steel production, as well as by a shortage of skill and capital. With few exceptions these industries are still organized on a small scale in most ECAFE countries and engaged primarily in repair and assembly operations. Outside mainland China, India, and Japan again, industrial machinery manufacturing and the machine tool industry, for instance, are insignificant or nonexistent. The Subcommittee felt, however, that there was considerable scope in most ECAFE countries for manufacturing simple general purpose metal and wood working machines and machines to produce spare parts and consumer goods or to process agricultural products. Likewise, more of them might develop a shipbuilding industry by first trying to construct the hulls and superstructures of small wooden and metal fishing vessels and barges of standard design. Whether they could also provide a complete fitting out, including the machinery, would depend on the parallel development of other engineering industries. They might set up small repair yards as well to maintain their vessels.[48] The Secretariat proposes to prepare for each session of the Subcommittee detailed studies on selected sectors of engineering in addition to the foundry and machine tool industries. These reports will cover supply and demand factors, costs of production, obstacles to development, and the scope for international cooperation. Certainly, if the experience of ECE is any guide, ECAFE will have to guard against a loss of precision as it moves more into the general engineering field. What Asian countries may well find more practically relevant, if it can be realized, is the idea now being explored of having a panel of engineers attached to ECAFE but paid for by BTAO to advise governments directly at their request on their plans and problems for developing or expanding metal-using industries.

In encouraging Asian countries to develop heavy industry,

46. Doc. E/CN.11/I&NR/L.21, 1960.

47. Doc. E/CN.11/I&NR/L.22, Dec. 15, 1960.

48. At present the shipbuilding and repair industries of the region are concentrated in Communist China, Hong Kong, India, Japan, Pakistan, the Philippines, and Singapore.

ECAFE has held before them the example of Japan's iron and steel industry, drawing raw materials from thousands of miles away, or of Switzerland, which has built up highly successful engineering industries on the basis of imported steel. Most ECAFE countries, however, will need far larger resources of skill and capital if they are to develop along similar lines. Many of them will also need to concert their policies and plans in order to enlarge their market for heavy industry so as to make possible the setting up of plants of optimum economic size. In 1958 nine South-east Asian countries[49] consumed, in crude steel equivalent, some 3,700,000 tons of steel products. This figure may well rise to 10,000,000 tons by 1970.[50] Yet there is not a single large-scale integrated iron and steel plant in any one of these countries.[51] Although none of them possesses an adequate supply of both iron ore and coking coal there is, as the Subcommittee has repeatedly declared, ample scope for increased intraregional trade in these materials.[52] It should also be possible to plan a pattern of international specialization among some of them to permit economies of large-scale production.[53]

A decade of economic development planning in the ECAFE region has not conclusively resolved the question whether it is better to proceed from heavy industry to light industry or the other way round. India is pushing ahead with heavy industry in order to achieve eventual freedom from dependence on imports and the constraints this imposes on sustained growth. For smaller Asian countries the limitations of planning their economic development on a purely national basis has left only one course open to them, namely, the production of light consumer goods. This

49. Burma, Ceylon, Laos, North Borneo, the Philippines, Sarawak, Singapore, South Viet-Nam, and Thailand.

50. Doc. E/CN.11/L.95, Jan. 31, 1961.

51. Ceylon and Indonesia, with the help of the Soviet Union, and the Philippines and Taiwan, are each planning to set up an integrated iron and steel plant.

52. E.g., Malaya has iron ore but no coking coal; Indonesia has coal but no good quality iron ore. Likewise Taiwan has coking coal without iron ore and the Philippines conversely.

53. Taiwan pointed out to the Industry and Trade Committee as far back as 1956 that because the most economical processes could still be too costly for some ECAFE countries, cooperation between two or three neighboring countries was necessary before certain iron and steel projects could be implemented; see Doc. E/CN.11/I&T/124, June 18, 1956.

has undoubtedly produced a more comfortable life for their peoples than the long-term economic strategy of India has so far allowed its citizens. On the other hand, their economic development "will continue to be subject to the vicissitudes of foreign trade and aid and so prone to instability from external factors over which they have little control." [54]

Small-Scale and Cottage Industries

Next to agriculture, handicraft, cottage, and small-scale industries employ the largest number of people in practically every country of the ECAFE region.[55] It is likely, in fact, that they account in most countries for a larger part of locally produced industrial goods than do factory industries. Their importance was increasingly to be recognized in the economic development plans Asian governments were preparing or implementing after 1949.[56] As in the case of agriculture, it was generally believed that a little capital invested in them would bring about a much larger increase in output.[57] These crafts and industries can be located near markets and the source of raw materials and in rural areas they provide valuable additional income for farming families. As their products embody traditional skills, whose intrinsic qualities are often greatly admired in Western industrial nations, they are potentially important earners of foreign exchange. Their preserva-

54. UN Sales No.:62.II.F.1.

55. E.g., in 1950 it was estimated that in textile manufacturing alone these industries provided full-time employment for approximately 2,500,000 workers in India, 300,000 in Pakistan, and 200,000 in Burma, and large numbers in other Asian countries, Doc. E/CN.11/I&T/30, Dec. 24, 1950. Small industries are differently defined in ECAFE countries but are usually classified according to the number of workers or amount of capital employed, though additional criteria like use or nonuse of motive power, location of activity in homes or workshops, may also be included. Roughly speaking, a cottage industry may be defined as one carried on wholly or primarily with the help of members of the family as a part-time or full-time occupation, while a small-scale industry is one operated mainly with hired labor, not exceeding 50 in number where no power is used or 20 in number where power is used. See Doc. E/CN.11/I&T/52, Sept. 5, 1951.

56. At present most ECAFE countries have plans and policies for developing small-scale industries, though India and Japan are the only two with a comprehensive program in full operation.

57. The Secretariat stated in 1950 that "development and modernization of cottage and small-scale industries have . . . become the key to economic strategy in many countries, particularly Burma, India, Pakistan, and Indonesia." Doc. E/CN.11/I&T/29, Dec. 9, 1950.

tion and well-being are also essential, it is argued, for the survival of traditional cultural and aesthetic values. Be that as it may, there is much to be said for an approach to economic development that emphasizes investment in human resources, the men and women of the countryside, their skills of brain and hand, and the local materials at their disposal.

The relative scarcity of capital and abundance of labor in Asia might suggest that labor-intensive techniques would be the best way of using these factor endowments. On the other hand, with low productivity, the ability of small-scale industries to withstand the competition of large-scale production—textiles is a good case in point—is in many instances doubtful. From the standpoint of rapid economic growth capital-intensive techniques would produce higher levels of productivity and consequently permit higher rates of capital accumulation, larger outputs, and, in the long run, greater employment opportunities. But government planners cannot base the choice of techniques solely on economic costs; they have to be mindful also of broad questions of welfare and, above all, of the necessity to relieve the open and disguised unemployment so prevalent in Asian countries. At the same time an indiscriminate policy of protecting cottage and small-scale industries against larger industries would be harmful to the wider interests by perpetuating a low income per head of population. Rather the aim must be to increase their productivity by encouraging and facilitating mechanization, greater skills, and better methods of organization and marketing. In these respects their problems are similar to those of small-scale agriculture. Handicraft production would also have to specialize in lines where it could compete with factory production and in traditional local designs rather than Western patterns. It is precisely on the problems and means of bringing about such improvements that ECAFE has been concentrating its studies and advice.

The Working Party on Industrial Development had insufficient time to complete a survey of small-scale and cottage industries; its report in 1948 merely drew attention to the importance of the rural weaving of textiles.[58] In 1950 the Industry and Trade Committee approved the Secretariat's intention to study [illegible] and cottage industries, particularly in relation to text

58. Doc. E/CN.11/131, Oct. 31, 1948.

same time a consultant with expert knowledge of the United States market was engaged to advise ECAFE countries on ways of improving the marketability of these products in hard-currency areas. It was as a result of these two surveys [59] that ECAFE the following year set up a Working Party on Cottage and Small-Scale Industries.[60]

The Working Party began by discussing certain general topics such as the problem of defining and classifying handicraft, cottage, and small-scale industries for planning purposes, government organization and services to deal with the interests and the problems of these industries, research and technical training institutes available for them, and handicraft marketing.[61] It was clear that governments were not organized or equipped to provide assistance and guidance to these industries. The Working Party therefore considered the kind of agencies required and the type of service they might provide. Handloom textiles was the first actual industry dealt with, and the Working Party discussed techniques for improving their production and quality. In India, for example, the majority of handlooms were still equipped with throw shuttles; yet fly shuttles, which could be substituted at small cost, would add, it was reckoned, at least 30 per cent to the operating efficiency of this industry. The difference this would make as a whole may be gauged from the fact reported in 1955 that nearly 10,000,000 people in India were dependent for their living on the handloom textile industry.[62] Thailand intended to set up a model textile plant along the lines suggested by the Working Party but was unable to do so for lack of funds. A similar ECAFE scheme for a pottery pilot plant met with better results, however, for Burma, Indonesia, the Philippines, and Thailand established such plants on the basis recommended. These earlier meetings also discussed in a general way the problems of other small-scale industries like fiber, handmade paper, ceramics, jaggery, smithy, and carpentry.

59. Docs. E/CN.11/I&T/30, Dec. 24, 1950, and I&T/45, Nov. 23, 1950.

60. Docs. E/CN.11/267, Feb. 25, 1951, and *ECAFE Annual Report to ECOSOC, 28 February–7 March 1951,* Doc. E/CN.11/306, Apr. 16, 1951. The name of the Working Party was subsequently changed to that on Small-Scale Industries and Handicraft Marketing.

61. Doc. E/CN.11/I&T/74, Oct. 3, 1952.

62. Indian statement to Industry and Trade Committee, Doc. E/CN.11/I&T/116, June 9, 1955.

The principal weakness of ECAFE's early efforts in this field was that they were spread too thinly over too large a canvas. From 1953 onward the Working Party consequently decided to devote each meeting to a specific industry, beginning with wood, rattan, bamboo, and lacquer ware. This particular meeting, for instance, stressed the importance of exploiting the distinctive character of these materials and of designing the finished product for utility rather than merely for prettiness and superficial effects. For wood products the aim should be to bring out unique and beautiful grains, not to produce finishes by using color, thick varnishes, or shellac.[63]

Western techniques have less to contribute in this particular field; Asians must learn from the best examples to be found in their own region. In 1954 ECAFE, therefore, arranged with the help of TAA for a group of directors of cottage industry development centers or agencies to make a Study Tour of Japan where small-scale industry is technically much more advanced than elsewhere in the region. The group examined the organization, financing, and marketing arrangements of these industries and the various sorts of public and private assistance given to them. It was subsequently reported to the Working Party that most Asian governments were taking steps to implement the recommendations of this Study Tour,[64] especially as regards the setting up of common facility centers on the Japanese model for centralizing raw material purchases and marketing and the founding also of small industry service, research, or training institutes.[65]

The Working Party's fourth meeting in 1955 was devoted to ceramics. Most parts of the region have a plentiful supply of clay, lime, gypsum, feldspar, and coloring oxides. But if better use is to be made of them, their physical and chemical properties must be determined, they must be classified by type and centers organized to process them. Burma, India, Indonesia, Japan, and the Philippines already have laboratories or institutes for just such a purpose. It is also essential to keep down the production costs of this industry, for consumers in many countries appear to prefer imported over locally produced ceramic ware. The Working

63. Doc. E/CN.11/CIWP.3/10, Sept. 25, 1953.
64. For report, see Doc. E/CN.11/I&T/108, Feb. 1, 1955.
65. Doc. E/CN.11/I&T/121, Dec. 1, 1955.

Party again urged producers to join forces in setting up common technical facility services.

In 1957 the Working Party met for the first time outside Bangkok, in Madras, to study various technical and economic aspects of the leather industry and its products. Madras had modern research facilities as well as traditional workshops and the industry there had made sufficient progress for inspection at first hand to be instructive. Great stress was laid at this meeting on the need for Asian countries to coordinate the related stages of animal husbandry, flaying and curing, and leather technology. There are, in fact, five institutes in the region doing research work on methods to improve this industry at the cottage level. What the Working Party might have concentrated more attention on, therefore, were the economic problems of marketing its products.[66]

Finally, the Working Party in 1960 took up the problems of cottage and small-scale food preserving industries.[67] An expansion of canning and bottling industries would help, among other things, to stabilize food supplies by preserving surpluses in times or areas of abundance for distribution in times or areas of want. One of the major obstacles to expansion, however, is the cost of containers, which often exceeds that of the food itself. Tin plate and glass jars are particularly hard to obtain in a number of Asian countries. As the tin plate demand of many of them is too small to establish national tin plate plants of optimum economic size, ECAFE has suggested that one such plant might be set up as a regional project to serve the wider needs of South-east Asia.[68]

In addition to examining the problems of selected industries the Working Party makes a regular review of general progress and difficulties in this field. Considerable gains in output could be achieved in many rural industries by the substitution, for instance, of simple improved equipment such as cast iron sugar cane crushers for stone rollers, ball bearing wheels for potters wheels, and semiautomatic looms for handlooms. The pace of mechanization of rural industries depends largely on the progress of rural electrification.[69] But the fear of displacing labor has often been

66. Doc. E/CN.11/I&NR/2, July 26, 1957.
67. Doc. E/CN.11/I&NR/30, Jan. 17, 1961.
68. Doc. E/CN.11/L.95, Jan. 31, 1961, and Doc. E/CN.11/I&NR/31, Feb. 16, 1961.
69. See pp. 167–68.

advanced as a further reason for proceeding cautiously with technological innovation in small industries. Judged by the experience of India and Indonesia, however, where evaluations have been made of their small industry mechanization programs, these fears appear to be exaggerated. On the other hand, without certain essential prerequisites—working capital, adequate raw material supplies and markets, managerial and technical skills—technological innovation could certainly lead to idle labor as well as productive capacity. ECAFE has accordingly examined the problems, techniques, and implications of mechanizing small industries.[70] The question of organizing credit for these industries is another common difficulty that needs a thorough investigation by ECAFE.

Exhibitions of handmade goods and market clinics for the products under discussion have been a regular feature of the Working Party's meetings. Experts examined the samples shown and indicated ways of improving size, utility, color, price, and marketing. In all these activities ECAFE has collaborated with FAO, ILO, UNESCO, and EPTA. The Secretariat has compiled a directory of cottage and small-scale industry research institutes in the region and included information on their research programs to encourage countries to exchange the results of their experiments on common problems and to avoid duplication of research effort. It has also been investigating training centers in the region, particularly those that might admit trainees from other countries.

That there are now departments in government administrations to deal with these industries where virtually none existed ten years ago is probably due in part to ECAFE's influence. Not that governments cannot further improve their services. In many cases the emphasis has been placed on techniques of production to the neglect of market analysis. One of the major marketing difficulties of these industries is how to get standardization, batch production, or quality control, while preserving the intrinsic qualities of the product. This is essential for securing large orders, and certainly for repeat orders, from big distribution outlets in the advanced countries. And when large orders are placed, how can governments counter the upward pressure on local raw material prices that often follows? Again, the technical

70. Docs. E/CN.11/I&NR/L.15, Jan. 5, 1960, and I&NR/22, Feb. 15, 1960.

aid of governments has been largely confined to urban and semi-urban areas and has not reached sufficiently far out into the countryside. Yet blueprints and five-year plans will get nowhere unless the rural populations of Asia are on the move in practice as they are said to be in political rhetoric. In the last resort practical results can only come from field work, extension services, and demonstration facilities. Many Asian countries are still badly handicapped in these respects, however, by a shortage of trained personnel.

ECAFE has likewise found it difficult to make much of a mark in this field and for much the same reasons. Covering a specific industry at each meeting of the Working Party, instead of thoroughly examining selected problems common to many industries like credit, standardization, raw material supplies, and prices has its disadvantages. While it enables a well-qualified specialist in the particular industry to attend, it prevents any continuity in representation. This weakness is further aggravated by the fact that the Secretariat has not the staff, time, or budget to permit much follow-up action on the Working Party's recommendations. The past tendency of the Secretariat to make two-year appointments in this field hardly gives the staff member concerned enough time to get to know the problems thoroughly and make contacts, much less to work to get recommendations implemented. Useful work has been done by the Secretariat outside the Working Party to put research institutes in touch with one another and to answer government requests for information and literature on what is being done where on particular problems.[71] One thing a number of directors of cottage industry centers would value are thorough case studies from ECAFE on interesting experiments, solutions, and developments in this field.

Public Enterprise

Over the last ten years in the ECAFE region the role of government in economic activity has steadily grown in importance. Pub-

71. In March 1962 the Commission approved a recommendation of its Industry and Natural Resources Committee that the Secretariat publish regularly a *Small Industry Bulletin*. This will disseminate information among other things on technological advancements in this field. For this purpose each country will designate a technical correspondent on small industries who will maintain close contact with the Secretariat.

lic investment in almost all Asian countries has become the most significant and decisive part of their total investment effort.[72] An indication and consequence of this trend can be seen in the extension of publicly owned enterprise. Before World War II state enterprise was not uncommon in, for instance, transport, public utility services, and irrigation works in Asia but was much rarer in manufacturing and trading. Its extension since then partly reflects the fact that the public sector of developing economies can more easily command financial resources and entrepreneurial talent than the private sector. Indeed, Asian governments have frequently had to pioneer manufacturing ventures that private enterprise is unable or unwilling to sponsor. In some cases, notably in Burma, Ceylon, and India, a preference for socialist policies has also worked strongly in the same direction. Whatever the motives and forces behind the extension of public ownership,[73] it certainly posed difficult problems of organization, administration, and control for all governments.

The success or failure of state enterprise could in many respects set the pace of economic development. It was indicative perhaps of the trouble Asian governments were experiencing that the Industry and Trade Committee requested the Secretariat in 1951 to make a comparative study of the structure of industrial organization in the public sector. The report that the Secretariat presented the following year[74] compared in general terms the advantages and disadvantages of various forms and methods of public organization, management, and control. The Committee accepted the report's suggestion that a regional seminar on the subject be arranged to provide governments with more detailed guidance.

Accordingly, a seminar on the organization and administration of public enterprises in the industrial field was held at Rangoon in 1954 under the auspices of ECAFE, TAA, and the International Institute of Administrative Sciences. This was the first meeting of its kind to be held anywhere. To ensure that the experience

72. UN Sales No.:61.II.F.1.

73. It should be mentioned that in some countries—for example, Pakistan, the Philippines, and Taiwan—the private sector has recently been taking over successful government-pioneered ventures, so reducing the importance of state enterprise.

74. Doc. E/CN.11/I&T/51, Nov. 12, 1951. See also, *Economic Bulletin*, 2, No. 3 (1951).

of advanced countries with public enterprise was readily available to the Asian delegates, TAA mobilized a strong team of experts from outside the region. Only eight Asian governments chose to be represented, however, and with the exception of Burma and Ceylon, the quality of their delegates left much to be desired. Pakistan for the whole of the seminar and India for part of it were represented by local diplomatic staff. Countries like Indonesia, Malaya, and Thailand, which should have shown a strong interest in the subject, were not represented at all. Interestingly enough, the Soviet Union, which preached the theory of public ownership at length, seemed unconcerned to offer the Asians guidance on its problems in practice; it, too, was represented only by a local diplomatic official. The presence of the consultants, however, enabled a useful report to be drafted.[75] This covered suitable forms of organization and administration for public undertakings, financing, commercial and economic aspects, and questions of public accountability.

Two further seminars on this subject or related aspects of it were subsequently convened by ECAFE in cooperation with BTAO and the United Nations Department of Economic and Social Affairs. The first in 1959 dealt with management problems in public industrial enterprises, including the criteria for measuring the effectiveness of management and techniques for improving its efficiency.[76] The participation of Asian governments, both in extent and quality, was a good deal better than at the Rangoon seminar in 1954; for the most part the delegates were actually in charge of public undertakings in their own countries. The second seminar, also well attended, was organized in 1961 at Madras and examined the aims, planning, organization, management, and financing of industrial estates.[77] As an instrument of planning, the industrial estate has a number of advantages. For one thing it encourages a decentralized pattern of industrial development and thus obviates the haphazard growth of urban slums. It is also a particularly useful means of promoting small-scale industry. India has spearheaded the foundation of industrial estates but now nearly all Asian

75. Doc. E/CN.11/I&T/103, Apr. 29, 1954.
76. For report, see Doc. E/CN.11/I&NR/21, 1959.
77. For report, see Doc. E/CN.11/I&NR/35, 1961.

governments are preparing, or have begun to implement, varying kinds of programs for establishing them. The ECAFE seminar was thus convened at an opportune moment.

Trained Personnel

A lack of skilled manpower is one of the most obvious manifestations and causes of economic backwardness. In the colonial period all Asian countries except Japan and Thailand relied to an important extent for their high-level administrative and technical personnel on European nationals. With the achievement of political independence they faced a huge task of producing large numbers of technicians from peoples whose background was essentially handicraft and nonmechanical. At its very first session ECAFE accepted this as a challenge international cooperation must also face.

In June 1947 the Commission requested the Secretariat to prepare a report which would enable it "to suggest the measures necessary to facilitate training in the economic field of administrative and technical personnel of the countries concerned and the obtaining of competent technicians from outside by countries in need of them." [78] In the short time available before the Commission met again in December of the same year, the Secretariat could only outline in a general way the training needs and facilities of the region.[79] With the exception of China and India, no Asian country had begun to take the measure of its shortage of trained manpower. The Executive Secretary suggested that ECAFE might undertake such an assessment, act as a clearinghouse of information on training demands and opportunities, and help governments negotiate with those countries willing to provide facilities. He further proposed that the Commission establish a committee on technical training.[80] Nearly all members of the Commission thought, however, that before ECAFE adopted these functions the Executive Secretary should consult ILO and UNESCO on the setting up of an office or other machinery for advising governments on training facilities and opportunities inside and outside the

78. Doc. E/CN.11/26, June 25, 1947.
79. Doc. E/CN.11/40, Oct. 27, 1947.
80. Doc. E/CN.11/41, Oct. 23, 1947.

region, how they might be expanded, and the best way of putting those needing them in touch with those willing to provide them.[81] Meanwhile the Secretariat should continue to collect the information required to perform these functions.

As a result of the Executive Secretary's consultations, ILO agreed to depute an expert to the ECAFE Secretariat to investigate training needs and opportunities, build up the basis for a rapid and regular exchange of information about them, and prepare a standard nomenclature for classifying occupational qualifications. But ILO was apparently not ready to agree to any special machinery being established within ECAFE for carrying out a program of work on technical training problems.[82] The Executive Secretary still hankered after a committee on technical training. No member country, however, apart from the Soviet Union and on one occasion the Philippines, wished to see ECAFE so obviously duplicate the responsibilities of ILO. At the same time, Asian countries were highly critical of the slowness of ILO in adopting any practical program of assistance to them and urged it to pay more attention to the needs of Asia.[83] The Commission asked the Executive Secretary, therefore, to renew and expedite discussions with ILO on setting up appropriate regional machinery for this purpose and meanwhile to establish a working section within the Secretariat to act as a clearinghouse of information, render direct advisory services, promote the expansion of training facilities, and help governments obtain expert assistance for their economic development projects.[84]

At the end of 1948 ILO announced its intention to establish an Asian field office on technical training at Bangalore in India and to convene an expert regional conference on the subject. Responsibility for direct negotiations with Asian governments on training requests and offers and all the relevant materials ECAFE had collected were transferred in 1949 to the ILO Asian Field Office. ECAFE could at least take some credit for galvanizing ILO into action on a program of assistance to Asia. The Commission, nevertheless, decided to maintain an interest in technical training

81. Doc. E/CN.11/70, Dec. 8, 1947.
82. Doc. E/CN.11/136, Oct. 18, 1948.
83. Doc. E/CN.11/SR.40, June 29, 1948.
84. Doc. E/CN.11/111, June 10, 1948.

problems and progress and asked ILO to report to it annually on these matters. In addition, the Executive Secretary was directed to prepare a survey of the fields of economic development handicapped by a shortage of trained personnel.[85]

The information needed for this inquiry was not easy to obtain. But with the help of ILO and UNESCO the Secretariat completed a remarkably comprehensive survey and presented the findings in 1951 to the Industry and Trade Committee.[86] These showed that in every major area of development, the execution and even, in many instances, the preparation of projects was being hampered by a serious lack of well-qualified administrators and technicians. The findings also revealed a no less desperate shortage of skilled and semiskilled workers, particularly in the construction and mechanical trades and the transport industry. In fact, the Secretariat's survey represented the first real attempt to produce a regional manpower budget for the occupations covered and provided valuable information for the developing operations of the Colombo Plan Consultative Committee and other technical assistance programs. The Industry and Trade Committee accepted the Secretariat's suggestion that a joint ECAFE/ILO/UNESCO working party at secretariat level be set up to keep under review the progress made in removing the more persistent shortages.

One of the principal concerns of this intersecretariat Working Party[87] was to urge Asian governments to make technical manpower budgeting an integral part of their economic development planning. By 1950 only India had made a systematic survey of its technical manpower needs and resources; but with the help of ILO in particular, a number of other Asian countries soon followed suit. The Working Party was able to report that several of them were making considerable progress in meeting their requirements for highly qualified expert personnel.[88] On the other hand, much less attention was being paid by countries to the need for training large numbers of intermediate and lower grade workers and

85. Doc. E/CN.11/176, Dec. 10, 1948.

86. *Fields of Economic Development Handicapped by Lack of Trained Personnel in Certain Countries of Asia and the Far East,* UN Sales No.:1951.II.F.6.

87. For reports, see Docs. E/CN.11/I&T/53, Nov. 12, 1951; I&T/76, Oct. 27, 1952; I&T/95, Nov. 4, 1953; I&T/111, Dec. 17, 1954; I&T/122, Jan. 5, 1955; and E/CN.11/451, Mar. 18, 1957.

88. Doc. E/CN.11/I&T/76, Oct. 27, 1952.

craftsmen. Nor was nearly enough being done to train managerial personnel.

Except in Japan and to a limited extent in China and India, no specialized training facilities existed in the region for producing the top managers required by the new industrial enterprises being planned. Despite the pronounced growth of state enterprises in several Asian countries the urgency of the problem was not sufficiently appreciated. Yet inefficient management practices, unchecked by the spur of competition, could easily force up costs and prices. The ECAFE Secretariat suggested that a regional management training institute be established to help meet this need.[89] But ILO and the Seminar on the Organization and Administration of Public Enterprises in the Industrial Field[90] convened by ECAFE in 1954 both thought it would be more useful in the first instance to develop national training facilities; international action should concentrate on organizing seminars and working parties on management problems[91] and on facilitating an exchange of management trainees. The last report of the Working Party in 1957, however, had much more to say about the inadequacies of existing efforts to meet this particular shortage than about the progress made in overcoming it.[92]

The intersecretariat Working Party has not met since 1957 because ECAFE decided that training problems and needs in its fields of activity could henceforth be more effectively kept under review by its own technical subcommittees and working parties.

89. Doc. E/CN.11/I&T/95, Nov. 4, 1953.
90. See p. 131.
91. E.g., see p. 132.
92. Doc. E/CN.11/451, Mar. 18, 1957.

CHAPTER 10

Natural Resources

Agriculture

In June 1947 the Commission passed a resolution requesting a study of the short-term demands of Asian countries for, among other things, food, seed, fertilizers, and agricultural equipment and the extent to which they could be met from domestic, regional, or other sources of supply.[1] ECAFE was thus immediately involved in activity closely related to, if not actually overlapping, the expanding work of FAO. The Executive Secretary accordingly asked the Commission a few months later to approve a standing joint ECAFE/FAO committee on food and agricultural production with power to engage in allocation work; pending the setting up of an FAO regional office it might be serviced by FAO officials attached to the ECAFE Secretariat.[2] He had not consulted the Director-General of FAO about the idea, but proposed to do so. The Secretariat also thought ECAFE should have a working party on the production and allocation of agricultural requisites, including fertilizers.[3]

The Philippines favored the Executive Secretary's proposals and seemed particularly anxious for ECAFE to arrange allocations of rice and agricultural equipment.[4] Even the United States at

1. Doc. E/CN.11/26, June 25, 1947.
2. Docs. E/CN.11/37 and 41, Oct. 23, 1947.
3. Doc. E/CN.11/39, Nov. 3, 1947.
4. The Philippines was greatly dissatisfied with the allocation work at Singapore of the organization of the United Kingdom Special Commissioner in South East

first envisaged ECAFE having a committee and taking some initiative on food and agricultural problems. Largely due to British insistence and lobbying, however, the Commission did not prejudge the issue and left the initiative very much to FAO. It merely suggested that FAO might consider setting up a regional committee on which ECAFE could be represented and perhaps attach some staff to the ECAFE Secretariat pending the opening of its regional office. The Commission also recommended that FAO formulate a food program for the region in 1948 and 1949. Apart from the instruction to consult the Director-General of FAO on the best means of promoting cooperation between the two organizations, the only discretionary authority the Commission gave to the Executive Secretary was to convene, when he judged appropriate, a conference of Asian officials engaged in agricultural reconstruction.[5]

The main practical result of the Executive Secretary's consultations with the Director-General of FAO was that the latter suggested, and ECAFE accepted, the idea of a joint working party to examine the requirements and availabilities of agricultural requisites in the region.[6] The only opposition to this came from the Soviet Union, which argued that all joint action with FAO was unconstitutional and urged ECAFE to set up its own agricultural committee.[7] In turn, FAO agreed to ECAFE's request to provide the Commission annually with a detailed factual report on food and agricultural conditions in the region.[8] The Director-General made it plain, however, that FAO must take the initiative on all questions concerning food and agriculture; the Executive Secretary readily recognized FAO's primary responsibility in this field but not its sole initiative.[9]

At the end of 1948, Lokanathan was still pressing the Commis-

---

Asia and the Rice Subcommittee of FAO's International Emergency Food Council in Washington. India, for much the same reason, was also interested in ECAFE becoming the main agency for allocating rice in the area.

5. See Docs. E/CN.11/AC.3/SR.2, Dec. 1, 1947, and SR.5–6, Dec. 5, 1947, and Doc. E/CN.11/59, Dec. 8, 1947.

6. Doc. E/CN.11/85, May 5, 1948, and Doc. E/CN.11/117, 1948.

7. Doc. E/CN.11/AC.8/5, July 13, 1948, and E/CN.11/AC.8/SR.43, 1948.

8. Doc. E/CN.11/116, 1948, and Doc. E/CN.11/134, Oct. 27, 1948.

9. Doc. E/CN.11/134, Oct. 27, 1948.

sion to set up a joint committee as ECE had done.[10] India and the Soviet Union supported him, but the majority, led once more by Britain, continued to insist that any such proposal must first come from FAO.[11] Those hoping for immediate ECAFE action in this field were left with the Executive Secretary's discretion to call a conference on agricultural reconstruction, though what exactly it was expected to achieve the Commission did not make clear.[12] Even so, ECAFE could hardly have organized it without the collaboration of FAO. In any event, nothing came of the idea, for as soon as FAO opened its regional office in Bangkok early in 1949 and began its own series of preconference regional meetings, it saw even less need for ECAFE to become involved with general agricultural problems.[13]

There was no hiding the fact that relations between the Executive Secretary and FAO were fast deteriorating. He blamed FAO officials for the lack of government support for his proposals; they thought ECAFE was trying to encroach on their preserves. The ECAFE Secretariat gave FAO officials the feeling that they regarded the secretariats of all the specialized agencies as second-class international civil servants; FAO, in turn, showed no high regard for the quality of the ECAFE Secretariat's work. Resentment was mutual. This was a deplorable state of affairs. Considering that agriculture is the principal economic activity of Asian peoples, ECAFE could hardly ignore the subject; it had entered this field before FAO began its regional activities and clearly meant to stay there. The sensible course, therefore, was for the secretariats of the two organizations to work out a reasonable division of labor. But personality differences and institutional rivalries prevented this and for some years ECAFE remained the only regional commission with which FAO had no such agreement.

The situation did not improve until 1952 when the FAO Director-General and the ECAFE Executive Secretary concluded a Memorandum of Understanding which put relations between the two secretariats on a more formal basis. They agreed that a joint

10. Doc. E/CN.11/138, Oct. 18, 1948.
11. Docs. E/CN.11/SR.50–51, Dec. 3–4, 1948.
12. Doc. E/CN.11/175, Dec. 10, 1948.
13. This development also ended for the time being all ideas of seconding FAO officials to the ECAFE Secretariat.

ECAFE/FAO Agricultural Division with an agreed program of work should be set up within the ECAFE Secretariat. FAO would provide a senior agricultural economist to take charge of it and act at the same time as the FAO Regional Economist; in the former capacity he was responsible to the Executive Secretary and in the latter to the Director-General. Other staff were to be provided by both organizations. This arrangement,[14] together with periodic consultations between the two secretariats, ensured a much more effective liaison between ECAFE and FAO.

Until this time cooperation between the two organizations had not amounted to much. In 1948 their joint Working Party on Agricultural Requisites issued a useful report[15] which aroused considerable interest. On its recommendation both organizations joined forces again in a study of the economic and social aspects of the production and utilization of chemical fertilizers.[16] FAO continued to present a report to each session of the Commission on food and agricultural conditions in the region until the joint Division took over the responsibility. Finally, in 1950 and 1952, the ECAFE Secretariat participated in meetings of FAO's Commission on Forestry and Forest Products in Asia and the Pacific.

Agriculture in the ECAFE region is characterized by small, often fragmented, land holdings, worked on a largely subsistence basis at low levels of productivity by mostly illiterate families who, in many cases, have no security of tenure. As the pace of industrialization in most Asian countries has not been great enough to absorb the natural increase in population, considerable reservoirs of underemployed labor remain in agriculture. When the joint ECAFE/FAO Agriculture Division was established, many governments were in the process of formulating or implementing long-term development plans. Consequently they were taking a keener interest than ever before in helping the small cultivator to raise his productivity. The productive base of agriculture was also being gradually raised by large schemes of land development, reclamation, irrigation, and flood control. The rate of growth of agricultural production, however, has not kept pace with the demands of

14. The Memorandum of Understanding, with some slight modifications, was renewed in 1954.

15. Doc. E/CN.11/135/Add.1, Nov. 13, 1948.

16. Doc. E/CN.11/I&T/33, Dec. 10, 1950; see also "Chemical Fertilizer Industry in Asia and the Far East," *Economic Bulletin, 1*, No. 1 (1950).

the industrial sector or of a rising consumption caused by increasing population and, in some countries, per capita incomes as well. The inability of many Asian countries to raise agricultural productivity even to the prewar level has led either to greater imports or, as in the case of cotton, tea, and sugar, for example, to a fall in the proportion of output available for export. Significantly, the major specific objective of the agricultural development plans of most Asian countries was to improve the balance of payments.[17] This, in brief, was the background against which the joint Division began to study the problems of agricultural development and planning.

A specimen study of agricultural development in one country, Thailand, was produced in 1955[18] and two years later the Working Party on Economic Development and Planning, in collaboration with FAO, devoted a whole session to the agricultural sector in relation to the planning process and economy as a whole.[19] The report of this meeting, while strong on the economic side, was unlikely to satisfy agricultural technicians. The Indian and Japanese delegations, for example, were interested in such refined planning techniques as the formula for assessing the response required from agriculture for a given rate of industrial change. For countries like Burma, Indonesia, Malaya, and Pakistan, on the other hand, the crucial questions were still how to get more production and what to produce. The absence, moreover, of representatives from treasury and commerce ministries suggested that the imperatives of agricultural development were not getting through to some vital areas of government policy-making. The Working Party's report was thus both a reflection of the newness of agricultural development planning and a timely reminder of its importance. Its general message was followed up in 1960 by an FAO/ECAFE expert group on the more technical problems of formulating and implementing agricultural plans.[20]

A related study which the joint Division began in 1957 was the

17. For the nature and progress of agricultural development planning in the region, see the report of the Working Party on Economic Development and Planning in *Economic Bulletin, 8,* No. 3 (1957); and "Some Aspects of Agricultural Planning in Asia and the Far East," ibid., *11,* No. 1 (1960).

18. Doc. ECAFE/L.88, Mar. 1955.

19. See note 17.

20. For report, see Doc. E/CN.11/L.91, Jan. 13, 1961.

agricultural aspects of community development programs. Its aim was to assess through field investigations in selected countries the impact of these programs on village agriculture and to provide basic agricultural data for a wider appraisal of their contribution to general economic development. More was known about the impact of community development schemes on rural initiative and social welfare than on agricultural productivity. Other members of the ECAFE Secretariat and the United Nations Bureau of Social Affairs [21] subsequently participated in the inquiry. The first field investigation was carried out in India by the Planning Research and Action Institute in eastern Uttar Pradesh where intensive community development programs had been conducted for more than three years, and in an adjacent area where no such experiments had been tried. In the light of the experience thus gained, Taiwan's National University and Joint Commission on Rural Reconstruction undertook a parallel investigation of the role of the Farmers' Associations in the agricultural and economic development of Taiwan. The whole inquiry showed that while the economic gains from community development programs have so far been rather modest, their potential contribution to economic development has by no means been fully realized.[22]

The effect of United States farm surplus disposal agreements on the economic development and normal trade of ECAFE countries is another controversial question on which the joint Division has thrown much valuable light. Between July 1954 and the end of 1959 twelve ECAFE countries [23] made agreements with the United States under Public Law 480 [24] for the purchase in local currency

21. See p. 269.

22. *Community Development and Economic Development:* Part I: A Study of the Contribution of Rural Community Development Programmes to National Economic Development in Asia and the Far East; Part IIA: A Case Study of the Ghoshi Community Development Block Uttar Pradesh, India; Part IIB: A Study of Farmers' Associations in Taiwan; UN Sales No.:60.II.F.6. (Separate pamphlets.)

23. Burma, Ceylon, India, Indonesia, Iran, Japan, Pakistan, the Philippines, South Korea, South Viet-Nam, Taiwan, and Thailand. In terms of value India has been the largest recipient, followed by Pakistan, South Korea, Indonesia, and Japan.

24. I.e., the Agricultural Trade Development and Assistance Act of 1954. Title I of this Act empowers the United States government to sell surplus agricultural commodities to friendly nations against local currency and to use these proceeds for making loans or grants to assist the economic development of the recipient countries.

of about $1.8 billion worth of surplus farm products.[25] Of this sum nearly 46 per cent was to be made available to the purchasing governments as loans and about 13 per cent as grants. A further 8 per cent was earmarked for loans to private enterprise. Other important food suppliers to the region like Burma and Thailand were clearly worried at first about the impact of this form of aid on the ordinary commercial imports of the recipient countries.[26] Australia, for equally self-interested reasons, doubted whether it was an effective way of promoting economic development.[27] Two carefully reasoned case studies prepared by the joint Division on the use of United States food surpluses in Japan [28] and Pakistan [29] showed that, as regards the transaction they described, these fears had been largely groundless. In Japan the local currency proceeds were largely invested in projects directly benefiting its rural population and economy; while for Pakistan, a much poorer country, the foreign exchange saving this aid represented greatly helped avoid an almost certain and severe curtailment of its economic development program.[30] In neither case was their trade with third countries materially affected.

In addition to agricultural development and planning, the hardy perennials in the joint Division's work program have been marketing, credit, and pricing policies. Poor marketing arrangements mean high prices to consumers without corresponding benefits to producers. In Asian countries, their mostly illiterate farmers are prey to the malpractices of traders who are also money-lenders; grades and weights are not necessarily standardized; and there are too few regulated buying centers and intermediaries. In 1956 the Division published a report on the marketing of major edible oils and oilseeds; [31] but more recently it has concentrated on

25. This amount excluded the value of surplus farm products the United States supplied to ECAFE countries for famine relief or under barter contracts, as authorized by other provisions of Public Law 480.

26. For statements of Burma and Thailand to the Commission, see, Doc. E/CN.11/408, May 24, 1955.

27. For Australian statement to Commission in 1956, see Doc. E/CN.11/451.

28. Doc. E/CN.11/L.60, 1958.

29. Doc. E/CN.11/L.100, 1961.

30. "If all the foodgrain imports (of Pakistan) during the three years 1956–58 had been paid for in foreign currencies, the foreign exchange reserve would have been totally eliminated." Ibid., p. 55.

31. UN Sales No.: 1956.II.F.5.

assisting national research institutes to undertake marketing surveys, especially for paddy and rice. In 1957 it advised, for example, the Indonesian University Institute of Economic and Social Research on a study of the internal marketing of rice. Two years later in New Delhi, FAO and ECAFE jointly sponsored a technical meeting on marketing problems with special reference to rice. The Division also investigated factors influencing the demand for foodstuffs. The Working Party on Economic Development and Planning in 1957 emphasized the importance of improving estimates of future requirements for agricultural products through, for instance, attempts to assess income elasticities of demand. The Commission, however, wanted the study defined in more general terms, presumably because only a few countries, such as India and Japan, were interested in highly methodological exercises.

The second hardy perennial of the joint Division is the problem of agricultural financing and credit. When, as in many Asian countries, the cultivators neither own the land nor have security of tenure and pay at times as much as 50 per cent or more of the crop as rent, a large proportion of them are compelled to borrow during the period between sowing and harvesting. Except in Japan, institutional sources of credit, such as cooperatives or special government agencies, cover only a small percentage of their needs. They have instead to rely heavily on the private moneylender, landlord, or merchant who frequently advances money on the security of the crop at exorbitant rates of interest, with the result that the farmer receives much less than the market price for his output. Combined with the well-known malpractices of moneylenders, shopkeepers, and merchants, such debts once contracted often keep on accumulating; a short-term loan may become a permanent burden. In these circumstances Asian governments could hardly avoid taking a direct interest in the problem. Accordingly, an FAO/ECAFE Centre on Agricultural Financing and Credit was held at Lahore in 1956 [32] and in the following year the Division published the paper it had prepared for this meeting.[33] It has since continued to meet requests for information

32. See FAO Report No. 631, Rome, 1957; mimeographed.

33. *Credit Problems of Small Farmers in Asia and the Far East,* UN Sales No.: 1957.II.F.2.

on the credit institutions and facilities being developed in the region.

Finally, the joint Division has been continuously concerned with the food and agricultural price policies of Asian countries. Most Asian governments interfere in varying degrees with the prices of food grains, principally in order to stabilize the cost of living. This is an understandable objective given the actual or potentially inflationary tendencies of developing economies. Experience has shown, however, that apart from Ceylon and Japan, the prices officially fixed for food grains have not given enough incentive to producers. Moreover, in a number of food importing countries government price policies often entailed a heavy burden on the taxpayer in the form of food subsidies or government trading losses. In 1955 the joint Division, in collaboration with FAO, prepared a study on the food and agricultural price policies of Far Eastern countries with special reference to rice,[34] and in 1958 a joint FAO/ECAFE Centre on Policies to Support and Stabilize Agricultural Prices and Incomes in Asia and the Far East was held at New Delhi.[35] A further Secretariat report on the subject, which had been prepared for this meeting, was published the same year.[36] The general verdict of these inquiries was that, while Asian governments would have to retain consumer price policies, at least as instruments for short-term protection, a fairer treatment of the producer, including the largest possible allocation of funds for the improvement of agricultural productivity, would be in the best long-run interests of the consumer as well.

On one important aspect of the development of agricultural resources, namely forest products, there has been much less co-operation so far between FAO and ECAFE. Early recommendations of the Commission on the desirability of standardizing timber terminology [37] were taken up by FAO's first regional Forestry and Timber Utilization Conference in 1949 and led, the year after, to an expert meeting on the standardization of the nomenclature, terminology, testing methods, grading, and dimensions of timber. But ECAFE has shown no propensity to initiate work on timber

34. Doc. ECAFE/L.87.

35. See EPTA Report No. 887 published by FAO.

36. *Food and Agricultural Price Policies in Asia and the Far East,* UN Sales No.:58.II.F.2.

37. Docs. E/CN.11/67, Dec. 8, 1947, and E/839, July 1, 1948.

problems, and the possibility of establishing a joint timber division, as in ECE, was never raised by either side. Indeed, when FAO somewhat belatedly proposed a joint study of timber trends and prospects in the region, along the lines of the ECE/FAO study published in 1953, the Secretariat was slow to respond at first; once involved, however, it fulfilled its commitment sooner than FAO. A draft of the study—*Timber Trends and Prospects in the Asia-Pacific Region*—was first issued in 1960 and has since been published.[38] Its findings made depressing reading.

While some parts are rich in forest resources, the ECAFE region as a whole is not. Its industrial wood consumption per head is extremely low, intraregional trade in forest products is negligible, and its imports of processed wood goods exceed its exports of primary forest products by around $300,000,000. On present demand and supply trends for industrial wood, the region will require net imports of the order of $2 billion in 1975 to meet its essential needs. Yet its forests are being steadily depleted by uncontrolled fellings, the ravages of pests, disease, fire, shifting cultivation, and the alienation of land to agriculture. A radical reappraisal of existing forest policies and a new approach to the planning of forest industries were overdue.

One such industry is pulp and paper. In 1960 FAO and ECAFE joined forces, again on the initiative of the former, in sponsoring at Tokyo a regional Conference on Pulp and Paper Development.[39] On the insistence of FAO, private business interests, not least from the major timber producing countries outside the region, were well represented. As a result of huge illiteracy eradication programs and rising population and living standards, the region's consumption of pulp and paper was expected to expand from 6,500,000 tons in 1960 to around 25,000,000 tons in 1975. To add another 18,000,000 tons or roughly $4 billion to its import bill in the next fifteen years is inconceivable; the expansion of supplies must come largely from within the region.[40] Many preinvestment surveys will be needed, however, before the necessary production capacity can be created. Because of the small size

38. See Doc. E/CN.11/I&NR/L.23, Dec. 19, 1960, and Add.1, Jan. 26, 1961.

39. For report, see Doc. E/CN.11/I&NR/28, Nov. 17, 1960.

40. Excluding Communist China, Japan, and Oceania, the Conference reckoned the total investment required to 1975 would be of the order of $1.3 billion, about half of which represented foreign exchange costs.

of many national markets, the possible economies of large-scale production, the localization of alternative materials for pulp and paper making, such as bamboo and bagasse, and the possibility of joint venture schemes, it would not be an optimum use of resources for Asian countries to approach this task along purely national lines. They should, in brief, coordinate their efforts. What is now needed is a joint ECAFE/FAO timber committee in which foresters, economists, and the timber trade can follow up the findings and recommendations of the Timber Trends Study and the Pulp and Paper Conference, formulate policies for developing forestry resources, and strive to get them accepted by the governments.[41] Neither organization, however, has so far risen to the challenge.

The joint Division is well aware that because of the poor development of agricultural economic services in the region, its studies are not receiving the attention they should in many Asian countries. By associating local research institutes with its work, as in the Indonesian rice-marketing survey and the field investigations undertaken in Uttar Pradesh and in Taiwan, the joint Division has been assisting and encouraging the training of more agricultural economists. It has also made an inventory of the existing status and scope of agricultural economics teaching, research, and advisory services in the region.[42] The difficulties it faces in trying to make a greater impact on governments are not peculiar to its field alone; but they do raise the question whether ECAFE and FAO have tackled them in the best way possible.

While collaboration between ECAFE and FAO through the joint Division has worked well, it has been less than satisfactory in other fields of ECAFE activity. In 1958 the Trade Committee, for example, requested the Secretariat to prepare a market survey for jute; yet FAO had been producing regular reports on the subject for years. That representatives of ministries of industries and trade failed to find out what ministries of agriculture could have told them is less surprising, perhaps, than that the Executive

41. India suggested to the Commission in 1956 that ECAFE should have a timber committee like that of ECE. Doc. E/CN.11/451. The idea was referred to the ECAFE Executive Secretary and the FAO Director-General, but no proposal emerged from their consultations.

42. *Agricultural Economic Research in Asia and the Far East,* UN Sales No.: 58.II.F.4.

Secretary should have accepted the inclusion of this item in ECAFE's work program.[43] In 1959 the Nutrition Division of FAO and the Industry and Trade Division of ECAFE belatedly discovered that they were both proposing to convene meetings that year on the canning and food processing industries and some mutual recrimination ensued. It so happened that the emphasis of each meeting was different; but it would have made fewer demands on governments if a joint meeting had been organized on all aspects of the subject. The Pulp and Paper Conference, although a joint effort, caused further friction between the two secretariats. It seemed to the FAO officials, who had prepared most of the United Nations papers submitted, that the ECAFE Secretariat, which had no technical specialists on this industry, claimed far too much credit for the Conference and regarded it largely, if not wholly, as a ECAFE achievement. In the Mekong Project, on the other hand, it was FAO officials who behaved arrogantly and tried to push ECAFE aside.[44]

The sense of rivalry and competition that too often animates relations between the specialized agencies and the United Nations has in this instance prevented ECAFE and FAO from remedying the most serious shortcoming of the collaboration epitomized by the joint Division, namely, that its direction and work are never properly discussed by any expert body of government representatives. The Division initiates its own program which is then approved in turn by the FAO Director-General and the ECAFE Executive Secretary and endorsed by the Commission. Directives can, though very rarely do, come from the Commission and are even less likely to emanate from the Council of FAO. Regional conferences of FAO have sometimes discussed at length various subjects of interest to the joint Division, such as agricultural planning and marketing problems, but they paid little attention to its actual studies or work program. Some of its reports have been considered at meetings like the FAO/ECAFE Centres on Credit and Prices and the session of the Working Party on Economic Development and Planning devoted to the agricultural sector; yet

43. In the event FAO supplied the Committee with reprints of an article on "Trends in World Demand for Jute Manufactures" which had appeared in its *Monthly Bulletin of Agricultural Economics and Statistics* for December 1960 and January 1961.

44. See p. 194.

others, such as the useful case studies of United States farm surplus disposal, have not been discussed by any specialist group in the region. The Commission's own attention to the work of the joint Division could hardly be more perfunctory. One possible remedy would be to change its agenda item "Report of the joint ECAFE/FAO Agriculture Division" to some important issue of agricultural development policy in the hope that this might induce governments to include agricultural economists in their delegations. But this would only partially solve the problem of providing a regular expert forum for the Division.

It is hard to escape the conclusion that if the work of the joint Division is to make a greater impact, there must be a joint ECAFE/FAO committee on agricultural economic problems similar to that of ECE. To keep down the number of meetings governments are asked to attend, it could meet every other year when FAO's Regional Conference did not, since the latter meets in alternate years. India actually proposed to the Commission in 1955 that such a committee should be established [45] and was supported by Burma, Indonesia, and the Soviet Union. The United States seemed favorably disposed but the Philippines and Taiwan were outrightly opposed, while Britain and Pakistan wanted to postpone a decision until the following year. On the suggestion of the Executive Secretary it was decided to leave him to explore the question further with the Director-General of FAO.[46] Their reported conclusion was that for the time being a joint committee was unnecessary.[47] Apparently FAO did not want its work program discussed by an ECAFE forum, though why there should be a greater risk of this happening in ECAFE than in ECE, which has joint Committees on Timber and Agriculture, is far from clear.

But even if FAO officials were prepared to reconsider the question, the signs are that the Executive Secretary is not keen on further joint action of this nature. True, the ECAFE Secretariat would have to shoulder the burden of servicing another committee. Various brushes with FAO officials may also have influenced the Executive Secretary's judgment. The fact remains, however,

45. ECAFE/L.92, Apr. 2, 1955. Ironically the Indian delegate who introduced the resolution, B. R. Sen, later became Director-General of FAO.

46. Doc. E/CN.11/408, May 24, 1955.

47. *ECAFE Annual Report to ECOSOC, 8 April 1955–14 April 1956*, Doc. E/CN.11/430, Mar. 1956.

that agricultural development is one of the region's most urgent and difficult tasks. ECAFE cannot hope to influence the way it is tackled by producing studies and guidance which are not properly considered by any representative body of government experts.

Minerals

Asia is endowed with a wide variety of minerals, but its known reserves are by no means fully exploited or its region fully surveyed. At the time ECAFE was established no country in the region, with the possible exception of Japan, had been extensively prospected for minerals [48] and reliable estimates of their reserves were not available. Exact knowledge tended to depend on the extent to which minerals had actually been used in the past. Thus much more was known about the mineral reserves it had been profitable to exploit for markets in Europe and North America than about those like coal which depended for their full exploitation on local industrialization. The mining industry in Asia developed essentially in response to the demands of the highly industrialized countries; in this way the region became the world's largest source of tin, antimony, tungsten, mica, and graphite. Nor had much attention been paid in the past to the wise conservation and rational use of mineral resources. For some years after the achievement of independence, coking coal, for example, which is very scarce in the region, was being used for non-metallurgical purposes, especially in India, while the region's large deposits of low-grade coal and iron ore remained underdeveloped for lack of improved techniques of production and utilization.

In 1948 the Working Party on Industrial Development urged Asian countries to speed up the rehabilitation of their mining industries and undertake extensive prospecting for coal, metals, and ores.[49] In discussing this report the following year, the Committee of the Whole decided the data available were not sufficient to enable it to define the scope for international action on mineral resources and left it to the Secretariat to make studies and raise

48. E.g., by 1950 only 28 per cent of India, which had a long-established and well-equipped Geological Survey, had been geologically surveyed on a one-inch scale, the smallest scale for practical use.

49. Doc. E/CN.11/131, Oct. 31, 1948.

problems in this field. The most urgent need, in short, was for accurate information on the actual and potential mineral wealth of the region.

By 1951 the Secretariat had completed a comprehensive review of the coal and iron resources of the region.[50] The Industry and Trade Committee thereupon instructed it to concentrate in the future on studying specific mineral development projects and problems, disseminating technical information, and rendering direct advisory services. The Committee agreed, however, that the time was opportune for calling a regional conference of experts on mineral resources.[51] The Conference on Mineral Resources Development, which was held at Tokyo in 1953, was the first occasion on which Asian geologists had met together to discuss their common interests. They recommended that a regional geological map be prepared and asked the Secretariat to compile a compendium of existing national laws and regulations affecting mineral development.[52] A majority of them also favored the creation of an ECAFE subcommittee on mineral resources in order to keep progress and problems in this field under review; but the British and United States delegates delayed complete agreement on a formal proposal by claiming they were without instructions on the question. When the idea was raised the following year in the Industry and Trade Committee, Britain suggested occasional expert meetings instead, while the United States thought the mandate of the Iron and Steel Subcommittee should be broadened to include minerals. As these were the only two opposing voices, however, the Committee had no difficulty approving the setting up of a separate Subcommittee on Minerals Resources Development.

The impetus behind national efforts in this field came from the rapidly growing energy demands of Asian countries and the importance they attached to the creation or expansion of the iron and steel industry. But in many cases it was evident that the raw material basis of their plans and aspirations had not been fully investigated. Since minerals are an exhaustible asset their rational

50. *Coal and Iron Resources of Asia and the Far East,* UN Sales No.:1952.II.F.1.

51. Doc. E/CN.11/267, Feb. 25, 1951.

52. For the proceedings of this Conference, see *Development of Mineral Resources in Asia and the Far East,* UN Sales No.:1953.II.F.5.

exploitation must be based on a long-term development plan; for this purpose a complete geological map showing main rock types is essential to an understanding of the best way of exploiting the minerals contained in them. In the early years of ECAFE a few Asian countries had still to attempt a national geological survey; practically all of them had still to complete one. In fact, Asia was the only continent in the world without a geological map for the whole region.

The regional conference of mineral experts agreed that this omission should be repaired. An ad hoc Working Party of Senior Geologists was accordingly set up in 1954 to formulate guiding principles and standards for the national surveys that were to form the basis of a regional map. The work was coordinated by the Director General of the Geological Survey of India, which actually prepared the map. This was a purely Asian effort financed entirely by voluntary contributions from British Borneo, Burma, India, Japan, Malaya, Pakistan, Taiwan, and Thailand. The amount each contributed depended mainly on the size of the space it occupied on the map. In 1961 the finished article was finally printed and put on sale.[53]

The project had some interesting consequences. In 1956 Afghanistan, with some advice from the Secretariat, established a Geological Survey Department to make a preliminary survey of the country for the regional map. A number of other country maps, formerly not available, were also completed. Acting on a recommendation of the Senior Geologists' Working Party that neighboring countries should concert their efforts on specific problems, Malaya and Thailand organized a joint survey of their border area and made some important mineral discoveries. British Borneo and Indonesia are proposing to follow suit. As aerial mapping is one of the new techniques available for this kind of work that provides ample scope for neighborly cooperation, ECAFE in 1960 convened a special seminar on the subject[54] and organized the following year, a Pilot Training Course on Techniques for Aerial Survey. Other regional maps are now being prepared. Borneo

53. It is also worth noting that Australia, France, the Netherlands, New Zealand, and the United States have been preparing a geological map for Oceania and the Pacific Islands which will complement the ECAFE map.

54. For report, see Doc. E/CN.11/I&NR/Sub.3/L.10, Mar. 25, 1960.

has been the coordinating agent for a regional petroleum map showing areas of known and potential petroleum and natural gas deposits, dry and active wells, refineries, and pipelines; Malaya assumed the responsibility for preparing a tectonic map showing geological structures; India and Japan are preparing maps of other known mineral deposits, after which one showing potential deposits will be made. All of this activity has been supervised by the Senior Geologists who lay down the standards by which the information included on the maps should be collected and presented. In 1959 their Working Party was made a permanent body of ECAFE and its functions broadened beyond map making to cover surveying, prospecting, and other geological problems.

In 1955, ECAFE and TAA arranged for a group of Asian geologists and mining engineers to make a Study Tour of Europe, including the Soviet Union, where they examined such matters as the method of organizing national geological surveys, survey and prospecting procedures and equipment, the exploration and development of coal and metalliferous ore deposits, and the training of geologists and mining engineers.[55] The visit to the Soviet Union was a particularly novel experience for the experts even though the language barrier prevented them from understanding its technical literature. It led, not surprisingly, to a United States invitation, though ECAFE and BTAO were unable to organize a Study Tour of North America until 1959.[56] Such are the inexorable rules of the Cold War, moreover, that in the Mineral Resources Subcommittee the United States delegation felt obliged to criticize severely the Soviet Union part of the report on the Study Tour to Europe and the Russians to give the same treatment to the report on the Study Tour to the United States. Both Study Tours can be fairly criticized, however, for trying to cover too much ground both literally and in subject matter. On the other hand, it was no small gain to ECAFE that a number of the experts who participated subsequently became the directors of their national geological surveys or mines departments.

The Secretariat, meanwhile, had been making regular reviews of mining developments in the region, including new mineral discoveries, the installation and expansion of processing plant,

55. For report, see Doc. ST/TAA/SER.C/27, n.d., 1958.
56. For report, see Doc. E/CN.11/I&NR/34, Nov. 15, 1961.

and trade in minerals.[57] One of the aims of this work has been to promote a uniform terminology, classification, and method of statistical reporting for the data collected. Comprehensive technical assessments have also been made on the methods of exploring, exploiting, conserving, and processing selected minerals. So far the Secretariat has studied coal, iron ore, sulphur, kaolin titanium, copper, lead, and zinc ore.

One interesting fact that emerged from the Secretariat's earlier investigations was that many Asian countries had considerable lignite or brown coal reserves but few details were available on their location, quality, and quantity. It was also apparent that while considerable quantities of this low-grade fuel were consumed in Europe and the United States, scarcely any was used in Asia outside Japan. The scarcity of high-quality coal, and especially of metallurgical fuel, made it essential for the region to make the most of its relatively abundant reserves of lignite. The subject figured prominently on the agenda of the regional conference of mineral experts in 1953 and the Mineral Resources Development Subcommittee subsequently instructed the Secretariat to prepare a comprehensive report on the possible role of lignite in the fuel economy of Asian countries. This investigation confirmed that with the possible exception of Cambodia, Laos, and Viet-Nam, all Asian countries possessed lignite reserves; it is for most of them their predominant, and for some their only, known mineral fuel.[58]

In 1954 ECAFE and TAA organized a Study Tour of Asian coal experts to Australia to observe modern techniques for developing and using lignite. The value of this particular visit as compared, for example, with the study tours the Asian geologists and mining engineers made to Europe and North America, undoubtedly gained from the fact that it explored a very specific subject. Most of the recommendations of its report[59] were subsequently accepted. Conversion into thermal power is perhaps the best way of

57. Five such surveys of *Mining Developments in Asia and the Far East,* covering the years 1953–58 have been published under UN Sales Nos.: 1953.II.F.5; 1954.II.F.4; 1957.II.F.3; 1959.II.F.4; and 1960.II.F.4.

58. *Lignite Resources of Asia and the Far East, Their Exploration, Exploitation and Utilization,* UN Sales No.: 1957.II.F.3.

59. *Australian Lignite Industry (Brown Coal) in Relation to the Development of Low Grade Coal Deposits in Asia,* Doc. ST/TAA/SER.C/15, Apr. 1, 1954.

using lignite. That Thailand, for instance, is now producing it for generating Bangkok's electric power supply is due in no small measure to the advice, facilities, and contacts provided by ECAFE.

Laboratory facilities for testing minerals are very inadequate in many Asian countries. The Industry and Trade Committee in 1951 was interested in the possibility of establishing a regional research center for the treatment of low-grade coal and iron ore. Britain advocated using national centers for regional purposes, but was firmly told by the Pakistani chairman that the "views of the countries of the region should carry most weight." [60] Actually the idea of a regional research center came to nothing and co-operation on this problem took more or less the form Britain had suggested. The Secretariat arranged with the ECE secretariat for samples of low-grade Asian coals to be tested in European laboratories. Through the good offices of the Secretariat, Japan tested coal from Burma and South Viet-Nam, peat from Ceylon, and lignite from Thailand; Australian and Indian laboratories also tested coal from South Viet-Nam; while Thailand's Bureau of Mines investigated samples of coal from Laos. In addition the Secretariat has advised the various countries concerned on specific problems connected with the development of their minerals. It is also worth noting that since the end of 1960 it has been the co-ordinating agent for the various programs of mineral prospecting going forward as part of the Mekong Project.[61] The Soviet Union at one time suggested that an "institute" of mineral resources experts, meaning presumably a panel, should be set up under ECAFE to give direct assistance to countries on geological surveys, the training of geologists, and the long-term development planning of their mineral resources.[62] What was being seriously explored at the end of 1961, however, was the prospect of establishing a regional geological survey center for South-east Asia to serve primarily, though not perhaps exclusively, the needs of Cambodia, Laos, South Viet-Nam, and Thailand, which do not have well-developed geological surveys. As regards the supply of geologists, an ECAFE/UNESCO working group of experts which reported

60. Docs. E/CN.11/I&T/17–32, May 10–Dec. 24, 1950. Papers prepared for the third session of the Industry and Trade Committee, Feb. 15, 1951, Lahore, Pakistan.

61. See p. 197.

62. Doc. E/CN.11/483, June 3, 1958.

in 1961 on the training needs of a number of specific countries and the region as a whole did not favor the setting up of a regional training institute.[63]

Liberation from colonial rule and the force of Asian nationalism demanded a revision of the terms on which minerals, including petroleum, had been exploited in the past. Indeed, many Asian countries began their political independence with no laws or regulations on the subject at all. The regional conference of mineral experts in 1953 asked the Secretariat, therefore, to make a comparative study of the laws and regulations in existence to see what amendments were desirable, as well as to inform private foreign capital of the legal conditions governing investment in mineral development. It was hoped the study might lead to the drafting of a uniform mining code for the region. The Secretariat, however, could not tackle so highly complex a subject unaided and TAA was unable to provide it with a consultant. In the end the United Nations Office of Legal Affairs undertook the assignment and the results of its preliminary survey were published in 1957.[64] A working group of experts is expected to be convened in 1962 to assess the effectiveness of various forms of legislation in helping promote the conservation and development of mineral resources. Unfortunately the long delay in formulating expert guidance meant that the problem became less urgent as countries went ahead and drafted or redrafted their own laws and regulations.

On the whole, the bulk of the activities and ideas initiated by ECAFE in this field have been of immediate practical relevance; but there have been exceptions. For instance, in 1951 the Industry and Trade Committee agreed with the Secretariat that it would be useful for the region to have a standard scientific system for classifying coals similar to that being worked out for Europe by ECE. In fact this was a somewhat pointless exercise for ECAFE. The ultimate aim of the ECE investigation was to produce a relatively simple standard method of identifying qualities of coal by its intrinsic properties, which would be practically useful in everyday commercial transactions.[65] But the ECAFE region produces

63. Doc. E/CN.11/I&NR/34, Nov. 15, 1961.

64. *Survey of Mining Legislation, with Special Reference to Asia and the Far East,* UN Sales No.:1957.II.F.5.

65. Wightman, *Economic Co-operation,* p. 89.

very little coal and has not, like Europe, a flourishing and complex international coal market. With the possible exception of India and Japan, which supported the project, a standard scientific classification system would be of little practical value to the region.

Much the same doubt can be fairly entertained about the energy balance sheets the Commission requested the Secretariat to draw up for ECAFE countries in 1958. This entailed tabulating and analyzing existing and prospective fuel and energy needs relative to present and prospective supplies. The aim presumably was to enable governments to formulate coordinated fuel and power policies. It proved to be rather an ambitious undertaking, however, since the statistics required for it are simply not available. It was premature also in the sense that the paramount problem for most Asian countries is not that of coordinating competing sources of energy, but of discovering and developing new sources of fuel, minerals, and power.

Apart from the occasional flight of fancy in the work program, the most striking feature of ECAFE's efforts in this field is that so small a part of its total activity should be so rich in examples of intergovernmental cooperation, not at the committee table discussing reports, exchanging information, and passing resolutions, but in the realm of practical action, which is where results really count. In 1958 it broke completely new ground by organizing a symposium on development of petroleum resources. Only three ECAFE countries, British Borneo, Indonesia, and Iran, produce and refine petroleum products substantially in excess of their requirements. Burma's production just about meets its own needs and the rest have to import these products at a substantial foreign exchange cost.[66] All countries in the region are therefore anxious to discover crude oil reserves or at least to establish or expand their own refining capacity and thereby save foreign exchange by importing crude oil rather than the more costly refined products.[67]

Until 1957 there had been hardly any suggestion that ECAFE should study the problems of exploring and developing the region's petroleum resources. The Working Party on Industrial Development realized in 1948 that for some years ahead the

66. Japan and Taiwan, although almost entirely dependent on imports of crude oil, export petroleum products because their refining capacity is larger than their domestic demand.

67. No refining capacity exists at present in Afghanistan, Cambodia, Ceylon, Hong Kong, South Korea, Laos, Malaya, Nepal, and South Viet-Nam.

region would be a heavy net importer of petroleum products and consequently urged Asian countries to develop substitutes such as power alcohol. In 1952 a seminar on the production and use of power alcohol was accordingly organized by ECAFE with the help of TAA.[68] That same year the Indian delegate to the Industry and Trade Committee suggested including petroleum in the work program,[69] but Britain and the United States thought it was a bad idea and no other country mentioned the subject.[70] In 1957 Thailand formally proposed to the Committee that ECAFE should organize a regional technical symposium on petroleum geology. The idea actually emanated from the Secretariat, which owed its inspiration, in turn, to a national petroleum geology symposium held by Taiwan the previous year. The Committee approved the proposal but broadened its scope to include the technical problems of petroleum production. The only surprising thing about this new ECAFE responsibility was that it had not come earlier, for a number of Asian countries seemed impatient with the assistance available for exploring and developing their petroleum reserves [71] and the terms on which petroleum products were supplied by Western oil companies.

The ECAFE Symposium on the Development of Petroleum Resources was held at New Delhi in 1958 [72] and aroused considerable interest, particularly among the world's leading oil-producing countries and companies, not least because it was the first ever held under United Nations auspices. The experience contributed by these outsiders added greatly to the value of the meeting. In addition to reviewing the petroleum industry and resources of the region, the symposium discussed various technical problems of oil exploration and production. Among the matters it suggested the Secretariat should follow up were the standardization of petroleum statistics and reports on exploration activity, and the possibility of establishing one or more regional petroleum institutes. It also requested the Senior Geologists' Working Party to

68. For report, see Doc. E/CN.11/I&T/71, Nov. 28, 1952.

69. This particular delegate later became, for a period, the chief of ECAFE's Industry and Trade Division.

70. Doc. E/CN.11/I&T/19, Mar. 21, 1950.

71. E.g., until 1961 the US government would give no technical assistance, loans, or grants for the development of petroleum resources in the ECAFE region.

72. For proceedings, see UN Sales No.:1959.II.F.3.

consider the preparation of a natural gas and oil map for the region.

ECAFE's first foray into the highly political world of petroleum had gone well and its symposium had helped to dispel the mists of secrecy which, in Asian eyes at any rate, seemed to surround this industry. But as ECAFE penetrates more deeply so it may expect to encounter stronger political undergrowth; even the comparatively simple question of a regional petroleum training institute could not escape. Iran, India, Pakistan, and, after an interval, Indonesia, each offered to act as its host country. The Secretariat circulated them all for precise details of their training facilities but by the end of 1960 only Iran had replied. At the 1961 session of the Industry and Natural Resources Committee the Iranian delegate consequently pressed the Executive Secretary for the recommendation the Secretariat had been asked to make following its questionnaire to the four countries. The only sensible recommendation he could make was that the Iranian bid should be accepted.

Iran had by far the most developed petroleum industry in the whole region and an extensive program for training the many specialists it required. India's training facilities were in the realm of intention rather than fact; the Pakistan bid was probably a reflex action to the Indian offer, while that of Indonesia looked very much like an afterthought for, like Pakistan, it had less to offer even than India. That these three countries had so little on which to found a regional institute doubtless explains their failure to reply to the Secretariat's questionnaire.[73] The Executive Secretary nevertheless refused to make the obvious recommendation, presumably for fear of offending India, Indonesia, and Pakistan, and merely enjoined all of them to go ahead with their plans to establish national training facilities as the region would need many such institutes, whether they were called regional or not. Discretion may have been the better part of valor in this instance, though the Executive Secretary would have avoided a blistering Iranian attack on his lack of leadership if the Secretariat had

73. It is worth pointing out in this connection that it is very expensive to establish and maintain a full range of training facilities for the petroleum industry. It seems an unnecessary and costly duplication, therefore, to create them on a purely national basis in the ECAFE region.

earlier declined to accept the responsibility for making a recommendation. Its great knowledge of this industry was about the one important experience Iran, a recently admitted member of the Commission, could and wanted to share with other ECAFE countries. Taiwan and Thailand supported its claim as the most obvious place to locate the first regional petroleum institute. But India was determined to prevent it being endorsed by the Industry and Natural Resources Committee. Consequently all the Committee could say to the Commission was that there was room for more than one regional institute.[74] This had always been thought possible; but it was plainly not an immediate prospect.

Iran was not, however, to be denied. At the 1961 Commission session it forced the issue to a decision by threatening to introduce a resolution endorsing its claim, for which it had canvassed a fair amount of support. The Executive Secretary was compelled to accept the obvious. The Commission accordingly requested the Secretariat to work out details with the Iranian government for the expeditious use of its training facilities as the first regional petroleum institute.[75]

This issue has been mentioned at length because it indicates something of what lies beneath the surface of cooperation on petroleum problems. Indian government officials privately recognized that Iran was the best place to locate the first regional training institute, but were politically inhibited from acknowledging the fact openly because the Iranian industry was dominated by international oil consortiums of the Western powers.

A second regional symposium on petroleum resources is expected to be held in 1962 at Teheran. What particularly distinguishes its agenda from the first is the inclusion of the economic aspects of petroleum production and distribution, including international trade and prices. The prices charged by Western oil companies, especially when compared with the cost of Soviet supplies, have been a cause of much recent dissatisfaction and hard bargaining with a number of Asian countries. The Soviet Union, believing evidently that the outcome would embarrass the Western powers and oil companies, proposed to the Trade

74. Doc. E/CN.11/I&NR/32, Dec. 19, 1961, and Doc. E/CN.11/I&NR/31, Feb. 16, 1961.

75. *ECAFE Annual Report to ECOSOC, 22 March 1960–20 March 1961*, Doc. E/CN.11/564, Apr. 22, 1961, para. 347.

Committee in 1961 that the Secretariat should make a marketing survey for petroleum and petroleum products. Both Britain and the United States thought the subject could more appropriately be considered by the second regional symposium but acquiesced all the same in its inclusion in the work program of the Trade Committee. The oil companies, which took violent exception to the findings of an ECE inquiry into oil prices in Western Europe some years previously,[76] will be watching very carefully, if not apprehensively, what ECAFE may produce on the same subject.

In view of the checkered political history of international oil operations, it would be no bad thing for the Secretariat to produce a report for Asian consumption on the factors influencing the market price for oil. It might well help to dispel the sense of mystery surrounding this question. The world market for petroleum products, like that for shipping, is an imperfect one in the economists' sense, so that at any one moment of time there is probably some oil company somewhere, prepared to offer large price discounts in order to be rid of a temporary surplus.

The price policies of Western oil companies are not, however, the most important supply problem facing Asian governments. What most needs an ECAFE investigation is rather the future total and pattern of Asian demand for petroleum products, how it can be met, and at what cost. If the per capita consumption of petroleum products in ECAFE countries rose only to that of Iran, an economically poor country still, though rich in oil resources, the region's total demand would grow enormously. What is the likely foreign exchange cost of meeting it? How much foreign exchange can be saved and at what capital cost by expanding refining capacity in the region? What is the optimum scale of refining operations for a given pattern of demand for petroleum products? These are the kinds of economic questions ECAFE could most usefully tackle regarding the long-term problems and prospects of developing the petroleum industry of Asian countries.

Electric Power

A large proportion of government expenditure on postwar reconstruction in the ECAFE region was devoted to making good war-damaged or worn out electricity generating plants. Even so,

76. Wightman, *Economic Co-operation,* p. 87, n.14.

its power supplies fell well short of current demands, and load shedding and power rationing were common occurrences. The report of the Working Party on Industrial Development reflected this concentration on the immediate tasks of rehabilitation. But it also urged countries to speed up their surveys of fuel and power resources and pay special attention to rural electrification, uniform technical standards, the location of hydro-power stations, and their coordination with thermal-power plants and with other multipurpose river development projects. The advanced countries were enjoined to help Asian countries by providing machinery, materials, and technical assistance. Realizing that a great deal of preliminary investigation would be needed before actual power schemes could be planned and implemented, the Working Party recommended that ECAFE establish a power division in the Secretariat to collect and analyze data on the technical and economic aspects of power development.[77]

In the discussion of this report at the Committee of the Whole in 1949, Britain, supported by India, proposed that ECAFE set up a subcommittee on electric power to consider in particular the standardization of power equipment, shortages of trained personnel, and the need for adjacent countries to coordinate their power development schemes. Pakistan even thought electric power should be a first priority for ECAFE. The Committee felt, however, that it was too soon to attempt to define the possible area of international action in this field.[78] In the first place, there was little exchange of power across national frontiers. The immediate concern of most Asian countries was to obtain power plant and equipment from the advanced countries to make good the damage and deterioration caused by the war to their generating capacity. Foreign exchange shortages and long delivery dates were problems ECAFE could do little about. Furthermore, the governments had still to formulate clear-cut plans or policies for the long-term development of their power resources.

It was the attention given by the Iron and Steel Subcommittee to the importance and cost of future power supplies for its own industry that brought ECAFE back to the question of what action

77. Doc. E/CN.11/131/Annex A, Oct. 26, 1948.

78. Doc. E/CN.11/AC.11/SR.3, March 30, 1949, and *ECAFE Annual Report to ECOSOC, 1 July 1948–5 April 1949,* Doc. E/CN.11/190, Apr. 29, 1949, para. 129.

it should take in the field of electric power. The Iron and Steel Subcommittee suggested that it consider setting up a full committee or subcommittee on power.[79] The idea was not accepted straightway. At the 1950 session of the Industry and Trade Committee, a number of countries, Australia, France, and Thailand especially, evidently still felt it was premature. Britain, India, Pakistan, and the Philippines, on the other hand, thought it would be useful to study at least the power resources and needs of the region and then see whether ECAFE should set up special machinery for further action. Rather surprisingly, Indian support was conditional on the work requiring no extra staff. This reversal of its earlier opinions brought a sharp reminder from Burma that smaller countries were less able than India to obtain expert advice. The Secretariat was directed nonetheless to make a factual survey of the power resources and needs of ECAFE countries and the ECE Secretariat offered to help out on the technical aspects of the study.[80]

By this time Asian governments were beginning to turn their attention from rehabilitation tasks to long-term development planning. For most of them electric power was the key to their aspirations for industrialization; in fact, a number of major industrial projects being planned depended on the availability of an adequate supply of power. Except in Japan, thermal-power plants accounted for the major part of the region's total output of electricity. Thermally generated power was fairly expensive, however, since fuel transport costs were high, especially for those countries which had to import coal or oil. Yet the region had tapped only an insignificant proportion of its apparently huge water resources. Much of this vast potential still remained to be properly investigated. In the long-term power programs being drafted, particularly those of India, Pakistan, and the Philippines, the emphasis was consequently placed on hydroelectric schemes. Measured by the capital cost actually or potentially involved and the benefits envisaged, these schemes were the largest industrial projects then being planned. As a result, the region's installed generating capacity was expected to double between 1949 and 1956. But even this high rate of expansion seemed unlikely to

79. Doc. E/CN.11/I&S/16, Apr. 17, 1950.
80. Docs. E/CN.11/I&T/SR.9–76, May 15–30, 1950.

match rising demands; nor was it likely to raise significantly the existing very low level of per capita consumption of electricity in the region or its share of total world output.[81] It was also clear that whatever the precise stage their planning had reached, practically all Asian countries needed, in addition to financial assistance, a great deal of expert advice on a host of specific problems connected with the exploration and exploitation of their potential power resources.

Having taken the measure of the power problems facing ECAFE countries,[82] the Secretariat suggested the creation of a power division to appraise particular schemes, including related industrial developments, and help work out proposals for technical assistance. It also recommended that ECAFE establish a subcommittee on electric power to consider, for example, problems of government planning, administration, control, and operation of power schemes; the development and extension of transmission systems over large areas, especially in rural areas; and requirements for power plant and machinery.[83] These proposals were presented to the 1951 session of the Industry and Trade Committee. Britain changed its earlier tune and declared that Asian governments could now get more help from TAA than from the Secretariat. It agreed with the Soviet Union that an electric power subcommittee should only be created on condition that no extra staff was demanded—a condition raised the previous year by India. On this understanding the Committee accepted the Secretariat's recommendation though without any marked enthusiasm on the part of its Asian members. The emphasis of ECAFE's function in this field was to be on providing practical guidance

81. With roughly half of the world's population, the ECAFE region accounted in 1950 for about 5 per cent of the world's output of electricity. This share has since been steadily increasing and in 1959 reached 6.4 per cent. All regional figures are heavily influenced by Japan, however, which in the case of electric power had twice as much generating capacity as the combined total for all other ECAFE countries. Over most of South-east Asia, for example, per capita consumption of electricity is under 50 kilowatt-hours as compared with over 1,000 kilowatt-hours in Japan, 2,000 kilowatt-hours in Britain, and nearly 5,000 kilowatt-hours in the US. *Electric Power Bulletin*, Doc. ST/ECAFE/SER.L/7, 1961.

82. *Electric Power Resources and Needs of ECAFE Countries*, Doc. E/CN.11/I&T/20, Mar. 20, 1950.

83. Doc. E/CN.11/I&T/32, Dec. 24, 1950.

on specific projects and problems. The scope of the work program subsequently undertaken is indicated in what follows.

While hydro-power schemes figured prominently in the first long-term development plans of a number of Asian countries, very little was known about the precise extent of their water resources. A scientific evaluation was a necessary condition of fixing rational priorities among various possible schemes and sites. Following a Secretariat paper on the subject,[84] an expert working party met in 1957 to recommend the best methods of calculating hydro-power potential.[85]

What is of immediate practical importance for the planners is less the theoretical or gross potential, the ceiling so to speak, of the water resources that can be technically developed than their economic potential. In any case most Asian governments simply do not have the funds, time, or trained manpower to survey all their river valleys, however much they appreciate the importance of this from a long-term point of view. So far only Japan has made a comprehensive hydroelectric survey of its water resources; India, Pakistan, the Philippines, and Taiwan have made preliminary investigations; the rest are compelled to proceed on a short-term view by going ahead with schemes of immediate importance on what they believe to be the most favorable sites.[86] In examining the problems of assessing hydro-power potential, ECAFE has benefited from the earlier work of ECE on the subject [87] and, with the latter's cooperation, is trying to assist countries whenever practicable to survey the theoretical or gross potential of their rivers.

The Working Party on the assessment of hydro-power resources advised countries to survey their short and long-run power demands as India and Japan had already done. The Secretariat had some years before prepared a paper on the techniques of making power market surveys.[88] While in general the demand for power has been constantly outstripping supply in ECAFE countries it is, nevertheless, essential that their specific power schemes should be

84. Doc. E/CN.11/I&NR/HPWP/11, 1957.

85. For report, see Doc. E/CN.11/I&NR/Sub.1/2, and Corr. 1, Dec. 12, 1957.

86. *Report of the Regional Seminar on Energy Resources and Electric Power Development,* Doc. E/CN.11/I&NR/Sub.1/L.21, 1961.

87. Wightman, *Economic Co-operation,* pp. 159–60.

88. Doc. E/CN.11/EP/14, Aug. 1, 1952.

paralleled by projects and developments that will use the energy produced. If the forecasts of expected load growth prove to be too optimistic, the heavy capital outlays on power installations will become an unnecessary financial burden. On the other hand, because the growth rates of the power industry have generally been higher than those of other services,[89] electrical engineers have often found it hard to persuade their finance ministries to provide sufficient funds for further expansion. Consequently, there has been a tendency for the planners to underestimate future power demands. Making accurate forecasts is no easy task, however, when, as is usually the case, comprehensive and reliable data are not available or where the production of primary products, which are subject to the vicissitudes of world markets, consumes an appreciable proportion of the power used.[90] In such comparatively unstable economies it is better, the Subcommittee on Electric Power agreed, to make separate forecasts for various groups of consumers—domestic, rural, commercial, industrial, or particular economic sectors—than attempt to relate consumption to trends in large economic aggregates like gross national product or the index of industrial production.[91]

Power schemes and industrial projects are thus interdependent and their planning requires close coordination. The Secretariat accordingly prepared for the Subcommittee several papers on the relation between energy generation and industrial development and particularly on the application of power to the metallurgical and chemical industries.[92] Electric smelting, the production of ferro-alloys, nitrogenous fertilizers, and caustic soda are examples of industrial activities that use relatively large amounts of power and thereby provide valuable revenue-producing loads for power generating projects. Asian governments seem to be well aware of

89. Power consumption growth rates in industrialized countries usually amount to 8 to 10 per cent per year. In Asian countries like India or Ceylon, with ambitious economic development programs, growth rates of from 16 to 19 per cent are expected over the next ten years. Countries such as Indonesia, Pakistan, the Philippines, Taiwan, and Thailand anticipate growth rates of the order of 12 to 14 per cent.

90. E.g., Malayan tin. Thus during 1958 and 1959 there was actually a reduction in Malaya's output of power because of restrictions on production enforced by the International Tin Council.

91. Docs. E/CN.11/I&NR/Sub.1/L.21, and I&NR/36, Jan. 11, 1962.

92. Docs. E/CN.11/I&T/Sub.1/2, July 5, 1954, and Sub.1/3, July 28, 1954.

the importance of this kind of coordination; as already mentioned the tendency has been for them to plan their power programs too conservatively rather than too optimistically.

The bulk of the electric power output of Asian countries is consumed by urban and industrial districts. A paramount objective of their economic development plans, however, is to raise the productivity and living standards of their predominantly rural population. This must entail, among other things, bringing electricity to village homes, farms, and industries. Asian governments have taken a keen interest in this prospect but, apart from Japan and Taiwan, they have made very little actual progress with rural electrification. In discussing their difficulties and formulating advice, the Subcommittee again benefited from the earlier work done by ECE on the subject.[93] In fact, rural electrification has been virtually a standing item on its agenda.

Reduced to its essentials the real problem of rural electrification in Asia is how to finance the cost of the power to very low-income consumers. How can the heavy capital outlays and operating costs be met when the loads are scattered over wide areas and the per capita demand is so limited? Even in advanced industrial countries with much higher living standards and larger farm holdings, the investment return on rural electrification schemes is comparatively small and various methods are used to subsidize them. If such methods are found to be necessary in Europe, how much more obviously are they required in Asia. Direct subsidies, interest-free loans, and similar kinds of financial assistance will have to be given, at any rate for the first ten years or so of any scheme, if electricity is to be brought to the rural populations of Asian countries.[94]

In addition to examining the financial aspects of the problem, the Subcommittee has recognized that the costs of rural electricity can be kept down by improvements in the design, construction methods, and operating practices of the equipment used. For instance, where steel and concrete are expensive and full-length wood poles scarce, fabricated wood poles can be used to support transmission lines. As several ECAFE countries required substantial quantities of wood poles for their power schemes, an ad hoc

93. Wightman, *Economic Co-operation,* pp. 164–65.

94. See *Rural Electrification,* UN Sales No.:1954.II.F.1.

working party of experts was convened with FAO at the 1957 session of the Subcommittee, to consider and make recommendations on their rational utilization, including methods of preserving them against the eroding effects of tropical climates.[95] For districts remote from existing power systems, the Subcommittee recommended that countries establish small generating units using local fuels or streams. Small diesel engine generators, for example, would help to build up power loads and act in this way as pilot installations. Asian governments have also become increasingly aware that the consumption of power in rural areas must be encouraged by village demonstration experiments and other promotional techniques. It cannot be assumed that economical power, once provided, will be used. In Burma, for example, the idea of using electricity was sold to the villagers by first lighting up their temples. Pakistan offered to conduct a pilot experiment in its North-West Frontier Province, where rural electricity is available, to test equipment thought likely to prove useful for rural electrification schemes in the region. Unfortunately, owing to administrative delays and difficulties and the inability of TAA to provide the financial assistance required, this modest regional project could not be organized. In 1959, however, the Subcommittee recommended that ECAFE establish a panel of experts in collaboration with BTAO, to visit countries at their request and advise them on the technical and economic aspects of their rural electrification schemes. It is hoped to begin this service in 1962.

Among various technical matters examined on the supply side of the electric power industry, the Subcommittee has evinced great interest in the possibilities of using lignite in thermal power plants.[96] As already indicated the exploitation and utilization of the region's lignite reserves has been an important item in ECAFE's work program on mineral resources. The Secretariat and the Subcommittee have also studied various aspects of the coordination or integration of hydro- and thermal-power supplies. A grid system, for instance, linking hydro- and thermal-power stations ensures a more reliable and uninterrupted supply of electricity at minimum cost. Great technological improvements have been made over the last decade in steam-power production. Taken to-

95. For report, see Doc. E/CN.11/I&NR./Sub.1/L.7, June 16, 1959.
96. See, e.g., Doc. E/CN.11/EP/27, Sept. 29, 1953, and Doc. ECAFE/EP/3, 1953.

gether with the fact that thermal plants can be built more cheaply and quickly than hydro-power stations, this has resulted in a marked rise in the share of thermally generated power in the region's total output of electricity.[97]

In 1956 ECAFE arranged with TAA for a group of Asian electrical engineers to make a Study Tour of Europe, including the Soviet Union and the United States, to observe the latest technical advances in the design, construction, and operation of power plants and in the practices generally of the electricity supply industry.[98] The Subcommittee subsequently reported that many of the recommendations of this Study Tour were being implemented in the region.[99] One important lesson the group brought back, which ECAFE has been impressing upon Asian countries, is the desirability of standardizing their power equipment and operating practices from the very outset of their power development programs. Standard types and sizes of machinery, voltages, frequencies, and methods of operation can do much to improve efficiency and lower costs. They help also to promote coordination between manufacturers and the power supply utilities, facilitate interchangeability of equipment and the exchange of power across national frontiers, and ensure proper quality control and greater safety for workers and consumers. At present, voltages and frequencies, for example, vary greatly in the region.[100] In 1959 the Subcommittee recommended that Asian countries as far as possible adopt 220-volt rather than 110-volt systems.[101] This is a question that excites much argument, since the standard adopted influences the design of electrical equipment and therefore the competitive position of the major electrical manufacturing countries. Thus the Subcommittee's recommended standard for the region happens to favor British electrical equipment suppliers more than French, Japanese, or United States manufacturers. The prospects of valuable trade orders from the big power development programs of Asian coun-

97. Hydro-power stations produced 73 per cent of the total output of public utilities in the ECAFE region in 1951 and 59 per cent in 1959. Over the same period the share of steam power rose from about 25 per cent to 39 per cent. *Electric Power Bulletin,* July 1961.

98. For report, see Doc. ST/TAA/SER.C/18, Oct. 11, 1957.

99. Doc. E/CN.11/I&NR/19, Oct. 27, 1959.

100. See Doc. E/CN.11/I&NR/Sub.1/L.6, May 6, 1959.

101. Doc. E/CN.11/I&NR/19, Oct. 27, 1959.

tries gives the outside powers a strong commercial interest in the work of ECAFE in this field. It is hoped sometime in the future to organize an expert working group on the possibilities and problems of standardizing power equipment and practices in the region.

The Secretariat and the Subcommittee have also examined organizational problems of the power supply services, electricity costs [102] and tariffs,[103] and safety precautions [104] in the use of electricity. The Secretariat periodically disseminates technical information, while its *Electric Power Bulletin* is the basis for a regular review by the Subcommittee of the progress of power development in Asian countries. This useful publication, which began in 1952, contains a wealth of statistics and other information on installed capacity, output, consumption, financial, and organizational aspects of the electricity supply industry in the region. The collection of comprehensive and uniform statistical data has been no easy task. ECAFE found that many governments had no organized system for maintaining statistics on the electricity supply industry. Where private companies operated under license there was no central agency to collect and compile statistics for the whole country. Again, some governments provided certain kinds of essential data but not others. Pakistan, for instance, which is not among the most underdeveloped countries of the region, does not even know how much power it produces. It sometimes takes months and many letters from the Secretariat before governments reply to an ECAFE request for information. Certainly the lack of common definitions, terms, and methods for collecting statistics has made the task more difficult. The Subcommittee has accordingly accepted the Secretariat's suggestion that an ad hoc working group of experts meet to examine this matter.[105] To a large extent, however, the real trouble is that governments simply have not the trained manpower to spare for such work. It exemplifies, in fact, a more general difficulty confronting ECAFE in its efforts to awake an interest and make an impact in this and other fields of activity.

102. Doc. E/CN.11/I&NR/Sub.1/L.10, June 22, 1959.
103. Doc. E/CN.11/I&NR/Sub.1/L.14, 1961.
104. Doc. E/CN.11/I&NR/Sub.1/L.18, 1961.
105. Doc. E/CN.11/I&NR/36, Jan. 11, 1961.

Outside Japan, the extent of power development and heavy electrical manufacturing in the region is still very small; there are hardly any regular exchanges of power across national frontiers, and apart from India, Japan, and the Philippines, all countries are short of electrical engineers. All this means that governments can contribute little to the substantive work of the Electric Power Subcommittee. The delegations have been of rather mixed quality and some, it is certain, have not been qualified enough even to appreciate and absorb the discussions. The governments, nevertheless, look to ECAFE for information and disinterested advice and it falls to the Secretariat to see that they get it. In this respect its close liaison with ECE has proved to be especially fruitful. The stubborn fact remains, however, that in many cases the governments are in no position to apply the guidance provided. The idea of using one or more national training institutes for electrical engineers, such as in Japan or India, to serve the training needs of other countries is being explored. The organization of a regional panel of rural electrification experts to render on-the-spot technical assistance is another way round the difficulty. But for some time ahead, ECAFE must inevitably continue to function in this field as an information service and tutor rather than an instrument of actual intergovernmental cooperation.

Water Resources Development

About half the population of the ECAFE region live in river valleys. For centuries they have suffered death, destruction, and misery from the uncontrolled flooding of important rivers like the Brahmaputra, Irrawaddy, Kosi, and Yellow.[106] With the notable exception of the Mississippi basin, the problem is one peculiar to monsoon Asia. Yet properly exploited, water power can add much to a people's wealth. It was to be expected, therefore, that Asian countries would turn to ECAFE for help in meeting the challenge. Whether, and if so how, it should help were questions not settled without a struggle.

In 1947, on the initiative of France, the Commission proposed

106. The Yellow and Kosi Rivers have also been notorious for their repeated changes of course. For an idea of the flood damage caused by the major rivers of the region, see *Flood Damage and Flood Control Activities in Asia and the Far East,* Appendix 1, ECAFE Flood Control Series No. 1, UN Sales No.:1951.II.F.2, or UN Sales No.:1950.II.F.1, Table 111.

to ECOSOC that the problem be tackled through the creation of a bureau of flood control.[107] The French permanent delegate to ECAFE, H. C. Maux, conceived the idea from his experience in China before World War II, when the League of Nations sent a team of experts to investigate the Yellow River. He suggested, in effect, a "board" of experts to do similar work in the ECAFE region. China, the country most severely affected by flood damage, strongly supported the French delegate and wanted a body that could give actual aid. ECOSOC required more details on the proposal, however, and asked the Executive Secretary and the specialized agencies to study it further.[108]

The Executive Secretary consulted FAO and two Chinese experts somewhat perfunctorily and reported the result to the Commission in June 1948.[109] All agreed that flood control must not be tackled in isolation but as part of the wider problem of conserving, controlling, and using water. A positive development approach was needed. But all disagreed on the means. FAO thought it premature to establish a bureau: any funds for this purpose should be spent on technical assistance for specific country projects rather than on general studies. The Chinese experts favored a fairly large bureau with far-reaching functions, including those of conducting research and rendering technical and material assistance. They envisaged it having a budget of over $250,000. By contrast, the Executive Secretary was surprisingly modest. He thought a bureau could help governments set up their own national organizations, which might then meet under ECAFE auspices to discuss common problems, including the international aspects of rivers flowing over national frontiers. A central body providing direct advisory services would, he felt, have to be organized on a large scale and might duplicate the work of existing national and international organizations.

A majority of the Commission still favored the idea of a bureau, though not organized on a substantial scale. A staff of between three and five highly qualified experts and a budget not exceeding $180,000 would be sufficient. It should not merely synthesize experience and promote the exchange of information but also pro-

107. Doc. E/CN.11/66, Dec. 8, 1947.
108. ECOSOC Res. 105(VI), Mar. 8, 1948.
109. Doc. E/CN.11/87, May 14, 1948.

vide advisory services and assistance at the request of governments.[110] The United States opposed the whole idea on the grounds that the means proposed were quite inadequate to tackle a complex problem that was best left to national organizations. The Soviet Union, though agreeing in principle with the majority, abstained from voting when the Commission did not accept its proposal that the bureau only help train flood control specialists who were citizens of the Asian country concerned.

This further recommendation to ECOSOC left the impression that the bureau was to be a semiautonomous body of experts, not part of the Secretariat, with no clearly defined relationship to the ECAFE Secretariat or any other source of direction. This was consistent with the wish of China and France to keep it free of the undesirable control, as they thought, of the Executive Secretary. This view came under heavy fire in ECOSOC. Strong criticism was directed in particular against the idea of a semiautonomous body providing technical assistance. It was generally agreed that flood control was a grave and urgent problem. But the critics, Britain, Canada, New Zealand, and the United States were against tackling it in the way ECAFE proposed, at any rate for the time being. With the backing of France and the Latin American members, the redoubtable P. C. Chang, the Chinese delegate and the staunch champion of Asia and ECAFE in the Council, fought hard to get the recommendation approved. The Soviet Union supported the idea of a bureau but not the administrative arrangements envisaged. A lengthy debate ended in compromise. The Council accepted the idea on principle but wanted an assurance that the bureau would form part of the Secretariat and be appointed by and responsible to the Secretary General.[111] To enable the bureau to start work in the meantime, it recommended that the General Assembly finance a budget of $100,000 for 1949.

At its fourth session in 1948, the Commission finally produced proposals that satisfied the Council.[112] The Bureau was to form part of the Secretariat as regards administrative and financial matters but enjoy autonomy on technical matters. The fact that its

110. Doc. E/CN.11/110, 1948.

111. ECOSOC,OR: 3rd Yr., 7th Sess., 191st, 192nd, 204th, 206th Mtgs., Aug. 6–19, 1948, and ECOSOC Res. 144D(VII), Aug. 19, 1948.

112. Doc. E/CN.11/178, Dec. 10, 1948.

annual reports to the Commission were to be submitted by its chief through the Executive Secretary and not by the latter himself, as in the case of other Secretariat activities, was a further indication of the Bureau's special standing. It was also specifically authorized to provide technical assistance to governments at their request.[113] In April 1949, an experienced administrator in this field in China was appointed chief of the Bureau, and during the next few months he gathered together a small but highly qualified staff. Apart from the fact that members of the Bureau, unlike other units in the Secretariat, all hold high-level posts, there is no distinction in practice between the designation bureau and division, or between a chief of the Bureau and a director of a division. In 1953, when it was redesignated the Bureau of Flood Control and Water Resources Development, Pakistan suggested calling it a division but this was opposed by Cambodia, India, the Philippines, Taiwan, and Thailand. Acting on a suggestion made by the Secretary-General's Survey Group on the Organization of the Secretariat, the Executive Secretary and Headquarters made a further attempt in 1957 to redesignate it a division. The chief of the Bureau strongly resisted and, by some adroit lobbying with the aid of the French permanent representative, mustered enough support at the Commission session to defeat the move. A change of title, it was argued, would be interpreted as a reflection on the prestige and standing of the Bureau.

The Commission agreed that the highest priority in the immediate work program of the Bureau should be given to an investigation of the needs of areas hardest hit by uncontrolled or partially controlled floods. Its first task, therefore, was to survey the extent and nature of flood damage and control practices in the region. Through field investigations and contacts with leading specialists and national institutions data was collected on nineteen major rivers in Burma, Ceylon, India, Indo-China, Indonesia, Pakistan, the Philippines, Southern China, and Thailand. Ironically, the Asian country that had pressed hardest for the creation of the Bureau, namely China, very soon lay for the most part out-

113. Under paragraph 1(g) of its terms of reference, the Bureau could "depute, upon request of member governments, experts to the national organizations with a view to advising them in the solution of certain specific problems."

side the scope of the Bureau's activities.[114] The early fruits of this survey were published in 1950.[115] This was followed by a study of methods and problems of flood control.[116] No two rivers have the same regime; no two floods on the same river are exactly the same. No country, therefore, has or can have a monopoly of the best methods of flood control: each has something to contribute and much to learn. On the basis of a survey of thirteen countries the ECAFE report discussed and analyzed the merits and demerits of different techniques.

Traditional methods of flood control have been primarily determined by pressure of population on food supplies. The main aim is to ensure that the food yield of a given cropping practice is sufficient to feed the population. In less densely populated areas such as the Mekong and Chao Phya river valleys one rice crop a year has been sufficient to satisfy local consumption and provide a surplus for export without the necessity of flood protection. Where population density is high as, for example, in the valleys of the Yangtze, Yellow, and Pearl rivers in China, or the Red River in North Viet-Nam, the practice is to plant two crops of rice and protect them by dikes. This has been the cheapest, most common, direct, and immediately effective method of flood control. About 300,000,000 people in the region live under their protection, which means that any breach of the dikes, especially through erosion, inevitably causes catastrophic damage. Bank protection and river training to safeguard the dikes and increase the capacity of existing channels are other control techniques. They are rather expensive, however, and hence not practiced to any great extent. The Bureau made a special further study of both these methods.[117]

For many rivers, it was clear that better results would come from reservoirs than from improved dikes. The availability of water in dry seasons is, in any case, just as crucial as controlling its abun-

114. At the 1954 Commission session India suggested that if Communist China approved, the Bureau should send a team to investigate the methods of water resources development there. Only the Soviet Union supported the suggestion.

115. *Flood Damage and Flood Control Activities in Asia and the Far East,* Flood Control Series No. 1, UN Sales No.:1951.II.F.2.

116. *Methods and Problems of Flood Control in Asia and the Far East,* Flood Control Series No. 2, UN Sales No.:1951.II.F.5.

117. *River Training and River Bank Protection,* Flood Control Series No. 4, UN Sales No.:1953.II.F.6.

dance in rainy seasons. Although parts of the region have numerous small reservoirs dating back centuries, none is large enough to detain or store flood flow to any appreciable extent. But except in special cases, larger reservoirs are not economically justified unless they can be made to yield additional benefits in the form of electric power, more irrigation, and improved navigation. In other words, flood control had to be thought of as part of multipurpose development over the entire basin of the river. This approach had been gaining favor in Asia following the spectacular success of the Tennessee Valley Authority (TVA) in the United States. Its essence is the impounding of water by a system of reservoirs in the rainy season, to be released in the dry season for irrigation and navigation, simultaneously producing hydroelectric power. Soil conservation, reforestation, fish culture, malaria control, and recreation facilities are also part of multipurpose river basin development. Many flood control plans in the region have been revised in the light of this approach. In 1951 a Regional Technical Conference on Flood Control, which the Bureau convened at New Delhi, agreed that "flood control is fundamentally a part of and cannot be separated from unified river basin development." [118] The scope of the Bureau's work was accordingly broadened by renaming it, as already mentioned, the Bureau of Flood Control and Water Resources Development.

Multipurpose dams are costly capital investments for underdeveloped countries. The time lag between their planning or commencement and their completion or utilization is fairly long. How can the investment be amortized? Financial return on capital is not, as it tended to be in the past, the criterion to emphasize. Water resources projects aim to set in motion a cumulative process of growth and for this reason have many of the characteristics of general economic planning. It is their wider economic and social benefits, direct and indirect, tangible and intangible, short and long, that have, therefore, to be estimated. In other words, the criteria must embrace an assessment of their over-all contribution to the economic growth of the area. Whether their cost should be borne by the users of the services provided, or by public funds, or by a combination of both, is a matter for public policy. As

118. *Proceedings of the Regional Technical Conference on Flood Control in Asia and the Far East,* Flood Control Series No. 3, UN Sales No.:1953.II.F.1.

with so much economic development in underdeveloped countries the planning and execution of multipurpose projects is held back by the lack of technical personnel, data, and know-how as well as financial resources. The Bureau systematically analyzed in concise form a great deal of experience and scattered knowledge on the subject and published it in 1955 as a manual for officials and specialists on the basic problems, principles, and techniques of planning and executing such projects, including methods of assessing their cost and benefits.[119] It was indicative of its reception that the Japanese and Taiwan authorities had it translated into their own languages.

The Damodar Valley Corporation in India and the Kitakami Special Area in Japan are as yet the only two notable examples in Asia of multipurpose river basin development. The Bureau has made case studies of them both.[120] As dams and reservoirs are, moreover, the most expensive structures in river basin development, it organized, with BTAO help, a symposium in September 1961 to discuss, among other topics, factors affecting the choice of damsites and of particular types of dam for a selected site.

Complementing the study of river basin planning and development the Bureau set out to make an inventory of the region's water resources. Country-by-country surveys were made giving present stage of utilization of these resources, future plans for their development, and difficulties encountered. Surveys have been published for Afghanistan, British Borneo, Burma, Ceylon, India, Indonesia, Iran, Japan, Korea, Malaya, Nepal, Pakistan, the Philippines, Taiwan, and Thailand.[121] In some cases these were pioneer studies requested by countries that had not made their own

119. *Multiple-Purpose River Basin Development,* Part I, "Manual of River Basin Planning," Flood Control Series No. 7, UN Sales No.:1955.II.F.1.

120. *A Case Study of the Damodar Valley Corporation and its Projects,* Flood Control Series No. 16, UN Sales No.:60.II.F.7.

121. *Multiple-Purpose River Basin Development,* Part 2A, Water Resources Development in Ceylon, China:Taiwan, Japan and the Philippines, Flood Control Series No. 8, UN Sales No.:1956.II.F.2; Part 2B, Water Resources Development in Burma, India and Pakistan, Flood Control Series No. 11, UN Sales No.:1956.II.F.8; Part 2C, Water Resources Development in British Borneo, Federation of Malaya, Indonesia and Thailand, Flood Control Series No. 14, UN Sales No.:59.II.F.5; and Part 2D, Water Resources Development in Afghanistan, Iran, Republic of Korea and Nepal, Flood Control Series No. 18, UN Sales No.:61.II.F.8. The Bureau's quarterly, *Flood Control Journal,* for June 1958 and March 1959 brought up to date the progress made by the Philippines and Thailand in water resources development.

national surveys. From these national studies it is planned to make a comprehensive regional review of progress in water resources development over the past decade.[122]

In addition to general and national surveys of water resources, the Bureau from time to time has made a number of studies of specific problems of common concern. As early as 1947, the Commission requested the Bureau, once established, to investigate the silt problems of rivers and reservoirs. The work was carried out jointly with the Punjab Irrigation Research Institute in India and the Royal Irrigation Department of Thailand. The findings were published in 1953.[123] The report briefly discusses the extent of soil erosion in the region and deals with various aspects of the sediment problem after the soil has entered natural streams or canals.

In 1951 the Bureau made a comprehensive review of existing practices in the region regarding the methods, records, and terminology of hydrological observations, on the basis of which new draft standards were prepared. Standardization was particularly desirable in the case of international rivers. After comments on the draft had been received from various technical organizations, revised standards were published in 1954.[124] Following this report the Commission recommended to the Bureau that it convene jointly with the World Meteorological Organization (WMO) an expert working group on the standardization of hydrologic terminology. A group of nine experts met in September 1955 and the glossary of terms they prepared was published the next year.[125] In 1957 the secretariats of ECAFE and WMO jointly presented to a third Regional Technical Conference on Water Resources Development a background paper on the deficiencies of hydrologic data in various ECAFE countries.[126] On the recommendation of this

122. Papers on ten years of development in various countries were presented to the fourth ECAFE Regional Technical Conference on Water Resources Development in December 1960. See Doc. E/CN.11/WRD/Conf.4/49.

123. *The Sediment Problem,* Flood Control Series No. 5, UN Sales No.:1953.II.F.7.

124. *Standards for Methods and Records of Hydrologic Measurements,* Flood Control Series No. 6, UN Sales No.:1954.II.F.3.

125. *Glossary of Hydrologic Terms Used in Asia and the Far East,* Flood Control Series No. 10, UN Sales No.:1956.II.F.7.

126. ECOSOC Res. 533(XVIII), Aug. 2, 1954, and Res. 599(XXI), May 3, 1956, urged that particular attention be given to remedying deficiencies in hydrologic data.

Conference the two secretariats in 1959 convened a joint Interregional Seminar on Hydrologic Networks and Methods. Twelve Asian and three non-Asian countries and several specialized agencies and NGOS were represented. The subjects discussed had to do with the design of such networks and hydrologic methods in the absence of adequate basic data.[127] A second seminar was held in November 1961 when field methods and equipment used in hydrology and hydrometeorology were discussed.

Apart from basic data and know-how, the lack of trained personnel is as great a problem in this as in other fields of ECAFE activity. A systematic practical training in the planning and operation of water resources development projects is nowhere to be had in the world. It was at one time thought that the Bureau might organize an international pool of experts, a sort of permanent cadre of engineers, for this purpose. Since 1952 when Burma and the Philippines introduced a joint resolution on the subject, the Commission has repeatedly emphasized the urgent need to establish a regional training center. But TAA felt unable to finance it and this long deferred project still awaits a sponsor. Instead, the University of Roorkee in India, on the Bureau's initiative, began regional training courses in 1956. Their aim is to enable serving engineers to study the latest techniques, including the economic and social aspects, of water resources development. The Bureau helped recruit the trainees and has provided short courses of lectures.

As a final example of the Bureau's work on specific problems the subject of earthmoving operations should be mentioned. Many heavy engineering projects in the region demand, at considerable cost, large amounts of earthwork. The right combination of labor and capital equipment appropriate to the region and type of project is crucial to the efficiency and cost of these operations. How should this combination be determined? Following a discussion of the subject at the second Regional Technical Conference in 1954, on-the-spot investigations were made in India, where cheap labor is abundant, and in Japan, where earthwork operations are largely mechanized because of the relatively high cost

127. The proceedings of this Seminar were published as *Hydrologic Networks and Methods,* Flood Control Series No. 15, UN Sales No.:60.II.F.2.

of labor. On the recommendation of the third Regional Technical Conference the whole subject was subsequently reviewed in 1959 by a Working Party on Earthmoving Operations which met at New Delhi. This was a curious meeting. Although eight Asian and five non-Asian countries attended, there were few qualified Asian delegates outside the large number of Indian engineers present. The discussion largely centered on ways of improving labor efficiency, including the general factors determining the scope and problems of mechanization. But too many of its stated conclusions were rather general and obvious. To report, for example, that "it was clear that the right type of equipment should be used for the right job" was unworthy of an expert group. Of more practical value was the Working Party's recommendation that experimental or pilot projects should be carried out to determine the proper choice and application of a large number of different implements used by manual labor in earthmoving operations. The Central Water and Power Commission of India and the East Pakistan Water Power Development Authority agreed to make the experiments with special implements supplied by the Philippines, Taiwan, and Thailand.[128]

Much of the work of the Bureau of Flood Control and Water Resources Development has been of a continuing nature. The problems studied admit no short-term solutions. They have been chosen partly by the Commission and the Secretariat, but mainly by the four Regional Technical Conferences the Bureau has so far convened.[129] The first in 1951 was probably the best. It certainly attracted the best representation, largely because organizations in related fields, such as the World Power Conference, convened meetings in New Delhi at about the same time. In addition to discussing flood control problems, this first Regional Conference recommended that the Bureau study ways and means of promoting cooperation in the development of the water resources of

128. For the report of the Working Party, see *Earthmoving by Manual Labour and Machines,* Flood Control Series No. 17, UN Sales No.:61.II.F.4.

129. The proceedings of the first three Conferences have been published as *Proceedings of the Regional Technical Conference on Flood Control in Asia and the Far East,* Flood Control Series No. 3, UN Sales No.:1953.II.F.1; Flood Control Series No. 9, UN Sales No.:1956.II.F.3; and Flood Control Series No. 13, UN Sales No.:1959.II.F.2. For the report on the fourth Conference, see Doc. E/CN.11/548, Jan. 19, 1961.

international rivers. The second conference in 1954, like the first, was largely concerned with multipurpose river basin development; the third, in 1957, with topics like deficiencies in hydrologic data, earthwork operations, and public or private methods of constructing projects; while a principal subject of the fourth Conference in 1960 was the development of groundwater resources. These latter resources are built up by that portion of precipitation which percolates downward to subterranean storage. Groundwater resources are often easier, quicker, and cheaper to exploit than storing surface water in reservoirs for irrigation. The fourth Conference discussed the problems and conditions of their effective development and recommended the setting up of a regional research and training center on groundwater resources. A special seminar or symposium on the subject is likely to be held in 1962. Another important subject discussed at this Conference, on which again a symposium may well be later organized, was the flood control of deltaic areas, especially as regards the problem of drainage and salt water intrusion.

These Regional Technical Conferences examine the reports of the Bureau and indicate future lines of work. They act, in effect, as the Bureau's committee. They are also a regional professional association for the planners, engineers, and other specialists engaged in water resource development. Most of the papers presented have been prepared by the delegates themselves; and the value of the discussions, as indeed of the Bureau's work as a whole, has been the greater for being concentrated on a few subjects of real importance. When problems needed to be examined in more detail, the Conferences invariably recommended the convening of a special working party, seminar, or symposium. All the same, it is rather surprising that it is now proposed to hold the Conferences every two years instead of three. The effectiveness of such Conferences depends very much on the quality of the papers and the participants. Good papers cannot be produced in a hurry; good delegates cannot always be spared for frequent attendance at international meetings of one sort or another. There has, in fact, already been a decline in the quality of both, and at the fourth Conference, in the extent of Asian representation as well. To hold these conferences at shorter intervals is thus a proposal of doubtful merit.

Part of the continuing work of the Bureau has been to act as a clearinghouse of technical experience and information through its studies and the *Flood Control Journal* which has been issued quarterly since 1950. With the help of TAA, sets of technical books and reports were distributed in 1951 and 1952 to various national organizations. It could happen only once since TAA did not like spending its funds in this way. One common method of learning about the most advanced techniques of multipurpose development at first hand, the study tour, was not arranged until 1958 when, with BTAO help, Austria, France, the Netherlands, and the United States were visited. The lack of any regional research center in this field led the Bureau to seek ways of filling the gap. It aimed, at first, to coordinate the hydraulic research being undertaken in many countries, but this has not advanced beyond the publication in the *Flood Control Journal* of information on the work of hydraulic research stations. For a few years it was the Bureau's practice to use part of its budget to commission a piece of research as, for example, in the case of the work on silt problems by the Punjab Irrigation Research Institute. Headquarters did not, however, approve of this kind of expenditure. In the course of field trips the staff of the Bureau has often provided technical assistance to governments at their request, sometimes with immensely beneficial results. As TAA was against the Bureau rendering technical assistance, these direct advisory services had to be confined to short assignments on matters related to its work program.

The Bureau of Flood Control and Water Resources Development has been one of ECAFE's most effective instruments of cooperation. Whether it will continue to be so may well depend on a change of emphasis in its activities, for it is unlikely to thrive solely on a diet of regional conferences. To provide more actual technical assistance and concentrate on international rivers would seem to be the most promising activities to pursue. There are, for example, eighteen major international rivers in the region. The Bureau has already held preliminary discussions with experts in India and Nepal on the scope and means of cooperation for the development of the Karnali River which both countries share. Its work to promote the multipurpose development of the Mekong shows what can be done. Nothing the Bureau has so far undertaken matches this project in ambition and complexity. No other activity in recent years has brought ECAFE so much international attention.

The Mekong Project

Many rivers in the ECAFE region flow through more than one country, the best known being the Brahmaputra, Ganges, Indus, Mekong, Red, and Salween. In 1951, when the Bureau began to study the technical problems of flood control on international rivers, it was the Indus that appeared to be most ripe for investigation and international action. But because of the bad political feeling between India and Pakistan, Lokanathan and Indian hydraulic engineers quickly warned against this choice,[130] and the Bureau selected the Mekong instead.

By any standard the Mekong is among the world's greatest rivers.[131] It flows about 2,600 miles in a broadly southerly direction from the Plateau of Tibet to the South China Sea near Saigon. Its lower basin, in which the Bureau was interested, drains 236,000 square miles—an area larger than California or France—extends over parts of Laos, Thailand, Cambodia, and South Viet-Nam,[132] and has a population of about 17,000,000.[133] On entering its lower basin, the river becomes much less turbulent, though there are still a falls and some rapids at a number of points before the delta area is reached.

For centuries the Mekong has been mainly a destructive force. Every year it floods several million acres of land, particularly in

130. Although Pakistan openly suggested to the Commission in 1948 that ECAFE should mediate in its argument with India over the control of certain irrigation and other river works in the Indus basin, it quickly abandoned the idea. With the help of the World Bank this long-standing dispute was eventually settled in September 1960 by the Indus Water Treaty.

131. Its precise ranking depends on whether length, or size of drainage, or quantity of flow is the criterion. Measured by low-water discharge, for instance, it is the third largest river in Asia, only the Yangtze and Ganges having a greater volume of water.

132. For 500 miles it forms the actual border between Laos and Thailand. About 40 per cent of the length and 23 per cent of the drainage area of the Mekong lie within China.

133. The total population of Cambodia, Laos, South Viet-Nam, and Thailand is probably around 42,000,000.

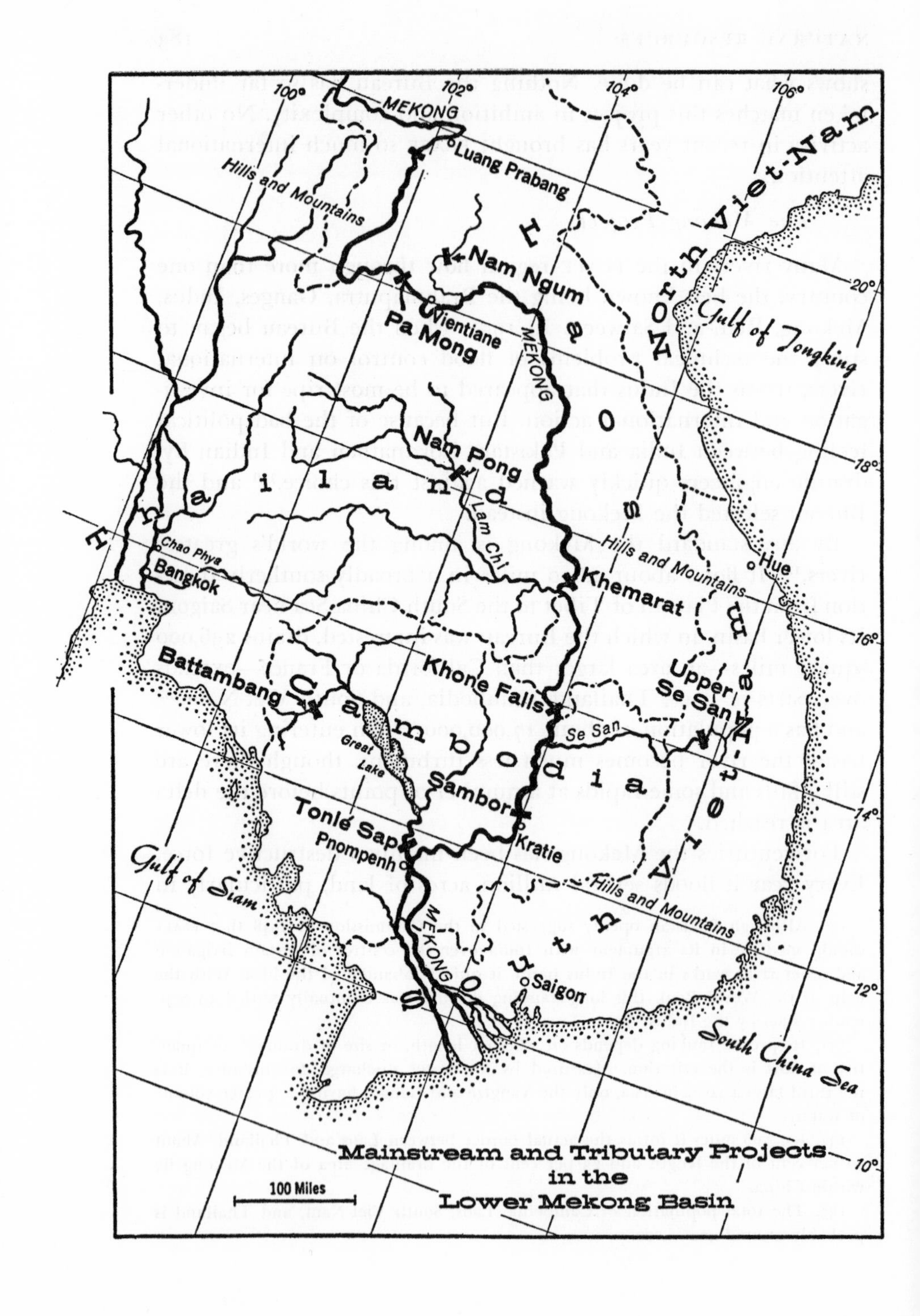

Mainstream and Tributary Projects in the Lower Mekong Basin

the delta area below Pnompenh.[134] In Cambodia and South Viet-Nam the peasant farmers adapt their agricultural practices to the floods rather than control the floods for specific crop requirements. One method is to plant floating or semifloating rice whose growth keeps pace with the rate of rise of the flood water. But this method allows for only one rice crop a year and its yield is unpredictable and low in quality compared to ordinary rice. Even then, exceptional flooding causes serious crop damage. Yet no large flood-control works exist in the delta. Indo-China and Thailand, in the past, did not even cooperate on a flood warning system. Over much of the basin the rainfall varies from less than adequate to just adequate for rice production. Serious crop damage is caused by years of less-than-average rainfall or by the uneven distribution of rainfall during the rice-growing period. Yet less than 3 per cent of the total land under cultivation is irrigated. In addition, in an area where lack of transport is an important obstacle to economic growth, where water is not only the cheapest but often the only mode of transport, long stretches of the Mekong are not navigable or are navigable only with great difficulty. Work on improving the main channel has been rather limited. Electric power is not available in rural areas and is fairly expensive when supplied to the towns because it is thermally generated from imported fuels. Nevertheless, the enormous hydro-power potential of the Mekong is untapped. This great resource, in short, was virtually neglected in the past. Not a dam, bridge, or control structure of any kind was built. No systematic hydrological observation of the river had been made.

In 1951 the four riparian countries approved the idea of the Bureau investigating the problems of flood control on the lower Mekong. Thailand and Indo-China nominated two consultants to cooperate on the study. However, when the Bureau issued its findings in the following year,[135] what excited attention was not its recommendations regarding flood-control methods, but rather

134. Before World War II this was one of the major rice-exporting areas of Asia. About 86 per cent of the cultivated land area of the Mekong basin is devoted to rice. Because of war and unsettled conditions, rice production in South Viet-Nam has still not reached its pre-World War II level.

135. *Preliminary Report on Technical Problems Relating to Flood Control and Water Resources Development of Mekong—an International River*, Flood/8, May 22, 1952.

its hopeful glimpse of the tremendous resources of the Mekong for power, irrigation, and navigation. The Bureau frankly admitted that little was known about these resources, and it proposed to investigate them in detail. What began as a technical study of flood-control problems broadened into a comprehensive investigation of the potentialities of the river for multipurpose development. Before field surveys could be organized, however, the war in Indo-China intervened, and for all practical purposes work came to a standstill until the Geneva Agreement of 1954 brought the war to an end. With the approval of the Commission preparations were begun in 1955 for an ECAFE reconnaissance of the river. They had not gone far before a further complication arose.

In 1955, the United States Operations Mission (USOM) in each of the four countries encouraged their governments to request the United States International Cooperation Administration (ICA) to organize a survey of the river. The ICA agreed and arranged for it to be done by the Bureau of Reclamation of the United States Department of the Interior. ECAFE was not consulted. An advance party of the United States team arrived in the area in December 1955 and asked the Secretariat for information and documents. ICA refused, however, to accept the Secretariat's offer to send one of its number to participate in the survey. Lokanathan regarded this attitude as high-handed and became even more determined to carry out the ECAFE plan.

The report of the United States team was published in March 1956.[136] It thoroughly examined the available engineering data on the river, emphasized that it was woefully inadequate for the orderly development of the basin, and outlined a program for collecting additional data. Its recommendations about the actual use of the Mekong were confined to minor improvements in navigation on the mainstream and to small tributary projects in each of the four riparian countries. On February 8, that is before the

136. *U.S. Bureau of Reclamation, Reconnaissance Report—Lower Mekong River Basin,* Mar. 1956. (Hereafter referred to as the ICA Report.) Its recommendations are also published as Annex I to ECAFE Flood Control Series No. 12, UN Sales No.: 1957.II.F.8, and in a forthcoming study, *The Lower Mekong,* by Russell H. Fifield and C. Hart Schaaf, to be published in 1963 by Van Nostrand Press, Princeton, N. J. The last-named author is the Executive Agent of the Mekong Co-ordination Committee.

report was published, ICA called a meeting of the four countries to discuss the recommendations made and how they should be implemented. Cambodia did not attend. The clear implication of its refusal was that cooperation between the four riparian countries was politically impossible under United States auspices. The field was left to ECAFE. Nevertheless, the United States and United Nations Headquarters, including TAA, strongly opposed the idea of an ECAFE reconnaissance.

More than one source of pressure lay behind the United States opposition. With an appropriation from Congress to justify, ICA had established a bureaucratic vested interest in the Mekong.[137] The Department of State mistrusted Lokanathan politically. Other United States officials thought ECAFE should not become "operational," meaning, presumably, that it should not engage in actual field work. This view was shared by the United Nations Department of Economic and Social Affairs and TAA. Some clumsy handling, particularly by a tactless United States liaison officer at Bangkok, inflated the issue still further. At the Bangalore session of the Commission in February 1956, the United Nations Undersecretary for Economic and Social Affairs and a senior official of TAA instructed Lokanathan to abandon the ECAFE plan. With rare defiance, the Executive Secretary replied that, if that was Headquarters policy, the Undersecretary should himself put it on record publicly before the Commission. This was too risky a challenge for Headquarters to accept. Instead, the Commission endorsed the Bureau's plan to make a reconnaissance of the Mekong, cautioned against unnecessary duplication with other surveys, and expressed the hope that it would be completed soon. An ECAFE team, drawn mainly from the Secretariat and strengthened by experienced Indian and Japanese engineers, was accordingly organized. The expedition was financed from ECAFE funds and absorbed its entire budget for consultants.

There was one question the team had to face right at the start: what was the point of covering the same ground as the United States team? A preview glance at the latter's recommendations

137. "A cooperative survey of the development potentialities on the Mekong River" is mentioned in the President's Report to Congress on the Mutual Security Program for the six months ended June 30, 1955.

provided the answer.[138] Insofar as they mentioned actual projects, the ICA team concentrated on those that could be carried out in and by each of the four countries themselves. Following the Bureau's work in 1952, the ECAFE team set out to emphasize the potentialities of projects requiring the cooperation of the four countries. They concentrated on the mainstream of the river. This was to be the United Nations approach to the Mekong Project. Accompanied by engineers from the four riparian countries the team reconnoitered the lower Mekong during April and May of 1956. Its report was presented to the Commission in March 1957 and published the following October.[139]

The ECAFE report differed from the ICA report in that, while both stressed the importance of collecting a considerable amount of basic data, the former presented a vision of the potential development of the Mekong and the latter did not. The ECAFE report outlined in some detail five possible mainstream projects: at Pa Mong, Khemarat, Khone Falls, Sambor, and on the Tonlé Sap. Dams on the first four of these sites would generate power and improve navigation. Furthermore, Pa Mong and Sambor would provide gravity irrigation. The suggested barrage across the Tonlé Sap had no power component but would help moderate the flooding of the delta area, improve navigation, and regulate river flow for irrigation and drainage purposes.[140] The report also outlined the benefits of these projects in terms of the amount and approximate cost of the firm power they could produce, the additional land they could irrigate, the increasing yield and quality of rice, the greater diversification of crops that regulated water supplies would make possible, and the improvement of naviga-

138. It should be mentioned that although dated Mar. 1956, the full ICA Report was not made available to the ECAFE investigating team until after they had completed their field work.

139. *Development of the Water Resources in the Lower Mekong Basin,* Flood Control Series No. 12, UN Sales No.:1957.II.F.8.

140. The Tonlé Sap project has some unusual features. Each year in the rainy season the rising waters of the Mekong reverse the flow of the Tonlé Sap into the Great Lake of Cambodia whose area and depth thereby increase. Shortly after the end of the rainy season the Great Lake begins to empty its stored supplies down the Tonlé Sap into the Mekong. In other words, the Great Lake acts as a flood retention reservoir; constructing a barrage across the Tonlé Sap would accentuate and regulate this effect. It is also hoped that it would reverse the present sharp decline in the Great Lake's fish yield and help to combat damaging salt water intrusion in the delta during low-water periods.

tion up to Luang Prabang which would particularly benefit land-locked Laos and its mineral and forest resources.[141] In these ways each of the projects, although located within one country, would benefit at least two or more countries. ECAFE suggested that they be investigated in detail and emphasized that the collection of the essential data should be organized internationally. "Since data on stream flow form the basis for planning and allocation of supplies," the report stated, "it is necessary that the accuracy of such measurements should be beyond doubt and that the figures should be acceptable to all countries concerned at all times."

This imaginative study deeply impressed the Commission. The next step was to formulate a work program on the many problems requiring detailed investigation. Much now depended on whether the four riparian countries would cooperate. A senior official from Headquarters suggested the idea of getting the four to make a joint declaration to this effect. The then Executive Secretary, C. V. Narasimhan, and the Undersecretary for Economic and Social Affairs, Philippe de Seynes, were doubtful if it could be done. But they agreed to approach the riparian countries and with the help of the French liaison officer to ECAFE,[142] the plan succeeded. The Laotian delegate, Princess Souvanna Phouma, wife of the Prime Minister of Laos, introduced a statement on behalf of the four countries, which expressed their wish that studies "be continued jointly with the four countries concerned in order to determine with more detail in what measure various projects concerning hydroelectric power, navigation, irrigation, drainage and flood control can be of use to several countries." [143] France, India, Japan, and the United States announced their willingness to provide technical assistance for these studies. The United States went further and intimated its readiness to receive proposals for financial aid from its Asian Economic Development Fund.[144] ECAFE lost no time in acting upon the joint declaration.

141. Less than one per cent of existing water traffic on the Mekong plies between Kratie and Luang Prabang.

142. This particular liaison officer also helped organize the ECAFE survey team the previous year. There has been much genuine French helpfulness to ECAFE over the Mekong, but one element in it also has been a sense of rivalry with the US.

143. *ECAFE Annual Report to ECOSOC, 15 February 1956–28 March 1957*, E/CN.11/454, May 8, 1957, p. 37.

144. See pp. 294–96.

In May 1957 a meeting in Bangkok of experts from the four countries recommended that their governments establish a Committee for Coordination of Investigations of the Lower Mekong Basin. The idea and name were suggested by Narasimhan. He persuaded the four governments that there would be no great difficulty in getting aid for the Mekong Project if they came together in this way. The experts also carefully considered the ECAFE report. Of the five mainstream projects suggested, they assigned first priority to Pa Mong, Sambor, and Tonlé Sap, second priority to Khone Falls, and third priority to Khemarat. It was agreed that for the development of the mainstream, the existing low-water discharge of the Mekong should not be reduced by any of these projects.[145]

The Coordination Committee was established the following October. It was to be no mere debating forum but a body with clear and considerable powers to decide and to act.[146] It was not, however, to be a supranational body. The four governments were to appoint their own representatives, and every decision taken had to be unanimous. At least three meetings a year were to be held and the chairman and venue were to rotate annually among the four countries, in alphabetical order, beginning with Cambodia.[147] The Committee was to submit annual reports to the Commission and to be serviced by the ECAFE Secretariat.

The new Committee got off to an encouraging start when a grant of about $100,000 from France was announced and accepted at its first session. The "Board of Directors" of the Mekong Project could make their first purchase of some of the hydrologic equipment required for the detailed investigations that now had to be made. They were in business. But what kind of a program of investigations should be followed? Should it be one directed toward establishing the feasibility of the mainstream projects proposed by the ECAFE team? But how was this approach to be reconciled with the recommendations of the ICA report? An independ-

145. *Joint Meeting on Lower Mekong Basin—Conclusions Reached and Recommendations Made by Joint Meeting,* ECAFE/WRD/1, May 3, 1957.

146. For the Statute of the Committee, see *Report of Co-ordination Committee to the 14th Session of ECAFE,* E/CN.11/475, Feb. 24, 1958.

147. The first chairman of the Committee was one of the two consultants who helped the Bureau with its technical study of flood control problems of the Mekong in 1951.

ent evaluation of the two reports and especially of the ECAFE vision seemed desirable. This was all the more necessary if United States financial support was to be forthcoming. On Narasimhan's advice the Committee, therefore, requested TAA to organize a team of four or five highly qualified engineers to review the studies already made, especially the ECAFE report, and to draft a full program of investigations required for the development of the basin as a whole and the Pa Mong, Sambor, and Tonlé Sap projects in particular. The Committee accepted the proposal of Narasimhan and TAA that Raymond A. Wheeler lead the mission.[148] This particular suggestion actually originated with Philippe de Seynes. It is worth noting that there was nothing in the Wheeler Mission's terms of reference to suggest any doubt about the viability of the Mekong Project.

The Wheeler Mission began its task in November 1957. Of the seven members of the team only two, Wheeler himself and a Canadian engineer, were strangers to the Mekong. Of the remaining five, one had been a member of the ICA team, the other four of the ECAFE team. Two schools of thought were thus reflected in the Mission, corresponding broadly to the ICA and ECAFE approaches to the Mekong, and an interesting debate ensued.[149] The first stressed the overriding need to collect basic data for the preparation of a master plan for the whole lower basin into which investigations for particular projects could be integrated. To encourage the four countries to undertake projects without adequate data, this school argued, was to risk failure, a waste of resources, and insufficient and uneconomical operations. The other school of thought accepted the need for basic data but argued that to await a master plan for the whole basin was to postpone the hopes for development to such a distant future as to drown the interests of the four countries right at the start. Underdeveloped countries cannot wait upon the ideal as regards data before undertaking development projects. In any case, no river anywhere, not even in the United States, had a master plan for its full develop-

148. Wheeler was an engineering consultant to the World Bank but is probably better known for his work on clearing and repairing the Suez Canal after the invasion of Suez in the autumn of 1956.

149. See, H. V. Darling, "Harmony on the Mekong River," *The Military Engineer* (May–June 1958), pp. 176–79. The author of this article was Wheeler's personal assistant in the Mission and had been a member of the ICA team.

ment. Data collection was a continuing, long-range task for which personnel had to be trained. The four countries were aware of this need. Meanwhile, this second school continued, they must be given some hope of realizing actual projects within a reasonable space of time. The Mission should not report, and indeed would not fulfill its terms of reference if it did so report, that nothing can be said about the feasibility of projects for the mainstream and its tributaries until a master plan could be prepared.[150]

The danger arose that this division of approach within the Mission would produce two reports; that would have doomed the Mekong Project at the outset. Actually, each school went a long way to accepting the approach of the other and a unanimous report, reflecting both points of view, was issued in January 1958.[151]

The report recommended a program of investigations resembling that advocated by the ICA team though much more sharply defined as a five-year undertaking, with first priority being given to the most promising sites on the main river, including those suggested by the ECAFE team. Investigations made during the first two years were to include hydrological observations, leveling, aerial mapping, and detailed topographic, hydrographic, and geological surveys of these promising sites. When sufficient data had been collected the preliminary planning of projects could begin in the third year. At the same time reconnaissance surveys of the main tributaries should be made. The investigations made during the first two years on the most promising sites of the main river should then be extended in the third and fourth years to these tributaries and to the remaining reaches of the Mekong itself, to be followed in the fifth year by the preliminary planning of further projects and the preparation of a skeleton basin plan. Special studies would also be needed of fisheries, agriculture, forestry, mineral resources, transport, power needs, and other prob-

150. Part of the argument centered on what was likely to prove an acceptable cost figure for any program of investigation. The first school of thought may perhaps have been influenced by an understanding Wheeler was believed to have received in Washington before leaving for the Mekong that the United States would contribute $3,000,000 for basic data collection.

151. Report of United Nations Survey Mission, "Programme of Studies and Investigations for Comprehensive Development, Lower Mekong Basin," Bangkok, Jan. 23, 1958.

lems relating to the general economy of the area. The Wheeler Mission set out the estimated cost of each constituent part of its recommended program and assessed the total cost at $9,200,000. Finally, the Mission recommended that the technical investigations be carried out by qualified engineering firms and that an international advisory board of distinguished engineers be set up to advise and assist the Coordination Committee.

In February 1958 the Coordination Committee accepted the conclusions and recommendations of the Wheeler report. At the same time, TAB announced a grant of $200,000 to meet the more urgent needs of the program. But how was the rest of the program to be financed? The Committee asked the Executive Secretary to negotiate on its behalf with interested governments and agencies the extent, form, and pattern of assistance they were prepared to offer. The response was heartening. At the Commission session in March 1958, New Zealand offered $100,000 and the United States $2,000,000.[152] Narasimhan worked hard on the Canadian government and subsequently obtained from it an offer of $1,300,000. Further contributions were later announced by Australia, Britain, India, Iran, Israel, Japan, the Netherlands, Pakistan, Philippines, and Taiwan. The Soviet Union indicated it was prepared to give technical assistance directly or through ECAFE in the designing of power stations. This offer was not accepted, however, because for one thing, the Committee was not interested in technical assistance pure and simple, but only when it was accompanied by valuable equipment as was the case with all the other bilateral contributions. In December 1959, the United Nations Special Fund granted nearly $1,400,000 for a survey of four Mekong tributaries.[153] By the beginning of 1961 the Committee's resources had practically reached the Wheeler Mission total of $9,200,000 and by the end of the year approached $14,000,000. Of this total, the four riparian countries had themselves by then

152. Later raised to $2,200,000. This contribution came from the Asian Economic Development Fund and was believed to be largely due to Wheeler himself. French *amour propre* was reportedly stung by the unexpected size of the United States contribution, which partly accounts for the second and much larger grant that France subsequently made to the Mekong Project.

153. The Battambang in Cambodia; the Nam Ngum in Laos; the Nam Pong in Thailand; and the Upper Se San in South Viet-Nam.

contributed at no small sacrifice about $1,500,000, in cash and kind, for local cost payments. It is a measure of their invested faith in the Mekong Project.

In addition to the investigations launched with these contributions, BTAO, at the Committee's request, provided experts to make studies on flood control, minerals, navigation improvements, the power market, and general economic development. By 1958 various specialized agencies had staked claims to a share in technical assistance for the Mekong. ILO reported on manpower; FAO on agriculture, forests and fisheries; UNESCO on an investigation of the delta basin model; WHO on health and sanitation; WMO on weather services; and the International Atomic Energy Agency (IAEA) on the use of radioactive isotopes for hydrological and sedimentation observations.[154]

The Committee soon had to call a halt to the spate of reports and surveys, not all of which made significant contributions. It reacted also to the pushing and lobbying of some of the specialized agencies. FAO officials behaved in a particularly arrogant fashion. The Mekong Project, they conceded, was a good ECAFE idea, but as it was essentially an agricultural development project and was now under way, FAO should take it over. They even tried to get the actual members of the Committee who were senior engineering officials replaced by representatives from the ministries of agriculture of the four countries. They also attempted to have FAO named by the Special Fund as the executing agency for the four tributary projects, but the Committee refused to accept the plan. To the four countries and ECAFE, the Mekong is a means to industrialization, not simply an agricultural development scheme.

The task of controlling, coordinating, and evaluating was becoming highly complex. By the middle of 1961 the Mekong Project had grown to 28 separate and distinct subprojects emanating from and financed by 11 different countries and 10 United Nations agencies. Before that stage was reached, however, the Committee had acted to meet the problem. At its request, TAB in 1958 ap-

154. For the latest information on the form of all government and agency assistance, see *Report of the Co-ordination Committee, March 1960–January 1962*, E/CN.11/577, Jan. 8, 1962. The main financial backing to date, in descending order of size of contribution, has come from the United States, UN Special Fund, Canada, France, Japan, Australia, Britain, and BTAO. See also Fifield and Schaaf, *The Lower Mekong*.

pointed an Advisory Board of three engineers[155] as the Wheeler Report had recommended. Members of the Advisory Board attend several sessions of the Committee each year to review and advise on major reports, developments, and problems, and occasionally to make field inspections. The following year the Committee further strengthened its power to control and coordinate by appointing an Executive Agent with ancillary staff and an office at Bangkok to make day-to-day decisions and to deal with donor governments and agencies. Perhaps his most extensive duty was to "direct and co-ordinate the work of any organisation, unit or bureau, that might be set up for the collection and analysis of all kinds of technical data, hydrological, meteorological, engineering, agricultural or other." [156] By a happy chance the man selected for the post was a former Deputy Executive Secretary of ECAFE. During the past few years a small staff of senior consultants has been recruited to help him.[157] The appointment of a senior United Nations official to act as Executive Agent to an intergovernmental body is among the more novel features of the Mekong Project. According to his terms of reference the Executive Agent, partly at his own urging and against, apparently, the wishes of BTAO at the time of his appointment, is subject to the direction and guidance of the ECAFE Executive Secretary on policy matters. Close liaison with the ECAFE Secretariat was further ensured when he insisted that his office should be located in the same building as ECAFE so that he could draw fully upon its technical and administrative services. Thus, although the organization and administration of the Mekong Committee had grown more self-sufficient, the umbrella function of ECAFE, despite the antipathies and jealousies of other agencies, was maintained and strengthened.

The investigations initiated by the Committee up to the end

155. Paul Bourriers of France; Kanwar Sain of India, formerly leader of the ECAFE survey team and a member of the Wheeler Mission; and Carl G. Paulsen of the US. At the end of 1959 the last-named was succeeded by Arthur Karasz, an economist and the World's Bank's representative in Thailand.

156. For detailed terms of reference of the Executive Agent, see *Report of Mekong Committee, February 1958–March 1959*, E/CN.11/500, Mar. 7, 1959.

157. Including as Senior Engineering Consultant, Kanwar Sain. Up until January 1961, the Office of the Executive Agent was provided by BTAO, but as from that date it has been financed under a separate section of the ECAFE budget supplemented by BTAO. The technical posts in the Executive Agent's Office are financed by the UN Special Fund and those of the Advisory Board by BTAO.

of 1961 have broadly followed the program recommended by the Wheeler Mission. In one interesting way, however, there has been a modification in priorities. To develop the resources of the Mekong is a long-term undertaking. Understandably, the four countries are anxious to get practical results in the shortest possible time. When, therefore, a Japanese team reconnoitered the major tributaries and reported that certain sites on them were so obviously promising that detailed investigations could begin straightway, the Committee readily agreed. Four sites, one in each country, were selected and the United Nations Special Fund made a grant for the preparation on each of them of a comprehensive feasibility report in a form suitable for loan applications.[158] Well-established engineering firms were chosen to make these reports [159] and it is hoped that on the basis of them an approach to the World Bank or the International Development Association can be made in 1963. These tributary projects can be realized more quickly and cheaply than those on the mainstream, and will give the Committee invaluable experience and a taste of achievement before tackling the larger projects. This suggestion actually came from United Nations Headquarters. Although it was not the emphasis of ECAFE's original approach, it has undoubtedly brought the prospect of practical results much nearer. Many more tributary projects are likely to be developed under the Mekong Project. Nor is the Committee waiting upon the construction of the mainstream projects before organizing improvements in navigation on the Mekong. Both the ECAFE and ICA reports suggested short-run improvements, and in 1960 the Committee adopted a program prepared by a TAA consultant and a member of the ECAFE Secretariat.[160]

Not that progress on the three mainstream projects has been slow. On the contrary, by 1961 it was possible to arrange for com-

158. See p. 193 above. A comprehensive feasibility report must include preliminary designs, specifications, and cost of structures, cost and benefit estimates of services the project can provide, such as power, irrigation, and prevention of flood or, in other words, sufficient detailed information upon which the source of finance can judge the merit of the investment.

159. A US firm for the tributary project in Thailand, a French firm for that in Cambodia, and a Japanese firm for those in Laos and South Viet-Nam.

160. For details, see *Report of Mekong Committee, 10th Session,* WRD/MKG/R.30, Rev. 1, Nov. 1960.

prehensive feasibility reports on them to be prepared as well. The United States offered to prepare one for the Pa Mong site, India for the Tonlé Sap project, and Japan will make a preliminary survey of the Sambor site. The Indian offer is particularly notable and generous.[161] It was also valuable in a political sense, for the Tonlé Sap project is potentially perhaps the most controversial of the three, insofar as the control and operation of the barrage—which will be in Cambodia—must affect to a vital degree the whole welfare of the delta area in South Viet-Nam. It was, therefore, agreed that the Indian comprehensive feasibility report should include proposals for operating the dam in a way beneficial to both countries.

The tinder of the ECAFE vision has been set alight. The engineers are confident it can be realized technically. But is it economically viable? That is the question economists have been asking, and no confident answer could be given by the end of 1961. Studies of the resources of the four countries, other than water, were being made before the Mekong Project was launched and have since been proceeding inside as well as outside its framework. For instance, with the help of the Special Fund and FAO, a special experimental demonstration farm is being constructed in Laos to determine the most suitable crops and the best irrigation and agricultural practices that perennial water supplies make possible. It cannot be left to the cultivator, unaided and unpersuaded, to make such adjustments. But is there a demand for the huge quantities of power the Mekong Project can produce? Processing minerals would be one big outlet and with the help of the Special Fund again, as well as of France and the United States, extensive geological surveying is proceeding in Cambodia, Laos, and Thailand. It is also true that the comprehensive feasibility report required of every project will include a detailed study of costs and benefits. All this does not, however, add up to an answer to the economists' question. The economic viability of the Mekong Project has not yet received an endorsement equivalent to that given by the Wheeler Mission in respect of its technical feasibility.

161. It is not fanciful to assume that Kanwar Sain was influential in securing this contribution.

An economic endorsement cannot be based simply on the expected return on the capital invested; that is too narrow a yardstick. It is the yield in terms of increased income and welfare that really matters. The most recent, though still tentative, thinking of the Executive Agent and ECAFE along these lines assumes the construction over a 25-year period of five mainstream and twelve tributary dams, including power houses, generating equipment, transmission lines, and pumping stations at a total cost in 1961 prices of $2 billion.[162] These constructions would make possible the hydraulic management of about 4,500,000 hectares (almost 11,200,000 acres). This, in turn, would permit a larger rice yield and a more diversified agriculture which, taken together, could, it is assumed, increase the value of farm output threefold. This benefit might be equivalent to the amortization costs of the total investment in constructions—including electrical installations—even assuming a fairly high rate of interest and a repayment period of 29 years when more favorable terms may well be obtained. The over-all investment of $2 billion also includes the installation of something like 5,000,000 kilowatts of electric power capacity with an estimated annual output of 28 billion kilowatt-hours of firm power. Just what kind of industrialization this large amount of relatively cheap power would make possible is difficult to envisage.[163] ECAFE thinking assumes that about two-fifths of the available power could be used to produce nitrogenous fertilizers for local consumption and export. Malayan bauxite and Mekong electricity might provide the basis for an aluminum industry. Much of the remaining proportion would be used for industries based on the mineral and forest resources of the area, as well as for industries like sugar and textiles. In other words, to ensure that the potential benefits of the Mekong Project are fully used will entail considerable additional investment. To

162. As a comparison, the annual United States aid to South Viet-Nam alone is about one-eighth of this figure.

163. In 1959 the four countries had a total installed capacity of 282,900 kw., which generated 745,500,000 kwh. of electric energy, *Electric Power Bulletin* (July 1961). The Pa Mong project alone can produce an estimated output of 10 billion kwh. of firm power annually and that of Sambor about 4.5 billion kwh. Compare this with a total output of 5,800,000 kwh. in Laos and 52,100,000 kwh. in Cambodia in 1959. It is likely, however, that the projects will be so designed that power generation and transmitting equipment can be installed in stages as power demands increase.

increase the capacity of the four countries to absorb substantial amounts of capital will mean fundamental changes in their policies, administrative arrangements, institutions, and modes of living. Nothing short of their complete modernization is involved. It is difficult, moreover, to see how the benefits of the Mekong Project can be achieved without a large measure of economic integration among them.

In 1961 the Committee decided the time was ripe to initiate a thorough study of the long-term economic feasibility of the Mekong Project and requested the Ford Foundation to organize an expert team to examine this question and its economic, social, and institutional implications, including the kind of studies and data that will be needed. The Ford team, which is headed by Gilbert White, an eminent economic geographer, is thus to do in the social science field what the Wheeler Mission did in the engineering field.

The Mekong Project is a unique example of Asian governments setting up a permanent organization for the joint planning and execution of a program that requires substantial external aid.[164] A notable degree of cooperation and mutual trust—not present at the beginning—has developed among the members of the Committee. In the earlier Committee meetings there was a strong tendency for the four countries to look at the Mekong Project in terms of what each got out of it in the way of aid. For instance, each first submitted its own country request to the Special Fund, which had then to point out that it would only allocate funds in accordance with priorities established by the Committee. The habit of looking at the river as a whole had to be fostered. A high degree of continuity in the representation of the Committee certainly helped the process along. The stiffest test of their spirit of cooperation will come when the costs, benefits, and methods of operating the projects have to be determined. The four governments are not yet prepared explicitly to accept commitments regarding the future cooperation required for this purpose. But at least they have recognized that at a not too distant

164. Sharp, *Field Administration*, p. 353. It is worth noting, in this connection, that unlike the Indus Water Agreement, which provides for a separate sharing of the Indus waters by India and Pakistan, the Mekong Project postulates a joint exploitation of the river.

date draft agreements on these matters will have to be concluded.[165]

The behavior pattern of the Committee is serious, hard-working, and businesslike. Searching questions rather than commendatory sentiment is what a prospective donor must face in the private informal talks that precede any public commitment to make a contribution. In fact, this way of proceeding avoids embarrassment, should the prospective donor not contribute. Once participating, the donors, or rather those making the investigation with the donors' contribution, can expect their work to be closely scrutinized. The United States, for example, undertook to collect basic hydrological data on the mainstream. This is, perhaps, the most crucial investigation of all, since the result measures the actual volume of water available for various purposes. For this reason, the methods of measurement have been subjected to some sharp questioning in the Committee and by the Advisory Board.

In the Coordination Committee, the Mekong Project has also created a unique instrument for channeling bilateral aid in support of a multilateral operation under United Nations auspices. If the Committee constitutes the "board of directors," the Commission, to which it annually reports, embodies the "shareholders." But what moved the shareholders to invest? The strategic and commercial importance of the area is obvious. In the case of the United States, for example, the strategic element was probably uppermost, whereas France and Japan have hardly disguised their strong commercial stake. The strong paternal feeling of France for its former colonial territory is also unmistakable. The motives and their importance no doubt differed with each donor. But in all cases, it is fair to say, the human challenge and opportunities presented by this international river have captured their imagination.

An unexpected feature of this aid effort is that the most difficult donors to deal with have proved to be not governments but agencies and branches of the United Nations itself. The Committee disciplined the buccaneering behavior of some specialized agencies. But it can do little to improve the slow, cumbersome procedures of bodies like the Special Fund. From a Special Fund

165. *ECAFE Annual Report to ECOSOC, 22 March 1960–20 March 1961,* E/CN.11/564, Apr. 22, 1961, para. 389.

announcement of a grant to the signing of the contract enabling operations to begin has taken, on the average, about a year. Because bilateral aid can be arranged more quickly the Committee is understandably impatient with United Nations procedures. Any feeling that a project dependent on United Nations action can be realized sooner by striking a bilateral bargain outside the Committee weakens the spirit of cooperation on the Mekong. Cambodia has already questioned the timetable for the construction of the Sambor dam.[166] This is not unthinking impetuosity on the Committee's part. Politically, they are not sure time is on their side.

It is, in fact, the political problems surrounding the Mekong Project that underline the importance of ECAFE's umbrella function. For a number of years United Nations Headquarters and the United States appeared not to realize that this largely technical operation began under ECAFE in the first place for essentially political reasons. They argued that ECAFE should not become "operational," meaning, presumably, that it should not engage in actual field work. Over the years the staff of ECAFE's Bureau of Flood Control and Water Resources Development had built up a fund of friendship, respect, and trust in these countries, often with people who later rose to policy-making positions and even to ministerial rank. For this reason ECAFE was able to bring the four countries together when the United States failed. Successive Executive Secretaries, each in his own way, have served them well. These were invaluable assets which arguments about constitutional arrangements and procedures tended to overlook. In any case, the Bureau's mandate authorized it to be operational;[167] indeed, it was providing technical assistance in the field before TAA even existed.

Some observers have remarked that the ECAFE Secretariat has acted too much like a nursemaid to the Mekong Project. If this means it has sometimes shown a possessive attitude to its brain child, there is some truth in the comment. But it has also to be

166. It is assumed that the projects at Pa Mong, Sambor, and Tonlé Sap could be built by 1973 and the first four tributary projects by 1966. These estimates, it should be noted, relate to the completion of construction, not the achievement of full utilization.

167. See p. 174.

remembered that, for a time, the Secretariat stood alone in advocating the project and, when it did get under way, attempts were made to push ECAFE aside. In any case, political nursing has certainly been necessary and will continue to be. It was needed in 1958 when Cambodia and Thailand broke off diplomatic relations over the disputed location of a temple and extraordinary arrangements had to be made to enable the Cambodian representative to attend an important meeting of the Committee at Bangkok. It was needed in 1960 when, with Laos torn by armed conflict, a special agreement was negotiated between Laos and Thailand to offer armed protection to an Australian investigating team at the Pa Mong damsite.[168]

There are other more dangerous political shoals to navigate. The Cold War, especially its effect on the internal stability of the area, is the most menacing. Thailand and South Viet-Nam are deeply worried about the political direction of Laos. South Viet-Nam is threatened by internal insurrection and concerned about the infiltration through Cambodia and Laos of subversive elements from North Viet-Nam. Any suggestion of a contribution from a Communist country to the Mekong Project, such as a reported Soviet offer to help construct the Sambor project, must be handled with great delicacy, particularly with Thailand and South Viet-Nam. In an area racked by internal strains and external pressures, the Mekong is potentially its greatest unifying factor. With peace and a measure of stability, with wise conservation and utilization of its water, it will, in the words of the Wheeler Mission, "contribute more towards improving welfare in this area than any other single undertaking."

168. Although grateful for the offer, the Australians nevertheless withdrew their investigating team at Pa Mong because they felt that Colombo Plan civilian experts should not work where armed protection was needed.

CHAPTER 11

Inland Transport

The task of postwar reconstruction in Asia was nowhere greater or more urgent than in the field of inland transport. World War II caused severe destruction and damage to the transport facilities of Burma, China, Indo-China, Indonesia, Japan, and Malaya and left those of Ceylon, India, and Pakistan in poor condition.[1] Shortages of equipment, materials, trained personnel, and foreign exchange militated against any rapid recovery. In many of the most devastated areas, continuing internal strife worsened the situation still further.[2] Moreover, it was not enough for Asian countries merely to restore prewar facilities and standards; increasing populations and new economic development programs demanded far larger transport resources. Yet, although expenditure on transport figured prominently in the postwar development plans of many ECAFE countries, Asian planners tended to underestimate the implications for transport of accelerated economic development.[3] This disposition to take transport for

1. For an indication of wartime damage and deterioration of transport installations and equipment in Asia, see Report of the Working Group for Asia and the Far East of the Temporary Sub-Commission on Economic Reconstruction of Devastated Areas, Doc. E/307/Rev.1, Mar. 4, 1947, and ECAFE Survey of Reconstruction Problems and Needs, Doc. E/CN.11/39, Nov. 3, 1949.

2. For the progress of recovery, see the *Economic Surveys of Asia and the Far East* for 1947 (Shanghai, United Nations); for 1948, UN Sales No.:1949.II.F.1; for 1949, UN Sales No.:1950.II.F.1; and for 1950, UN Sales No.:1951.II.F.4.

3. "Considering the heavy demands made on the transport and communication systems in these countries, it is felt that even larger amounts than those allocated in the plans could have been usefully spent on transport development." Report

granted reflected to some extent the legacy of a colonial past when many Asians believed that transport existed primarily to serve the trading interests of the imperial power. The ECAFE Secretariat at first showed no greater foresight.

Transport in the ECAFE region, it is true, was not so obviously suitable or ripe for international organization as in Europe. Distances are much greater and not easily overcome. Few international rail connections existed and there were virtually no international highways. The level and standard of transport development varied widely, though nowhere outside Japan was it high.[4] It should also be remembered that Asian countries and the Secretariat were concerned at first to elaborate a case for external aid to the region. As far as transport was concerned, the most urgent task, they thought, was to assess the availabilities of transport equipment and supplies in relation to the region's requirements. When the Executive Secretary in 1947 proposed the creation of a transport committee,[5] this was apparently envisaged as its only function. No attempt was made to relate transport problems to the general objectives of ECAFE. Most of its member governments either believed there was no scope for international cooperation in this field or had no views on the question. Only India and, to a lesser extent, Pakistan thought the transport industry had special problems deserving of study in their own right. Two principal developments subsequently impelled ECAFE in this direction.

In April 1948, the United Nations Transport and Communications Commission recommended to ECAFE that an early meeting of experts be convened to examine the problems of transport rehabilitation and coordination and the best way to tackle them.[6] This suggestion, which ECOSOC later endorsed, came before the Commission in June 1948. Ceylon, India, and Pakistan favored it and so did the Executive Secretary. The majority shared the British view that such matters should be left to the Working

of the Working Party on Economic Development and Planning, Doc. E/CN.11/L.86, Oct. 19, 1960.

4. See, e.g., The Present Status and Problems of Transport in Countries of the ECAFE Region, Doc. E/CN.11/DPWP.6/L.3, Aug. 11, 1960.

5. Doc. E/CN.11/41, Oct. 23, 1947.

6. Doc. E/CN.11/71, Add. 1, May 4, 1948.

Party on Industrial Development; no special conference was needed because transport was not an international issue. The supporters managed, however, to win a close decision to place the results of the Working Party's investigation of transport problems before a special meeting of transport experts.[7]

The Working Party's report [8] was, in fact, the second influential factor pushing ECAFE into the field of transport proper, for it took the whole subject right out of the restricted framework of merely budgeting for reconstruction needs. In addition to assessing requirements for equipment and materials as directed, it emphasized the importance of studying inland transport as a whole and of coordinating its three modes under one administration. Among the subjects listed as needing investigation were the methods of constructing, operating, and standardizing railway equipment; the use of alternative fuels in steam locomotives; road vehicle maintenance; an immediate improvement in the condition of highways and bridges; and the further development of inland waterways. These were all subjects in the work program of the Transport Committee ECAFE was later to establish. Meanwhile, the Working Party recommended that they should be examined by a special expert conference for which the Secretariat should set up a transport division to make the necessary preparations.

This special meeting was held at Singapore in October 1949.[9] It was the first time Asian transport specialists had met together to discuss their common concerns and was the first regional conference convened by ECAFE. The experts refined and elaborated the suggestions of the Working Party into a program of work for the Secretariat and recommended the setting up of an inland transport committee. It was upon this last proposal that discussion largely turned when their report came before the Commission a few days later. Britain and France, supported by the Philippines and Thailand, thought that it would be premature to establish a committee. Another meeting of experts should discuss the Secretariat's studies and report their conclusions directly to the Industry and Trade Committee; China, India, Indonesia, and Pak-

7. Doc. E/CN.11/SR.36, June 4, 1948, and Doc. E/CN.11/AC.5/5, June 10, 1948.
8. Doc. E/CN.11/131, Oct. 31, 1948.
9. For its report, see Doc. E/CN.11/204, Oct. 13, 1949.

istan pressed for the immediate creation of a transport committee but were narrowly defeated on a vote. In deference to their wishes, however, it was agreed that the second meeting of experts should be called an ad hoc Committee of Inland Transport Experts and could consider the desirability of setting up a permanent committee.

The ad hoc Committee met toward the end of 1950.[10] Britain was represented only by its liaison officer to ECAFE. More surprising was the relatively poor Indian representation and the absence of Pakistan. The experts discussed a wide range of short- and long-term problems of rail, road, and inland water transport and indicated those which should be given high priority in the Secretariat's work program. These included single-line railway operations; the use of alternative fuel in steam locomotives; dieselization; telecommunications; operation of railway workshops and terminals; highway registers, classification, and financing; vehicle maintenance; the training of motor mechanics; the design and operation of new types of inland water craft; pushing and towing methods on waterways; coordination problems; the collection and dissemination of transport statistics and technical information; and the provision of a library service. The experts suggested that a nongovernmental Asian and Far Eastern railway association be established to deal with some of the more technical problems of interest to railway administrations. Most of them also favored the creation of a permanent and strong transport committee like that of ECE, with subcommittees on highways and road transport, and an inland waterways subcommittee. The Western powers, however, continued to prevaricate on this issue. Australia, Britain, and the United States said they might not participate in such a committee "because it would pertain largely to activities within the region." [11] Australia still felt there was little scope for cooperation in this field. Britain doubted whether it could spare any experts to attend but thought its liaison officer might be able to do so from time to time; it might provide expert representation, however, if the proposed committee "should discuss questions related to certain aspects of inland transport in the

10. For its report, see Doc. E/CN.11/262, Nov. 10, 1950.

11. Australia was the one country which participated only sporadically in the first few sessions of the Inland Transport Committee, when established.

United Kingdom." [12] These were very odd reasons to give for refusing wholehearted support to the proposal; Britain went even further and actually tried to reduce the effectiveness of the new Committee.

When the ad hoc Committee began drafting the terms of reference of a permanent committee, most Asian delegates favored a clause empowering it to make recommendations on transport matters directly to its member governments. This was in line with the mandate given to the other subsidiary bodies of ECAFE and with the general character of all three regional commissions. Britain, however, voted twice against this particular clause, once on its own behalf and once on behalf of Malaya and British North Borneo, which its liaison officer also represented on this occasion.[13] This resulted in a tie vote. The Indian delegate thereupon strongly challenged the right of Britain to exercise two votes. If the metropolitan powers began to cast proxy votes on behalf of their associated territories, he argued, they would be able to dictate every decision in ECAFE. The Ceylonese delegate pressed home the attack by questioning the credentials of the British delegate. When the authorization to represent Malaya and British North Borneo was found to be inconsistent with United Nations standard practice, the British delegate withdrew the second vote and the clause was passed. This bizarre demonstration of British opposition to Asian wishes proved to be the final provocation that led to the conclusion of the Lahore Agreement.[14]

In 1951 the Commission finally approved the creation of an Inland Transport Committee. A number of Asian countries doubted the wisdom, however, of having a nongovernmental rail-

12. Doc. E/CN.11/SR.80, Mar. 8, 1951.

13. Australia at the 1951 Commission session also questioned the right of the Transport Committee, created at that session, and its subsidiary bodies to recommend directly to governments.

14. See above, p. 51. There were other curious aspects to this incident. For instance, it is doubtful if the Secretariat had the right to make public to all the delegates present the form of the credentials of a government representative. As part of the understanding by which the British delegate withdrew the second vote, the whole discussion of the incident was deleted from the official records of this meeting. This again seems a questionable practice. The only public clue to what had transpired is a paper the UN Legal Department presented to the 1951 Commission session, which argued forcibly against dual representation and voting in UN organizations. Doc. E/CN.11/275, Dec. 8, 1950.

way organization for the region. The Commission therefore decided to establish a Railway Subcommittee and leave it to consider the idea further. In the end the formation of an Asian and Far Eastern railway association was not recommended. Agreement would not have been easy to reach on either its functions or its location. The smaller Asian countries had little or no research facilities, but feared that if such an organization was located in India or Japan, which were much better equipped to undertake research, it would too readily reflect the interests of those countries. An alternative suggestion was for Asian countries to join the International Union of Railways (UIC) whose headquarters were in Europe, or the Association of American Railroads (AAR). While a few did, in fact, join one or both, the technical work of these organizations was too advanced for most Asian countries. ECAFE itself would have to meet their needs. This meant pursuing highly technical problems which its sister commission in Europe was able to leave to nongovernmental transport organizations. The creation of an Asian and Far Eastern railway association may well have to wait until the national railway systems and international rail connections of the region are much more developed than at present.[15]

The first session of the Inland Transport Committee in December 1951 completed its structure by setting up a Subcommittee on Highways as well as on Railways and Waterways. In its present form the Secretariat's Transport Division began functioning early the following year.

The general direction of ECAFE activities in this field had been determined. In the face of a continuing and acute shortage of transport capacity, the immediate concern of Asian countries was to improve the quality and efficiency of existing facilities. Considerable emphasis was consequently placed on the study and dissemination of modern techniques of operating and maintaining transport installations and equipment. The activities pursued under this general heading may, for purposes of illustration, be most conveniently divided into those relating to railways, high-

15. A conference of Asian national railways was actually held in Japan in May 1958 at the invitation of the directors of the Japanese National Railways. It seems probable, however, that its primary purpose was to advertise Japanese railway equipment.

ways, inland waterways, and problems of concern to more than one means of transport.

Railways

During the last decade most Asian countries have been contending with unprecedented increases in rail traffic.[16] Because of inadequately strong tracks, outmoded operating and signaling techniques, insufficient locomotive power, deficiencies in the number and type of rolling stock, and rising construction, operating, and maintenance costs, their carrying capacities have not kept pace. With the exception of Communist China and India no significant changes have been made in the size of their railway networks. This lack of adequate transport resources and the inability to use existing resources efficiently have been obvious impediments to economic development.

The bulk of the region's railways are single track and on many sections of line the traffic density had reached saturation point. To ease the strain by doubling the track would have taken too long and been immensely expensive. Railways had to concentrate instead on raising the capacity of single-line working by introducing modern equipment and operating practices. These could not be adopted, however, without the necessary trained personnel. To help meet this demand the Commission decided in 1951 to organize with TAA a regional Training Centre for Railway Operating and Signalling Officials at Lahore. For this purpose ECAFE and TAA first arranged for a group of senior railway officials to make a Study Tour of some of the important railways of Europe, Japan, and the United States. This experience enabled the group to suggest the curriculum and equipment the Lahore Centre would need for training personnel in the operating and signaling techniques it thought suitable for the ECAFE region, as well as recommend more efficient operating practices to their own administrations.[17]

With the cooperation of Pakistan, lecturers financed mainly by TAA and equipment provided by TAA and the developed coun-

16. While railway traffic in the world as a whole increased by less than 60 per cent in net ton kilometers between 1948 and 1957, in Asia it increased by more than 200 per cent. See UN *Statistical Yearbook 1958,* UN Sales No.:58.XVII.1.

17. See Doc. E/CN.11/TRANS/Sub.1/21, Sept. 24, 1952.

tries, notably Britain and France, the Lahore Training Centre was opened in April 1954. Participation at first was disappointingly small, but by the end of 1961 well over 200 senior railway officials had been trained there. Pakistan supplied the largest single group, though Burma, Indonesia, Malaya, Taiwan, and Thailand have also sent trainees in good numbers. India, which was the first to ask ECAFE and TAA to arrange a signaling course, has sent no trainees since the second half of 1957. The Railway Subcommittee of ECAFE generally directed the work of the Centre and the Advisory Board issued policy directives, until January 1, 1958, when Pakistan assumed the entire responsibility for its management except for the international instructors BTAO continued to finance. The change did not affect its regional character, however, for the Secretariat, BTAO, and two other Asian countries by rotation continued to be represented on the Advisory Board. It is believed that many of the ideas and techniques learned at the Centre are being gradually put into effect in the region. Trainees from Middle Eastern countries have also been accepted and the idea of opening the Centre to African countries is being considered.

Regional interest in the Lahore Centre appears to have been waning recently. In December 1959 the Advisory Board reported a gradual decline in the status of the trainees and during 1960 and 1961 there was a sharp drop in the number of participants from countries other than Pakistan, with the result that the Centre was by no means fully used.[18] This trend, it is true, reflects to some extent its very success in increasing the number of well-trained officials in the region. But that is not the whole story and Asian countries could certainly give it more support. The last Secretariat review[19] of training requirements and availabilities showed that most Asian countries still needed to train many more railway officials abroad. Moreover, neither TAB nor Pakistan can be expected to accept indefinitely an arrangement whereby the lecturers for the Centre are counted as part of Pakistan's country program under EPTA. It looks as if the Centre will either become a purely Pakistan affair or, as the Secretariat hopes, survive as a regional project by arranging for fewer senior courses, to be given

18. See, e.g., Pakistan's statement to the 1961 Commission session. Doc. E/CN.11/566, July 4, 1961, p. 179.

19. Doc. E/CN.11/TRANS/Sub.1/L.11, Sept. 2, 1959.

by lecturers who do not need to be recruited from outside the region with United Nations technical assistance funds. A further possibility already mentioned would be to open it to African railways.

In addition to the work of the Lahore Centre, the Secretariat has been studying the operational aspects of railway signaling with special reference to speed, safety, and increasing line capacity.[20] Modern signaling could be very expensive to install and maintain, however, and in any case is not the only way to increase the capacity of single lines. Traffic density is also affected by such factors as operating rules, the length of block sections, speeds, loads, terminal layouts, and condition of the track. Consequently it was proposed in 1962 to convene a working party of operating and signaling officials to examine methods of achieving optimum efficiency under such varying conditions.

Another obvious way to increase carrying capacity is to use existing rolling stock more intensively through a quicker turnaround of wagons, speedier repairs and maintenance in workshops, and better wagon control operations in marshaling yards. These improvements would also help in many cases reduce the demand for foreign exchange to buy new wagons. The Railway Subcommittee has investigated and made recommendations on all these problems.[21]

Track construction and maintenance form the biggest capital outlay and running costs of railways. After World War II railway track all over the ECAFE region was in poor condition and its maintenance absorbed as much as 40 per cent of railway revenues. There was ample scope for large savings in this expenditure. More, faster, and heavier trains also required better track. One obstacle to this was the growing shortage and high price of hard, durable wood for timber sleepers. To help make available supplies go further, a joint ECAFE/FAO Working Party recommended some relaxation in the specifications of timber sleepers and drew the attention of railway adminstrations to methods of preserving sleepers made from softer woods.[22] The Malayan railways subsequently amended their specifications as suggested and a number of other

20. See, e.g., Doc. E/CN.11/TRANS/Sub.1/L.13, Sept. 28, 1959.
21. See Docs. E/CN.11/TRANS/Sub.1/4, 8, 9, 10, 11, 13, Sept. 1–Nov. 19, 1951.
22. Doc. E/CN.11/TRANS/Sub.1/47, Jan. 2, 1957.

countries are expected to follow suit. ECAFE has also investigated the merits and problems of concrete and metal sleepers and such other modern methods of track maintenance as the mechanization of rail replacement, ballast screening, measured shovel packing, and mechanical sleeper tamping. Considerable savings on track construction are possible by welding rail joints,[23] and a number of Asian countries have actually embarked on fairly large-scale welding programs. Because the problems involved were extremely technical, the Secretariat suggested that the advanced countries might send experts to make on-the-spot investigations and give advice. Under its own technical assistance program France sent a team for this purpose in 1961 to Cambodia, Indonesia, Malaya, South Viet-Nam, Taiwan, and Thailand.

Faster and heavier trains demanded more powerful locomotives. Several railways in the region have been compelled to burn firewood in their steam locomotives because of the scarcity and high cost of better grades of imported fuel. The practice was primitive but seemed likely to persist for a long time. To remedy the lack of sufficient engine power in these cases meant raising the thermal efficiency of the low grade of fuel available. The Secretariat investigated the matter and was able to help the railways of East Pakistan, Malaya, South Viet-Nam, and Thailand achieve fairly good results from the technical improvements recommended. The formation of excessive scale in boilers as a result of hard and impure water also reduced engine power. The treatment of this condition increased the frequency and cost of cleaning and washing boiler tubes and, hence, the time locomotives were out of service. The Secretariat studied the problem in consultation with an expert and published the results in a report [24] which is now used as a reference manual by a number of railways.

A more straightforward method of increasing motive power which ECAFE countries have been fast adopting, especially where good quality coal is scarce and expensive, is to switch over to diesel traction. Diesel locomotives and railcars pull heavier loads at faster speeds and lower operating costs than steam locomotives. On the other hand, their capital and maintenance costs are greater and

23. See, e.g., Doc. E/CN.11/TRANS/Sub.1/L.9, July 27, 1959.

24. Doc. E/CN.11/TRANS/Sub.1/40, Sept. 10, 1954, and UN Sales No.:1956.II.F.6.

operating them requires imported fuel and a much higher level of technical skill. Bearing in mind different operation requirements, maintenance facilities, physical and climatic conditions, and the availability of trained personnel, what kind of diesel locomotives and railcars would be most suitable for what countries? This question was first examined by the Secretariat in collaboration with a group of experts drawn from Britain, France, India, Indonesia, Japan, and Pakistan which the Railway Subcommittee appointed in 1953. The comprehensive reports [25] of the group formed the material from which in 1959 a Working Party of Mechanical Engineers made recommendations on various aspects of diesel locomotive operations and maintenance.

As part of the same effort to help railway administrations keep down running expenses, ECAFE has studied the prevention and quick disposal of claims in respect of the loss, damage, or pilferage of goods; [26] measures to reduce accidents; [27] and the mechanization of accounts.[28] It has also been disseminating information on management techniques. The introduction of transport containers is one way the railways in developed countries have tried to provide a door-to-door service as flexible and competitive as that of road haulage. This has resulted in greater efficiency, speed, safety, and economy in freight handling. As Japan is the only country using them to any extent in the ECAFE region, the Secretariat is studying the technical and economic feasibility of introducing them on other Asian railways.[29]

The experience of Asian railways has shown that a number of highly technical problems usually have to be solved and modern equipment modified to suit local conditions before they can introduce more advanced methods of operation. Most of them, how-

25. See Docs. E/CN.11/TRANS/Sub.1/L.6, Sept. 13, 1957, and L.7, Oct. 9, 1957.

26. Doc. E/CN.11/TRANS/Sub.1/38, Aug. 30, 1954. The Indian railways subsequently reported that the application of ECAFE's recommendations had considerably reduced their expenses on this account.

27. Docs. E/CN.11/TRANS/Sub.1/11, Oct. 30, 1951; and L.5/Corr.1, Oct. 3, 1957.

28. Doc. E/CN.11/TRANS/L.17, Jan. 28, 1958. ECAFE left this problem to the manufacturers of statistical and accounting machines when it was learned that they were willing on request to make survey reports and recommendations without obligation or cost.

29. For a preliminary report on the subject, see Doc. E/CN.11/TRANS/Sub.1/L.14, Sept. 29, 1959.

ever, lack research facilities for this purpose. India and Japan are much better placed in this respect,[30] but it has proved politically impossible to transform their facilities into regional centers. ECAFE therefore adopted a different approach to the problem and decided that a regional research adviser should be attached to the Secretariat to assess the research needs of Asian countries and then try to have the work done by the most suitable research institutions. This appointment, with BTAO financing, was expected to be made in 1962.

While Asian countries have made considerable efforts during the last decade to rehabilitate and modernize their railway systems, they have done very much less to develop international rail connections and traffic. India has rail links with the two wings of Pakistan, and Thailand with Cambodia and Malaya. It is technically feasible to envisage the construction of links between Thailand and Burma and between Cambodia and South Viet-Nam. But even with the existing connections, Thailand and Malaya are the only countries that have a regular exchange of traffic. No trains run between Thailand and Cambodia. Though some interchange of rolling stock takes place between India and Pakistan, no through trains run across India between East and West Pakistan.

The development of international rail connections and traffic depends partly on a greater degree of standardization of railway equipment and installations such as couplings and gauges and on the conclusion of agreements about maximum moving dimensions and the interchange of rolling stock.[31] The introduction of transport containers would also facilitate international traffic. As early as 1950 a group of mechanical engineers from Indo-China, Malaya, and Thailand made some tentative recommendations regarding standardization of couplings on their rolling stock. The Secretariat has since kept the problems of standardization under review. Although Asian governments have paid repeated lip service to the importance of developing international rail links and traffic, little actual progress has been made in this direction. It is not the tech-

30. See, e.g., Research Facilities in the ECAFE Region, Doc. E/CN.11/TRANS/Sub.1/L.10, Aug. 25, 1959.

31. Thailand, for example, has such an agreement with Malaya but not with Cambodia.

nical problems involved that have held them back but their lack of sufficient political confidence and trust in each other.

Roads

The expansion of road transport in most parts of the region since World War II has been even more striking than that of rail traffic;[32] and, as in the case of railways, road construction and improvement have not kept pace with needs. New construction has mainly taken the form of purely local roads or of bypasses to avoid congested sectors on trunk roads; even then roads are often completely neglected after being built. Yet the cost of road construction and maintenance, including its foreign exchange element, is generally smaller than for railways. Furthermore, roads are perhaps the most effective way of opening up the minds of rural populations to the idea of economic progress. The number of road vehicles has rapidly increased in almost all ECAFE countries; but the maintenance of vehicles is invariably poor, with the result that costs are needlessly excessive, the speed and quality of road services are adversely affected, the life of vehicles is shortened, and the demand for spare parts greatly increased. ECAFE therefore began its work on road transport problems by studying the most economical methods of constructing, repairing, and maintaining roads, and of improving the utilization of road transport equipment.

One of the principal difficulties hampering the planning and development of roads in most Asian countries has been the lack of accurate and complete data on the state of existing roads and on the relative cost of several types of construction, from simple earth roads to soil-stabilized and macadamized surfaces or asphalt and concrete surfaces. To help meet this deficiency the Secretariat designed a standard form of highway register, a kind of health card, for recording the condition of road surfaces and structures, the type of construction, the maintenance performed and needed, and other useful data.[33] Systematic surveys of this kind are the

32. For a rough estimate of the increase in freight transport by road as compared with rail, see The Present Status and Problems of Transport in Countries of the ECAFE Region, Doc. E/CN.11/DPWP.6/L.3, Aug. 11, 1960.

33. Doc. E/CN.11/TRANS/Sub.2/3, Mar. 19, 1952.

first essential condition of a properly phased program of construction and improvement. India, Malaya, Pakistan, and Thailand subsequently adopted this type of record. ECAFE recommended similar standard forms for recording data on bridges [34] and concrete paved roads [35] and agreed that to speed up administrative appraisal and approval a standard method of preparing and presenting road projects should also be adopted.[36]

As a first step toward remedying the lack of information on the costs of road construction, the Secretariat formulated in 1953 a set of principles for assessing the comparative cost of different types of construction. The report [37] was politely welcomed and then shelved. Yet eight years later the Highways and Highway Transport Subcommittee, as it had come to be called, asked the Secretariat to study the different methods used for determining the economic benefits from road building and improvement.[38] This suggests that road transport officials had underestimated the difficulties of trying to justify road works to their finance ministries and perhaps to the providers of foreign aid as well. Asian governments have certainly become more conscious that their methods of highway administration and financing must keep in step with the demands of a rapidly growing volume of traffic. The Secretariat was asked in 1953 to study the problems involved but did not produce its findings until 1960.[39] Among the more important practices the Secretariat and the Subcommittee have emphasized is the necessity for governments to put their road funds on a continuing basis so as to permit long-term planning.[40]

ECAFE's first approach to the economic problems of highway engineering also prompted the governments to ask for detailed studies on the techniques of building water-bound macadam roads [41] and bituminous roads.[42] New road construction in Asia

34. Doc. E/CN.11/TRANS/Sub.2/14, Apr. 16, 1953.
35. Doc. E/CN.11/TRANS/Sub.2/15, Apr. 16, 1953.
36. Doc. E/CN.11/TRANS/Sub.2/16, Apr. 24, 1953.
37. Doc. E/CN.11/TRANS/Sub.2/18, July 13, 1953.
38. Report of the Highways and Highway Transport Subcommittee, Doc. E/CN.11/TRANS/145, Jan. 3, 1961.
39. Doc. E/CN.11/TRANS/Sub.2/L.8, Aug. 11, 1960.
40. See Doc. E/CN.11/TRANS/145, Jan. 3, 1961.
41. Doc. E/CN.11/TRANS/Sub.2/25, May 31, 1954.
42. Docs. ECAFE/TRANS/Sub.2/4, Aug. 31, 1955; and E/CN.11/TRANS/Sub.2/L.1, Sept. 11, 1958.

means, above all, low-cost roads; very limited resources have to produce very long mileages. Following a Secretariat investigation of the methods of building low-cost roads by modern soil stabilization techniques,[43] a special seminar on the subject was arranged in cooperation with TAA and held at New Delhi in 1958. The comprehensive findings of this seminar form a useful manual for highway engineers and administrators.[44] Judged only by the subsequent large demand for copies, it obviously met a widely felt need. That countries such as India, Laos, Malaya, and Thailand have recently applied modern soil stabilization techniques, sometimes on experimental sections of road, probably owes something to ECAFE's influence.

As regards road transport equipment, the most obviously urgent problem was the widespread tendency in the ECAFE region to run motor vehicles with a minimum attention to maintenance and repairs. This resulted in uneconomic use, rapid deterioration, and early scrapping, or in a relatively large expenditure of foreign exchange on importing spare parts and replacements. The answer lay in raising the technical competence of motor vehicle drivers and mechanics. A simple standard instruction manual on vehicle maintenance and repairs was prepared by an ILO expert in collaboration with the ECAFE Secretariat and published in 1954. It was also arranged for ILO to provide visual and oral instruction by means of mobile demonstration vans. The Secretariat and Subcommittee have periodically reviewed the needs and facilities for training highway engineers and other specialists and intend now to explore the possibility of organizing a regional training center. For the basic research requirements of the region, however, the governments favor the Secretariat disseminating information on the work being carried out by national road laboratories and institutes.

With road traffic outstripping the rate of highway construction and improvement, the problem of road safety became more acute. In many urban areas of Asia, the intermingling of slow-moving animal-drawn vehicles with fast-moving mechanical ones, the low standard of vehicle maintenance and repair, and the fitful enforcement of traffic regulations have resulted in severe traf-

43. Doc. ECAFE/TRANS/Sub.2/3, Aug. 23, 1955, and Corr.1, Sept. 28, 1955.
44. Doc. E/CN.11/TRANS/Sub.2/30, Jan. 31, 1958.

fic congestion and high accident rates. After the Secretariat reported on the engineering and traffic aspects of road safety,[45] a seminar on the subject was organized at Tokyo in 1957. The report of this seminar[46] provides an instructive manual for highway engineers and all those concerned with road safety. It recommended, among other things, that countries organize road safety weeks which delegates from other countries might attend. India, in fact, held one at Bombay in 1959 and the Philippines at Manila in 1961. Finally, the Secretariat, with the help of Australia, Britain, and India, has prepared an educational manual on highway safety.

In 1959 the Subcommittee on Highways was redesignated the Subcommittee on Highways and Highway Transport to mark and reflect its growing interest in the economic efficiency of the road transport industry. The Secretariat has made a comparative study of the organization, operation, and public control of passenger road transport in the region[47] and this was discussed by a road transport seminar held at Madras in 1961. Similar attention will next be given to the freight side of the business. Among recently developed activities, however, this enlargement in the scope of the work program pales by comparison with ECAFE's grand design for a network of Asian highways stretching from Saigon and Singapore to the Turkish border. Indeed, no achievement of ECAFE in the whole field of transport has aroused so much enthusiasm as this proposal.

By comparison with the European and North American continents little had been done in Asia to develop international highways. Although the idea was written into ECAFE's work program in 1954, the political confidence needed to pursue it was not forthcoming until 1958. The Secretariat added extra sales appeal to the project by labeling it the Asian Highway. They suggested that it be based on existing main national routes and indicated the basic requirements of an international highway network.[48]

Because of its immense size and the variety of conditions en-

45. Doc. E/CN.11/TRANS/Sub.2/26, May 28, 1954.
46. Doc. E/CN.11/TRANS/Sub.2/29, Sept. 25, 1957, and UN Sales No.:58.II.F.3.
47. Doc. E/CN.11/TRANS/Sub.2/HT/L.1, 1961.
48. See Doc. E/CN.11/TRANS/Sub.2/L.3, Sept. 19, 1958.

countered, the area covered by the project was divided into three zones and separate expert working groups were set up to consider the special problems of each. The first included Burma, Cambodia, Laos, Malaya, Singapore, South Viet-Nam, and Thailand; the second, Ceylon, Nepal, East Pakistan, and India; the third, Afghanistan, Iran, and West Pakistan. Not the least interesting and valuable feature of these groups [49] is that they are purely Asian in composition, with no outside powers present. It should be added that BTAO has helped finance their meetings.

The Asian Highway will connect capital cities, industrial and commercial centers, and a number of places of interest to tourists and pilgrims. It would have been unrealistic, however, to expect that its location would not also be influenced by political and strategic considerations. It has, for example, studiously avoided Kashmir and any suggestion of a possible future link with Communist China, while Burma modified the original Secretariat suggestions by omitting for strategic reasons a section in the northern part of the country. The International Chamber of Commerce (ICC), indeed, thought the routes selected showed that political and strategic considerations had actually outweighed economic considerations; [50] but considering there is so little international traffic at present, this seems too positive a judgment. In 1961 the grand design was further extended by including Indonesia, which will be linked to it by a ferry service to the Malayan peninsula.

There is no question in this project of building a new road all the way. True, some missing links will have to be constructed, especially in Burma, East Pakistan, and Thailand. The principal task, however, is to raise the technical specifications of the routes selected up to those required of an international highway. All the same, this is still a costly undertaking and for this reason it will not be possible to develop immediately the entire route within each country up to the full and final specifications already agreed upon. To speed up progress, therefore, priority routes have been

49. For their reports, see Docs. E/CN.11/TRANS/Sub.2/L.6, Feb. 8, 1960; L.9, Aug. 24, 1960, and L.15, Jan. 25, 1961.

50. For its statement to the ninth session of the Transport Committee, see Doc. E/CN.11/TRANS/148, June 5, 1961.

selected and a stage-by-stage improvement of standards accepted. For instance, as a minimum objective the participating countries have been urged to bring their priority routes up to the standard of a motorable surface as quickly as possible. As and when funds permit and the traffic increases, the minimum standard can subsequently be upgraded.[51] Reduced to its essential, the Asian Highway project is, in fact, an international exercise in the technical coordination of national highway development plans. When completed, this internationally integrated network of national highways will total nearly 35,000 miles, though the priority routes will total only 13,000 to 14,000 miles.

It will take some years to complete this grand design and the participating countries are eager to move quickly. But progress so far has been less than was hoped. By 1961 much work remained to be done on the priority routes, several missing links, and many bridges. The countries concerned, however, lack the funds and foreign exchange required to purchase the necessary materials and equipment. Some of them also need technical assistance. It was, therefore, decided to investigate in detail the difficulties hampering early completion of the priority routes and assess the technical and financial assistance required to overcome them. For instance, a reconnaissance survey of the routes from Calcutta to Bangkok by a team of experts early in 1962 showed that the cost of constructing the missing links, building bridges, realigning certain portions, and bringing others up to acceptable minimum international standards would be approximately $128,000,000, of which the countries concerned had planned to spend the equivalent of $38,000,000. Of the remaining $90,000,000, the foreign exchange requirement amounted to $25,000,000. Armed with this information the Executive Secretary will then approach donor countries and agencies, including the United Nations Special Fund, to see what assistance, if any, they are prepared to offer. Taking a cue from European experience, ECAFE hopes, as well, to arrange a meeting at ministerial level in order to stimulate the participating governments to greater efforts on behalf of the project.

In addition to these decisions, the expert working groups have

51. Four specification standards have, in fact, been agreed upon.

agreed on a uniform code of road signs, signals, and pavement markings.[52] The Asian Highway will also need ancillary services such as gasoline stations, garages, restaurants, hotels, and telecommunication lines. Agreements will have to be concluded on such matters as the permissible maximum dimensions and weight of vehicles on the routes, safety regulations, and the mutual recognition of license plates and operating rights. Finally, frontier formalities, including customs regulations, must be simplified if the grand design is to fulfill its purpose. This is likely to prove the most difficult hurdle since it is at bottom a political problem.

The technical foundations of the project are thus being laid and an encouraging climate of cooperation has been created. Skeptics have wondered, however, about its economic justification. That is admittedly hard to produce. When it launched the project in 1958, the Highway Subcommittee recognized that an economic analysis of its benefits would be desirable, but this has not yet been attempted. It is accepted that for some time ahead the volume of international traffic on the Asian Highway, both passengers and goods, will be small; the routes forming the network will continue to carry mainly national traffic. Unlike Europe, for instance, international highways in Asia are not an obvious response to a large and rapidly growing volume of international traffic. On the contrary, like so many development projects, they have to create their own demand: their role is a promotional one.

Historically, the impact of the West on Asia came from the sea and was most marked in the ports and their environs. It is precisely where it was least felt, namely in the hinterlands, that the consequences of road building could well be far-reaching. The importance of the Asian Highway for landlocked Afghanistan, Laos, and Nepal, for instance, needs no emphasis. The Secretariat thinks of it as a modern revival of the ancient caravan routes along which traveled not only goods but peoples and ideas. It is as much for these purposes as for their economic benefits that better and cheaper international communications are sorely needed in the ECAFE region.

52. These are based on the UN Protocol on Road Signs and Signals of 1949; the UN Convention on Road Signs and Signals of 1952; and the recommendations of the ECAFE Seminar on the Engineering and Traffic Aspects of Highway Safety of 1957.

Waterways

With the exception of Afghanistan, Ceylon, Indonesia, Japan, Nepal, and the Philippines, all ECAFE countries have important river systems in their most populous areas. In some cases as, for example, in Burma, Cambodia, East Pakistan, South Viet-Nam, and Thailand, waterways dominate the pattern of transport. This is also true of Indonesia and the Philippines if coastal and inter-insular shipping is considered. Despite the importance and relative cheapness of water transport, however, especially for bulky cargoes, Asian governments have generally spent far too little on developing its facilities. River and canal conservancy in most countries is practically nonexistent, adequate aids to safe navigation are commonly lacking, and inland water and coastal vessels frequently obsolete and uneconomical. ECAFE's first task in persuading and helping governments to overcome these deficiencies was to emphasize the potentialities of this form of transport.

A United Nations study tour sometimes helps raise the standing and influence of the participants in the eyes of their own government administrations. Accordingly, in 1951 and 1952, a Study Tour of inland waterway officials to Europe and the United States was organized in cooperation with TAA. Its chief purpose was to create a nucleus of Asian officials familiar with the most advanced practices and in a stronger position to influence their own governments in favor of doing more to improve and maintain inland waterway facilities. The comprehensive report and recommendations of this group [53] became, indeed, a standard reference manual in the region and formed the basis of the inland waterway plans of, for example, Burma, India, Pakistan, and Thailand. It also led to a strengthening of the inland waterway administrations of Burma, India, and Pakistan. After an irksome delay, a further Study Tour was organized in 1959 to the Soviet Union and the Danube basin.[54]

As much as 90 per cent of the inland water traffic of the ECAFE region is carried by slow-moving and indigenous craft of tradi-

53. UN Sales No.:1953.VIII.1. Following and arising from this report the Secretariat published a reference manual on Selective Plans of Inland Waterway Vessels, UN Sales No.:1955.VIII.2.

54. For its report, see UN Sales No.:61.VIII.1.

tional design, country boats operated by the owners and their families. These boatmen are not organized and governments take them for granted. They are frequently illiterate so that no transport documents can be issued to them and their cargoes are uninsurable. For these reasons industrial and commercial firms are usually reluctant to entrust their goods to country boats outside their own supervision. The Secretariat drew the attention of governments to the importance of improving the design, construction, and turnaround ability of these owner-operated country boats and showed how by proper organization, including various methods of towing by small tugs, their efficiency could be improved. This probably influenced Pakistan to ask a TAA expert to examine various aspects of country boat construction and operation and India to begin towing experiments on the Ganges River.

While country boats are clearly important, the full advantages of cheap water transport can only be realized by introducing modern craft and operating practices. In 1950 the ad hoc Committee of Inland Transport Experts suggested the organization of a pilot demonstration scheme, including practical experiments with tugs and pusher craft, to discover the most suitable designs and operating methods. The idea was later discussed extensively by the experts participating in the Study Tour of Europe and the United States. India and Pakistan were particularly keen to organize a scheme. A TAA consultant worked out a plan on the basis of which India organized and itself financed the first experiment with modern craft and operating practices on the Ganges and Gogra rivers. Pakistan, however, could neither afford the necessary equipment nor obtain it from TAA and proposed instead to organize a demonstration project with fast passenger hydrofoil craft. These vessels are quite expensive, so it was essential to be sure of their technical and economic feasibility under local conditions before introducing them commercially. Unfortunately and precisely because of their cost, it has again proved impossible for United Nations technical assistance funds to provide such a craft, while private manufacturers are interested in sales, not demonstration projects. Negotiations aimed at obtaining one are continuing and the Special Fund may well be approached.

Following the experiments which the Study Tour to Europe and the United States helped to define, services with pusher craft commenced on an experimental basis in India and Pakistan. Burma went further and reaped substantial economies from the introduction of pusher flotillas on a commercial basis on the Irrawaddy River. Since other ECAFE countries were invited to observe the original experiments, they became, in effect, regional demonstration projects. As a logical extension of these developments, ECAFE has been working to produce a standard design for a suitable prototype coastal vessel for the region.[55]

To encourage countries to mechanize inland water transport, the Secretariat prepared a report[56] on various types of diesel marine engines, which are often a more economical solution for marine propulsion than steam engines. This study, or rather reference manual, sets out the relative advantages and disadvantages of different types and recommends those thought most suitable for the region. One of the main limitations on the extensive introduction of such engines, however, is the shortage of trained operating and maintenance workers. To help meet this need, Burma, in April 1956, opened the training center that ILO had organized at Rangoon to trainees from other ECAFE countries. The location was well chosen, for almost 90 per cent of Burma's large inland water fleet was diesel-powered and it was rapidly modernizing its maintenance facilities for them. Despite these advantages, the Training Centre for Diesel Marine Mechanics has not, in fact, been well patronized by other ECAFE countries. Its Advisory Board, on which ILO and ECAFE were represented, sometimes even had to cancel scheduled meetings because of insufficient support. ECAFE has not, however, been much involved with the Centre and in 1960 Burma assumed entire responsibility for its operation and supervision. At the same time, other Asian countries are setting up their own training centers for diesel mechanics and thereby helping to spread the knowledge of the instructors trained at Rangoon.

One of the main obstacles to improved operational efficiency on the inland waterways of the ECAFE region is the inadequacy of inland port facilities. In some cases boats spend as much as 85 per cent of their time at terminals. Following a Secretariat study

55. In 1953 coastal shipping was included in the terms of reference of the Waterways Subcommittee. The Soviet Union also wanted it to deal with ocean shipping.

56. UN Sales No.:1955.II.F.2.

on inland ports,[57] an ad hoc working group made various practical suggestions on their design, construction, operation, administration, and financing, and on ways to reduce terminal delays. It is known that the design of several inland ports, particularly in India and Pakistan, were subsequently revised in the light of these recommendations.

More efficient water transport also depends on removing hazards to safe navigation. The failure, for example, to mark the frequently shifting channels of rivers has been a common cause of boats running aground. In 1954 the Inland Waterways Subcommittee accordingly accepted the Secretariat's proposal for a uniform system of buoys and shore marks. As a convention seemed too formidable an instrument for such an agreement, the proposals were published in pamphlet form [58] and countries were merely asked whether they were prepared to accept them. Most have in fact done so. In addition, the Permanent International Association of Navigation Congresses (PIANC) has investigated, at the Secretariat's request, the problems of dredging waterways and ports.[59]

The need for some element of organization of water transport in the ECAFE region is perhaps most clearly seen in the fact that no country knows how many boats operate on its inland waterways, much less their carrying capacity, while international waterway traffic has been hampered by the lack of any internationally recognized certificate of registration. ECAFE accordingly designed uniform methods of measuring craft for national census and registration purposes and suggested ways of making these registration certificates mutually acceptable to riparian countries. This should help reduce frontier delays and thereby increase the carrying capacity of a given fleet of vessels. A Convention [60] embodying these recommendations was signed at Bangkok in 1956 by Cambodia, Indonesia, Laos, South Viet-Nam, Taiwan, and Thailand. It is the only convention ECAFE has prepared and was intended to come into force within four years after ratification by at least four coun-

57. Doc. E/CN.11/TRANS/Sub.3/17, Oct. 17, 1957.

58. UN Sales No.:1957.II.F.7. The proposals were based on a League of Nations Agreement for Maritime Buoyage of 1937.

59. Doc. ECAFE/TRANS/Sub.3/17, Feb. 3, 1954.

60. *Convention Regarding the Measurement and Registration of Vessels Employed in Inland Navigation,* UN Sales No.: 1957.II.F.9.

tries. In fact, none has so far done so. While there has been increasing mutual recognition of national documents in practice, Asian countries are apparently reluctant to surrender the right to control international water traffic whenever political circumstances dictate. ECAFE has also been working to establish a standard schedule for classifying waterways and desirable standard dimensions for each class of waterway, their structures, and the craft using them. The main aim is to avoid bottlenecks and unnecessary expense in the construction of through routes or sections which may form part of through routes.

Finally, as many Asian governments have been anxious to set up special administrative services to cope with inland water transport, including river and canal conservancy, or to strengthen existing services, the Secretariat made a comparative study of various forms of public organization of water transport in Western Europe and the ECAFE region.[61] On the basis of this information an ad hoc working group in 1959 recommended suitable regulatory machinery ECAFE countries might adopt for this mode of transport.[62]

Common Problems

To complete the record of ECAFE in the field of transport some considerations must be given to those activities which involve more than one means of transport. For instance, the Secretariat, in collaboration with the Institute of Refrigeration, has examined the technical and economic feasibility of refrigerated transport for the ECAFE region.[63] This special form of transport is little used in the region yet could obviously help to stimulate a larger consumption of perishable foodstuffs like meat, fresh fruit, and vegetables. The Transport Committee recommended that it be introduced according to an over-all plan for a cold chain from producer to consumer, with refrigeration by road, rail, and waterways and proper cold storage capacity in the larger cities. Railways, it was suggested, might take the lead in promoting such a chain. The Indian railways have, in fact, been experimenting with refrigera-

61. See Docs. E/CN.11/TRANS/Sub.3/L.5, Oct. 1, 1957; and E/CN.11/TRANS/Sub.3/14, Nov. 21, 1955, and Sub.3/16, June 7, 1957.

62. See Report of the Inland Waterways Subcommittee, Fifth Session, Doc. E/CN.11/TRANS/140, Nov. 19, 1959, Appendix 4.

63. Doc. ECAFE/TRANS/11, Dec. 6, 1956.

tor cars, while the Japanese railways have introduced refrigerated containers for less-than-carload traffic and a new type of refrigerator car. Otherwise, ECAFE countries have not made much progress in implementing the Committee's recommendations.

Tourism and telecommunications are two other subjects which found their way into the general work program of the Transport Committee, though neither involves problems peculiar to the transport industry.

ECAFE first took up the problems of tourism as part of its trade promotion work. In 1949 a Working Group on Travel Facilities, consisting of representatives of carriers and travel agents, met to consider the customs, passport, health, and foreign exchange regulations of Asian countries which impeded the free movements of students, traders, and tourists. On the basis of their report,[64] an ad hoc Subcommittee on Travel was convened a few months later to formulate specific recommendations.[65] The fruits of its labors were embodied in a resolution [66] the Commission passed a few days later, which consisted, in fact, of 71 separate recommendations relating to the promotion of tourist travel, the relaxation of controls affecting the traveling public, and the quantity and quality of hotel accommodation.

One of the recommendations urged the International Union of Official Travel Organizations (IUOTO) to establish a regional travel organization in Asia.[67] This was acted upon in 1952 when IUOTO set up an Asia and Far East Travel Commission (AFETC) with its headquarters initially at New Delhi. All the travel promotion activities of ECAFE were thereupon transferred to the new nongovernmental regional organization.[68] But AFETC was not apparently very effective and in 1955 IUOTO divided it into two subregional travel commissions, one for South Asia and the other for East Asia. At the same time it asked ECAFE to set up a section within the Secretariat to deal with all aspects of tourism. This

64. Doc. ECAFE/TRA/W.6/1, 1949.

65. For its report, see Doc. E/CN.11/205, Oct. 19, 1949.

66. Doc. E/CN.11/218, Oct. 27, 1949.

67. This was another instance of ECAFE prodding an international organization based in Europe to pay more attention to Asia. The General Assembly of IUOTO met in Asia for the first time only in 1955.

68. Including a monthly publication, *Asian Travelways,* which the Secretariat inaugurated in July 1950.

could not be done, however, owing to the shortage of staff. After shifting its headquarters around several times, the East Asia Travel Commission merged with the Pacific Area Travel Association, a wealthy United States affiliate of IUOTO based at San Francisco, and became the Pacific and East Asia Travel Commission. Its other half, the South Asia Travel Commission, remained more or less moribund.

The Secretariat continued to maintain liaison with IUOTO and no separate activity on tourism was contemplated until 1959, when the South Asia Travel Commission pressed for a more active relationship. That more effective work needed to be done to promote tourism was patently obvious. Neither of the two subregional travel organizations had even made a systematic survey of the tourist potentialities of their areas. Governments were nevertheless becoming increasingly conscious of the importance of foreign exchange earnings from tourism, and on the initiative of the Philippines practically all ECAFE countries agreed to designate 1961 as "Visit the Orient Year." To help make this campaign a success, ECAFE, in cooperation with BTAO and IUOTO, organized a seminar on the promotion of tourism at New Delhi in April and May 1961, which concentrated on the techniques of tourist promotion and publicity, travel barriers, transport and accommodation facilities, and training for those employed in the industry.

As regards ECAFE's involvement with the problems of tourism the wheel has turned full circle, though now the subject is part of the work program of its Transport Committee. This is a questionable development. The promotion of tourism in the ECAFE region involves many problems that lie far outside the field of transport and can hardly be thought a priority claim on scarce Secretariat resources. The actual and potential values of developing the industry are not disputed; nor the fact that this is intimately connected with transport. But the typical tourist in Asia travels to and around the region by air and ship. Neither mode of transport concerns ECAFE. More important, there seems no compelling reason why Asian governments should not themselves carry out the work they have requested ECAFE to undertake in this field. It is a strange sense of priorities that leads the Transport Committee to direct the Executive Secretary to explore, for instance, the possibility of establishing a regional training center for hotel managers.[69]

Good telecommunications are indispensable to traders, to meteorology, and to the broadcasting and electric power industries as well as to transport. In the provision of these facilities the ECAFE region lags far behind Europe. Yet the International Telecommunication Union (ITU), the proper international authority for this field, had done virtually nothing for specifically Asian needs and problems. On the initial suggestion of India and Japan, the Commission in 1956 approved the inclusion of telecommunications within the scope of the Transport Committee and two years later renamed it the Inland Transport and Communications Committee. The effect was to induce ITU to pay more attention to Asia, if only because it disliked the idea of ECAFE encroaching upon its preserves. It has, in fact, proved difficult to define a working relationship that is acceptable to both organizations.

In 1957 the Transport Committee asked the Secretariat to approach ITU and TAA to obtain expert assistance for a study of the national and regional requirements of ECAFE countries. The following year two ITU experts provided by TAA, one on line communications and the other on radio communications, set to work. On the completion of their survey an ECAFE Working Party of Telecommunications Experts met at Tokyo in 1959 to formulate specific recommendations and lay down future lines of work.[70] ECAFE was to concentrate on the economic aspects of telecommunications, including methods of financing, leaving ITU to deal with the purely technical problems. Further progress was then held up while the Secretariats of both organizations wrangled about the precise form their cooperation should take. The Transport and Communications Committee favored the idea of a joint unit within the ECAFE Secretariat similar to the ECAFE/FAO Agricultural Division,[71] but no agreement on this had been reached by the end of 1961. It was reported only that two ITU experts had commenced work in Bangkok on their part of the program.

69. See Report of Inland Transport and Communications Committee, Ninth Session, Doc. E/CN.11/556, Feb. 26, 1961.

70. For its report, see Doc. E/CN.11/TRANS/138, June 26, 1959.

71. See pp. 139–40.

Much of ECAFE's work on transport problems has been concerned with channeling technical advances thought most suitable for the stage of development of particular Asian countries. In addition to the activities mentioned, the Secretariat, through the loan of technical books and documentary films, the distribution of technical publications, and its *Transport and Communications Bulletin,* has fed them continuously with the fruits of technical experience and research. In the course of field trips and correspondence it has given them much advice directly. Special mention should be made in this respect of the assistance given to the navigation improvement program of the Mekong Project.[72] Moreover, the common practice of arranging on-the-spot inspection tours in conjunction with meetings held in different parts of the region has enabled countries to learn from one another in a most practical way. Finally, considerable progress has been made in defining the terminology and form of compilation of transport statistics, especially those required at various administrative levels for measuring efficiency. Cambodia, the Philippines, South Korea, and South Viet-Nam are known to have accepted the recommendations made on these problems, and other ECAFE countries may be expected to follow suit as their statistical services improve.[73] It is hoped that the Conference of Asian Statisticians will consider the statistical data required for planning transport development.

There is no denying that the technical work of ECAFE in the field of transport was generally welcomed by Asian governments and consequently pushed by the Secretariat. In the absence of regional research organizations for railways, highways, and waterways, ECAFE had to do what it could to help countries without adequate research facilities of their own. All the same, an ineluctable impression remains that too much emphasis was given to this kind of work. The time spent on some highly specialized problems, the burning of wood fuel in boiler locomotives, for example, was out of all proportion to the relative importance of their claim on scarce Secretariat resources. There has been a tendency, which the Secretariat has aided and abetted, to take on too much with the result that efforts have been spread too thinly. But

72. See p. 196.
73. See, e.g., Doc. ECAFE/TRANS/12, Dec. 12, 1956.

only the outside powers, notably Britain and the United States, have pointed this out.[74] Furthermore, in concentrating on the technical problems hampering improvement in the productivity of transport resources, ECAFE had neglected the relation of transport to agricultural and industrial development. Where should transport facilities be located? How can the future demand for transport be estimated and what should be its pricing policy? In short, it had still to come to grips with fundamental questions of transport policy.

To government officials the central problem of transport policy is the coordination of transport. In 1950, the ad hoc Committee of Inland Transport Experts thought this should receive high priority from a permanent committee. In fact, it was not until 1956 that the Transport Committee discussed a preliminary report by the Secretariat on the problem and indicated which aspects of it were of immediate interest to Asian governments. In the light of this directive a team of experts, in collaboration with the Secretariat, studied the methodological problems involved in calculating true transport costs,[75] while a Working Party on Coordination was convened in 1958 to concentrate on analyzing the objectives and methods of sound coordination policies. The most important recommendation of this latter meeting was that Asian governments should establish an over-all regulatory agency with power to authorize and make proposals for the coordinated development of all means of transport. This appears to be consistent with the trend of government thinking on this question.

If ECAFE's slowness in coming to grips with coordination problems reflected a proper caution in the face of huge complexities, the sentiment is understandable. These problems have been pursued for many years in Europe, and not least by ECE, without con-

74. The US delegate to the Commission in 1958 stated that the Secretariat "could not hope to provide competent technical advice on the whole range of technical problems raised by transport authorities. At best, it could provide only summary, and at times rather superficial, reports on technical research and developments. It should not therefore devote a disproportionate amount of its limited resources to the study of such problems." The then Executive Secretary, Narasimhan, implicitly acknowledged the force of this criticism. Doc. E/CN.11/483, June 3, 1958, p. 144.

75. For its report, see Doc. E/CN.11/TRANS/81, Jan. 4, 1952.

clusive results. The word coordination, to which bureaucrats are so attached, means all things to all men and is often a refuge for those with no clear ideas. When applied to transport, it usually means tying a millstone around the neck of road transport so as to match the burdens and obligations public policy has imposed on rail transport. This temptation becomes almost irresistible if the railways are state owned and losing business to the roads. In Western Europe the trend of transport policy has been away from this restrictive outlook and toward the creation of conditions in which the railways may compete for the business they are best able to do. But in the ECAFE region, governments still feel they cannot, in the words of one prominent member of the Transport Committee, "afford the luxury of competition in the transport field, particularly between private and public enterprises." [76] Because their transport capacity still falls far short of demand, Asian governments see the problem rather as one of coordinating the development of adequate transport facilities. This approach nevertheless still faces them with the same question that baffled transport policy in Europe for so long, namely, how to provide a rational economic basis for determining the distribution of investment between different means of transport?

Mindful, no doubt, of the experience of ECE, whose work on transport coordination problems became bogged down in a morass of pious hopes and abstract principles, ECAFE has so far confined itself to preparing the basic knowledge required to answer this question. On the suggestion of the Working Party on Coordination, the Secretariat has made a preliminary comparative study of the pricing policies of Asian railways [77] and engaged a consultant for a study on uniformity in accounting and statistical procedures. Government policies that affect transport development and operations and the techniques and organization of intercarrier traffic are also being investigated.

Finally, in 1960 the Working Party on Economic Development and Planning devoted a whole session to the relation of transport to economic development in general. It considered such problems as estimating future transport needs, the criteria for allocating in-

76. For the Pakistan delegate's statement to the ninth session of the Committee, see Doc. E/CN.11/TRANS/SR.58, 1961 (Incorporated in Doc. E/CN.11/TRANS/SR.55–61, June 5, 1961).

77. Doc. E/CN.11/TRANS/L.28, Jan. 5, 1961.

vestment between different means of transport, and methods of financing transport development.[78] This was a useful meeting if only for demonstrating how much work needs to be done by Asian governments and ECAFE on the economic problems of transport. Declarations about planned coordination and unorganized competition are no substitute.

The emphasis of ECAFE's work in the field of transport has thus been gradually changing with the growing awareness of the need for transport to serve and promote general economic objectives. Perhaps this trend will also transform the Transport Committee into a forum which leaves largely technical discussions to its specialized subsidiary bodies and concentrates instead on the basic issues of high-level policy-making. Its failure to do so in the past has been its most conspicuous weakness.

78. For its report, see Doc. E/CN.11/L.86, Oct. 19, 1960.

CHAPTER 12

International Trade

International trade illustrates well the potentialities and difficulties of economic cooperation in the ECAFE region. The fact that all Asian countries have a material stake in international trade should have made it easier to identify the common ground of useful cooperation. Actually ECAFE had an uphill struggle even to persuade them of the relevance of foreign trade for their own economic development. In this as in other fields of ECAFE activity, colonialism had bred attitudes not easily overcome. Foreign trade was the begetter of colonial domination. It was essentially a Western stake organized by Western interests. It was also the means by which Asian economies became distorted into a highly vulnerable dependence on the export of a few primary products. Consequently, when Asian countries became independent they tended to believe that any importance attached to foreign trade implied a shift of emphasis away from economic development, to which they were passionately committed. They shared a widespread feeling that home-produced goods should be kept at home rather than exported. The ECAFE Working Party on Industrial Development,[1] for example, said nothing about the need for industrializing countries to expand their exports. As these inherited prejudices faded in time, new political inhibitions came to exercise a powerful influence on Asian views about the scope for useful cooperation in this field.

ECAFE was much preoccupied at first with the foreign exchange problems of Asian countries. As a result of war damage and con-

1. See p. 41.

tinuing inflation, population expansion, and internal strife, their import needs rose much faster than their export earnings. The exceptional demand for imports, especially for food, was heavily concentrated on the United States where supplies were available, with the further result that virtually all Asian countries developed substantial dollar deficits within their total deficits on current trading account. In this situation little foreign exchange was available for importing the capital goods needed for economic recovery and development.

ECAFE examined the character and magnitude of the region's postwar dollar shortage and indicated some broad considerations that should guide the foreign exchange policies of Asian countries.[2] The long-run answer to the problem was to raise the productivity of their resources. Meanwhile, some immediate relief seemed possible through an expansion of trade within the ECAFE region. Intraregional trade was well below its pre-World War II level and one important reason for this was the almost complete disruption of trade with Japan. For many of the import demands of ECAFE countries Japan had excess productive capacity,[3] but needed their food and raw materials to get production going again. A basis for mutually beneficial exchanges clearly existed. In the absence of a "Marshall Plan" for Asia, increased trade with Japan became indeed the most hopeful means of accelerating the industrialization of the region.[4]

For several years this line of thought was pursued within ECAFE. Resolutions were passed and reports issued[5] urging Asian countries to maximize their trade with Japan or to conclude trade

2. See, e.g., Nature and Extent of Dollar Shortage and Possible Remedial Measures, Doc. E/CN.11/I&T/24, Mar. 31, 1950, and the annual *Economic Surveys* for these earlier years.

3. Taking 1932–36 as 100, the index of industrial activity in Japan was 57.1 in 1947 and 74.1 in 1948. In 1949 its production of major items of capital goods was mostly well below 50 per cent of existing capacity. See Problems and Prospects of Accelerated Economic Development in the ECAFE Region Through Increased Trade with Japan, Doc. E/CN.11/I&T/21, Mar. 27, 1950.

4. Doc. E/CN.11/113, June 11, 1948, states that "within the limits set by the Far Eastern Commission and the Peace Settlement, when concluded, Japan's trade and industrial plans should be adjusted to the needs and requirements of the economic development of Member and Associate Member countries."

5. E.g., Problems and Prospects of Accelerated Economic Development in the ECAFE Region Through Increased Trade with Japan, Doc. E/CN.11/I&T/21, Mar. 27, 1950.

agreements where none existed, so as to achieve a fuller utilization of Japan's productive capacity.

The logic of the argument was undeniable. Nevertheless, the Commission was far from united in its wisdom. In the first place, Japan was virtually a hard-currency country. Because its economy depended heavily on United States supplies,[6] the Supreme Commander of the Allied Powers (SCAP) insisted on receiving dollars or at least essential imports in exchange for Japanese exports. Any diversion of food and raw materials from the region to Japan, however, would simply transfer part of the dollar problem of the latter to the former. Furthermore, apart from Burma and Thailand which were trading their rice for Japanese manufactures, Asian countries did not wish to encourage an undue dependence on Japan. The memory of its prewar co-prosperity policy and essentially colonial-type domination was still fresh in their memory. Britan, France, and the Netherlands, for obvious reasons of commercial self-interest, supported this cautious approach. The United States, for no less obvious reasons, wished to promote Japanese trade with the ECAFE region. The SCAP representatives to ECAFE meetings virtually became salesmen for Japanese goods.[7] But any suggestion of special pleading or preferred treatment for Japanese recovery was not well received by Asian countries, particularly by India and China. The outside powers, on the other hand, were equally sensitive to any suggestion that ECAFE lay down guiding principles for this recovery or otherwise interfere with the work of the occupation authority, namely, the Far Eastern Commission. The Soviet Union went further and argued that ECAFE had no right to consult or have any relations with the occupation authority.

By the end of 1950 the Commission sensibly recognized that the limits of useful study of this problem had been reached. Further action was left to interested Asian countries and a number of them, in fact, sent trade missions to Japan. Actually, the Korean war did more than organized cooperation to bring about the

6. From September 1945 to December 1949 US aid to Japan totaled $1.6 billion, of which about $1 billion was imports of food and beverages, ibid.

7. An attempt by SCAP at the meeting of the Industry and Trade Committee in 1951 to introduce a Japanese observer to speak was vigorously and successfully resisted by the British and Soviet delegates who argued that observers had no right to make a statement unless called upon by the Committee.

development ECAFE had so halfheartedly pursued. The export prices of the region's primary products rose steeply, thereby momentarily easing its foreign exchange position. At the same time it was compelled to concentrate more of its import demands on Japan, because rearmament reduced supplies from the West. Finally, with the conclusion of a peace treaty in September 1951, Japan assumed full responsibility again for its own commercial relations.

The inconvertibility of currencies other than the dollar made it difficult to finance trade not only with Japan but between all countries in the region which belonged to different monetary blocs. Western European countries faced the same difficulty when they began to foster trade among themselves and tackled it by evolving compensation and transferability arrangements which led ultimately to the formation of the European Payments Union (EPU). In June 1948, the Commission authorized the Secretariat, with the help of government experts and officials from IMF and the World Bank, to study the problem for the ECAFE region. The report of this group was issued a few months later.[8] It gave a few general examples of financial arrangements that would facilitate trade in conditions of foreign exchange shortage and currency inconvertibility, but was unable in the time available to make any positive proposal other than that IMF should investigate the practicability of a multilateral clearing union for the region. Although Britain and the United States strongly opposed the suggestion, the Commission nevertheless accepted it. In 1949 the Fund presented ECAFE with extensive material on intraregional trade [9] and reported, on admittedly inadequate evidence, that a regional clearing union was impractical. It might have added, but did not, that in any case the idea offended its principles. The Commission thereupon dropped the subject, though not for long.

In 1953 Japan suggested to a regional Conference on Trade Promotion [10] that ECAFE should examine the payments problems of the region. Another group of experts, drawn this time from the central banks of nine Asian countries as well as from IMF and the

8. Report on Financial Arrangements to Facilitate the Trade of the Countries of the ECAFE Region, E/CN.11/128, Oct. 9, 1948.

9. Intraregional Trade of ECAFE Countries, Doc. E/CN.11/206/Annex A/Add.1, Oct. 27, 1949.

10. See p. 241.

Secretariat, was accordingly convened for the purpose. But this group also felt unable to recommend the creation of an Asian payments union.[11] Nearly three-quarters of intraregional trade and an even larger proportion of the region's trade with the rest of the world was conducted in sterling or dollars. As the latter were fully convertible, the answer to multilateral compensation problems lay less in regional solutions than in the progress of sterling toward full convertibility.[12] India and Pakistan certainly preferred to remain in the sterling area rather than get involved in new monetary arrangements, while most of the other Asian countries had no strong views on the matter. Moreover, a payments union presupposes that some members have a surplus in their current trading accounts; virtually all ECAFE countries had persistent deficits. In this situation a large amount of working capital would be necessary to establish such a union and further underwriting might well be needed to keep it going. Only the United States could have supplied the capital and it was wholly unsympathetic to the idea of an Asian payments union. Like Britain, it repeatedly stressed the global character of international trade and was not prepared to encourage, much less finance, purely regional trading arrangements.[13] Thus, while it was useful for ECAFE to have discovered the limits of possible action on payments problems, practical trade cooperation had to be sought in other directions.

In June 1948 the United States prodded the Commission into creating in the Secretariat a Trade Promotion Section to undertake research, act as a clearinghouse of commercial information, and advise governments at their request on the setting up of trade promotion machinery. It could also organize trade conferences. Owing to lack of staff, however, no real impetus was given to the

11. Report of the Working Group of Experts on Payments Problems of the ECAFE Region, Doc. E/CN.11/I&T/112, Dec. 9, 1954.

12. "Scope for Multilateral Compensation Payments of ECAFE Countries," *Economic Bulletin, 5,* No. 1 (May 1954). With the dissolution of EPU in 1958, all Western European currencies, including sterling, became fully convertible into dollars as far as nonresident holders were concerned. This meant that ECAFE countries could export against currencies that were once more interchangeable.

13. Not all US delegates consistently followed this line. At a meeting in the Committee on Industry and Trade in 1949, for example, the US delegate suggested that a study on ways of stimulating intraregional trade, such as by a customs union, would be most valuable. Docs. E/CN.11/I&T/SR.1–8, Oct. 12–18, 1949.

work of the section until the following year when it was put in charge of a trade promotion specialist and upgraded to a division.[14]

It was the Division's clearinghouse function that developed most rapidly. For instance, in 1950 a *Handbook on Trade Promotion Facilities* was published giving information on government commercial services within and outside the region, a list of the principal trade organizations, and the publications most commonly used as standard references. In the same year a monthly publication, *Trade Promotion News,* was launched.[15] These were followed in 1954 by a *Glossary of Commodity Terms.*[16] A considerable amount of commercial information and literature, including pamphlets, circulars, trade and exchange control regulations, export availabilities, and import needs was published in the form of a Trade Promotion Series.[17] The Secretariat also directly advised various governments trying to develop their own trade promotion machinery. Not all the information which the Secretariat disseminated was obviously relevant and important. The inevitable delay in getting commercial intelligence to governments sometimes nullified its value. Taken together, however, these activities amounted to something like the services of a trade commissioner or regional chamber of commerce and were widely appreciated. The smaller Asian countries, which had little or no facilities for obtaining anything like so extensive a range of information, were especially grateful. But none supported the Division more enthusiastically than the Western powers. In fact, they applauded its efforts so much that it began to look as if their real purpose was to steer ECAFE clear of more fundamental prob-

14. At the same time, economic research on trade problems was transferred to a separate Research and Statistics Division. In January 1952 the Trade Promotion Division was merged with a Division of Economic Studies to form a Trade and Finance Division, and in January 1954 an Industry and Trade Development Division was created. Within this latter Division a specially designated Trade Branch was formed in 1957.

15. In 1952 *Trade Promotion News* absorbed a monthly *Calendar of Conferences, Fairs and Exhibitions* and became a bimonthly publication.

16. UN Sales No.: 1954.II.F.4.

17. From the end of 1954 this series was distributed in alternate months to *Trade Promotion News* and was largely devoted to the publication of government invitations to tender. In 1956 the series was discontinued and *Trade Promotion News* was again issued monthly.

lems of regional trade cooperation. The Soviet Union, on the other hand, scathingly dismissed its activities as mere gratuitous advertising for British and United States firms and, at best, of purely secondary importance.[18] A fair assessment of their value would fix it somewhere between these two extremes.

Although this clearinghouse function was undoubtedly useful, it did not amount to actual cooperation between government representatives. Four years passed before ECAFE organized the first intergovernmental meeting devoted solely to trade. During 1948, the Executive Secretary contacted governments and the ICC about the idea of a regional conference of businessmen but was doubtful if it should be arranged by ECAFE. After some hesitation, the Commission decided that a trade conference of government officials and business should, in fact, be held under ECAFE auspices. This Regional Conference on Trade Promotion, as it was called, met at Singapore in October 1951.[19] With over 150 delegates it was the largest meeting ECAFE had so far organized. All members of the Commission except Nepal and Pakistan were represented, as were Belgium, Canada, Denmark, Sweden, FAO, WHO, and a number of NGO's. Many businessmen were included in the government delegations in addition to those representing NGO's. The Soviet Union, not unexpectedly, tried to seat Communist China, and was ruled out of order.

The Conference discussed a wide range of subjects and produced some clearly defined proposals. The training courses of technical assistance programs should include trade promotion techniques and procedures. The Secretariat should make regional market surveys and investigate the idea of establishing a permanent exhibition of the region's products. A convention on simplified customs regulations was desirable. National arbitration associations should be organized where none existed and legislation passed to give validity to their awards. ECAFE should collect and disseminate information on standardization and, together with the International Standards Organization (ISO) and FAO, convene a conference on standardization problems. A number of Asian

18. For Soviet statement on the work of the Trade Promotion Division to the Industry and Trade Committee, see Docs. E/CN.11/I&T/SR.17–32, Feb. 20–Mar. 3, 1951, and to the Commission the following month, Doc. E/CN.11/SR.83, Mar. 8, 1951.

19. For its report, see Doc. E/CN.11/I&T/59, Nov. 1, 1951, and Corr.1, Dec. 3, 1951.

delegates supported the idea of establishing a regional organization of national trade associations and chambers of commerce, but expressed a variety of opinions as to what it should do. (In any case, ICC answered them the following year by setting up a Commission on Asian and Far Eastern Affairs (CAFEA) with its headquarters at New Delhi.) The conference did, however, recommend that countries inside and outside the region discuss periodically their trade plans, export availabilities, and import needs. Finally, it unanimously agreed that another Regional Trade Promotion Conference should be held.

At the invitation of the Philippines this second conference was held at Manila in 1953.[20] It was about as large as the first one, and roughly one-third of the delegates again represented private business interests. A feature of the representation this time, however, was the much larger attendance of nonmember countries of ECAFE, including, with the special permission of ECOSOC,[21] three countries—Finland, Hungary, and Italy—which were not even members of the United Nations. The Executive Secretaries of ECE and ECAFE both thought the conference's prospects of success would be enhanced by a wider participation of non-Asian countries interested in trade with the ECAFE region. But were these to include those European countries that were members of ECE but not of the United Nations?[22] The ECAFE Executive Secretary felt it would be impossible to invite them and ignore Communist China. Britain and the United States wished to minimize the chances of anything like a repetition of the Moscow Economic Conference of businessmen held in 1952, which would certainly have suited the Soviet Union. The Philippines, as host country, was also concerned about the political implications of opening the conference door too widely. The formula finally approved by ECOSOC limited the invitations to members of the United Nations and the three regional commissions. This at least closed the door on Communist China. Of the other Communist bloc countries only Czechoslovakia, Hungary, Poland, and the Soviet Union were represented. The familiar

20. For its report, see Doc. E/CN.11/I&T/84, Mar. 23, 1953.

21. ECOSOC Res. 459(XIV), Dec. 19, 1952.

22. They were at this time: Albania, Austria, Bulgaria, Finland, Hungary, Ireland, Italy, Portugal, Romania, and Switzerland.

motion to seat Communist China was again ruled out of order. The Soviet delegate did not press the issue and presumably mentioned it simply for the record. In fact there were no political fireworks; both the West and the Communist bloc concentrated instead on wooing Asian sympathy.

The substantive recommendations of this second conference largely reaffirmed those passed at Singapore. The Secretariat was asked to report periodically on the progress made in implementing them and also to investigate the long-term demand for the region's exports and the scope for increasing intraregional trade.

The Singapore and Manila Conferences were widely voted a great success. Some of their suggestions were rather thin but there was enough of substance to form a useful program of work for the Secretariat to follow. Both Conferences, however, were concerned with the technical problems of trade promotion rather than the broad issues of commercial policy. The Manila meeting ended without even recommending that a further conference be held. True, an Industry and Trade Committee had existed in ECAFE since 1949. But experience showed that it was more concerned with problems of industrialization than of trade. In order, therefore, to "permit more penetrating and continuous work on trade matters" the Executive Secretary suggested in 1954 that the Industry and Trade Committee create a permanent subcommittee on trade.[23] Most Asian countries favored the proposal. Australia, Britain, Japan, Pakistan, and the United States were against it; Thailand remained skeptical. That the opposition included those with the largest stake in the region's trade did not escape notice. Britain and the United States believed that commercial policy was a global matter best discussed within the framework of the General Agreement on Tariffs and Trade (GATT). Many Asians, however, regarded this organization as a club whose rules were more appropriate to relations among rich countries than those between rich and poor countries. Not many ECAFE countries, in fact, belonged to GATT.[24] What Britain and the United States ap-

23. Doc. E/CN.11/I&T/98, Nov. 13, 1953.

24. The following are not members: Afghanistan, Iran, Laos, Nepal, the Philippines, South Korea, South Viet-Nam, Taiwan, and Thailand. Cambodia participates under special arrangements. Associate members of ECAFE whose international relations are a British responsibility are included in GATT by virtue of British membership.

peared to fear was the creation of a special ECAFE trade forum in which Asians could be organized as a pressure group to question the doctrines of GATT and the policies based upon them. But this was so obviously a situation for which the Lahore Agreement [25] had been designed that they acquiesced in the decision to accept the proposal.

By 1956 the Executive Secretary had come to the conclusion that the inordinate length of the Industry and Trade Committee's annual session was discouraging governments from sparing their top-level officials to attend. One way to shorten its agenda, he suggested, was to make the Trade Subcommittee a full committee, thereby removing one stage in the process of reporting to the Commission. A number of countries argued, however, that industry and trade should not be considered in separate committees. Some believed a new committee would place even greater burdens on governments. India thought a subcommittee was more efficient and less formal than a committee. The governments clearly needed more time to consider the idea and did not, in fact, approve it until the following year. Interestingly enough, the formal proposer on this second occasion was Japan which, a few years earlier, had opposed a trade subcommittee.

What the Executive Secretary had suggested in 1948 [26] had at last been approved. No doubt it would have been premature to have created a trade committee so early. On the other hand, a gestation period of nine years suggests the lack of any real drive behind the development of cooperation in this field. Some of the difficulties may be illustrated by considering what happened to the recommendations of the Singapore and Manila Trade Promotion Conferences.

As Asian countries reached independence and became responsible for their own commercial policies they were faced with the task of building up machinery for trade promotion and regulation. For this purpose they urgently needed more officials competent to undertake the duties of commercial counselors and attachés. In 1949, for example, only nine Asian governments had trade promotion departments and only India maintained extensive trade offices abroad. Several smaller countries had no over-

25. See p. 51.
26. See p. 44.

seas trade representation at all. The Singapore conference recommended that the training courses of technical assistance programs, whether under United Nations, Colombo Plan, or United States auspices, include trade promotion techniques and procedures. At the Secretariat's request such training had already been included in the United Nations fellowship program. The Manila Conference felt that more needed to be done and urged ECAFE and TAA to organize on-the-spot training as soon as possible. It was not until 1956, however, that the Secretariat put forward any scheme.[27] Under the somewhat misleading title of a training center, two eight-week training courses were to be organized, one in 1957, the other in 1958. The first would be held in India, the second in Japan, and TAA would help to finance both by providing fellowships for the trainees. A number of countries still thought the size of the problem warranted the establishment of a permanent regional training center and Pakistan offered host facilities for its location. The Secretariat reckoned this would cost at a modest estimate about $175,000 a year. That amount of money would be difficult to obtain on a continuing basis from any single source. If TAA provided the funds initially, it would be unable to finance other ECAFE regional projects of high priority. It was therefore decided to await an assessment of the two proposed training courses before making any attempt to establish a permanent center.[28] As it turned out United Nations technical assistance funds were unable even to finance the first of the two courses until 1959. It was then held in Japan and not India, as the original scheme suggested. Nineteen officials from twelve ECAFE countries and territories attended. Japan provided the bulk of the lecturers, though some lectures were also given by British, French, Soviet, and United States officials. A second and similar training center was organized at New Delhi in 1961. As far as the United Nations was concerned it had taken eight years to organize a modest response to the recommendation passed by the Singapore conference.

Largely as a result of the Singapore and Manila conferences ECAFE became increasingly concerned about removing or reducing obstacles in the way of the smooth functioning of foreign

27. Doc. E/CN.11/I&T/120, Nov. 23, 1955.
28. See Report of Committee on Trade, Doc. E/CN.11/472, Jan. 30, 1958.

trade. The emphasis of the Secretariat's work shifted from research on intraregional trade and payments to the study of certain technical trading problems and the performance of practical services. Commercial arbitration is a good case in point.

Asian countries had no need of arbitration facilities as long as their overseas trade was being handled by foreign firms with head offices elsewhere. But when this trade passed into Asian hands their lack of adequately developed arbitration facilities became increasingly obvious from the upward trend in the number of trade disputes. The Singapore and Manila conferences had recommended that countries develop arbitration associations and facilities and negotiate arbitration agreements with each other. The ICC continued to urge the need for these developments.[29] The ECAFE Trade Subcommittee decided, however, that exhortation needed to be backed by detailed proposals. The Secretariat should first publish the texts of all relevant laws, treaties, and court decisions bearing upon commercial arbitration. This compilation should also include the rules of all arbitral bodies in the region, a description of their activities, and a commentary on the arbitration system of each country. From this material the Secretariat should then identify the main legal and practical problems affecting the functioning of international commercial arbitration in the region. This highly technical study was actually entrusted to the United Nations Office of Legal Affairs. On its completion a working party of arbitration experts was expected to draft specific recommendations.

Progress reports on the investigation were presented to the Trade Committee in 1959 and 1961.[30] Experts or expert bodies from eighteen ECAFE countries and territories helped the United Nations Office of Legal Affairs to collect some of the data required and assess the uses, adequacy, and difficulties of commercial arbitration. The results showed, among other things, that no at-

29. An ICC initiative to bring conventions concluded under the League of Nations up to date led ECOSOC to convene a United Nations Conference on Commercial Arbitration in 1958 at which a draft convention on the Recognition and Enforcement of Foreign Arbitral Awards was agreed. Among ECAFE countries only Ceylon, India, and Japan indicated a willingness to participate in this Conference.

30. See Arbitral Legislation and Facilities in Certain Countries of the ECAFE Region, Doc. E/CN.11/Trade/L.19, and Add.1; and Commercial Arbitration in the ECAFE Region, Doc. E/CN.11/Trade/L.38, Nov. 23, 1960.

tempt had been made in the region to evolve a standard arbitration clause for inclusion in trade contracts; in a few countries no legislation existed to give validity to arbitral awards, and there was no uniformity about the provisions of the legislation that did exist. By the beginning of 1962 the investigation was sufficiently advanced for an expert working party to begin formulating specific recommendations. The length of time taken to reach this point is largely explained by the magnitude and complexity of the subject. Even ECE, in much more developed conditions, has been dealing with it continuously for over eight years.

Another hindrance to domestic and foreign traders that ECAFE sought increasingly to remove or reduce was the needless complexity of the foreign trade regulations and procedures administered by Asian governments. In the aftermath of colonial rule the spirit in which these were applied was often biased against the private trader for much the same reason as prejudices were manifested against private foreign investment. The problem was as much to remove discriminatory restrictions, even when they were used selectively to promote and protect domestic industry and employment, as to simplify and streamline formalities and procedures regarding the administration of these controls.

The Singapore conference agreed that an effort should be made to draft a convention for the simplification of customs regulations. Five years later the Secretariat investigated the progress made in this direction. Its report [31] covered such matters as import and export licensing, customs procedures and administration, quality control of exports, business travel, trade complaints, industrial property rights, and government purchase. The Trade Subcommittee accepted the Secretariat's suggestion that a Working Party on Customs Administration be convened to study intensively selected aspects of customs formalities and procedures and make practical proposals for their improvement and simplification. The GATT and the Brussels Customs Co-operation Council offered to assist the Working Party, though in fact their cooperation did not amount to much.[32] The Secretariat meanwhile

31. Regulations and Procedures concerning the Conduct of International Trade, Doc. E/CN.11/I&T/Sub.4/7, Oct. 4, 1956.

32. Each prepared a paper for the first session of the Working Party and in addition the Customs Co-operation Council, though not GATT, sent an observer to the meeting.

continued to report the progress made by ECAFE countries in simplifying their export and import licensing procedures.[33]

The Working Party on Customs Administration, which consisted largely of senior customs officials, held its first session in 1958.[34] It made a number of recommendations on, for example, simplifying and improving export and import formalities; documentary requirements; streamlining procedures relating to the examination, testing, classification, detention, and bonding of goods; customs valuation; procedures affecting businessmen and tourists; and, on cooperation between customs administrations. It also urged countries to adopt certain GATT conventions and agreements relating to the freer movement of goods and passengers to which the Secretariat had already drawn their attention.[35]

The most important decision taken at the second meeting of the Working Party in 1960 was to accept a Secretariat proposal that the recommendations already agreed upon should be formulated into an ECAFE Code of Recommended Customs Procedures.[36] This would have a number of advantages. It would give the recommendations a more permanent character, consolidate the progress made, and impart a sense of purpose and direction to future work on this whole problem. The Code, which contains 41 recommendations, is not a code of law but of practice or, rather, of the principles on which practice should be based. Nor is it mandatory. Governments were merely asked to notify the Executive Secretary within six months whether they generally endorsed it and which, if any, of its recommendations they could not accept. Great importance is attached to this follow-up action. Thus, while an endorsement does not mean an obligation to implement the Code in its entirety, the Working Party or Trade Committee will certainly expect countries not accepting all its provisions to explain the exceptions they make. In this way the

33. For report made to the first session of the Trade Committee, see Doc. E/CN.11/Trade/L.6, 1958.

34. For report, see Doc. E/CN.11/Trade/L.17, 1958.

35. E.g., Code of Standard Practice for Consular Formalities (1952); Recommendations on Standard Practices for Documentary Requirements for the Importation of Goods (1952); and International Convention to Facilitate the Importation of Commercial Samples and Advertising Material (1955).

36. For the complete Code, see Doc. E/CN.11/Trade/L.40, 1960.

Code seeks by moral pressure to produce not only greater uniformity out of widely differing practices but a more liberal treatment of traders and travelers whom customs authorities have tended in the past to harass unduly. It calls, in other words, for a change in entrenched attitudes as well as habits.

Among the other matters that the Working Party is due to consider are the simplification of documentary requirements; relations between trade associations and customs authorities; cooperation in the exchange and training of customs staff, including the possibility of establishing a regional training and research center in customs administration; customs terminology; and customs valuation. This last subject is particularly crucial because changes in the methods of customs valuation can completely offset the effect of any agreement to change tariff levels. It is hoped in 1963, with BTAO assistance, to start a training course in customs administration.

Many of the noticeably growing number of trade disputes in the region seemed to relate to quality specifications and reflected an insufficient awareness among Asian countries of the importance of adopting appropriate standards for their export commodities. Greater standardization, by permitting better grading and quality control, would help to increase export income as well as avoid disputes. The Singapore and Manila conferences discussed the subject and on their recommendation ECAFE, in cooperation with the International Standards Organisation (ISO), has acted as a clearinghouse of information on the standards being adopted in the region. Countries have been urged to set up national standards organizations and join ISO, which is the international body best placed to help them.[37] It is fair to add, however, that the work programs of various ECAFE subcommittees and working parties include the technical problems of standardizing a number of commodities and materials. It is also possible through international cooperation to standardize general conditions of sale or to produce a standard form of contract for the region's export products. ECE has been engaged in this work for some years, and in 1961 India suggested to the Trade Committee that ECAFE follow suit.

37. Only India, Indonesia, Iran, Japan, and Pakistan have national standards institutions and all except Pakistan belong to ISO.

A number of other ways in which ECAFE has been helping the cause of trade promotion deserves a brief mention. On the recommendation of the Singapore and Manila conferences the Secretariat began, somewhat belatedly, to produce a series of marketing surveys for some of the region's principal exports. The commodities selected were those for which relatively less information on their marketing problems was available than, say, for tin or rubber. Surveys have thus been made for major edible oils and oil seeds,[38] hides and skins,[39] spices and spice products,[40] and, with the cooperation of FAO, on the coconut industry.[41] FAO also supplied one on jute.[42]

The possibility of organizing an Asian trade fair is another suggestion which has been a long time maturing. The Singapore Conference thought a permanent exhibition of the region's commercial products would help to promote trade and asked the Secretariat to prepare a report on the idea. Nothing appears to have been done until 1956 when the Secretariat presented to the Trade Committee a number of recommendations on the organization of international fairs and exhibitions.[43] Over a year later the United States suggested that ECAFE organize an Asian regional fair rather than trade promotion talks. But no positive decision was taken on the proposal until 1961. Even then the first inclination of the governments was to leave the preparatory explorations entirely to the Secretariat. The Executive Secretary refused, however, to accept this evasion of governmental responsibility and succeeded in persuading them to nominate representatives to work with the Secretariat on the problems of organizing such a fair.[44] It has been agreed to hold a fair in November and December 1963 and to accept the invitation of Pakistan to hold it in Karachi. Only members and associate members of ECAFE will be eligible to participate.

Much of the work program laid down by the Singapore and

38. UN Sales No.:1956.II.F.5.

39. Doc. E/CN.11/I&T/Sub.4/4, Sept. 25, 1956, and Corr.1, 1956.

40. Doc. E/CN.11/Trade/L.13, Dec. 26, 1958.

41. Doc. ECAFE/I&T/Sub.4/4, Sept. 25, 1956.

42. This was a reprint from the FAO *Monthly Bulletin of Agricultural Eonomics and Statistics, 9,* No. 12, and *10,* No. 1.

43. Doc. ECAFE/I&T/Sub.4/5, Sept. 14, 1956.

44. Report of the fourth session of the Committee on Trade, E/CN.11/Trade/11, Dec. 16, 1957.

Manila Conferences aimed at improving the "climate" for trade expansion. If results came slowly, it was largely because no great priority was given to it in the distribution of the Secretariat's resources. But a more important shortcoming of these activities was that they did not attack the fundamental trade problems of ECAFE countries in the light of their long-run prospects for economic development. They did not, for example, bring Asian governments together to consider how best to strengthen their mutual trade relations. And that, after all, was one of the stated aims of ECAFE.

In 1954 the Industry and Trade Committee asked the Secretariat to examine the scope for expanding intraregional trade in specific commodities. The results were issued two years later as brief background notes on iron ore, coal, salt, fish, and fish products.[45] The report did not present any strong case for intergovernmental cooperation to raise the level of this trade. The most comprehensive trade study made by the Secretariat up to this time dealt, instead, with trade between Asia and Europe and was prepared in collaboration with the secretariats of ECE and FAO.[46] Indeed, it was really an ECE initiative that first started ECAFE debating the idea of organized intergovernmental meetings to discuss actual trading opportunities and problems.

In 1954, ECE drew the attention of ECOSOC to the valuable experience gained from its intra-European trade consultations[47] and suggested that the technique could usefully be extended by organizing interregional trade consultations under the auspices of the three regional commissions.[48] The Council asked the Secretary-General to examine the practicability of the proposal and present the assessment to ECAFE and ECLA for their opinion.[49] Before this report was issued, however, a senior ECE official informally explained the ECE technique to the chief delegates at an ECAFE Trade Subcommittee meeting in January 1955. Their re-

45. Doc. E/CN.11/I&T/Sub.4/15, 1954. A further study of trade in minerals, which included other commodities besides coal and iron ore, was issued in 1960. Doc. E/CN.11/Trade/L.30, Dec. 14, 1959.

46. *Trade Between Asia and Europe,* UN Sales No.:1953.II.F.3.

47. On the character of these consultations, see Wightman, *Economic Co-operation.*

48. ECE Res. 5(IX), 1954.

49. ECOSOC Res. 535B(XVIII), Aug. 5, 1954.

actions provided an instructive pointer to the position countries were likely to adopt when the proposal formally came before the Commission a few months later.

The United States delegate, with angry emotion, castigated the idea as a bureaucratic fantasy. Trade, he said, was a matter for private business and could not be promoted by government officials. The ECE consultations, moreover, encouraged bilateral trading, which was bad. The United Kingdom and Netherlands response was also negative. The Japanese and Indonesian delegates, on the other hand, enthusiastically supported the idea, and those of Afghanistan, Burma, Cambodia, Hong Kong, Laos, Malaya, the Philippines, and South Viet-Nam were distinctly interested. French and Soviet views were also positive, while the Indian delegate appeared to favor whatever proposal of this kind other Asian countries thought valuable. The probable positions of Pakistan, South Korea, Taiwan, and Thailand remained uncertain.

Just before the Commission session in March 1955 the question was briefly discussed as an agenda item of the Industry and Trade Committee. While few significant changes of attitude were revealed on this occasion, political mistrust was much nearer the surface, especially when Burma, India, and the Soviet Union suggested that Communist China be included in any organized trade consultations. Some countries, the South Korean delegate bluntly replied, "seemed to understand that inter-regional cooperation meant trade with Red China"; Taiwan seconded his remark.[50] In an atmosphere of deepening suspicion even Japan greeted the proposal cautiously. As no general consensus emerged from the discussion, the Committee made no recommendation.[51]

The Commission seemed unlikely to do much better when, a few days later, it considered the Secretary-General's assessment of the ECE proposal. The report[52] merely described the ECE technique and indicated somewhat vaguely the possible value of interregional trade consultations, but left the countries them-

50. Trade with Communist China, said the Philippines delegate to the Trade Committee in 1958, would lead to an infiltration into the Philippines of an alien ideology and serve to encourage the peace-disturbing minority of Huks who were now in the last stage of liquidation. Doc. Trade/SR/3, Jan. 22, 1958.

51. Doc. E/CN.11/I&T/116, June 9, 1955.

52. Doc. E/CN.11/403, Feb. 15, 1955.

selves to judge the merits of the proposal. After private informal discussions and little public debate, the Commission accepted a compromise resolution jointly sponsored by India and the United States, which endorsed in principle the idea of trade consultations between interested member countries of the United Nations in general, not just of the regional commissions, and asked ECOSOC to consider the "most effective means of exploring new techniques and avenues for the expansion of international trade." [53] ECAFE had simply returned the ball to ECOSOC. This was not helpful to the Council, which felt it was a matter for the regional commissions to decide.[54] All it could do was to put the ball right back in the ECAFE court.

The following year the Commission and the Trade Subcommittee accordingly returned to the question. No new points were argued and the lines of division became, if anything, even more sharply defined. On the whole, the pro-Western countries were firmly against interregional trade talks; the "neutral" or non-aligned Asian countries and the Soviet Union favored them. This suggested that the real difference between the two sides lay in their approach to relations with the Communist bloc. The opposition feared the proposal would give the Communists a ready-made opportunity to seduce Asians politically with trade offers. It might also provide Communist China with a backdoor entry into the United Nations. The deadlock became so complete on the issue that in 1957 it was finally dropped.

Meanwhile, Japan had suggested that the Secretariat explore, instead, the possibility of organizing trade promotion talks between Asian countries only. If all the outside powers were excluded there would be no case for any Communist country to participate. To make sure the point was clearly understood, Japan proposed that the talks should be held *in camera* with no minutes recorded or observers present and should, in effect, exclude any consideration of trade with Communist China.[55] If

53. *ECAFE Annual Report to ECOSOC, 19 February 1954–7 April 1955*, Doc. E/CN.11/407, Apr. 7, 1955, p. 25.

54. It is fair to add in this connection that in September 1955 ECLA also refused to commit itself.

55. One of the Japanese conditions for the talks provides that they should be held within the framework of UN resolutions and without prejudice to the international obligations of the participants. See Doc. E/CN.11/I&T/133, May 24, 1957. On

Japan hoped these terms would settle all further doubts it was quickly disabused; it took much argument and several delaying moves to decide the issue.

Asian reactions to the proposal immediately disclosed a continuing division along political lines. The "neutrals" favored it; most of the pro-Western group did not. Each side disagreed with the other on the scope for expansion of intraregional trade and hence on the relevance and likely results of adopting the ECE technique. The supporters saw the talks as a convenient and inexpensive means by which countries without extensive commercial services could discuss actual trading opportunities and problems on a bilateral basis in a multilateral setting. The opponents believed the proposal ran counter to the professed aim of all ECAFE countries to encourage world-wide multilateral trading. Even on the supporters' own argument, they maintained, the talks were unnecessary since Asian countries could easily engage in bilateral trade consultations without using ECAFE.[56] Some still apparently feared that regional trade consultations might involve dealings with Communist China despite the fact that the United Nations General Assembly had long ago made it impossible for ECAFE to recognize the existence, much less invite the participation, of the government of mainland China. Pakistan wondered whether India and Japan, the two most powerful supporters, had some hidden purpose in mind and so sought to delay a decision in the hope of finding out. Even the Secretariat was divided. Executive Secretary Lokanathan thought the whole idea unsuitable for the ECAFE region and did not see how Asian governments could be made to talk to one another as the ECE technique implied. The chief of the Industry and Trade Division, on the other hand, enthusiastically supported the Japanese proposal.

two counts this condition clearly excluded any discussion of trade with Communist China, much less its participation: 1) since General Assembly Res. 396(V), Dec. 14, 1950, recommended that the "attitude adopted by the General Assembly . . . concerning any such question [when more than one authority claimed to be the government entitled to represent a member state in the UN] should be taken into account in other organs of the United Nations," and the Assembly never took up this specific question, and, 2) since General Assembly Res. 500(V), May 18, 1951, recommended that all UN members embargo exports of implements of war and strategic goods to Communist China.

56. For a summary of the arguments, see Report of the Committee on Trade, first session, Doc. E/CN.11/472, Jan. 30, 1958.

The West neither opposed nor encouraged the idea of purely Asian trade talks but doubted their usefulness. Britain certainly, and perhaps other Western countries as well, feared they would give Japan a commercial advantage. Australia, New Zealand, and the Soviet Union disliked being excluded. Some wondered whether Japan was not bent upon the ultimate creation of an Asian customs union or common market. If the Japanese government had been primarily motivated by a desire to gain a commercial advantage over the West the proposal would most probably have originated in the Economic Affairs Bureau of its Ministry of Foreign Affairs or in its Ministry of International Trade and Industry (MITI). In fact, both departments seriously doubted whether such talks would benefit Japan at all. The idea actually originated in the United Nations Bureau of the Ministry of Foreign Affairs. This group of officials had grown dissatisfied with the work of ECAFE and was keen, if only for reasons of bureaucratic self-importance, to see its functions develop beyond those of research and disseminating information. When the proposal was not acted upon at the committee level, saving face became an added incentive to get it accepted by the Commission. Japan worked hard on the United States, Pakistan, and other possible obstructionists to persuade them at least to abstain when a final vote was taken.

The issue came to a head at the Commission session of 1958. The opposition still sought to postpone a decision. This time, however, Executive Secretary Narasimhan, unlike his predecessor, threw his influence behind the proposal. After privately reminding the outside powers of the Lahore Agreement, he strongly appealed to the Commission for a final vote. His intervention earned a public rebuke from Pakistan, which still suspected an Indian plot somewhere. Nevertheless, the decisive vote was taken and, with the outside powers abstaining, the supporters carried the day. Except for Australia and New Zealand which voted against, the outside powers abstained.[57]

The first intraregional trade promotion talks were held in January 1959. Despite some groping, the experiment was thought sufficiently worthwhile, even by those who had originally op-

57. Doc. E/CN.11/483, June 3, 1958. For the terms of the resolution passed, see Doc. E/CN.11/479, Mar. 11, 1958.

posed the idea, that it has since become an annual event. The talks are held at the beginning of the year as a prelude to the Trade Committee. Of the 18 ECAFE countries and territories entitled to attend, between 13 and 15 have actually participated. Only Nepal has never been represented. Each session follows much the same pattern. An opening plenary discussion on problems of common concern is followed by a series of bilateral and multilateral talks on specific commodities and interests. When the latter are concluded the delegates reassemble in plenary for a preliminary general appraisal of the whole session.[58]

The multilateral talks inevitably considered many problems such as shipping services, ocean freight rates, trade restrictions, quality control, commercial disputes, and price stabilization, which figured on the agenda and work program of the Trade Committee. The essential point about these sessions, however, and perhaps their greatest value, is the opportunity they gave to Asian countries to achieve a greater sense of identity and develop a "club atmosphere," unhampered and uninhibited by the presence of outsiders. Indeed, the chief complaint of government officials is that they are not sufficiently informal. The agenda has been too long and the officials too numerous for other than formal statements. A thorough discussion of a few topics in a less formal atmosphere would be more effective.

Unlike the ECE technique, every delegation was not expected to talk to every other delegation.[59] Not that those politically estranged were at all sensitive; for instance a number of countries that had maintained diplomatic relations with Communist China, nevertheless had talks with Taiwan. In addition, the consultations provided convenient and inexpensive commercial contacts and intelligence for the many Asian countries without consular or trade representation in other countries of the region. The size, composition, and quality of the delegations have varied considerably and it may well have been difficult, in some of the bilateral talks, for the smaller and weaker ones to deal with the larger and more powerful ones. On the other hand, the talks do

58. See, e.g., the Executive Secretary's report on the first session, Doc. E/CN.11/Trade/L.22, Jan. 22, 1959. Subsequent reports were included in ECAFE's *Annual Report to ECOSOC.*

59. Wightman, *Economic Co-operation,* p. 224.

not replace actual trade negotiations; they merely facilitate the type of contacts that precede them. Unlike official trade delegations sent from one capital to another, trading opportunities can be explored in an atmosphere less dominated by the need to conduct specific negotiations. Their value is well illustrated by the experience of Japan.

In 1959 Japan approached the first session of trade talks seeking export opportunities. This was clear from the inclusion in its delegation of representatives of private export interests. The problem it quickly came up against, however, was Japanese imports. Most South-east Asian countries were anxious to reduce their trade deficits with Japan by persuading it to import more of their goods. A larger demand for Japanese goods could only be created by larger Japanese purchases. Burma and Thailand, for example, pressed it to buy more of their rice. But rice consumption per head in Japan has been falling and the country is now more or less self-sufficient in this food grain. Other commodities would have to be found and made competitive in quality, specifications, and price. One such product discovered through these talks was Thai corn and Japan has since been importing it in increasing quantities. It is also very much interested in raw materials like rubber, minerals, and timber and is prepared to give technical assistance to South-east Asian countries for improving the productivity of their agriculture, mines, and forests. As a result of this first session, Japanese delegations to subsequent talks included more representatives of private buying interests. Thus, while not indispensable, the talks have proved sufficiently useful to Japan that it would miss them if they were not held.

The impact on other countries is harder to assess. Much depended on the subsequent action taken by governments or private business. Cambodia, India, Indonesia, the Philippines, South Viet-Nam, and Thailand reported practical results in terms of trade and travel impediments lifted or reduced, contracts placed, and trade agreements concluded, but the details are not available. There have been cases such as Taiwan, where officials frankly admitted that, once back in their own capitals, they became too preoccupied with day-to-day work to find time for specific follow-up action. Philippine officials claim that what they learned at the talks helped their subsequent trade negotiations with Japan and South Korea. Sometimes private business is left to exploit any trade opening revealed by them. It is not, however, easy for most Asian countries to build up quickly new trading connections and habits. Simply exploring the possibilities and special problems of intraregional trade is still a comparatively new experience. But ECAFE has at least emancipated their thinking from an exclusive concern with the problems of interregional trade.

A complete picture of ECAFE activities in the field of trade cannot overlook its role as a court of opinion which hears and judges the hopes, fears, and complaints of its members. Sometimes the issues raised proved to be of only passing concern. For instance, in 1951 Asian governments suddenly became worried that Western rearmament would cause a shortage of capital goods and disrupt their development plans. Pakistan wanted a special conference of exporters and importers to discuss the situation and ensure adequate supplies and an equitable distribution of these goods. The West opposed new machinery for this purpose and preferred to settle difficulties bilaterally. Under pressure, however, they promised to review and improve the channels of supply and agreed that the Secretariat's good offices should be used to facilitate consultations between buyers and sellers.[60] The Secretariat kept the position under review until supplies became much easier a few years later. The instability of primary commodity prices, on the other hand, has been a constant complaint about which ECAFE could do little more than regularly record a general sentiment in favor of greater stability.[61] Other complaints have been prosecuted to greater effect. One such case is that of ocean freight rates.

During the last decade Asian governments have repeatedly complained about excessive and discriminatory freight rates allegedly charged by shipping lines that belonged to combines or were parties to conference agreements. Discriminatory rates, they argued, tended to direct trade along certain channels and made it harder to develop others. In short, they perverted the theory of

60. Docs. E/CN.11/SR.83, Mar. 8, 1951 and SR.89, Mar. 11, 1951, and Doc. E/CN.11/305, Mar. 7, 1951.

61. It has also kept governments regularly informed of the considerable attention given to this problem by other international organizations.

multilateral trading. The big maritime powers, with Britain as their chief spokesman,[62] admitted that market sharing and price fixing agreements existed, but insisted that the real problem was inadequate and inefficient port facilities. Congested ports like Colombo, for example, made for slow turnarounds and higher operating costs. The policy of the conference lines was to maximize long-term earnings rather than charge what the traffic will immediately bear. They aimed to offer a regular service at stable rates.

In 1955, the Trade Subcommittee requested the Secretariat to make a study of ocean freight rates affecting the trade of the region. Britain thought that "intergovernmental bodies or individual governments should not concern themselves with the subject," but acquiesced in the proposal provided the inquiry was carried out in close consultation with the United Nations Transport and Communications Commission.[63] In any event, the Secretariat could only make a preliminary assessment of the problem, as the information made available to it was not sufficient for detailed analysis. Nevertheless, its report [64] showed that neither plaintiff nor defendant was without a case to argue.

The ECAFE region is only part of the world-wide market for shipping. A host of complex factors, therefore, determined the rate to or from a particular port or for a particular commodity. Abnormal congestion, which existed in almost every port of the region, was certainly one of them. For this reason governments should give the highest possible priority to expanding and modernizing port facilities. It was no less clear, however, that shipping cartels used punitive and discriminatory practices to frighten away potential competitors and were influenced by the highest cost operators in fixing their rates. Unfortunately the history of shipping shows no happy medium between rate wars and combination. The long-run answer was for Asian countries to build up their own merchant fleets perhaps in some cases by organizing jointly-owned shipping lines. Meanwhile, the real problem was to prevent the abuses of combination. For this pur-

62. The Japanese flag is the only Asian flag in the shipping conferences concerned with the trade of the ECAFE region.

63. Official Records, Committee on Industry and Trade, eighth session, Doc. E/CN.11/I&T/124, June 18, 1956.

64. Doc. E/CN.11/I&T/Sub.4/3, Sept. 12, 1956.

pose the Secretariat suggested that governments set up freight study units to investigate complaints. They should also encourage the formation of exporters' associations and support their negotiations with the shipping lines. Finally, the shipping conferences should file copies of their agreements, including their tariff rates, with Asian governments. The aim of these recommendations, in other words, was to make the conference lines justify their rates to the Asian shipper.

Not surprisingly the maritime powers disliked the Secretariat's suggestions and continued to assert that shipping difficulties should be settled through private commercial channels. British delegates were instructed at first to oppose tooth and nail any resolution inviting governments to interfere. The less governments intervened, Britain argued, "the less was the free flow of international trade and shipping likely to be artificially distorted." [65] Governments could more appropriately act to improve port facilities. But Asian countries remained unpersuaded and demanded further study and action. In the face of so much determination, the maritime powers relented to the extent of tacitly accepting a recommendation that countries might usefully set up consultative machinery between the shippers and conference lines with, if necessary, a government representative as chairman.[66] By the end of 1961 India had set up such machinery and Pakistan a Freight Study Unit. In addition it is known that other Asian governments have held ad hoc consultations with shipping lines from time to time and obtained some redress of their complaints. Even so, Asian countries in general remain dissatisfied with the services and charges of the conference lines.[67] The whole subject is being kept under review. What ECAFE has achieved so far is at least to make the conference lines much more public relations conscious.

In the ECAFE court of opinion the defendant has not always

65. Official Records, Trade Committee, third session, Doc. E/CN.11/Trade/9, Dec. 13, 1957.

66. See Trade Committee Report, third session, Doc. E/CN.11/521, Feb. 17, 1960.

67. There is a deeper dilemma underlying shipping costs in the region. So long as intraregional trade remains comparatively small (see p. 301), freight charges are liable to remain comparatively high. This again reflects the general problem of economic underdevelopment. The way around it is to take consciously planned action to increase intraregional trade.

been the outside powers. On occasion an Asian country has found itself in the dock. For instance, in 1956 Afghanistan bitterly arraigned Pakistan for allegedly closing its frontiers to the transit of Afghan goods.[68] Pakistan hotly denied the charge and resented Afghanistan's action in prosecuting the issue before ECAFE.[69] As transit facilities vitally affected Laos and Nepal as well, ECAFE was able to raise the issue to a more general plane by asking the Secretariat to study the problem for all landlocked countries in the region. The Secretariat's report[70] recommended that the countries concerned negotiate bilateral agreements in conformity with the principles of certain existing international agreements and statutes.[71] Afghanistan refused at first to accept the suggestion but subsequently concluded a transit agreement with Pakistan. Agreements were also made by Laos with Thailand and South Viet-Nam.

Undoubtedly the most portentous ECAFE trade debates recently have been on the implications for the region of the formation of the European Economic Community (EEC), or Common Market, and the European Free Trade Association (EFTA).[72] The Secretariat has steadily kept Asian governments informed on the progress and policies of these significant experiments in European economic integration. Asian countries fear, above all, that EEC by design or force of circumstances will discriminate against their exports. This could happen in more than one way. The common external tariff and agricultural policy of EEC, its possible substitution of high internal taxes for customs duties, might reduce its

68. See, e.g., Doc. E/CN.11/451, Mar. 18, 1957, and Official Records, Committee on Industry and Trade, eighth session, Doc. E/CN.11/I&T/124, June 18, 1956. The complaint was first made by Afghanistan to the Second Committee of the General Assembly in December 1955.

69. Officials in Karachi maintained that tighter Pakistan control over smuggling across its borders with Afghanistan was the root cause of the latter's complaint, especially as foreign trade is an Afghan government monopoly. Trade and politics have been badly entangled in Afghanistan's relations with Pakistan since World War II. The Pathan tribes who inhabit both sides of the frontier, and Afghanistan's proposal that they should form an independent "Paktoonistan," are two important sources of trouble.

70. Doc. ECAFE/I&T/Sub.4/2, Aug. 29, 1956.

71. E.g., Barcelona Statute on Freedom of Transit (1922) and Article V of GATT.

72. For perhaps the two best debates, see Official Records, Trade Committee, first and fourth sessions, Docs. E/CN.11/Trade/3, June 6, 1958, and Trade/12, Dec. 18, 1957.

demand for commodities such as tea, coffee, tobacco, hides and skins, coconut and vegetable oil products, textiles, and other low-cost manufactures. In addition, the special preferences granted by EEC to its associated territories overseas might divert some of this demand from Asia to Africa. They could also divert European capital away from Asia.[73]

Australia and New Zealand, as big exporters of primary products, shared many of the fears expressed. For Japan, the possible indirect effects were as worrying as the direct because any reduction in the export earnings of South-east Asia adversely affected a market for Japanese goods far larger than the Western European. In the long run, moreover, Japan might well face stiffer competition in the ECAFE region from the exports of EEC countries. To the Soviet Union all these forebodings were useful grist for its political mill. The alternative it preached, however, was state trading and long-term bilateral contracts with the Communist bloc.

The French gave the impression at first that, whatever ECAFE might think, EEC would do as it pleased and left the Netherlands to bear the brunt of the Asian assault. But when ECAFE countries showed no disposition to exempt EEC from the obligation at least to explain its actions, France became more public relations minded and assumed the main responsibility for reassuring them. It thought the Asians were being excessively pessimistic and apprehensive. If, as it expected, the European Common Market brought about a more rapid economic growth of its member countries, that was bound to create more trade for the ECAFE region than it diverted away. By 1961 the French were quoting figures to show this was already happening.[74] But the Asians and Australians were not convinced that the point had already been

73. For a number of reasons Asian countries have been less worried about the possible consequences of the European Free Trade Association (EFTA). The members of EFTA have no common external tariff and do not propose to give their overseas territories any special trade or investment preferences. Their exports to non-member countries are far larger than their exports to each other. Finally, EFTA agreed that a great number of primary products would be treated as if they originated within EFTA's area irrespective of their actual origin. If Britain joins the European Common Market, EFTA will presumably cease to exist but Asian anxieties will almost certainly be heightened.

74. Official Records, Trade Committee, fourth session, Doc. E/CN.11/Trade/12, Dec. 18, 1957.

proven or was likely to prove true in the future. There was no use in EEC being prepared to consider their export interests only when real evidence of damage was produced, they argued, for by then it would be too late to rectify the harm done.

Every Asian country naturally viewed EEC from the standpoint of the possible effects on its own export products. The prospect each faced was not exactly the same. Behind the differences, however, has lain a common recognition that EEC would inevitably strengthen the relative bargaining power of the rich countries at a time when ECAFE countries are passing through a critical stage in their economic development. Their export earnings are growing too slowly to provide adequate foreign exchange resources for their mounting import requirements. Except for a few commodities such as rubber, oil, and minerals, the prospects for raising these earnings seem bleak. The gap between their capacity to import and the volume of imports needed to maintain a reasonable rate of economic growth is widening.

This long-term foreign exchange problem would exist even if EEC and EFTA did not. There has perhaps been a tendency for Asian governments to attribute to these blocs trading difficulties that are not, in fact, of their making. But at least this defensive reaction has left them better prepared than before to consider how various forms of regional economic integration could help accelerate their own economic development. As this challenging task holds large implications for the future character and scope of cooperation through ECAFE, further consideration of it has been left to a later section.[75]

75. See pp. 299–305.

CHAPTER 13

Social Problems

Although social problems were not explicitly included at first in the terms of reference of the regional commissions for Asia, Europe, and Latin America, ECOSOC early drew their attention to the social aspects of economic development.[1] In doing so it clearly implied that such matters were not outside their competence. But apart from housing, it was some years before the social aspects of economic development became an integral part of ECAFE's work program. The initiative behind this development came largely from the United Nations Bureau of Social Affairs.

The first step was taken in 1949, when regional social welfare advisers were stationed at Bangkok, Geneva, and Santiago to help organize the Advisory Social Welfare Services part of the United Nations regular program of technical assistance. In 1954 the Bureau suggested that small social affairs units should be permanently established within the secretariats of the regional commissions. These would enable the Bureau to keep in closer touch with social development and problems in the regions, to collect more reliable up-to-date information, to give its staff more actual field experience, and to assist the operational work of TAA more effectively. Perhaps also a tinge of envy at the secure footing of the Division of Economic Affairs in the regions, and a sense of inferiority toward it, lay behind the Bureau's desire to create stronger outposts in the regional commissions. The Secretary-

1. E.g., ECOSOC Res. 155(VII), Aug. 13, 1948, and 179(VIII), Mar. 4, 1949.

General accepted the suggestion[2] and in 1955 a small social affairs unit was accordingly established in the ECAFE Secretariat. In the following year it was made a full division.

This development did not meet with unqualified approval in ECOSOC. The United States, in particular, feared it portended a potentially dangerous trend toward decentralization that might well inflate the importance of the regional commissions. In the United States view it was essential, therefore, that the outposted social affairs staff should continue to receive their instructions only from Headquarters.[3] It was not easy, however, to reconcile control from New York with the notion that they formed an integral part of the regional secretariats. The Executive Secretary and senior staff of ECAFE did not accept as full colleagues a group which received directives on substantive matters direct from Headquarters; the Division, for its part, was plainly unhappy at being regarded as the "ugly duckling" of the Secretariat but seemed unsure where its main loyalties should lie. This situation did not change noticeably for the better until 1959. Following an explicit mention of the social aspects of economic development in the terms of reference approved for the new Economic Commission for Africa (ECA) in 1958, ECOSOC asked the other regional commissions whether a similar provision should be included in their mandates. ECAFE unanimously agreed that it should and its terms of reference were amended accordingly.[4] Although this action merely formalized an accomplished fact, it nevertheless helped raise the standing of the Division of Social Affairs and dispel the conflicts of divided authority and loyalty which had bedeviled its earlier relations with the rest of the ECAFE Secretariat.

For purpose of exposition, ECAFE's involvement with social problems may be conveniently considered under the headings of social policy, population, and community development. Housing is also included among these problems though it actually forms

2. It had also been recommended in 1955 by his Survey Group on the Organization of the Secretariat in Overseas Offices and TAA; General Assembly Doc. A/3041, Nov. 23, 1955.

3. Sharp, *Field Administration,* pp. 189–91.

4. *ECAFE Annual Report to ECOSOC, 16 March 1958–19 March 1959,* Doc. E/CN.11/506, n.d.

part of the work program of the Industry and National Resources Committee.

Social Policy

The most important single function of the Division of Social Affairs has been to impress upon ECAFE and its member countries the social problems and implications of economic development and to help Asian governments tackle their more obvious consequences. Part of its function, for instance, has been to work closely with UNICEF, WHO, and FAO experts on family and child welfare problems. It has advised governments directly on their welfare services, helped conduct regional seminars on the planning, organization, and administration of such services, and supported United Nations technical assistance activities in the general field of social welfare.

To help assess the importance of specific social objectives in current development planning, case studies were made of the allocation of public funds to the social services in Burma and Ceylon. The results of both investigations have been used by the Bureau of Social Affairs in preparing its report on the world social situation. They also provided useful data on one of the more perplexing questions confronting economic planners.

Earlier approaches to economic planning tended to emphasize only one productive factor—capital. The trend of more recent economic development theory, however, has been to stress the importance of investment in "human capital," that is, in human capacities to create wealth. There is no longer a simple conflict of choice between capital expenditure and social expenditure. It became fashionable in United Nations debates, reports, and resolutions to speak instead of the need for balanced social and economic development. This is an emotionally satisfying but analytically worthless concept.[5] It provides no objective criterion for determining the allocation of development expenditure between capital formation and social improvement. At present the amount Asian countries spend on social services varies from 15 per cent of the national product in the case of Ceylon and Japan, to 3

5. For a useful discussion of it, see Doc. E/CN.11/DPWP.5/L.2, July 22, 1959.

per cent in the case of India and Pakistan.[6] The Working Party on Economic Development and Planning, which spent the whole of its 1959 meeting discussing the relationship between social and economic development,[7] was compelled to conclude that there were no generally valid criteria for determining what this proportion should be. Certainly, as the Working Party admitted, the concept of balanced social and economic development provides no practical guidance. But that has not apparently diminished its appeal.[8]

Finally, the Commission has approved a proposal to convene in 1963 a meeting of experts to explore the feasibility of applying programing techniques derived from economic planning[9] to selected sectors of social policy.

Population

Considering the dramatic proportions of the population explosion in its region, ECAFE was surprisingly slow off the mark in analyzing its economic implications. Only in 1954 was a study of the relationship between population growth and economic development first listed in the work program. The following year ECAFE joined forces with TAA and the Bureau of Social Affairs in sponsoring a regional seminar on population.[10] Articles on the subject appeared in its *Economic Bulletin* but did not have their origins in ECAFE.[11] It was not, in fact, until 1959 that the first of a projected series of studies on the economic implications of Asian population trends appeared from the ECAFE stable.[12]

6. *Economic Survey of Asia and the Far East 1960,* UN Sales No.:61.II.F.1.

7. For report, see *Economic Bulletin, 10,* No. 3 (1959).

8. E.g., General Assembly Res. 1674(XVI), Dec. 18, 1961, recommends that the regional commissions "continue to pay special attention to problems of balanced economic and social development, taking into account the interaction of economic growth and social development and all valuable experience of countries of various economic and social systems."

9. See p. 107.

10. For report, see Doc. E/CN.11/415, Jan. 6, 1955.

11. E.g., "Acceleration of Population Growth in ECAFE Countries Since the Second World War," *Economic Bulletin, 6,* No. 1 (1955), which was prepared by the Population Branch of the Bureau of Social Affairs; and "Population and Food Supplies in Asia and the Far East," ibid., 7, No. 1 (1956), which was prepared by FAO.

12. "Population Trends and Related Problems of Economic Development in the ECAFE Region," ibid., *10,* No. 1 (1959). This was followed by "Population Growth and the Problems of Employment in the ECAFE Region," ibid., *12,* No. 2 (1961).

Population trends in the ECAFE region since World War II ; been dominated by an accelerating decline in death rates and f; constant birth rates.[13] On the conservative assumption of a con tinuation in prevailing mortality and fertility rates, it was estimated in the mid-1950s that the population of South-east Asia would double itself between 1950 and 1980 and thus equal by the latter date the total population of the whole world today.[14] The already heavy burden of dependency due to the large proportion of young age groups in the population[15] is bound to grow still heavier. This means that practically all ECAFE countries will have to spend a rising share of their national incomes on food and will have a smaller share left for capital formation. Faster rates of population growth both hold down savings and increase capital requirements. Other things being equal, a country with a higher rate of population growth must make a greater development effort to achieve any given rate of increase in real per capita income. Whether the Malthusian specter looming over Asia will slow down the rate of economic development of ECAFE countries depends on the success of their efforts and of international assistance in keeping national incomes rising as fast or faster than population.

The first results of the 1960–61 population censuses taken in a number of countries show this to be an even more terrifying race than anyone had suspected. For instance, the 1961 census count in India implied a total population of around 30,000,000 above the official estimate and some 10,000,000 above the total assumed by its third Five Year Development Plan. In Pakistan the census enumeration exceeded the official reckoning by 4,000,000 and in the Philippines and Thailand by 2,000,000 to 3,000,000 or by 9 and 13 per cent respectively. An annual rate of population growth of around 3 per cent or more, which several Asian

13. This is not true of Japan where the birth rate has been halved in the last ten years.

14. See *The Population of South East Asia (Including Ceylon and China:Taiwan) 1950–1980*, Doc. ST/SOA/Series A/30, 1958; and *The Population of Asia and the Far East 1950–1980*, Doc. ST/SOA/Series A/31, 1959. These reports define South-east Asia as excluding Afghanistan, India, and Pakistan where population was expected to increase by 80 per cent in the period 1950–80.

15. The ratio of dependent persons to persons of working age is about 2:3 in the ECAFE region as compared with 1:3 in economically advanced countries.

countries already experience,[16] will soon become typical for the majority of them.[17] This means a doubling of their population in 23 years or less. The antimalarial campaigns, public health programs, and measures to improve diet and sanitation so painstakingly carried out since the war have succeeded beyond all expectations in postponing death.

The Secretariat has given much direct advice to governments in connection with their preparations for the 1960 World Censuses of Population and Agriculture[18] and in 1960 cosponsored with the Bureau of Social Affairs and BTAO a regional seminar on the evaluation and utilization of population census data. It is likely that Asian governments will demand more of this kind of guidance. Accordingly, ECAFE is beginning to organize a team of regional advisers on, for instance, demographic studies; early in 1962 the first member had been appointed. The Secretariat has also been assisting the work of the regional Demographic Training and Research Centre which was established in Bombay by the United Nations in collaboration with India. Finally, ECAFE proposes to hold an Asian conference in 1963, by which time the majority of Asian governments should have detailed results of their censuses, to examine thoroughly the population trends of the region and their social and economic implications.

Rapid urbanization is another demographic characteristic of the ECAFE region. Although the level of urbanization is less than in any other continent except Africa, it is high in relation to the extent of economic development in most ECAFE countries.[19] In other words, the heavy migrations from rural to urban areas are not a reflection of the superior income and employment opportunities of the city compared with the countryside. For one thing the movement has been swollen by multitudes of refugees from areas of political and social unrest. Whatever the motives, however, the resulting social condition of the cities is only too apparent to the eyes and nostrils of the most casual traveler. There are, moreover, no obvious practical answers to the appalling social problems of Asian cities. In 1956 UNESCO, ECAFE, and the Bureau

16. Hong Kong, Malaya, the Philippines, Singapore, South Korea, Taiwan, and Thailand.

17. Doc. E/CN.11/578, Feb. 9, 1962.

18. See p. 96.

19. "Aspects of Urbanization in ECAFE Countries," *Economic Bulletin, 4,* No. 1 (1953).

of Social Affairs cosponsored a seminar on the physical, social, and economic problems of urbanization in the region.[20] Following up one of its recommendations, a further meeting was organized two years later to discuss physical planning and the location of industry. Finally, ECAFE expected in 1962 to hold a regional seminar to explore whether and how the techniques of rural community development programs could be applied to urban areas.

Community Development

The apathy, ignorance, poverty, stagnation, and isolation of so many rural communities in Asian countries constitute one of their biggest obstacles to economic growth. Over the last ten years community development has become the generally accepted prescription for the malady. This somewhat amorphous movement has come to mean any program of leadership and education in primitive villages which uses the labor, skills, and materials readily available on the spot to improve rural living conditions. It seeks, in other words, to find voluntary answers to problems that Communist governments have tackled by collectivizing the farms and regimenting the peasants. By 1959 sixteen ECAFE countries were operating community development schemes of varying scope and emphasis; in Ceylon, India, and Taiwan they covered more than half the villages.[21]

Many international agencies have been concerned with studying and assisting this movement, each in characteristically independent fashion rather than as part of one single, vigorous combined effort.[22] Until recently, ECAFE's own contribution has been rather modest. Its Division of Social Affairs has organized conferences and seminars and disseminated information and literature on the subject, advised governments on their problems and projects, helped conduct national and regional study tours, and supported United Nations technical assistance operations. It also collaborated on pilot investigations into the impact made by the movement on national economic development.[23] The findings showed the economic gains to be rather meager as yet.

20. For report, see *Economic Bulletin, 8,* No. 1 (1957).
21. *Economic Survey of Asia and the Far East 1961,* UN Sales No.:62.II.F.1.
22. Andrew Shonfield, *The Attack on World Poverty* (New York, Random House, 1960).
23. See p. 142.

In 1959 the Division helped organize a United Nations seminar on the planning and administration of rural community development programs for the benefit of Burma, Laos, Malaya, Thailand, and South Viet-Nam. A similar seminar in 1961 for all ECAFE countries was followed immediately by a regional conference to review the progress made in this field.[24] Whereas some years earlier attention had been focused mainly on proper organization and direction at the center, the emphasis is now placed on the need for a larger measure of decentralization of administrative, financial, and technical responsibility in the operation of these programs. The conference recommended, among other things, that teams of visiting consultants be organized to advise governments at their request on the planning, implementation, and evaluation of community development schemes. The Secretariat is to study the use of underemployed labor in them, the role of local government bodies and voluntary agencies in the movement, and uniform methods for assessing its economic impact.[25] In March 1962, the Commission requested the Executive Secretary to convene about every two years a high-level Asian conference on the social aspects of economic development, including major aspects of community development.[26] With a new and continuing intergovernmental body behind it, ECAFE's contribution to the total international effort being made on behalf of the movement may be expected to expand.

Housing

The housing situation of the ECAFE region is probably the worst in the world. No one knows exactly how many Asian families live under what, by any minimum standard, can only be called slum conditions; including rural housing it cannot be less than 100,000,000 and may be nearer 150,000,000. Over most of the region rapid population increases are constantly creating large additional demands for housing. The growth of cities is outpacing the means available to provide decent living conditions in them.[27]

24. For report, *see* Doc. E/CN.11/569, 1961.

25. Doc. E/CN.11/L.96, Jan. 24, 1961, and *ECAFE Annual Report to ECOSOC, 22 March 1960–20 March 1961,* Doc. E/CN.11/564, Apr. 22, 1961, p. 149.

26. Doc. E/CN.11/592, Mar. 16, 1962.

27. Much of the city growth of Asian countries has been the result not of "pull

Urban misery and rural poverty, however, are two sides of the same coin—economic underdevelopment. It is their very low income per head of population that makes the provision of housing such a dispiritingly difficult problem in practically all Asian countries. Few of them are within even striking distance of a solution. ECAFE has been trying to help by providing technical and economic guidance. It was other organizations, however, that first prodded it into action.

In 1950 WHO drew the attention of the Industry and Trade Committee to the difficulties of Asian countries in obtaining essential building materials such as cement, steel, and teak, and the need to help them tackle their shortage of low-cost housing.[28] On the initiative of the United States the Committee directed the Secretariat to collect and analyze information on alternative methods of construction using locally available materials and to consult with housing authorities and the building materials industry on ways of manufacturing these materials.[29] But with no staff to spare, the Secretariat could do no more than disseminate some technical notes on building materials. ECOSOC and its Social Commission meanwhile had passed resolutions urging the regional economic commissions and the specialized agencies to help governments provide housing, particularly for lower income groups.[30] In 1952 the Secretariat accordingly proposed, and the Industry and Trade Committee accepted, the setting up of a Working Party on Housing and Building Materials to consist of representatives of ECAFE, FAO, ILO, TAA, the United Nations Division of Social Affairs, UNESCO and WHO. In this way ECAFE assumed responsibility, in effect, for coordinating the regional work of the principal international agencies active in this field.

The intersecretariat Working Party held its first meeting in

---

factors" like employment opportunities and expectations of higher income from the development of industries, commerce, or services but rather of "push factors" such as low levels of rural living and, sometimes, conditions of physical insecurity. *Economic Bulletin, 8,* No. 1 (1957).

28. Doc. E/CN.11/I&T/46, Jan. 5, 1951.

29. Industry and Trade Committee Report, third session, Doc. E/CN.11/I&T/48, Feb. 23, 1951.

30. E.g., ECOSOC Res. 434(XIV), July 28, 1952; Social Commission: Report of the seventh session, Doc. E/1982, Apr. 14, 1951, and eighth session, Doc. E/2247, June 2, 1952.

1952 and its second in 1954. When it met for the third time in 1955, however, experts from five ECAFE countries—Burma, India, Indonesia, Laos, and South Viet-Nam—also participated.[31] In the following year it became a full-fledged intergovernmental body. Had the Secretariat's resources permitted, this would doubtless have happened sooner. The first meeting of the Working Party unanimously recommended the creation within the ECAFE Secretariat of a Division on housing and building materials with staff assigned to it from the specialized agencies.[32] Yet, when this proposal came before the Industry and Trade Committee, the agencies dragged their feet; they thought it was premature and seemed reluctant to cooperate with ECAFE. The Executive Secretary recognized that ECAFE could not commit the agencies; he explained that the Committee could merely endorse the proposal in principle: it would then be up to him to explore with the agencies how it might be implemented. The Pakistan delegate deplored this hesitation and the way it was being exploited by the agencies and, together with Burma, India, Indonesia, and Japan, strongly supported the setting up of a housing division.[33] The upshot, nevertheless, was the creation of a section, not a division, and even then for four years it consisted of only one staff member. At present it has two. Inevitably, ECAFE has been compelled to proceed modestly in this field.

The Secretariat with the help of two consultants presented to the Working Party in 1952 a preliminary report on housing and building materials in the ECAFE region.[34] A periodic review of the housing situation and programs of Asian countries became a regular function of the Working Party. It was clear from the first that, despite the scarcity and comparatively high cost of cement, steel, and teak, there was a general tendency in the region to rely too heavily on these construction materials. Low-cost housing for low-income population would need cheaper materials and methods

31. Working Party on Housing and Building Materials Report, third meeting, Doc. E/CN.11/I&T/117, July 21, 1955.

32. Working Party on Housing and Building Materials Report, first meeting, Doc. E/CN.11/I&T/77, Dec. 9, 1952.

33. Official Records, Industry and Trade Committee, fifth session, Doc. E/CN.11/I&T/78, July 9, 1953.

34. Doc. E/CN.11/I&T/HBWP/L.2, Oct. 27, 1957.

of construction. The region has plentiful resources of clay, inorganic binders, tall grasses, reeds, and forest waste if only they could be manufactured into building materials.[35] It also has an abundant supply of labor and, over most of it, a climate that does not necessitate the heavier and more solid structures of colder parts of the world.

One pressing need then was to evolve new building techniques or modify old ones to suit local resources. The Working Party in 1952 urged governments to include research on low-cost housing materials within their housing budgets.[36] This should provide as well for the practical demonstrations of research results—the translation of theory into practice—to the public, the housing administrator, and the building and professional trades. Pilot projects to help bridge the gap between the fruits of research and actual building practices are crucial to any attempt to change the methods and materials of so conservative an industry. Few Asian governments, however, have the organization, funds, or men required to run such demonstration projects and services.

On the side of research itself a great deal more has been done. Building and similar research institutes in Burma, Ceylon, India, Indonesia, Japan, and Malaya have been investigating new materials and the scope for standardizing housing components. Following an early recommendation of the Working Party,[37] two Regional Housing Research Centres were established, one in New Delhi to deal with the housing problems of hot, dry climates, the other at Bandung to cover those of hot, humid climates. Both have engaged in research, training, documentation, and other educational activity; both have received support from TAA, the Bandung more so than the Delhi center, although the experts provided have been counted against the technical assistance country programs of India and Indonesia. It is disappointing, therefore, that other ECAFE countries have not made good use of these facilities. In an effort to arouse their interest, the Working Party recommended the setting up of a liaison body to be called the

35. *Survey of Housing and Building Materials in Asia and the Far East, 1956.* Doc. E/CN.11/432 or UN Sales No.:1956.II.F.9.

36. Working Party on Housing and Building Materials Report, first meeting, Doc. E/CN.11/I&T/77, Dec. 9, 1952.

37. Cf., ibid.

Regional Housing Advisory Committee.[38] This body, which held its first meeting in 1958, consists of representatives of four ECAFE countries, the ECAFE Secretariat, the United Nations Bureau of Social Affairs, and the directors of the two centers. Its chief function is to review and guide the work programs of the centers.[39] To provide a channel of technical information on national housing research problems and progress, the Advisory Committee invited governments to appoint liaison officers to the centers. Every country has now done so though by the middle of 1961 only twelve liaison reports had been received by the centers. It was hoped that a two-way channel of contact would be developed between national research institutes and the Regional Housing Centres, with practical housing problems passing from the former to the latter and a flow of technical answers moving in the opposite direction. In practice the channel has so far tended to be only one way. The two centers have sent out free of charge their own technical literature on Indian and Indonesian problems in the hope that they might prove of more general interest, but have received very few inquiries and problems from other ECAFE countries in return. The latter have simply not shown sufficient interest in making proper use of the two centers.

The Secretariat has also distributed technical information on building materials, including suggested guiding principles for building codes and standards. The development of national and regional research centers meant, however, that the Working Party could concentrate more on economic and administrative problems. Thus, the Secretariat recently made a comparative analysis of building costs in ECAFE countries.[40] It found that the most meaningful index of costs and the best indication of building efficiency was the number of days' wages an unskilled worker required to produce one square meter of finished building. The results revealed enormous variations in building costs in Asia [41] with Ma-

38. Working Party on Housing and Building Materials Report, third meeting, Doc. E/CN.11/I&T/117, July 21, 1955.

39. See, e.g., Advisory Committee Report, third meeting, Doc. E/CN.11/I&NR/HBWP.6/L.7, Nov. 24, 1960.

40. Doc. E/CN.11/I&NR/HBWP.6/L.2, Aug. 1, 1960.

41. As the Secretariat points out, the formula cannot take account of variations resulting from differences in transport costs or in the prices of materials like

laya, Singapore, and South Viet-Nam generally having the lowest and Indonesia, Pakistan, and Thailand the highest. The Secretariat's report goes on to examine the probable reasons for these differences. The cost of housing to the users consists first of interest on the capital cost; second, amortization charges; and third, maintenance costs, including taxes. Lower housing standards and specifications would reduce the first item but increase the other two; while unduly high standards would reduce the last two items, but increase the first. Housing authorities have to strike the balance where the long-term recurring cost to the user is lowest. It is obviously desirable to tackle the problem by lowering real costs—through better organization and designs, raising the productivity of building labor, and the use of larger quantities of locally available and cheaper materials instead of the more costly imported ones—rather than by lowering housing standards and specifications.

Asian governments cannot mount a real attack on low-cost housing problems without proper organization and direction at the top. As a first step the Working Party urged them to establish ministries or departments expressly concerned with housing and town and country planning.[42] Five ECAFE members now have housing ministries[43] and another seven housing departments[44] within ministries. In other words, direct government responsibility for housing the poorer sections of the community is of very recent origin in the ECAFE region; this is one reason why its progress in developing low-cost housing has generally been so slow. Perhaps some credit for this change in government policy should go to ECAFE insofar as it strengthened the power of the delegates attending the Working Party to influence their own national administrations.

In 1960 ECAFE arranged with the help of BTAO and the cooperation of ECE for a party of housing administrators, planners, archi-

---

cement or steel whose costs are not directly related to the wages of unskilled workers.

42. Working Party on Housing and Building Materials, fifth session, Doc. E/CN.11/I&NR/10, Sept. 8, 1958.

43. Burma, Ceylon, India, Malaya, and Singapore.

44. Hong Kong, Indonesia, Japan, the Philippines, South Korea, South Viet-Nam, and Taiwan.

tects, and civil engineers from the region to make a Study Tour to Europe. The party concentrated more on studying the methods of planning, organizing, and financing large-scale housing programs including land policies for housing in the advanced countries than on their modern building materials and techniques.[45] Housing conditions and problems in Asia, however, are greatly influenced by special factors—unexampled population pressures, customs, climate, and the availability of funds—not found in Europe. It is thus a moot point whether the fairly large amount of time, effort, and money put into the Study Tour of Europe might not have been better invested in group visits to the best examples of Asian housing schemes and developments. Interestingly enough, the report of the Study Tour to Europe recommended that ECAFE organize housing study tours to Asian countries at the end of its working party meetings, on the same lines as those arranged by the ECE Housing Committee.

A further contribution to reducing housing costs in the ECAFE region can usefully be made by mobilizing through self-help and mutual help the householders' labor and skills for building and improving their own homes and community. The Working Party recommended that governments foster and finance self-help programs.[46] Burma, India, Indonesia, and other countries have attempted to assist rural housing in this way but no satisfactory progress seems to have been made. Toward the end of 1961 the Secretariat participated in a United Nations Mission, consisting of experts from Headquarters, ILO, FAO, UNESCO, and WHO, to survey and evaluate self-help housing methods and practices in Southeast Asia. Community services such as protected water supply, drainage, roads, and electricity are also an integral part of well-conceived housing programs. Yet it is not unusual in the ECAFE region for housebuilding to precede, not follow, the provision of such services, as governments simply cannot cope with the task of providing them in large and rapidly growing urban areas. It was therefore planned to convene a seminar in 1962, with the help of BTAO and the cooperation of WHO, on the administrative, finan-

45. For report, see Doc. E/CN.11/I&NR/HBWP.6/L.4, Oct. 5, 1960.

46. Working Party on Housing and Building Materials, second and fourth meetings, Docs. E/CN.11/I&T/102, Apr. 1, 1954, and I&T/127, Aug. 30, 1956.

cial, and technical problems of providing proper community facilities.

Lack of long-term finance is another obvious and important reason why the supply of decent housing has lagged far behind demand in most ECAFE countries. The Working Party in 1956 recommended that countries establish national housing finance corporations or similar institutions for this purpose.[47] There has not been, however, very much progress along these lines. In the Philippines a Home Finance Corporation, a statutory body, guarantees bank loans to private individuals and housing cooperatives and has thereby helped construct a large number of owner-occupied houses. In India funds from the Life Insurance Corporation are being used for middle-class housing and the development of land for housing. But these are hardly shining examples of the way to finance low-cost houses to rent. The Working Party also advised governments to strengthen their powers of expropriation to forestall speculation in building sites required for slum clearance and to formulate rent control and taxation policies that encourage investment in low-cost housing to rent.[48] Finally, private builders should be encouraged through the provision, for example, of technical services, building materials, and credit at reasonable rates, and building land at cost.[49]

The fact that decent housing for low-income groups can only be provided with the help of direct or indirect government subsidies in itself puts a brake on the launching of large-scale low-cost housing programs. Governments have been understandably reluctant to devote scarce resources to a non-self-financing, and hence technically "uneconomic," project. Housing, moreover, has become a serious competitor for scarce construction materials needed for transport, dams, and factories. The Working Party has repeatedly pointed out that better housing is not just a crying social need, but an investment in human resources to improve human efficiency and reduce social costs. It asked the Secretariat to try to find a formula for estimating this over-all benefit for

47. Ibid., fourth meeting, Doc. E/CN.11/I&T/127.

48. Ibid.

49. Working Party on Housing and Building Materials Report, fifth session, Doc. E/CN.11/I&NR/10, Sept. 8, 1958.

the common man to be derived from new housing.[50] Unfortunately the Secretariat had not the staff, nor is there a clear methodology, for this kind of investigation.

Housing is a less neglected subject in the region than it was when ECAFE first entered the field. In all Asian countries the private sector has made considerable efforts, with or without government assistance, to build middle and upper class houses. A number of Asian governments have special housing ministries or departments and make definite long-term financial allocations for housing in their development plans.[51] These allocations are still relatively meager, however, and in many cases are not fully spent because of difficulties in obtaining land, materials, and qualified personnel for large housing schemes. Furthermore, if financial stringency is forced upon governments, social expenditure, including that on housing, is invariably the first to suffer.

Actual housebuilding progress in the region has been very uneven. Ceylon, Hong Kong, Singapore, and Thailand have enjoyed building booms on a scale that may well make housing their most important item of national investment. Japan has also experienced high rates of construction. But of these countries only Ceylon, Japan, and Singapore can foresee their present unsatisfied housing demands being met. At the other end of the scale are countries such as Burma and Pakistan, which simply do not know the extent of their housing shortages. The typical annual rate of construction in the region is something like one or two houses per 1,000 of the population as against, in advanced countries, anything from five to fifteen per 1,000 according to the priority given to housing.[52] This has not been enough in most cases to meet current demands let alone wipe out the backlog of replacement needs.[53] A depressing impression remains that over

50. Working Party on Housing and Building Materials, third meeting, Doc. E/CN.11/I&T/117, July 21, 1955.

51. E.g., Burma, Ceylon, Hong Kong, India, Japan, Malaya, Pakistan, the Philippines, South Viet-Nam, and Taiwan.

52. Working Party on Housing and Building Materials Report, sixth session, Doc. E/CN.11/I&NR/29, Dec. 7, 1960. The gross densities of new housing schemes in some Asian countries are 1,000 or more per acre, whereas even in the most thickly populated European countries, it is exceptional to find more than 150 persons to the acre.

53. E.g., in India a shortage of 2,500,000 urban houses in 1951 was expected to grow to 5,900,000 by 1961. See Doc. ST/ECAFE/SER.M/18, 1961. India has given

the last decade urban housing conditions have generally deteriorated in many parts of the region.[54] The outlook is anything but encouraging.

The planners are not necessarily wrong in refusing to give larger resources to housing. They reason quite rightly that poverty is the crux of this and other social questions; the overwhelming effort of the nation must therefore be directed to raising real income per head. On the other hand they would also do well to remember, as the early phases of industrialization in the West can confirm, that mounting social costs quickly become economic costs, if rapid urban growth is insufficiently regulated.

---

housing a very low priority in its development planning and exercises control over it by rationing building materials.

54. Even a minimum standard of three square meters of covered space per person cannot be enforced in most metropolitan areas for it would leave large numbers of people without accommodation. Working Party on Housing and Building Materials, sixth session, Doc. E/CN.11/I&NR/29, Dec. 7, 1960. It should also be mentioned that there has been a marked tendency for Asian countries to emphasize urban housing needs although roughly speaking more than three-quarters of domestic structures in the region may be classified as rural.

PART FOUR

PERSPECTIVE VIEW

CHAPTER 14

The Changing Scope of Cooperation

The demand for equality of opportunity with other peoples was an important element in the Asian nationalism which liberated vast numbers of subject peoples from colonial rule after World War II. It was out of this revolution of rising expectations, as it has been aptly called, that ECAFE was born. But the hopes aroused for regional cooperation by this unity of political feeling in Asia proved difficult to realize. Only rather slowly and somewhat variably did a sense of ECAFE's relevance to the economic problems of the region develop. The ECAFE region is certainly a difficult one to organize. The policy of the Western powers and emerging political divisions among Asian countries made the task very much harder.

In the first place ECAFE was not at the outset a predominantly Asian organization: only four of its ten founder members were Asian countries. Consequently a large part of its proceedings for the first years was devoted to a political effort by its Asian members to make it more representative of Asian peoples and aspirations. Not until Indonesia, after a long drawn out struggle, became a full member in 1951 did Asians have a voting majority in the Commission. The policy and attitude of the Western powers had given them good grounds for thinking that any worthwhile future for ECAFE depended on this shift in the balance of voting power.[1]

Secondly, ECAFE was denied the opportunity and means of making any tangible contribution to immediate postwar reconstruc-

1. For further comment on the political elements affecting regional economic cooperation, see Chap. 16.

tion in Asia. After the demise of UNRRA the principal international efforts in this direction were being organized by the Office of the United Kingdom Special Commissioner in South East Asia [2] and the Far Eastern Commission, the occupation authority, in Japan. The Executive Secretary toyed with the idea of taking over some of the allocation functions of the former but ECAFE was plainly not equipped for or offered this kind of activity. Its sister commission in Europe was engaged in allocation work at this time only because it had inherited this function from the emergency European economic organizations which it had absorbed as going concerns.[3] The Western powers reacted no less strongly to any suggestion of ECAFE interfering in the affairs of the occupation authority in Japan.[4] They also scotched the notion of the Executive Secretary, Lokanathan, and some Asian countries, notably Pakistan and India, that ECAFE might help Asian governments prepare schemes for financial assistance from the World Bank. This was a matter, Britain and the United States insisted, for direct dealings between governments and the Bank. When it was suggested that the Bank might be asked to clarify its conception of a "sound project," they tartly asserted that it was not ECAFE's business to advise the Bank on its loan policy.[5] The most serious setback to early Asian hopes of ECAFE, however, came from another cause.

From the beginning Asian states set great store on using ECAFE as a lever to prize out of the Western powers a recovery program similar to the Marshall Plan for Europe. It was, after all, "in order to give effective aid to countries devastated by war" that the General Assembly had instructed ECOSOC to establish an ECAFE.[6] The Commission's Working Party on Industrial Development accordingly set out to elaborate a case for substantial external assistance. This demand was also implicit in many of the earlier suggestions of Asian delegates and the Secretariat regarding the future work of ECAFE. Within two years of its creation, however,

2. See p. 40.

3. See Wightman, *Economic Co-operation.*

4. See p. 236.

5. This view was constitutionally incorrect since the Commission's mandate authorizes it to make recommendations directly to the specialized agencies of which the Bank is one.

6. General Assembly Res. 46(I), Dec. 11, 1946.

the United States had rejected this idea uncompromisingly. The Asians were offered nothing, not even sweet words of hope and encouragement. They were advised instead to practice the virtues of promoting a sound currency, expanding exports, and giving adequate incentives to private foreign investment. Not surprisingly, they became momentarily disillusioned about the value and purposes of ECAFE.

A further opportunity to use ECAFE as a channel of aid came with the inauguration in 1949 of EPTA. It was not so much a question then of giving ECAFE technical assistance funds to allocate, although that was what Lokanathan wanted.[7] The initial distribution of these funds was a delicate political matter best settled at Headquarters. But all the important administrative procedures and decisions regarding the program were also centralized in New York. Despite the lip service paid to using the experience and resources of the regional economic commissions, no significant tasks were given to them. The Western powers which donated the bulk of the funds favored a high degree of centralization and so, in consequence, did a number of Asian governments. Technical assistance was the first tangible benefit the underdeveloped countries obtained from the United Nations. The failure to give ECAFE any important role in the program confirmed the view of the skeptics within Asian governments that the Commission was a mere talking shop and of little practical worth.[8] Economic cooperation through ECAFE, the Asians learned, would have to be an extended exercise in self-help. But even this function proved difficult to organize.

ECAFE was created at a time of intense organizational activity, great initiatives, and high expectations within the United Nations. But few, if any, saw clearly what a regional economic commission without funds or executive powers and with few Secretariat resources could be expected to accomplish. This was due partly to the already substantial vested interest in functional commissions as the proper United Nations approach to economic and social problems. Moreover, even if there was genuine feeling at Headquarters for the emerging aspirations of Asia—and it is doubtful

7. See p. 48.
8. For further comment on the relation between ECAFE and UN technical assistance operations, see Chap. 15.

if many grasped their significance—it was difficult to see what a regional organization of absurdly limited Asian membership could do about them. In trying to make the first agendas, documentation, and preliminaries meaningful, Headquarters could only draw upon the experience of the League of Nations committees. This suggested a pattern of Secretariat studies, an annual economic survey, and, as the big occasion, a formal Commission session as the proper way to proceed. The Western powers supported this view. Lokanathan, however, early made it plain that he was not prepared to preside over a mere study group. Nor, as already indicated, did this narrow conception of ECAFE appeal to its Asian members.

The experience and achievements of ECE under the forthright leadership and infectious enthusiasm of Gunnar Myrdal soon provided quite a different model for ECAFE to follow. By getting away from the upper levels of political representation and tackling specific problems through expert groups, ECE showed that practically relevant, if unspectacular, results were possible. That many of Lokanathan's first thoughts on the possible functions and organization of ECAFE should have closely resembled those of ECE was no coincidence.[9] Even then the Western powers, particularly Britain and the United States, continued to maintain a negative attitude toward proposals for extending the functions of ECAFE beyond those of collecting information and publishing studies. In its most plausible form this position argued that the right way to proceed was first to identify and define the problems and then consider the machinery needed to tackle them. Lokanathan, they maintained, was putting the cart before the horse in wanting to establish a whole range of subsidiary bodies straightway. Furthermore, the Secretariat had not the resources to service them; nor were Asian governments so well off in qualified experts and foreign exchange that they could afford to send delegates to all the meetings he appeared to envisage. Senior officials at Headquarters shared these criticisms of Lokanathan's earlier ideas and were ir-

9. It might be argued that ECLA, which set up very few subsidiary bodies and put the bulk of its efforts behind economic studies, direct economic advice, and the elaboration of the rationale of Latin American economic integration, would have been a better model for ECAFE to have followed. But this is to ignore the very different political profile and less homogeneous character of Asia as compared with Latin America.

ritated when he ignored their advice to emphasize problems rather than machinery. This distinction between problems and machinery was, however, much too simple.

There is no doubt that Lokanathan was too ambitious in aspiring to copy the ECE committee structure all at once. But to set up no subsidiary bodies at all was tantamount to saying that ECAFE had no practical contribution to make to the economic problems of its region or that Asian governments were not prepared to get together on matters of common concern. Not everything they and Lokanathan proposed was wise, practical, or opportune. Nor was ECAFE always the proper body to do what they wanted. It was also true that the economic map of the ECAFE region had only begun to be charted. Asian countries did not properly know their own, let alone each other's, economic problems. They hardly knew each other. Nevertheless, they were clear that if ECAFE was to be of practical use, it needed to create subsidiary bodies in which government representatives could pool their experiences and difficulties and formulate relevant guidance on specific problems. This was the way to bring greater realism into ECAFE's work. What the critics of Lokanathan's earlier ambitions overlooked was that only by getting government experts together in the first place could ECAFE hope to identify and define their specific problems.

Asian governments were particularly anxious for ECAFE to provide them with guidance on their industrial plans or projects. They tended to equate industrialization with heavy industry. The Western powers, with a misconception of their own long-run economic interests, were opposed to the development of heavy industry in Asia. They emphasized instead the importance of surveys, agriculture, cottage industries, trained manpower, a scientific outlook, trade promotion, domestic savings, and adequate incentives to private foreign capital—the preconditions, in other words, of industrialization. The advice was not wrongheaded; it was merely unimaginative. Asian countries grew wise to the importance of these factors from their own experience. At the time, however, the Western position appeared to them to shut the door on their aspirations for industrial development. Each side deeply misunderstood the attitude of the other. The Soviet Union, on the other hand, preached to the Asians at length on the necessity of developing heavy industry as the only sure foundation for real independence. Worse still, the Western powers used their superior voting strength and not the arts of persuasion to gain endorsement of their views. Only under the strongest pressure did they agree to the creation in 1949 of an omnibus Committee on Industry and Trade and a Subcommittee on Iron and Steel. These were the first extensions of ECAFE's functions to emerge from the Asian aspiration to industrialize.

During the same year the important ECAFE Bureau on Flood Control was started and a program of work mapped out on inland transport problems. The period of fumbling and uncertainty had passed. From then onward ECAFE acquired a momentum that expressed itself in an ever widening range of activities and an increasing number of permanent and ad hoc subsidiary bodies. The ECE model was being well and truly followed. Meanwhile, the Asian members were becoming more realistic, confident, and assertive. They spoke out more against the domination of ECAFE by the Western powers and of the Cold War atmosphere introduced into its proceedings by the constant political clashes between the West and the Soviet Union. They identified ECAFE with Asian prestige; it was their organization. Their growing impatience with the negative and highly political role of the outside powers finally boiled over at the Lahore session of the Commission in 1951 and resulted in what became known as the Lahore Agreement or Convention.[10] Other formidable obstacles, however, still lay in the path of any rapid development in the substance and scope of regional economic cooperation.

The ECAFE region was not an easy one to organize compared with Europe or Latin America. Although embodying much that Asians share in common, its geographical limits, as fixed by ECOSOC in 1947, were somewhat artificial. With large contrasts in levels of economic development and in the capacity of governments to make good use of ECAFE, it has not been easy to select problems and formulate guidance of practical relevance to most Asian countries. For long isolated from one another, their mutual economic ties are weak. Their traditional links have been with the developed countries that dominated their economies. The international communications of the region were also adapted to this

10. See p. 51.

matrix of enforced bilateralism. This situation of mutual isolation could not be changed easily or rapidly. The task of ECAFE has been as much to foster new economic relations as to organize existing ones more rationally. Even under favorable political conditions this would have been no easy task; but the political climate was not in fact favorable.

No sooner had Asian countries gained control of ECAFE than their political solidarity was eroded by the Cold War. On issues such as Chinese representation, the inclusion of mainland China within the scope of the Secretariat's research program, and membership for North Korea and North Viet-Nam, they became hopelessly divided. The creation of SEATO in 1954 hardened the lines of division. The voting pattern on many important issues began to reflect with predictable regularity the opposed positions of SEATO members and the politically nonaligned countries. The poor relations between India and Pakistan, which the latter's membership in SEATO undoubtedly aggravated, was an especially great misfortune for ECAFE.

Despite these daunting circumstances the catalogue of useful things accomplished through ECAFE steadily lengthened. It has produced countless reports and studies, made scores of recommendations, and given much advice to many countries on a variety of problems. A great many of its activities to begin with had inevitably to be concerned with collecting data and defining problems. For this purpose its omnibus Committee on Industry and Trade was clearly too unwieldy an instrument. In any case, there are no general problems of economic development: only a multitude of specific ones. A mounting number of specialized groups were accordingly convened to collect and analyze data and to formulate advice on particular questions. Reviewing plans, projects, and problems became a regular function of all the permanent subsidiary bodies. In the process of focusing attention on the theoretical necessity for economic development and the measures required to promote it, ECAFE has tried to refine some slipshod, though widely held, notions about economic planning, deficit financing, and the role of agriculture and foreign trade. It has encouraged and helped countries investigate the extent and quality of their natural resources. It has performed the functions of a technical adviser by making available knowledge of more advanced techniques and encouraging their application.[11] Gradually the main economic problems and potentialities of the region became more sharply defined. The barely perceptible economic profile that existed in 1947 has been filled out immeasurably. In these ways ECAFE has not only helped deepen a sense of regional economic consciousness but also temper the dangers of chauvinism in Asian nationalism.

Much of the substantive work of ECAFE has reflected, in fact, preinvestment tasks of national economic development. It would not be wide of the mark to describe it as largely technical assistance in character. Valuable and necessary as this was, it did not, however, amount to actual government cooperation on fundamental issues of economic policy. Especially is this true in the field of economic development, planning, and trade. Here the potentialities for regional cooperation through ECAFE have barely been exploited. On the one hand, economic progress and planning in the region have been repeatedly frustrated by serious fluctuations in the volume and value of its exports of primary products. On the other hand, the domestic markets of most Asian countries are not large enough to support efficiently the range of industries that would permit a greater diversification of production of their economies and more rapid economic growth. Even India has a rather small market economically. Regional cooperation offers a way out of this dilemma between dependence on the vicissitudes of world markets and the limitations of a narrowly nationalistic approach to economic development.[12] For a number of reasons, some of which have already been indicated, Asian countries have been slow to pursue this solution.

In the early years of ECAFE a few isolated and expansive declarations were voiced about the need for countries to coordinate their national development plans.[13] One or two Asian governments saw even then the danger of Asian countries all trying to establish the same range of industries or expand too much the

11. For further comment, see Chap. 15.

12. David L. Gordon, "Regional Approaches to Economic Development," a paper presented at the annual meeting of the American Political Science Association, New York, September 1960.

13. See p. 99.

same industry.[14] They recognized, in short, the desirability of promoting international specialization in the region's industrial development. The predominant trend, however, has been the other way, toward narrowly nationalistic economic planning and a refusal to accept the notion that beyond disseminating information about these plans and advising countries at their request on specific projects, ECAFE had a role to play. ECAFE's function, according to this view, was to identify and define the scope of regional cooperation on the assumption that national plans were sacrosanct.

Underdeveloped countries have better reasons than rich ones for nationalistic economic policies.[15] Such policies may also be required to infuse a sense of national unity, cohesion, and common purpose in the face of the centrifugal forces released by the achievement of political independence. But economic policies do not become rational simply by appealing to national sentiment. True, there is an almost inevitable flavor of autarky about national economic planning for the simple reason that demand and supply conditions are easier to assess and influence within national frontiers.[16] Even so, the further the trend proceeds the more irrational it becomes.

The fragmentation of the ECAFE region since the war into smaller political and economic units[17] has thus made the task of economic development more difficult for many Asian countries. The first postwar decade of economic progress in the region was not inspiring. The economic development pattern of most Asian countries continued along old colonial lines. Their planners con-

14. For Malayan statement to the Commission's fourth session, see Docs. E/CN.11/SR.47–48, Nov.–Dec., 1948.

15. E.g., to protect their domestic markets, reserve foreign exchange for essential imports, and build up effective demand to absorb their labor force.

16. "In a situation where there is no supra-national authority and only a minimum of inter-state co-operation and bargaining almost any policy of intervention in economic automatism becomes autarkic in its consequences." Gunnar Myrdal, *Beyond the Welfare State* (London, Duckworth, 1960), p. 118.

17. E.g., the partition of India in 1947; the breakup of Indo-China into Cambodia, Laos, and Viet-Nam; the separation of Singapore from Malaya; the Cold War division of Viet-Nam and Korea into north and south states. It should also be noted that Korea and Taiwan before World War II were closely integrated into the Japanese economy but became separate economic units after the war.

tinued to grapple with fundamental questions for which they had no clear answers. They appeared to lack a solid body of techniques for assessing the record and shaping the future. By the end of 1954 Lokanathan decided that this situation required some new and challenging initiatives from ECAFE.

There were also reasons of a political nature why some significant enlargement in the scope of ECAFE's functions appeared urgent at that time. The founding of SEATO in September 1954, a meeting of the Colombo powers in December of the same year, and the projected African-Asian conference at Bandung the following year were regarded by some senior United Nations officials as symptomatic of Asian disillusionment with international cooperation through the United Nations and hence of a search for new groupings and solutions outside its framework.[18] The possibility of a larger volume of United States aid, organized and distributed in new ways, was thought likely to strengthen these symptoms.[19] It was in response to this background that Lokanathan put before the heads of delegations attending the Commission session at Tokyo in 1955 an Aide Mémoire on the intensification of regional cooperation through ECAFE.

Executive Secretary Lokanathan's proposals signposted three principal directions in which more effective regional cooperation could be pursued. The first pointed to the problems and limitations of national economic planning. These should be tackled by a new Secretariat research program and through a mutual examination and, if necessary, adjustment or coordination of national plans in the interests of a better regional specialization.[20]

Secondly, there was considerable scope for beneficial intergovernmental cooperation in special fields. For instance, ECAFE could help governments conclude agreements for sharing through joint ventures the output of a commodity or service where an expansion of the market was an indispensable condition of efficient production. Geological surveying, especially of border areas, trade consultations and multilateral payments arrangements, the development of international highways and rail connections, the

18. For further comment, see Chap. 16.
19. See pp. 294–95.
20. See p. 104.

multipurpose development of international rivers such as the Mekong, were other possibilities mentioned by the Aide Mémoire. ECAFE should also continue and intensify activities of a more general regional character such as the formulation of uniform standards, the creation of regional training and research centers, the organization of study tours and seminars in collaboration with TAA, the coordination of research and demonstration experiments, and the preparation of geological and other maps. At the same time, Lokanathan argued, because most countries were still at the stage where "national projects loom naturally large in their schemes of things," ECAFE's direct advisory services should be strengthened. Finally, Lokanathan invited governments to consider ways of associating the Commission more closely with bodies like the Colombo Plan, especially if this or other forms of aid to the region were about to expand. The weight and influence of ECAFE would be greater if they provided a higher level of representation, preferably ministers, at the Commission sessions and relatively senior officials as liaison officers at Bangkok and in their capitals.

The most striking quality of this Aide Mémoire is the clarity and prescience with which it charted the future course of regional cooperation through ECAFE. It is no exaggeration to say that all the major advances subsequently made by ECAFE have been concerned with translating its ideas into practical action. In many cases, however, some important political hurdle had first to be surmounted. The Mekong Project got under way in 1957 once the four riparian countries had declared their willingness to cooperate under ECAFE auspices.[21] The political confidence required to pursue the Asian Highway scheme was not forthcoming until the following year.[22] Considerable political suspicion and several delaying moves prevented the holding of trade promotion talks until 1959.[23] Regional projects of a largely technical character such as geological mapping[24] and the formulation of an ECAFE Code of Recommended Customs Procedures[25] were initiated more easily because they touched no sensitive political nerve. All these

21. See p. 189.
22. See p. 218.
23. See p. 254.
24. See p. 152.
25. See p. 247.

efforts were valuable demonstrations that ECAFE was and could be more than merely a body of inquiry and advice. Furthermore, the work on geological mapping, international highways, trade promotion, and the Mekong Project showed how mutual trust and confidence among Asian countries could be encouraged by organizing them together on practical tasks. In addition, ECAFE has been constantly trying to evolve more effective ways of making the organized sharing of experiences and guidance more directly relevant to the specific difficulties confronting government policy-makers and administrators.[26]

The outcome of Lokanathan's proposals in the field of economic development planning has been very different. As already indicated, the governments refused to commit themselves at the Tokyo session of the Commission in 1955 to the desirability of adjusting national plans in the interests of a better regional specialization, much less to accepting the particular steps Lokanathan suggested for bringing this about.[27] What emerged instead was a new Working Party on Economic Development and Planning, a somewhat academic body as it turned out, and a more extensive Secretariat research program on the problems and techniques of economic planning. Even these decisions were not taken without doubts and misgivings.[28] This was rather less than Lokanathan had hoped.

Asian antipathy to regional planning was also demonstrated forcibly at this time at another and very different conference. On the initiative of Harold E. Stassen, the head of the United States Foreign Operations Administration (FOA),[29] President Eisenhower, in April 1955, included in his recommendations to Congress on the Mutual Security Program for 1956 a proposal to set aside $200,000,000 for the creation of a President's Fund for Asian Eco-

26. This problem is further discussed in Chap. 15.

27. See p. 104.

28. Significantly the general consensus on the Aide Mémoire was expressed in the "account of the proceedings" of the Commission, because resolutions to the same effect might well have been voted down or become deadlocked. See *ECAFE Annual Report to ECOSOC, 19 February 1954–7 April 1955*, Doc. E/CN.11/407, Apr. 7, 1955, paras. 220–24. In this connection the helpful drafting work of the head of the Pakistan delegation, A. Khaleeli, who was a good deal more far-sighted than his official instructions (see pp. 105–06) should not go unrecorded.

29. Superseded, from July 1, 1955, by the International Co-operation Administration (ICA), and from Nov. 1961 by the Agency for International Development (AID).

nomic Development.[30] The object of the Fund was to promote regional economic cooperation. United States officials concerned were not sure how this might be done but appeared to think a sort of OEEC-type organization might be established.[31]

At the prompting of Stassen, India invited the Asian members of the Colombo Plan to meet at Simla in May 1955 to discuss how the Fund might be used.[32] India made the mistake of not instructing its diplomatic representatives to sound out the governments first before issuing invitations. The United States Department of State failed to back Stassen and by its silence left the impression that it was indifferent to regional cooperation. Burma was not interested in the proposal on any terms and did not attend the conference. Neither did Ceylon, which did not see why India should interpose itself between Ceylon and the United States as regards the latter's aid. Pakistan had no need to foster suspicions about the Indian initiative: they already existed.

Two positive approaches dominated the Simla Conference. India suggested a number of examples of development projects of benefit to more than one country, such as international rivers and communications, for which the Fund might be used. Japan thought it should be used to establish a regional settlements bank to provide short-term credit during periods of seasonal fluctuations in trade and to finance intraregional trade, meaning in practice trade between itself and other Asian countries. Neither approach proved acceptable.

In the first place, it was difficult to identify any regional project at a sufficiently advanced stage of preparation to permit immediate realization with Fund resources. National projects seemed of far greater urgency. Second, the Fund was much too small to establish an Asian payments union or commodity price stabilization schemes as Japan had suggested.[33] Underlying these difficulties, however, was the much more profound fear of the smaller

30. US Dept. of State *Bulletin, 32,* No. 827 (May 21, 1955).

31. Congress actually voted $100,000,000 for the Fund, of which not less than 50 per cent was to be used as loans and not more than 25 per cent given to any single country.

32. The following countries were represented: Cambodia, India, Indonesia, Japan, Laos, Nepal, Pakistan, the Philippines, South Viet-Nam, Thailand, and the territories of Malaya, North Borneo, and Sarawak.

33. India reminded the Conference that an ECAFE expert group on regional payments problems had reported the previous year that it would require substantial working capital to establish an Asian payments union. See p. 238.

Asian countries that any regional schemes or organization launched with the help of the Fund would be dominated by India or Japan, or both. They were therefore opposed to the creation of new machinery on the model of OEEC by strengthening, for instance, the Colombo Plan Bureau [34] and, indeed, to the interposing of any new level between them and the source of aid. On the contrary, country programs of technical and financial assistance should be strengthened. The notion that in matters of aid and trade the bargain to be struck had to be a bilateral one with a rich outside power had become deeply rooted in the ECAFE region. The only consolation for ECAFE that emerged from the Conference was that no rival organization for regional economic cooperation was established.[35]

By arguing within ECAFE and at Simla that little impetus could be given to economic development by a regional approach, Asian countries had not yet faced up to the limitations of their narrowly nationalistic economic planning. The economically small size of their domestic markets did not make it practically easy or very economical to build up a complete structure of industries. The passage of time makes this more difficult in those cases where the progress of modern technology gives increasing advantage to large industrial concerns. Asian countries could undoubtedly make more rapid progress if, through trade, they could promote greater specialization among themselves and reap the benefits of economies of scale. It is surprising, therefore, that after the Tokyo Commission session and the Simla Conference the Secretariat did

34. There was some concern expressed also that this might weaken the case for a Special United Nations Fund for Economic Development (SUNFED).

35. For the final communiqué of the Conference, see the *Times of India,* May 14, 1955, and for some perceptive comments on it, *The Times* (London), May 16, and *The Economist,* May 21, 1955. Actually ICA had some difficulty trying to spend the President's Fund for Asian Economic Development. Among the largest projects were: road and telecommunication links between India and Nepal, the improvement of rail and road connections between Afghanistan and Pakistan, a SEATO Engineering School at Bangkok, and telecommunications and an English language training center for Laos, South Viet-Nam, and Thailand. A US contribution of $2,200,000 to the Mekong Project also came from the Fund (see p. 193). The President's Report to Congress on the Mutual Security Program for the six months ended December 31, 1957, confessed that "the development of suitable projects has been slow, primarily because the concept of joint economic undertakings among Asian countries is new and often runs into political and economic differences which take time for them to reconcile."

not ram home the lesson by convincing and forceful analysis. A touch of questing boldness on this theme would not have been amiss at this juncture. The Secretariat's energies and resources became fully absorbed, however, in preparing and launching a reconnaissance survey of the Mekong River.[36]

The narrowly nationalistic approach of Asian countries to economic development was not the only limiting trend in their future prospects for growth. Apart from cyclical fluctuations in export earnings plaguing development efforts, it was becoming evident that these earnings were growing much too slowly in relation to the mounting import requirements of economic development.[37] In its *Economic Survey* for 1959 the ECAFE Secretariat produced its first searching analysis of the problem. This showed that except for a few commodities like oil, rubber, and minerals, the prospects for raising the region's export earnings were bleak. The gap between its capacity to import and the volume of imports needed to maintain a reasonable rate of economic growth is widening.[38] External aid can bridge it to some extent but obviously cannot form the permanent basis of sustained economic growth. Some relief could be obtained through a further intensification of import substitution of consumer's and producer's goods; but the smallness of their own domestic markets sets strict limits to this policy.[39]

Thus, the real answer is to conceive and execute the policy

36. See p. 187.

37. Cf. *World Economic Survey 1956,* UN Sales No.:1957.II.C.1, and *Trends in International Trade,* Sales No.:GATT/1958.3. Between 1950 and 1957 the ECAFE region's combined export earnings rose by 40 per cent; but its import outlays rose by 115 per cent. The proportion of manufactures secured in exchange for the region's foodstuffs and raw materials actually declined in the 1950s.

38. "On any reasonable assumption as to the desirable rate of growth of their national product, it appears, therefore, that hardly any country of the region can look forward to an economic development in which the growth of exports of primary products to the industrial countries plays the leading role." *Economic Survey of Asia and the Far East 1959,* UN Sales No.:1960.II.F.1, p. 96.

39. Only those Asian countries with a relatively large home market carried out any appreciable degree of import substitution in the 1950s. Even then, because of the need to obtain development goods from outside the region, this took place, with few exceptions, at the expense of intraregional trade. In short, mutual Asian economic ties have in general grown weaker, not stronger, during the last decade. See *The Scope for Regional Economic Co-operation in Asia and the Far East,* Doc. E/CN.11/CAEF.1/L.4, 1961.

on a broader basis. This could be done by preferential trade arrangements which discriminate against outside supplies, encourage regional specialization, and permit economies of scale, thereby keeping down cost differentials between regionally produced and imported goods.[40] Asian countries need, in short, to plan their economic development and arrange their industrial protection together, not separately. National economic development and regional cooperation are intimately linked: each is a favorable condition of the other. But since World War II mutual economic dependence among Asian countries has steadily declined.

Without more intensive economic relations among themselves, Asian efforts to form a common front in international organizations on general economic issues are bound to be largely empty demonstrations.[41] As the rich Western countries organize their own common market and aid-donors club [42] the bargaining power of Asia must deteriorate still further. And not only vis-à-vis the developed countries. The Latin Americans have made progress toward the ultimate creation of a common market for their continent.[43] The new African states seem keen to move in the same direction. Is Asia to be left behind, stuck in the rut of its own divisions, unable to emancipate itself from essentially colonial economic relationships, merely accommodating itself as best it can to the policies of rich countries? [44]

40. *Economic Survey,* UN Sales No.:1960.II.F.1.

41. Myrdal, *Beyond the Welfare State,* p. 170.

42. I.e., the Organization for Economic Co-operation and Development (OECD) and its Development Assistance Committee (DAC).

43. *The Latin American Common Market,* UN Sales No.:59.II.G.4. Latin American economic integration was first seriously proposed by ECLA as early as 1949; but the real impetus came from the Trade Committee it established in 1955.

44. The delegate of Viet-Nam summed up the problem so perceptively to the Commission as early as 1956, that his words are worth quoting in full: "At the present stage, extra-regional trade relations could be no more than bilateral relationships between an underdeveloped country with low productivity and an advanced country with high productivity. As its productivity and prices were uncompetitive, the underdeveloped country had to confine itself to a few agricultural and manufacturing commodities traditionally associated with the colonial era. Under such circumstances, the development of new lines of production was dependent on the domestic market, whose capacity was, however, limited by the low purchasing power of the masses. Therefore the economies of the region could only be developed and diversified through the expansion of intra-regional trade relations which enabled a new pattern of trade to be created. . . . Diversification of the economies between the countries of the region was feasible and the widen-

There have been signs in recent years within ECAFE, especially at meetings of its Working Party on Economic Development and Planning, that government experts recognized what needed to be done to meet this situation and prospects for growth.[45] It was not, however, until the 1960 Commission session that Asian countries woke up in some alarm. During the previous two years the Secretariat had been feeding them information on the economic integration schemes going forward in Western Europe and Latin America. They were getting worried about the likely effect of the European Common Market on their export prospects. Then came the *Economic Survey* for 1959. The disturbing implications for economic growth revealed by its analysis of the long-term trade outlook of the region fell upon prepared ground.

From the ensuing Commission debate,[46] it emerged that most Asian governments were now prepared to consider seriously more intensive forms of regional economic cooperation. The Secretariat was ready with an appropriate form of words to express this new resolve. The resolution, which India introduced[47] and seven other Asian governments[48] cosponsored, recommended that Asian countries "seek suitable measures for increasing intra-regional trade, in the context of enlarged world trade, to enable a sustained increase in production, resulting from larger markets and to explore in this regard the possibilities of promoting regional cooperation in efforts for economic development and improvement of productive efficiency." It appealed to industrially advanced countries to facilitate and encourage imports from Asian countries and to cooperate in finding ways of stabilizing the prices of primary exports "at fair and adequate levels." The United Nations Special Fund and Technical Assistance Committee (TAC) and other international organizations were requested "to provide larger allocations for regional projects." Finally, it directed the

---

ing of the market through intra-regional trade relations would permit the emergence of new industries which could then be worked to their optimum economic capacities." He suggested that the Secretariat should collect and disseminate information on the European Coal and Steel Community (ECSC), the decision to organize a European Common Market, and similar developments in Latin America.

45. See pp. 109–10.

46. Doc. E/CN.11/532, May 26, 1960.

47. Doc. E/CN.11/525, Mar. 14, 1960.

48. Burma, Indonesia, Japan, Nepal, Pakistan, the Philippines, and Thailand.

Executive Secretary to "explore the scope and practical measures for promoting co-operation for economic and social development in the region as a whole and if necessary among individual countries . . . particularly in the fields of agriculture, industry, transport and trade."

Cambodia, Iran, and the Soviet Union supported this resolution but the United States thought it was "not balanced and practicable as it made no reference to the generation and proper use of domestic savings. The element of reciprocity was missing. In the field of commodity stabilization insufficient importance was given to the operation of immutable economic laws." Moreover "some of the topics it covered were already being dealt with by other international bodies." The United States, with the support of Britain and South Korea, wanted more opportunity, therefore, to consider and presumably amend the resolution. Its sponsors desired an immediate decision, however, and had their way. Not to be outdone, the United States later in the proceedings introduced and got accepted another resolution on regional cooperation incorporating the points it evidently wanted to see included in the first resolution. Faced with the absurdity of two texts on much the same theme, the drafting committee preparing the annual report to ECOSOC had little choice but to reconcile them.[49]

Unanimity was thus finally achieved though only at the expense of a certain dilution in the force and clarity of the original declaration.[50] The final result nevertheless marked a notable landmark in ECAFE's uphill struggle to inspire a sense of common economic purpose among its Asian members. The Secretariat had, in effect, been given a broad mandate to explore all possible forms of economic integration from specific joint projects to an Asian common market. What kind of approach seems most

49. See Doc. E/CN.11/528/Rev. 1. Mar. 21, 1960.

50. E.g., the final wording also recommends Asian countries, *inter alia,* "to study the possibility of a suitable pattern of regional co-operation *consistent with the principles of GATT*" (author's italics) and to make greater efforts to mobilize and attract domestic and foreign capital. That favorite phrase of economic orthodoxy—"economically sound"—appeared in more than one place. The UN agencies concerned were not requested "to provide larger allocations for regional projects" but only "to provide adequate allocations." The US touch is unmistakable in all these additions and amendments to the original resolution.

promising is a question that has excited much discussion within the Commission and its Committees on Trade and Industry and Natural Resources during the past two years.

Asian countries realize that the formation of anything so ambitious as a common market in the ECAFE region would be immensely difficult. Profound differences in their political alignments and levels of economic development, their heavy dependence on customs revenues, their need for convertible currencies, and the inadequacy of intraregional communications are among the more obvious problems. They believe in a modest, empirical approach to the question of how best to promote a greater measure of economic integration in the region. For these reasons the example and inspiration of ECLA is likely to be more persuasive than that of Western Europe.

In the first place, although intraregional trade accounted on the average for about one-third of the ECAFE region's total trade during the period 1957–59,[51] it was largely concentrated among very few countries. Excluding Japan[52] and the entrepot trade of Malaya, Singapore, and Hong Kong, there is actually very little trade between Asian countries. The most important regionally traded commodities by value are textiles, rice, petroleum and its products, and rubber. Of these rice is the most dependent on regional markets.[53] With few exceptions trade with countries outside the region is of decidedly greater importance. The present structure and low level of trade between most Asian countries reflect the fact that their economies developed in response to the import demands and export supplies of Western Europe and

51. Excluding trade between Malaya and Singapore and for lack of data, Afghanistan, Brunei, and Nepal. See *Economic Bulletin, 12,* No. 1 (1961). The corresponding proportion for Western Europe in the same period was 55–60 per cent and for Latin America 10 per cent.

52. Which alone accounted for about 30 per cent of intraregional exports and 20 per cent of intraregional imports in 1957–59.

53. These facts account for the exceptional degree of dependence on regional markets or supplies of some Asian countries. Thus rice explains why about 70 per cent of Burma's exports went to Asian markets in the years 1957–59. Trade with Japan or Hong Kong or both accounted for a similar proportion of the exports of South Korea and Taiwan. That roughly 50 per cent of the total imports of Burma, Cambodia, and Thailand came from Asian sources is largely due to Hong Kong, Singapore, and Japan.

North America.[54] Its smallness is not a law of nature, however, and to assume it will always remain so is to judge Asian countries incapable of economic development.

Nor is the fact that most Asian countries produce the same or similar commodities an insuperable barrier to greater trade between them. The limiting factor is not so much their supposed lack of complementarity in resources endowment but the degree of existing restrictions on the potential volume of intraregional trade.[55] Indeed, the gains from economic integration are likely to be larger the greater the extent to which the same or similar commodities are produced under protective conditions.

A more serious difficulty is the wide contrasts in the level of economic development between Asian countries. In this situation full economic integration between the smaller and weaker Asian countries and more powerful ones like India and Japan would simply condemn the former to perpetual underdevelopment.[56] These two powers could no more be full members of a wider economic association of Asian states than the United States could be of a Latin American common market. The gains from economic integration will have to be shared out equitably. Furthermore, since the promotion of rapid economic growth inevitably places great strains on the balance of payments, Asian governments cannot be expected to abandon all controls over foreign trade in any scheme of economic integration. A considerable amount of mutual consultation and conscious negotiation will be needed to overcome these difficulties. The much greater degree of state control over the distribution of resources in the ECAFE region as compared with Western Europe points to the same conclusion. As the price mechanism works extremely weakly, if at all, in most

54. There are still some glaring irrationalities in this situation. Thus, in the period 1957–59 the ECAFE region was a net exporter of rice; yet some Asian countries still bought rice from outside the region. It was also a net importer of sugar; yet half its sugar exports went to markets outside the region. This gives some indication of the scope for substituting intraregional for interregional supplies.

55. *The Scope for Regional Economic Co-operation in Asia and the Far East,* Doc. E/CN.11/CAEF.1/L.4, 1961.

56. E.g., Ceylon pointed out to the Industry and Natural Resources Committee in 1961 that India, Japan, Hong Kong, and Singapore dominated its imports from the ECAFE region in many products it hoped to produce itself. To develop its economy Ceylon must, therefore, protect itself against the competition of comparatively simple, low-cost manufactures from more developed Asian countries.

Asian countries, trade liberalization alone will not bring about the desired pattern of regional specialization. In other words, cooperation confined to trade will produce no significant results unless it is reinforced by some degree of mutual adjustment of national economic plans.[57]

Whether Asian governments were ready to accept this conclusion was the question which lent special interest to the Conference of Asian Planners ECAFE convened at New Delhi in 1961. Although a few continued[58] to stress the inviolability of national targets, there was general consensus on the need at least for some process of consultation on the regional implications of national economic planning. Following this meeting the Executive Secretary, toward the end of 1961, invited three outstanding experts from the region to examine the feasibility of various forms of possible economic integration for the ECAFE region.[59]

Their findings constitute an inspiring case for a collective Asian endeavor to tackle the highly complex problems of regional economic integration. Recognizing that a fully developed customs union or free trade area would not be immediately feasible in the ECAFE region, the experts advocated instead the creation of a joint regime of intraregional trade promotion. Its principal task would be to devise ways of achieving greater intraregional trade through, for instance, tariff reductions and enlarged quotas. But, in addition to a broad-based effort to liberalize trade in regional products among regional members, there were many rewarding opportunities for establishing subregional industrial units catering to multinational markets. These would entail sectoral or partial economic integration in certain commodity markets and

57. E.g., the largest textile producing countries in the region, India, Japan, and Pakistan, to say nothing of the unknown intentions of Hong Kong, are planning to export far larger quantities of textiles than the rest of the region is expecting to import. As other Asian countries develop a textile industry, the big producers will either have to find larger markets outside the region or revise their textile production targets.

58. E.g., Pakistan. On trade cooperation also, Pakistan continues to hold back. At the 1961 meeting of the Trade Committee, it accepted the desirability of creating more complementary economies in the region, but was against trade groupings which conflicted with GATT. But neither Pakistan nor any other country has explained how a strict adherence to the principles of GATT would bring about more rapid economic growth in the ECAFE region.

59. See Doc. E/CN.11/615, Feb. 13, 1963.

industries. For this purpose mutual consultations on national development plans would be necessary if only to relate production increases to export possibilities. The need was even more apparent in the case of agriculture. For agricultural and mineral products, moreover, long-term trade agreements and contracts offered considerable scope for mutually beneficial cooperation among Asian countries. Again, while commodity stabilization problems were largely global in character, regional consultations would be well worthwhile on the marketing problems of such regional products as coconut and copra, pepper, raw jute, and perhaps tea. As regards the strengthening of intraregional communications, the experts more or less endorsed the activities and proposals already being pursued through ECAFE bodies. In brief, the time was ripe, they thought, for a decisive move toward closer regional cooperation in Asia. The paths governments are prepared to explore in practice, however, are more likely to be shaped by their political attitudes and relations.

The form and degree of economic integration Western Europe has achieved was made possible by its strong sense of common political purpose. This again suggests that Asian countries should first build up confidence and mutual trust through piecemeal bargaining. Especially is this true for the smaller Asian countries which understandably fear that any broad schemes would be dominated by India and Japan.[60] There have been some tangible signs recently of a readiness to follow this approach.

An Association of Southeast Asia (ASA), which Malaya and the Philippines initiated in January 1959 and Thailand joined the following September, was officially inaugurated in July 1961. Its declared aims embrace cultural and social as well as economic cooperation. The intended areas of economic cooperation cover trade liberalization and promotion, joint industrial ventures, the sharing of technical experts, training facilities and know-how, tourist promotion, and transport and communication facilities.

60. Fearing that the European Common Market and talk of a possible US trade negotiation with it will lead to the economic isolation of Japan, the business community there has been reportedly urging the Japanese government to take the lead in bringing about greater economic integration in the ECAFE region. See *The Guardian* (Manchester), Mar. 1, 1962. Memories of its pre-war Co-Prosperity Sphere are still, however, a potent source of mistrust of Japan among smaller Asian countries.

Thus, while the long-term objective of ASA supposedly includes the creation of a common market, the initial approach is piecemeal and empirical.

Malaya and Singapore, on the other hand, have recently been studying the feasibility of a complete merger, economic and political, of the two countries. These explorations soon became dwarfed, however, by the more ambitious idea proposed by the Prime Minister of Malaya in May 1961 of a Greater Malaysia comprising Malaya, Singapore, and the territories of Brunei, North Borneo, and Sarawak. While accepting the desirability of such a federation in principle, Britain agreed with Malaya in November 1961 that the views of the peoples of North Borneo and Sarawak and those of the Sultan of Brunei should be consulted before the next steps were decided.[61]

The idea of Asian economic integration is much more thought-provoking to Asians than association with Europe is to Britain and will take much more debate before the precise methods of integrating are agreed upon. But that a number of Asian countries are now prepared to explore in a thoughtful and realistic manner a problem which only a few years ago they were not even willing to discuss within ECAFE may be counted a significant advance in the spirit of cooperation within the region. Perhaps the new mood has been induced more by a defensive reaction to trade blocs being formed in other regions than by a positive enthusiasm for strengthening economic ties among themselves. But it is no bad thing if economic compulsions begin to soften the lines of political division. Only by more intensive economic relations among themselves can Asian countries hope to accelerate their own economic development and strengthen their bargaining power in the world community. Only with greater bargaining power will they achieve more equality of opportunity with other peoples. And this, after all, was the demand that characterized the political renaissance of Asia after the war.

61. One possible obstacle to the creation of a Greater Malaysia could be a developing conviction among the Chinese population of Malaya and Singapore that it is simply a move by entrenched Malayan conservatives to avoid being overwhelmed by a large left-wing Chinese majority in any merger between Malaya and Singapore. This is a reminder that problems of economic integration in the ECAFE region are further complicated by the powerful centrifugal forces at work in some Asian states.

CHAPTER 15

The Techniques of Cooperation

In the last resort the effectiveness of ECAFE depends on its ability to influence and shape government policies and actions. With no executive powers of its own it must necessarily be constantly concerned to evolve methods of cooperation which serve the aims its activities are designed to achieve. It has first to create opinions and habits favorable to collaboration and then find the means to implement agreements once reached. These can take various forms. They may be embodied in a convention, the most formal of all. The only example of such agreement prepared by ECAFE, that relating to the measurement and registration of inland water craft,[1] has nowhere been ratified in the region. A less formidable procedure is simply to ask governments to indicate formally whether they accept in principle the agreement reached by their experts as was done in the case of the ECAFE Code of Recommended Customs Procedures.[2]

The overwhelming bulk of agreements within ECAFE, however, have been expressed in the form of recommendations or resolutions. Although their effectiveness rests largely on nothing more than moral force, they can also have something more rational to support them. In the first place, delegates accept them on behalf of their governments and may be expected to see that they are carried out. The only trouble is that, on returning from an ECAFE meeting, delegates often find that the personnel, organization, facilities, and information required for a line of recommended

1. See p. 225.
2. See p. 247.

action are inadequate or nonexistent. Sometimes this prompts them to set about trying to remedy the deficiency; but in a depressingly large number of instances it is evident that little, if anything, is or can be done. Second, governments can be asked at subsequent meetings what steps they have taken to implement earlier recommendations. In 1951 the Secretariat was formally instructed to report their answers periodically to the Commission.[3] Two such reports were made; [4] but neither was very illuminating. During these earlier years, ECAFE displayed an excessive faith in the virtue of resolutions without always distinguishing between those capable of producing results and those representing little more than formal declarations.[5] In any case, as a guide to the impact of ECAFE, which is what the Commission seems to have wanted, these reports were highly misleading since much of its activity and influence did not get expressed in resolutions. Moreover, the governments soon found it burdensome, and perhaps embarrassing, to answer the questionnaire the Secretariat sent them on the subject. In 1954, therefore, Lokanathan proposed and the governments agreed that the Commission itself should periodically prepare instead a broad assessment of its activities.[6]

Finally, in 1957 the Commission explicitly charged its subsidiary bodies with the duty of assessing the degree of government compliance with ECAFE resolutions. The Secretariat, whenever it can find out, refers to the subject in its documents and delegates sometimes mention in a general way the actions their governments have taken on particular recommendations. But no regular and systematic assessments of the effectiveness of ECAFE resolutions are, in fact, made by either its subsidiary bodies or the Secretariat.

In exercising its functions as a body of inquiry and advice, ECAFE has not found it easy to make generalizations that will seem

3. Doc. E/CN.11/301, Mar. 7, 1951.

4. Docs. E/CN.11/274, Jan. 24, 1951, and 382, Dec. 23, 1953.

5. E.g., in 1950 a subcommittee of the Commission found that out of 80 resolutions passed since ECAFE was established, only 8 were of a type where some further report from the governments appeared to be needed.

6. See, e.g., *ECAFE Annual Report to ECOSOC, 3 April 1955–14 February 1956*, Doc. E/CN.11/430, Mar. 1956, Part IV, and the *Annual Report, 16 March 1958–19 March 1959*, Doc. E/CN.11/506, n.d., Annex IV. In the 1951 *Annual Report* a similar appraisal was attempted in preparation for the review ECOSOC was due to make that year of all three regional commissions.

relevant and significant for most countries in the region. Economic planners in large countries like India in principle face much the same difficulty. What is an appropriate idea for one part of the region may be too advanced or too simple for another. No country can use knowledge and techniques, however readily available, that lie wholly outside its field of experience. In these circumstances a thoroughly well-made case study would sometimes be more instructive than a compendium of rather thin generalizations.

Thus, where ECAFE recommendations consist of broad exhortations, the impact is bound to be indirect, diffuse, and hard to fathom. The most tangible results are likely only from its most specific recommendations. Writing nearly a decade ago on ECAFE, one of its former Deputy Executive Secretaries argued that "its usefulness will increase in proportion to its willingness to make some of its recommendations increasingly specific." [7] That is still true today. Such recommendations are more difficult to formulate, however, since they invariably require much more careful study and preparation before governments will accept them. This type of agreement may actually border on negotiations or at least quasi-negotiations and therefore involves a more formal commitment than the acceptance of more general recommendations. The Asian Highway, the Mekong Project, and the intraregional trade promotion talks fall into this category. In these cases the element of actual negotiation is sufficiently developed to require private meetings. The formulation of new technical standards also involves very specific recommendations. This can become a protracted process when, as for instance with the standardization of electrical voltages or diesel locomotives, there is an important commercial stake within and outside the region in the end result. But on the whole private interests are rarely represented in the delegations. The dominant and active role of the state in most Asian economies, their condition of underdevelopment, and the relative absence of NGO's in the region mean that collaboration through ECAFE is much less a matter, as it is in Europe, of reconciling the conflicting and competing interests of well-organized

7. C. Hart Schaaf, "The United Nations Economic Commission for Asia and the Far East," *International Organization*, 7, No. 4 (1953).

private groups.[8] It is rather through the spokesmen of the industrially advanced countries, including Japan, and on such topics as shipping, petroleum, and commercial policy that powerful private economic interests make their presence felt.

ECAFE is thus, in fact as well as in theory, very much the servant of Asian governments. If it is to grow in stature it is precisely in the direction of encouraging and facilitating actual government negotiations that it must continue to move. But the more it is used for this purpose the more will its methods of collaboration have to change in consequence. For one thing promotional publicity will have to defer to the demands of quiet diplomacy.

The aims of ECAFE may be adequately served also by periodic study and discussion. While it is extremely difficult to see the influence of this process on subsequent government policies and actions, some of its most vigorous meetings have been of just such a nature. Their importance is the same as that of all international forums: they help to keep alive significant international issues. The Secretariat studies problems and blueprints proposals on which governments feel obliged to take up positions. In this way the international forum exerts gradual pressures in favor of governments taking certain preliminary steps to tackle international problems through international action. The immediacy and impact of this process must not, however, be exaggerated. Governments are not usually given to major changes in policy simply because of the enlightenment or criticisms their representatives encounter at meetings of bodies like ECAFE. But in due course there often occurs some erosion of their instructions at the edges. The gradually less uncompromising attitude of the British on the subject of ocean freight rates in the ECAFE region is a good case in point.[9]

These forums serve other useful purposes. Without them national projects and policies would certainly go ahead in any case; but finding out about the relevant experiences and solutions of other countries would be more difficult. A United Nations forum avoids the embarrassment of suppliant and benefactor for all are present on an equal footing. ECAFE has brought together, often

8. See Wightman, *European Co-operation.*

9. See p. 259.

for the first time, many kinds of expert groups to pool common experiences and formulate useful guidance. For a number of specialist groups it has acted, in effect, as their own regional professional association. Many of them have freely acknowledged to the present writer how at ECAFE meetings they discovered new ways of looking at old problems. Contacts once established in this way can then be maintained by direct exchanges. The bonds of attachment thus forged between these specialist groups and ECAFE largely explains why they appear, in general, to be more knowledgeable and appreciative of its work than the economic policy-maker in Asian governments. Their confidence in the functions and purposes of ECAFE can be, as the genesis of the Mekong Project demonstrates,[10] a not unimportant element in the inauguration of some major new exercise in international collaboration. ECAFE meetings have also been the means of giving young administrators, who may be future leaders, a greater breadth and maturity of outlook and more self-assurance, thereby helping to make them better committee men in their own national administrations.

The value of these meetings clearly depends on careful timing and preparation and well-organized discussions. Their number and duration need constantly to be related to the amount and quality of the effort the Secretariat and governments can put into them. There is no special merit about a large calendar of meetings. In recent years there have been signs indeed that the mounting work load from this cause has become too uncomfortable for the Secretariat.[11] For instance, the big regional technical conferences ECAFE periodically convenes rely for their success to a large extent on the quality of the papers presented. Good papers cannot be prepared in a hurry; nor good participants spared at frequent intervals to attend international conferences of one sort or another. The decision to convene future regional Technical Conferences on Water Resources Development every two instead of three years is, therefore, of doubtful wisdom.

One characteristic disease of the United Nations which wastes a great deal of time is the seemingly endless process of reporting to some higher level body with a consequent tendency to repeti-

10. See p. 201.
11. See p. 73.

tion in government speeches. In the case of ECAFE this is most evident in the Committees on Transport and Industry and Natural Resources and at the Commission session. Governments usually feel obliged to say something about most reports on the agenda even if their representatives have said it all before at some lower level. Few of them can muster the size and quality of delegation that would be needed if all these reports were to be expertly appraised.[12] As each report comes up for notice and approval the proceedings become more like a prize-giving ceremony than a high-level policy debate. Even this ritual puts a strain on small delegations which, unlike large ones, cannot parcel out the various items among their members. Furthermore, the discussion invariably takes the form of prepared statements. Where these relate to the relevant experience of the country concerned, which can admittedly be instructive, it would seem better to circulate them. But for other kinds of intervention the set speech is almost inevitable since English or French, the working languages of ECAFE, is not the first language of most delegates. Extemporaneous debate is, therefore, understandably difficult for them. Those from Ceylon, India, Malaya, and Pakistan usually speak well. On the other hand delegates from Japan, competent but possessing little linguistic ability, often do not make the impact their contributions warrant, while representatives of smaller countries sometimes have to be prodded to speak at all.

One possible way to encourage delegates to think aloud more at committee sessions would be to abolish their summary records. It would also save paper, translation, and other secretariat services. The Executive Secretary actually suggested this in 1958[13] but the governments refused to agree. Summary records, they maintained, enabled delegates to follow previous discussions at which they were not present and to study individual statements. Moreover, it would be a great strain on the smaller delegations if governments had to prepare their own notes on the proceedings.

A reasonable degree of continuity in government representation and the "club atmosphere" this helps to establish also facilitate

12. E.g., at the 1961 session of the Industry and Natural Resources Committee, more than half the member countries of ECAFE were either absent or represented by delegates with no special competence in the topics under discussion.

13. *ECAFE Annual Report to ECOSOC, 29 March 1957–15 March 1958,* Doc. E/CN.11/482, n.d., para. 262.

the smooth flow of business and a less formal style of discussion. On the other hand, the hidden norms of behavior and unspoken understandings that develop in a "club atmosphere" may merely encourage that narrow, cautious consideration of the national interest which bureaucrats instinctively understand, and even approve, in one another. One of the obstacles to achieving greater continuity of representation at ECAFE meetings is that senior government officials in many Asian governments do not, and cannot expect to, remain in the same department or ministry for years on end. Where promotion is by seniority a transfer from one field to another may be the only method of advancement even though it results in the misuse of highly specialized and expensively trained manpower. It must be remembered, too, that all Asian governments are in varying degrees short of well-qualified officials and the ablest tend to be grossly overworked.

A strong chairman can obviously exercise a decisive influence on the character and outcome of a meeting. The practice in ECAFE of electing the leader of the host delegation to the chair, while an agreeable courtesy, frequently produces a poor chairman. This is especially true of meetings held at Bangkok since Thai delegates generally have no assured command of either English or French. In this situation it falls to the Secretariat to provide the firm guidance that may be needed to produce a clear definition of the question to be decided and a conclusive result. This becomes easier when the Secretariat has prepared a study whose conclusions and proposals can form the basis of discussion.

Too many Secretariat studies in the past, though less so in recent years, were little more than a rehash of information supplied by the governments or parroted from technical journals. This was partly the fault of governments in dumping problems on ECAFE with scant regard for priorities or the resources available to investigate them. In some instances, however, staff members undoubtedly aided and abetted the process on well-known empire-building principles. The failure of governments to review the over-all work program which resulted is one of the most blatant weaknesses of the Commission and its subsidiary bodies. The criticisms of ECAFE reports officials make privately in their offices are rarely reflected in government speeches at meetings. They wonder about the usefulness of ECAFE instead of asking themselves what they could do to make it more useful. No one wishes to seem uncooperative or, as the Asians put it, to hurt the heart.

Until 1950 the Secretariat worked on studies it thought the governments should or would want, as well as those the Commission actually requested. On the initiative of the then Deputy Executive Secretary, C. Hart Schaaf, who in turn got the idea from a senior official at Headquarters, the Commission that year drafted a consolidated work program and listed the priorities.[14] In fact ECAFE pioneered this practice. Furthermore, the Executive Secretary was given authority to defer items and modify priorities. But as the work program expanded, so did the number of items awaiting completion. Some remained in that state for years on end. Governments showed little disposition to match commitments against resources in a realistic timetable. It was not uncommon for them to forget to inquire about items they themselves had actually suggested the year before. Occasionally the outside powers, notably Britain and the United States, would express apprehension about the financial implications of further proposals. This did not, however, prevent a sizable margin of excess fat from accumulating around the work program.

Shortly after his appointment as Executive Secretary in 1956, Narasimhan, with the Commission's approval and a warm commendation from New York, lopped 25 per cent off this inheritance. He stressed the need to concentrate in depth on continuing problems of a truly regional character by reducing the time spent on purely factual or technical studies and on various clearinghouse functions. Yet despite his formulation of a set of principles for determining the admissibility and priority of particular items, the work program bequeathed to his successor, Nyun, again bore no close relation to what the Secretariat could be expected to accomplish well in a reasonable space of time. The notion of priority had become almost meaningless, in fact, for by 1961 around 90 per cent of the items were listed in this category. On the prompting of New Zealand, the Executive Secretary, with some evident reluctance, brought together during the

14. At the 1949 Commission session Britain suggested some sort of priority in the work program and was supported by France, but Asian members refused to discuss the matter. Doc. E/CN.11/SR.71, Oct. 29, 1949.

Commission session that year a group of Asian delegates to review and evaluate the work program as a whole. One of the more extraordinary features of this meeting was the way some division chiefs then defended every detail in their own programs. In the event there was time only for a partial review; but at least it was agreed that in the future there should be a proper appraisal immediately before the opening of each Commission session.

One other cause of this constant tendency to inflation in the work program is that ECAFE has not been able to the same extent as ECE, for instance, to push work on to the governments themselves as well as on to NGO's. Government experts have often contributed technical papers to meetings and there have been some instances of Asian governments actually taking the initiative in organizing regional seminars and study groups.[15] But if ECAFE is to concentrate on the really important regional issues, much more of its work program will have to be shouldered by the governments themselves. The making of regional geological and other maps [16] shows what can be done.

Relations between governments and ECAFE are also conducted through liaison officers or permanent representatives stationed at Bangkok. These people help keep their governments in close touch with the activities of the organization, many of which are of a continuing nature, and make it easier for the Secretariat to consult governments without committing them. They may also be instrumental in expediting replies to Secretariat questionnaires and letters and helping to ensure some degree of continuity in representation at meetings held in Bangkok. For the most part, these liaison officers are local diplomatic staff who have been given this additional duty. It does not make for effective cooperation, however, when they represent governments at meetings where they have no special competence. Nevertheless, an able liaison officer filled with the urge to accomplish positive results can exercise a considerable influence. Such was the respect accorded to the first French permanent representative, for instance, that he became the only non-Asian to be elected chairman of an ECAFE committee. A later French liaison officer played a useful role in

15. E.g., road safety weeks. See p. 218.
16. See p. 152.

getting the Mekong Project under way.[17] Still it is hard to escape the impression that, more often than not, the liaison officers have no special interest in ECAFE or are too junior to command attention.

This cursory examination of the functioning of ECAFE forums underlines the obvious, though still imperfectly understood, point that what governments get out of them depends greatly on what they put in. At the very least they have to send delegates fully able to profit from the experience. Their capacity to make good use of ECAFE in this sense has differed markedly. Countries formerly under British rule, with the possible exception of Burma, inherited on independence a larger nucleus of trained administrators and skills than those formerly under French or Dutch rule. The retreat from the mainland provided Taiwan with a sudden and comparatively large supply of well-trained officials. But administration for most civil servants immediately after independence consisted of applying settled policies. Men trained to maintain law and order and collect revenue had to turn their minds and procedures to the actions required to develop human and material resources. This in itself was an immensely absorbing task even without the disorder and chaos that accompanied independence and prevailed for years afterward in countries such as Burma, Indonesia, and those formerly constituting Indo-China.

It is hardly surprising, therefore, that Asian delegations in the earlier years of ECAFE had no official instructions except perhaps on some foreseeably important political issues. But not all the political issues voted upon were predictable and very few Asian governments were sufficiently well organized to reply the same or next day to a cabled request for instructions. Consequently the delegates were often left to guess what the reply might have been. Where that became too difficult abstention or absence from a crucial vote seemed the better part of discretion. Thus a number of the earlier voting patterns in ECAFE, especially on political questions, regularly included a fair sprinkling of abstainers and absentees. In short, Asian governments were not in a position at first to put much into ECAFE. Lokanathan was compelled to

17. After a somewhat tactless US liaison officer had succeeded in widening the differences between Lokanathan and the US on this same issue. See p. 187.

plead strongly with them to send fully qualified experts to technical meetings, to define their problems more precisely, to make constructive suggestions for future activity, and to recognize more their responsibility for taking and implementing decisions. The Secretariat itself, he complained, had to collect data with little or no assistance from the governments for studies they themselves had requested.[18]

The emergence of good, well-informed briefs from Asian governments at ECAFE meetings tended to reflect the evolution and status of national economic development planning. India was well ahead of other Asian countries in this respect. From the early 1950s its delegates were eager for ECAFE to tackle problems its planners had come up against in drafting and implementing India's First Five Year Plan. Other Asian governments, however, had yet to encounter them. Indeed, for the smaller countries the initial pace, standard, and demands of ECAFE were often too high relative to their available information, administrative organization, and personnel. They were more inclined, and still are to some extent, to look for direct practical assistance from ECAFE. They hope it will do something for them individually[19]—a nationalistic approach, in other words, which overlooks the fact that ECAFE exists primarily to further regional cooperation. It is bound to fall short of such expectations as compared, for example, with the specialized agencies or BTAO which have country programs whose effects can visibly be seen at work. Furthermore, unlike the specialized agencies, which can cultivate ministries such as agriculture, health, and education and groups such as the farmers, doctors, and teachers, ECAFE has no comparable ministry or group to champion its cause with the governments.

What is less easily explained is why the quality of representation from the same country varies from one year to the next. Again, no simple generalization will cover all cases, but the following pattern seems broadly true. A newly elected member country seeks to create a good impression and is therefore well represented

18. See Executive Secretary's statement to the Industry and Trade Committee, first session, Docs. E/CN.11/I&T/SR.1–8, Oct. 12–18, 1949.

19. Technical specialists in some of the smaller Asian countries have remarked to the author that they would like to see something going on in their country—a pilot experiment or demonstration project—with an ECAFE label attached.

at first. Otherwise the trend apparently has been for the quality of representation to decline in the 1950s and then pick up again in recent years. For small countries the choice of delegates may be rather limited. But foreign exchange shortages and such irrelevant considerations as status, saving face, or the wish for a trip have been known to complicate the selection. The annual Commission session is usually deemed to be sufficiently important for the delegation and its leader to require cabinet approval. In some countries the cabinet also approves a complete list of ECAFE meetings at which the government should be represented. The prime minister or president may even insist on endorsing the actual choice of delegates for them. But for ECAFE subsidiary bodies it is more common to leave this decision, though not the size of the delegation, to the ministry or department most concerned.

All member governments have a specially designated office as the channel of communication with ECAFE. Most of these offices keep the appropriate ministries and departments informed of forthcoming ECAFE meetings, solicit their comments on the agendas of these meetings, brief the delegates, and distribute their reports to those most concerned. Although these liaison offices are sometimes located within the foreign ministry as, for example, in Japan,[20] they are more usually found in ministries of finance or industry and commerce. Even in the latter cases, however, it is often helpful to ECAFE if the foreign ministry, which is naturally more sensitive to diplomatic considerations, chooses to exert its influence on government policy toward the organization. Instances have arisen where the foreign ministry felt strongly that the country should be represented though the ministry of finance would rather have saved the foreign exchange cost of sending a delegation. It is upon the foreign ministry that ECAFE may also have to rely at times for the decisions that break essentially political stalemates over major new proposals. This, in turn, is facilitated when the prime minister or president holds the port-

20. The Economic Affairs Bureau of the Japanese Foreign Ministry deals only with the Commission and the Trade Committee. Delegates to subordinate ECAFE bodies report directly to the agency or department concerned. Because it is not acquainted with the results of technical meetings, the Foreign Ministry does not, therefore, have a fully rounded view of ECAFE.

folio of, or takes an active interest in, foreign affairs as, for instance, in Ceylon, Indonesia, India, and Taiwan. In the case of Pakistan, on the other hand, the foreign ministry appears to have little influence or interest in ECAFE affairs. In the Philippines also the foreign ministry knows little about the potentialities of ECAFE which is very much the monopoly of the Department of Industry and Commerce.

In practically all Asian governments the process by which delegates are briefed is, at best, imperfectly developed. Many officials admitted to the present writer that because they only learned of their assignment or saw the relevant documents at the very last moment,[21] their briefing was woefully inadequate. Consequently they were in no position to make a substantial contribution to the meeting. Furthermore no procedure was found to exist in any country whereby what a delegate learns from an ECAFE meeting is properly disseminated to, much less discussed by, other interested members of his own administration. Nor has any government developed the practice of making its own periodic appraisal of ECAFE activities as a whole.

The Philippines in 1951 established a committee for ECAFE matters with the express purpose, apparently, of taking follow-up action on ECAFE recommendations. It first met twice weekly under the chairmanship of the secretary of the Department of Industry and Commerce. But since 1954, when there was a change of political regime, it seems not to have functioned properly and, indeed, has hardly ever met. Taiwan has a commission for ECAFE on which are represented about ten different agencies. It meets as occasion demands, if necessary two or three times a month, according to the volume of work and number of impending ECAFE meetings. But in practice neither of these two experiments in interdepartmental consultation on ECAFE affairs—the only examples of their kind in the region—has ensured systematic follow-up action on ECAFE recommendations and resolutions. Without exception this is undoubtedly the weakest link in the whole chain of connection between governments and ECAFE. Even the

21. The writer has himself seen on more than one occasion piles of ECAFE documents gathering dust in the corner of liaison offices. It is evident that the documents do not always circulate as widely as they should or are simply not read by those for whom they were intended.

highly developed administrations of India and Japan cannot be exempted from the criticism. In brief, no government in the region has yet devised well-functioning machinery and procedures for making the best use of ECAFE.

If the governments are dilatory about taking follow-up action, members of the Secretariat have the opportunity during the course of their field trips to apply further persuasion. A complaint commonly made by government officials to the writer, however, was that staff members seemed more concerned to collect information and material than to inquire about the progress made or problems encountered in implementing ECAFE recommendations and resolutions. Some officials remarked, perhaps a little unkindly, that staff members seemed more concerned to justify the trip than to justify ECAFE. In fairness to the Secretariat it should be pointed out that a personal visit is frequently the only way to obtain essential information from the governments. As protocol is of some importance in these matters a questionnaire will not always elicit a reply. All the same, the impression that staff members on field trips are better fact collectors than ambassadors for ECAFE is one the Secretariat should not find difficult to correct.

Like all international organizations, ECAFE must try to project its image and purposes to the peoples governments represent. The difficulties of the task in Asia are at once apparent. The public educated enough to be reached is extremely small. Much of ECAFE's activity is not in any case newsworthy. But even when good copy is forthcoming, the almost prohibitively high cable rates from Bangkok will invariably cut it short. One interesting, indeed unique, example of a private effort to publicize ECAFE on a national scale is the Japan ECAFE Association. This body was founded in 1953 to spread knowledge of ECAFE activities in Japan, promote research along ECAFE lines, and collaborate with the Commission and other international organizations in exchanging and collecting information on the economic and social development of Asia and the Far East. It regularly produces Japanese editions of the *Economic Survey* and *Bulletin,* including the reports of the Working Party on Economic Development and Planning, and *Mining Developments in Asia and the Far East.* In addition, numerous other ECAFE reports and studies are translated for inclusion in the Association's periodical, *Japan* ECAFE

Information. These translated publications are distributed to its members, various departments of the Japanese government, and research institutes at home and abroad. The Board of Directors of the Association consists almost entirely of representatives of Japanese business, commerce, and banking.

Despite the obvious difficulties of advertising ECAFE in the region, the somewhat staid publicity methods of United Nations Information Centres in the region do not seem designed to make the most of the opportunities offered. It is a little shocking, for instance, to be told by senior government officials in cities where United Nations Information Centres exist, that their ministers, on being reminded of an immediately pending appointment with the Executive Secretary, knew absolutely nothing about him. The ECAFE Executive Secretary should not be an unknown entity to the leading government figures of his own region. It should be the business of local United Nations information services to sell him well, if necessary by the sort of publicity ballyhoo which counts, so that he is known on arrival to be a person of considerable standing with an important mission to accomplish. Tossing the local press the usual dry biscuit of a press release is hardly a substitute.

In a body such as ECAFE, the role of the Secretariat is of crucial importance. The Secretariat can make proposals and withdraw them without damaging the prestige of any government. It can likewise secure amendments and deletions to the work program which governments may be reluctant to suggest for fear of being thought uncooperative. It is also the business of the Secretariat to see that its own activities do not overlap those of other international organizations. ECOSOC has persistently tried to coordinate the activities of its subsidiary bodies. The lawyers attached to the delegations represented at its Coordinating Committee doubtless imagined they were bringing order into United Nations economic and social activities the world over. In fact, it is not within ECOSOC but within government administrations that the real problem of coordination lies. When the right hand of government is unaware of what its left hand has proposed at international meetings, some overlapping between the activities of international organizations can very easily result.

In practice, therefore, the task of coordinating international activities usually falls to international secretariats and is often of a delicate diplomatic nature. ECAFE's earlier relations with FAO showed [22] how difficult it was to draw precise lines of demarcation between agencies whose interests must inevitably overlap to some extent. The solution eventually accepted was to pool resources on a jointly agreed program of work. This was implemented through a joint ECAFE/FAO Agriculture Division. There is a good case, as was argued earlier,[23] for extending this arrangement to include a joint intergovernmental forum to deal specifically with the economic problems of Asian agriculture. Where friction has occurred between the two organizations on other matters, it has been mainly the result of the self-centered behavior of a few officials on either side, but not of their respective chiefs. There have been occasions also when ECAFE initiative impelled an international agency into doing more for Asia. It so happens that all the major international institutions with global responsibilities, including the United Nations specialized agencies, are based in Europe or North America. They cannot entirely escape from the aseptic influence of their environment,[24] and Asian governments and the Secretariat have rightly felt at times that some of them should pay more attention to Asia. Thus ECAFE's earlier incursions into the field of trained manpower probably helped to galvanize ILO into launching a program of work for the region; [25] while more recently the inclusion of telecommunications within the scope of ECAFE has highlighted ITU's relative neglect of specifically Asian problems.[26] It was ECAFE also which prodded the International Union of Official Travel Organizations (IUOTO) into creating a regional travel organization for Asia.[27]

It is worth noting, however, that ECAFE has no serious rival in its region. Although the Manila Pact of 1954 defined a basis

22. See pp. 137–40.
23. See p. 149.
24. "The remoteness of these institutions from the scenes of misery and heart-rending daily human tragedies may make their activities leisurely, *recherché*, and methodological." Statement of Ghanaian delegate summarized in GAOR: 15th Sess., 2nd Cmtte., 687th Mtg., Nov. 21, 1960.
25. See p. 134.
26. See p. 229.
27. See p. 227.

of economic cooperation, no rival program to that of ECAFE has been developed within SEATO. In any case only three Asian countries are members of SEATO.[28] The Colombo Plan, which has acquired unusual prestige by not doing any planning, complements the work of ECAFE. It is not, like ECAFE, primarily concerned with promoting regional cooperation but concentrates generally on national situations and prospects. At first the Colombo Plan had no relations with the Commission and the Executive Secretary was not invited to meetings of its Consultative Committee. Some United Nations officials regarded the omission as a calculated snub to ECAFE, but the first Director of the Colombo Plan Bureau maintains that, in the busy process of getting started, the Bureau did not straightway develop its liaison activities. Since 1952, however, the Executive Secretary has attended meetings of the Consultative Committee and the director of the Bureau, those of the Commission, as official observers. In addition, ECAFE studies and reports have been made readily available to the Consultative Committee.

A number of government officials in the region believe the proceedings of the Colombo Plan to be more informal than those of ECAFE and attribute this to the family atmosphere established by the original nucleus of British Commonwealth members.[29] Discussions among the experts preparing the country drafts that are included in the annual report of the Consultative Committee are said to be very frank. But that is probably true of small expert groups convened by ECAFE or any other organization. The tone of the Consultative Committee, other Asian delegates admit, is rather formal and very British. Furthermore, whatever the degree of informality that may characterize the early stages of editing, the final draft of the country chapters must be acceptable in each case to the country concerned. Just where, in fact, the Colombo Plan got its inflated reputation is, as others have remarked,[30] something of a mystery. A much superior public relations job appears to have been done for it than for ECAFE.

28. Pakistan, the Philippines, and Thailand. Its treaty area, however, also specifically includes Cambodia, Laos, and South Viet-Nam.

29. It should be added, however, that some Colombo Plan delegates from non-Commonwealth countries confessed to the author their dislike of feeling outside the "family" and not privy to its closeness.

30. E.g., Shonfield, *The Attack on World Poverty,* p. 184.

Among the range of relations ECAFE has maintained with other agencies, those with ECE have probably been the closest. They are certainly among the more fruitful. ECE provided the model on which ECAFE's methods of operation were largely fashioned. The ECAFE Secretariat has drawn heavily on the ECE secretariat for information, inspiration, and actual guidance in such fields as trade, coal, electric power, iron and steel, housing and building, and inland transport. ECE helped to arrange laboratory investigations of low-grade Asian coal [31] and a number of study tours initiated by ECAFE. Its staff have occasionally attended ECAFE meetings and been seconded to Bangkok. ECAFE contacts with ECLA have, in contrast, been less active, being confined mainly to an exchange of information. On the other hand, the rationale of economic integration at present being developed for Asia owes far more to ECLA than to ECE. But among the more decisive influences making for bonds of understanding and sympathy between the regional secretariats have been issues of centralization versus decentralization in United Nations economic and social activities.

That relations between Headquarters, or the center, and the regions should sometimes give rise to awkward questions of responsibility and even of loyalty is not hard to understand. The regional commissions have the power to recommend directly to their member governments and are primarily responsible to them; yet they are also accountable to ECOSOC and the General Assembly, either of which may adopt a different policy. Their secretariats are the servants of the commissions, yet also form part of the United Nations Department of Economic and Social Affairs and owe allegiance to the United Nations Secretary-General. It is not uncommon in international organizations for their secretariats to solicit resolutions from the governments. But what happens if this leads to, say, an ECAFE resolution that contradicts Headquarters Secretariat policy? The position becomes more complicated when the political pressures exerted in the center are different from those at work in the region. The Western powers have sometimes suggested that certain lines of proposed action which, in truth, they disliked would be better pursued globally than regionally, because their power to nullify them in

31. See p. 155.

ECOSOC or by lobbying at Headquarters was far greater than in the regions. The recent growth in the voting power of the African-Asian bloc in the General Assembly, however, has now made this a rather less easy maneuver to execute.

The general approach of the first Assistant Secretary-General for Economic Affairs,[32] David K. Owen, to the regional secretariats was to try to pick good Executive Secretaries, give them wide latitude, and see how and what they developed. This characteristically empirical attitude proved to be both sound and expedient: sound because to attempt to hold them on a tight rein would almost certainly have brought Headquarters into ultimate conflict with the wishes of governments in the regions; expedient because there were few, if any, men at Headquarters who could match Myrdal at ECE, Raúl Prebisch at ECLA, and Lokanathan at ECAFE in intellectual stature or toughness of fiber. All the same this policy did not and could not mean that the regional secretariats were free to do more or less as they pleased. They were, after all, part of a global organization. The good relations of the United Nations with the governments and other organizations, as well as efficient administration, demanded that they observe certain standard practices and procedures.[33] It was also very desirable for them to be in constant touch with Headquarters about major policy initiatives, especially those having important political implications. Apart from written communications and occasional visits of senior officials, for instance, to Bangkok and ECAFE meetings, the chief method of conducting these policy consultations has been through regular meetings between the Undersecretary for Economic and Social Affairs and all the Executive Secretaries at the time ECOSOC receives the reports of its regional commissions. Headquarters guidance and policy may in turn originate from resolutions of ECOSOC and the General Assembly on such matters as the need to establish clear priorities in the

32. This post is now called Undersecretary for Economic and Social Affairs.

33. In the case of the regional economic commissions it is already apparent that the "central problem in the relationship between . . . Headquarters and the secretariats of the regional economic commissions is the appropriate measure of regional autonomy consistent, on the one hand, with a unified United Nations policy." GAOR: 10th Sess., 1955, Annexes, Agenda items 38 and 47 (A/3050, para. 7); see also ibid. (A/3041).

work program,[34] to limit and control documentation,[35] or the number, frequency, and length of meetings.[36]

In the case of ECAFE, which was a very weak organization to begin with, various units at Headquarters contributed to its annual *Economic Survey*, prepared papers for its meetings, and even cosponsored some of them. Having no legal affairs officer of its own, ECAFE has relied entirely on Headquarters for clarifications and interpretations of its terms of reference, rules of procedure, and other constitutional questions. Consequently it was not always unreasonable for Headquarters to feel that its views should be taken into account by the ECAFE Secretariat. Lokanathan, however, sometimes issued documents on matters involving major United Nations policy issues without first consulting Headquarters. Furthermore, it was early apparent that he was not good at interagency diplomacy and tended, for instance, to ignore the interests of the specialized agencies and resented TAA interference in the organization of meetings it helped to finance.

But while firm guidance and directives from Headquarters were justified at times, there were other elements in the relationship which gave Lokanathan and, for that matter, the ECE and ECLA secretariats as well good grounds for believing that Headquarters was becoming unduly meddlesome. Although the Cold War rapidly eroded the scope for global United Nations initiatives, it was still possible to do useful work in the regions, especially in Asia and Latin America. The canker of McCarthyism which the first Secretary-General, Trygve Lie, allowed to penetrate into the very corridors of the Headquarters building, deprived the Secretariat of some large and able minds and shattered the morale of others. Without a challenging program of their own to keep them fully preoccupied, it was tempting for senior officials at Headquarters to assert their authority and will over the regional secretariats. Perhaps a tinge of envy of the regional commissions which were, and still are, much more connected with actual intergovernmental activity than Headquarters contributed to the trend. In addition, Headquarters was under mount-

34. ECOSOC Res. 451A(XIV), July 28, 1952.
35. ECOSOC Res. 557A(XVIII), Aug. 5, 1954.
36. ECOSOC Res. 590(XX), Aug. 5, 1955.

ing pressure from the United States to curb what United States officials regarded as dangerous symptoms of autonomy in the regional commissions and their secretariats.[37] Understandably, Lokanathan suspected that some of the directives received from New York were the result of this pressure. On his appointment as Secretary-General, Hammarskjold and the Undersecretary for Economic and Social Affairs, Philippe de Seynes, attempted to tighten the rein on the regional secretariats and bring them under more intellectual and administrative discipline. But political and economic forces have been against any strong centralization of United Nations operations and in favor of greater regional initiatives and groupings. The political emancipation of Africa has noticeably strengthened them in recent years.

Headquarters still decides or approves a whole range of questions of importance to the regional secretariats from the recruitment, promotion, and transfer of staff, to their travel program and the printing of their documents. There is an unmistakable sense among experienced members of the ECAFE Secretariat that, as regards the manner and spirit in which this power has been exercised, they are the poor and distant relations or forgotten children of Headquarters.[38] Although these feelings appear to betray a sense of inadequacy which needs to find causes outside itself, they are by no means irrational. There are aspects of Headquarters' operations which are, in fact, hard to understand or justify.

In 1952 the General Assembly's Advisory Committee on Administrative and Budgetary Questions suggested that an expansion of staff in the regions be accompanied by a reduction at Headquarters.[39] It implied that there was a large-scale duplication of activities between Headquarters and the regions. The Secretary-General firmly denied this and thought the suggestion impracticable. Since then, as a result of ECOSOC decisions, there has been a significant expansion in the substantive work of Headquarters in such fields as water resources and industrial development. A Water Resources Development Centre was established at Headquarters in 1959 and

37. For further comment, see pp. 349–51.

38. Also noticed by Sharp, *Field Administration*, p. 152.

39. Advisory Cmtte., 1st Report, GAOR: 7th Sess., Suppl. No. 7, 1952.

a Committee for Industrial Development held its first meeting there in 1961 and recommended, *inter alia,* the setting up of a United Nations Industrial Development Centre which was done the following year. ECOSOC and the General Assembly have charged this Committee with the main responsibility for United Nations activities aimed at assisting industrialization. Naturally, Headquarters had to find the staff to service these new responsibilities. For instance, in 1962 the Secretary-General appointed a Commissioner for Industrial Development at the undersecretary level to be in charge of the Development Centre. But considering the difficulties faced by ECAFE in trying to make an impact on government policies and actions, it is far from clear what exactly the substantive activities at Headquarters hope to accomplish. Admittedly, a central location for certain functions, such as pooling information, experience, and guidance, can be both useful and necessary. Furthermore, a body like the Committee on Industrial Development may help to dramatize the necessity for more effort and resources to be devoted to accelerating the industrialization of underdeveloped countries. All the same the development of industries and natural resources cannot be effectively tackled on a global plane since the problems are local and therefore closer to the regions.

In 1961 a Committee of Experts appointed by the Secretary-General to review the activities and organization of the United Nations Secretariat as a whole [40] suggested that the Department of Economic and Social Affairs be divested of all operational responsibilities and the staff concerned transferred to the regions. "As the regional secretariats become built up," the committee added, "there would be benefits both at Headquarters and regionally if some members of regional staffs were transferred to Headquarters." [41] It noted that in the past the flow of staff has tended to be all one way, namely from Headquarters to the regions. This has, in fact, been one of the more strongly pressed grievances of the ECAFE staff though little, if anything, appears to have been done about it in recent years. In commenting on the experts' suggestion, the Secretary-General admitted that as regards

40. In accordance with General Assembly Res. 1446(XIV), Dec. 5, 1959.

41. GAOR: 16th Sess., 1961–62, Annexes, Agenda item 61 (A/4776, para. 113).

the redeployment of regional staff, "there may be some scope for action."[42] Existing arrangements, however, allowed "the regional commissions to build up their resources in priority areas while being able to count on Headquarters support in areas which do not warrant the establishment of quadruplicate regional services." Moreover, ECOSOC and its functional commissions have been demanding increasingly centralized research and information services, particularly in the fields of natural resources and industry. For this reason "it would seem out of reach to develop a full body of technical competence at each regional office in such broad and highly diversified fields." The Secretary-General should therefore continue to use total Secretariat resources in the most efficient way for the benefit of United Nations member countries, "the question of geographical attachment of staff and distribution of financial resources being only a related consideration."

These high sounding statements may or may not have real substance. But to the outsider unversed in the niceties of United Nations administrative practices and uninfluenced by the bureaucratic vested interests or innate resistances that may lie behind them, it would seem to be of most practical benefit to underdeveloped countries to locate substantive staff as near as possible to the specific problems faced by their policy-makers and administrators. The "feel" for local situations, which can be acquired only by firsthand experience, is an indispensable quality of sensible diagnosis and prescription. When the Mekong Project got under way, for instance, some staff at Headquarters behaved as if the Mekong flowed into the East River under their very noses. There is a tendency to an aura of omniscience at Headquarters which even the least self-centered minds there must find hard to resist. It is this impression of knowing what is best that often annoys the man on the spot. But perhaps the complexity of the whole question of centralization versus decentralization of United Nations operations emerges more clearly from an examination of ECAFE's relations with United Nations technical assistance activities.

On its inauguration in 1949 the United Nations Expanded Programme of Technical Assistance was decentralized with the specialized agencies and the United Nations itself carrying on the

42. Ibid. (A/4794).

work. In theory the regional commission secretariats were to participate actively in that part of the program for which United Nations Headquarters was responsible.[43] In practice this was interpreted to mean giving them a sense of participation without actual policy-making functions or operational responsibilities. In July 1950 full control over the development and implementation of the United Nations part of the program was vested in a new body, TAA, which reported direct to the Secretary-General and functioned more like a specialized agency than an integral part of United Nations economic and social activities. The first Director-General of TAA was, in any case, unsympathetic to regional points of view. The major financial contributors to EPTA also strongly supported a high degree of centralization. Not surprisingly, the relevance of ECAFE to United Nations technical assistance activities was consequently rather limited.[44]

First, TAA and later BTAO reported annually to the Commission session on their activities in the ECAFE region. This gave Asian countries, particularly those that were not members of ECOSOC, an opportunity to win regional support for their views on the scope and character of these activities, for it has always been open to the Commission to make recommendations to ECOSOC on the subject. The early debates on TAA activities also served to encourage a better response from those Asian governments that were slow at first to request technical assistance. Later on, the quality of experts, the cost of operations, and the lack of continuity in technical assistance came in for a lot of criticism in the Commis-

43. "In the execution of its programme of technical assistance," the Secretary-General stated in 1949, "the United Nations would make full use of the resources not only of the Secretariat at headquarters but also of the secretariats of the regional economic commissions." *Technical Assistance for Economic Development*, UN Sales No.:1949.II.B.I. p. 52.

44. The Undersecretary for Economic and Social Affairs confessed to the Second Committee of the General Assembly on November 21, 1960, that "we were more or less dominated over a long period, by a way of thinking which doubtless originated in a desire to simplify and clarify matters. According to that way of thinking the regional economic commissions were organs which should devote themselves to research and study and which should be barred from what are termed operational responsibilities." He added that the effects, far from simplifying matters, made them singularly complicated. "It prevented the regional commissions from gaining the full impetus and full dynamism which they nevertheless seemed designed to possess in view of the terms of reference assigned to them by the Economic and Social Council and the confidence placed in them by Governments."

sion.[45] Several Asian governments clearly desired a more important role for ECAFE in the program.[46] Pakistan favored the status quo; [47] so did most of the outside powers.

Second, the advisory services that the Commission's mandate authorizes its Secretariat to perform have, in effect, been a form of technical assistance. Headquarters insisted, however, that they must only be given in connection with approved projects in the ECAFE work program and limited to about two weeks on any one project in a single country in any one year. In no circumstances should extra staff or consultants be engaged with the primary object of providing such services. Despite these limitations the advisory services have often been very helpful to governments. Some ECAFE staff, nevertheless, exaggerate their intrinsic value.[48] Most of the technical specialists in the Secretariat, particularly those who have not actually practiced their skills for a long time, are not top-flight experts. Their function is more that of the "family doctor" who knows when and what kind of a "specialist" is required. Countries can then cite ECAFE in support of their requests for technical assistance.

For the most part the value of these advisory services lies less in their intrinsic worth than in the friendly feelings and attachments they help to cultivate for ECAFE. They have been supplemented in some instances by the secondment of experts to the Secretariat mainly for the purpose of supporting United Nations technical assistance operations in the region. The work of the regional census advisers [49] and the outposting of social affairs officers [50] are good cases in point. Both proved to be useful demonstrations also of the advantages of decentralization. A number of ECAFE subsidiary bodies have now recommended that panels of expert advisers be available in or through ECAFE to visit countries

45. E.g., at the 1954 Commission session. See Doc. E/CN.11/389, Mar. 25, 1954.

46. See, e.g., 1951 and 1956 Commission session debates. Docs. E/CN.11/SR.86, Mar. 10, 1951, and E/CN.11/451, Mar. 18, 1957.

47. For Pakistan statement to 1952 and 1956 Commission sessions, see Docs. E/CN.11/344, Apr. 21, 1952, E/CN.11/363, Apr. 15, 1953, and E/CN.11/451, Mar. 18, 1957.

48. The author has come across cases where a request for Secretariat advisory services and a testimonial to their value was actually solicited from government officials unknown to the minister in charge of the department concerned.

49. See p. 96.

50. See p. 263.

at their request for on-the-spot consultations. These should not only help to spread the benefits of technical advice but also to enhance the practical value of many ECAFE activities.

The third principal way in which ECAFE's work has been relevant to United Nations technical assistance operations is through the identification and organization of regional projects such as study tours, demonstration experiments, seminars, and training centers, requiring the financial backing of TAA or BTAO. Regional projects, as well as bringing nations together, are, as TAA recognized, "more economical and effective than a series of separate schemes." [51] Yet at the 1954 Commission session, when India introduced a resolution emphasizing their importance and asking the Executive Secretary to expand them if possible, other Asian countries, notably Burma, Ceylon, and Pakistan, were quick to remove any possible implication that regional projects should receive priority over country programs. In addition the United States and TAA felt that the Indian resolution invited the Executive Secretary to assume functions which were primarily the responsibility of TAA. Accordingly, the United States secured the deletion from it of the part requesting him to continue and, if possible, expand regional projects.[52] The following year the Technical Assistance Committee of ECOSOC (TAC) decided that not more than 10 per cent of the total cost of EPTA could be spent on such projects. On the recommendation of TAB this was raised to 15 per cent in 1962.[53]

Of the various types of regional project, the study tour has probably been the most popular. But whether such tours always constitute real value for money may be questioned. Doubts on this score are further strengthened in those instances where the itinerary has been dictated as much as anything by a politically motivated invitation from either the Soviet Union or the United States. A definite answer is not possible since there has not been

51. TAA statement to 1956 Commission session. See Doc. E/CN.11/451, Mar. 18, 1957.

52. Doc. E/CN.11/389, Mar. 25, 1954.

53. Regional projects financed under the UN regular program of technical assistance, as opposed to EPTA, are not subject to this legislative limit. There is much to be said against ceilings on the outlays for regional projects since concerted regional activities are bound to grow in number. See Sharp, *Field Administration*, pp. 546–47.

nearly enough reported follow-up action on the results and impact of ECAFE study tours.

Asian countries have also been very ready to propose or accept the idea of regional training and research centers. But bringing them into existence has proved far from simple. The policy of TAA and BTAO has been to create regional training centers on the basis of national training facilities. The difficulty is that India and Japan are invariably best placed to offer such facilities, while smaller Asian countries tend to feel that regional projects of this nature should be shared more equitably. Moreover, great prestige value is attached to being host to a regional center although it is not always realized that it can be quite expensive for the host as well. In the case of regional research centers, where again India and Japan usually have the best national facilities, there is even more inhibition about locating them in either place for fear that Indian or Japanese interests would be the dominating influence on their activities. Even when centers are established, as at Lahore for Railway Operating and Signaling Officials [54] and at Rangoon for Diesel Marine Mechanics,[55] they have not been consistently well supported by Asian governments. The same is true of the regional housing centers at Delhi and Bandung.[56] For technical training there is still a marked preference, which the Colombo Plan Bureau can confirm, to seek it outside the region even though equally good, if not better, facilities are available in some other Asian country. Partly this reflects the continuing power of historical connections and partly the greater prestige attached to training in Europe and North America.

In 1960 the Commission passed a resolution asking the United Nations agencies to provide adequate allocations for regional projects.[57] Although under EPTA the percentage share of regional projects in the total cost of technical assistance to the ECAFE region rose slightly from 1956 to 1960, it was less than for Latin America and for Africa as well in 1960.[58] This suggests that the real prob-

54. See p. 210.
55. See p. 224.
56. See p. 274.
57. See p. 300 n. 50; also *ECAFE Annual Reports to ECOSOC, 20 March 1959–21 March 1960,* Doc. E/CN.11/530, n.d., para. 344, and *22 March 1960–20 March 1961,* Doc. E/CN.11/564, Apr. 22, 1961, para. 416.
58. The percentage share rose from 5.7 per cent in 1956 to 7.2 per cent in 1958

lem for the ECAFE region as compared, for instance, with the ECLA region is less a lack of funds for regional projects than of well-conceived projects or at least of determination to translate ideas into realities. Centralization of technical assistance operations is no longer an obstacle, since the choice, organization, and priorities for all United Nations regional technical assistance projects in the ECAFE region now rest with ECAFE itself. They are, in effect, ECAFE projects. There seems no good reason why devolution of responsibility should not be completed by allowing ECAFE to administer the budget for them. It is in respect of national programs, however, that the failure of ECAFE activities and United Nations technical assistance operations to support and complement one another has been most marked.

In 1955 a Survey Group established by the Secretary-General reported that "technical assistance activities in countries within the geographical scope of the Regional Commissions have failed to benefit from the wealth of specialized knowledge and experience within the Commissions' secretariats, in spite of the fact that many of these activities are closely related to the work of the Commissions and in certain important respects are mutually complementary. . . . The Regional Commissions and their staff, for their part, have been largely detached from technical assistance in countries in which they work, to which they themselves occasionally provide technical advisory services, and in which they have come to be regarded as the regional arm of the United Nations." [59] The Survey Group accordingly suggested that technical assistance and social affairs units be established within the regional secretariats. The Secretary-General agreed that this "would improve our services and enhance a profitable use of funds." [60] The proposal was not liked by various governments, however, especially among the largest contributors to EPTA; nor by TAA, which feared it might give the regional secretariats too much influence over United Na-

---

and 7.8 per cent in 1960. See *Annual Report of the Technical Assistance Board to the Technical Assistance Committee* for 1960, Doc. E/3471, May 1961.

59. Organization of the Secretariat. Report of the Secretary-General's Survey Group, Doc. A/3041, Nov. 23, 1955.

60. Ibid. This opinion was endorsed in the *ECAFE Annual Report to ECOSOC, 8 April 1955–14 February 1956,* Doc. E/CN.11/430, Mar. 1956, paras. 295–96. Some Asian governments at the 1956 Commission session wanted to enshrine it in a resolution, but others did not agree. See Doc. E/CN.11/451, Mar. 18, 1957.

tions technical assistance programing.[61] In the end, a social affairs unit was established within the ECAFE Secretariat.[62] Yet there were a number of obvious weaknesses about the highly centralized control and administration of United Nations technical assistance operations which the Survey Group's suggestion might have helped to correct.

As is now recognized, the substantive briefing of technical assistance experts cannot be done well from New York. The ECAFE Secretariat is much closer and more familiar with local situations and has a better "feel" for them than Headquarters. Once in the field, the expert needs continuing support services or, to use United Nations terminology, "backstopping services," from BTAO. But Headquarters simply cannot give adequate attention to all its country program activities. The field trips of BTAO officials are too infrequent and usually too hurried with the result that many experts feel remote from and uncared for by Headquarters. The creation of a technical assistance unit in the region and regular contacts between experts and the ECAFE Secretariat would have helped to remedy this situation and at lower cost than any attempt to do so from Headquarters. The ECAFE Secretariat was not allowed in the past to make contact with experts in the field. A few experts attended ECAFE meetings, occasionally as members of government delegations, but the practice was on the whole exceptional. The value of their services would be enhanced if ECAFE were provided with funds to invite them to those meetings where their experience and competence would make a valuable contribution to the discussions.[63]

The Secretariat has been asked to make comments to Headquarters on the reports of experts. It is a little embarrassing, however, to criticize an expert's work to his "employers" behind his back. A better procedure would be for the comments to go directly to the expert for consideration before sending his final report to

61. Sharp, *Field Administration,* p. 188.

62. See p. 263. The Secretary-General was authorized to carry out on a trial basis a partial decentralization of TAA's functions in Latin America only. The experiment was not, however, a great success, principally because all decision-making power, including that relating to routine day-to-day administration, was retained by Headquarters. See Sharp, *Field Administration,* pp. 270–80.

63. This can only be done in respect of regional projects.

BTAO. Moreover, there seems no good reason why those who read these reports at Headquarters should not read them in the regions. The ECAFE Secretariat used also to suggest experts to Headquarters, but appears to have given up doing so because its recommendations were largely ignored. Whatever may be the advantages of centralizing the recruitment of experts, it is not clear why the drafting of the job description and hence of the kind of expert required should not be done in the region. Headquarters also receives and decides applications for United Nations fellowships; ECAFE has been consulted only about fellowships for regional projects. But why should Headquarters be more competent to decide the merits of, say, a Cambodian applicant, than the ECAFE staff? True, on all such matters BTAO consults the substantive division at Headquarters and will not recommend without its approval. But that does not dispose of the point that the regional staff is closer and more familiar with local situations than Headquarters staff. In short, there appears to be no compelling reason why the section for Asia and the Far East of BTAO should not be transferred to Bangkok.

The failure of ECAFE activities and United Nations technical assistance programs to support and complement one another was most apparent, however, in the absence of regular consultations between the ECAFE Secretariat and TAB Resident Representatives.[64] There have been many instances where technical assistance could well have helped governments to implement recommendations they themselves accepted at ECAFE meetings. It is theoretically possible for the Secretariat to persuade a government to request specific assistance for this purpose; but this rarely happens in practice. To be effective the persuasion must be done through the Resident Representative at the time country programs are being formulated.

For the most part United Nations technical assistance operations have heretofore not helped to consummate the advantages of international economic cooperation. Even if strong central control was desirable at the outset, because the regional commissions out-

64. For a useful account of the origins and functions of TAB Resident Representatives, see C. Hart Schaaf, "The Role of Resident Representatives of the United Nations Technical Assistance Board," *International Organization, 14*, No. 4 (1960).

side Europe were weak organizations or because no one could foresee all the administrative problems involved, neither reason justified its continuation for over ten years. To have clung to procedures and practices which diffused and wasted the resources and efforts of both governments and the United Nations itself was a singularly paradoxical way of tackling the problems of economic underdevelopment.[65]

Within the past two years a strong wind has blown up, particularly from the direction of ECA and the new African members of the United Nations, in favor of a larger measure of decentralization of United Nations technical assistance operations. In August 1960, ECOSOC unanimously passed a resolution recognizing that the regional commissions "have an increasingly important role to play in assisting in the initiation, implementation and co-ordination of economic and social programmes and activities at the regional level, including appropriate technical assistance projects." It accordingly urged the governments and the Secretary-General to make all possible use of their services and facilities.[66] The General Assembly the following November reinforced the authority of ECOSOC's directive in a resolution sponsored by 25 underdeveloped countries, which requested the Secretary-General to consult the regional commissions on the decentralization of United Nations economic and social activities.[67] A significant number of underdeveloped countries have demanded, in other words, a reversal of the trend toward ever more centralized control and administration of United Nations operational responsibilities. The ECAFE Commission session in 1961 welcomed these initiatives in a resolution and recommended closer association between United Nations technical assistance and Special

65. It is noteworthy that the specialized agencies never divorced their substantive departments and regional offices from their technical assistance operations.

66. ECOSOC Res. 793(XXX), Aug. 3, 1960. This resolution was prompted by the findings of an expert appraisal of UN economic and social activities contained in *Five Year Perspective, 1960–1964*, Doc. E/3347/Rev.1, 1960.

67. General Assembly Res. 1518(XV), Dec. 15, 1960. The Ghanaian delegate in introducing this resolution before the Second Committee on November 21 mentioned that its sponsors would like to see support for the regional commissions also take the form of "adjusting, in consultations with the Secretariats of the Commissions, international multilateral and bilateral economic and technical aid for various countries within the regions to the order of priorities established by the Commissions in their work programmes."

Fund activities and ECAFE and an enlargement of the Secretariat's advisory services.[68] It added, however, that any "administrative arrangements to implement the resolutions on the decentralization of United Nations economic and social activities . . . should avoid complicated and confusing procedures and should aim at the speedy, efficient and maximum use of the total resources available in the United Nations Secretariat." [69] This is certainly an important consideration to bear in mind since bilateral programs outside the United Nations often respond more quickly to requests for assistance.

Finally, in July 1961, a further ECOSOC resolution sponsored by four underdeveloped countries and, significantly, the United States requested the Secretary-General to submit to the General Assembly "an up-to-date account of the administrative and organizational measures and changes that have been taken, and are required to be taken, to advance the process of decentralisation of the United Nations economic and social activities including the proposed expansion of the supporting substantive and administrative staff of the regional economic commissions, in such a way as to ensure efficiency, economy and the most effective execution of the United Nations operational programmes." [70] ECOSOC also authorized the setting up of technical assistance units within the regional commissions.

The precise form and manner of decentralization had not yet been determined at the beginning of 1962 but it seemed destined to be fairly far-reaching. Signs of change had been accumulating during the previous two years. In 1960, for the first time, United Nations country programs of technical assistance for 1961–62 were sent to the ECAFE Secretariat for study in relation to present work programs and future activities. The first of a projected series of regular meetings between resident representatives in the region and the Secretariat was held in 1962. It is believed that more technical assistance experts are being routed through Bangkok for briefing by the Secretariat. The fact that United Nations regional technical assistance projects are now ECAFE projects has already

68. See *ECAFE Annual Report to ECOSOC, 22 March 1960–20 March 1961,* Doc. E/CN.11/564, Apr. 22, 1961, p. 150.

69. Ibid., para. 422.

70. Doc. E/L.909/Rev.1, July 20, 1961.

been mentioned. The decision to make the ECAFE Secretariat the executive agent of the United Nations for the Mekong Project has been fully vindicated. Much more responsibility is likely to follow.

In 1961 a committee of outside experts set up by the Secretary-General to review the activities and organization of the whole United Nations Secretariat, suggested [71] that regional secretariats be responsible for executing United Nations technical assistance programs, selecting and placing applicants for fellowships, and recruiting experts from the region. For these purposes some transfer of Headquarters staff to the regions, including the relevant geographical sections of BTAO and part of the Technical Assistance Recruiting Services (TARS), would be necessary. The regional secretariats should also have the authority and means to invite United Nations technical assistance experts to meetings. Some of the experts even thought they should administer the United Nations share of EPTA, as well as an allocation from the United Nations budget for its regular technical assistance program.[72]

The Secretary-General, while fully agreeing with the objectives of decentralization, thought these ideas too far-reaching.[73] Regional administration of the United Nations technical assistance system, he contended, "would inescapably lead to a compartmentalisation of programmes and the loss of a major benefit associated with the United Nations programmes, namely, the truly international interchange of experience, skills and techniques." The role of the regional commissions should be developed primarily at the planning and programing stage of technical assistance. Whether actual technical assistance administrative units should be set up

71. GAOR: 16th Sess., 1961–62, Annexes, Agenda item 61 (A/4776).

72. The Committee disagreed on this point. The US expert, L. M. Goodrich, doubted whether the regional secretariats were now or would be for some time to come in a position to determine wisely or efficiently a regional allocation of technical assistance. He feared that political considerations would become decisive, because there were no recognized criteria for making an allocation except the merits of a particular project and wondered if the regional secretariats wanted the responsibility for determining the priority of projects. It is not altogether clear exactly what Goodrich meant or why his argument did not apply equally to allocations from Headquarters. Certainly, it would be rash to assume that allocations from the center are free from suspicion on the part of the recipients. There is something to be said for transferring part of the onus for dealing with aid from donors to recipients. See Gordon, "Regional Approaches to Economic Development."

73. GAOR: 16th Sess., 1961–62, Annexes, Agenda item 61 (A/4794).

within them was a question he preferred to leave to the Executive Secretaries. ECOSOC agreed with him on this point.[74] In a further discussion on decentralization the General Assembly thought that unified policy guidance and financial controls and management should be maintained at Headquarters. It was emphatic, however, in wishing to see operational responsibility for United Nations technical assistance decentralized.

In the last resort the real test of decentralization will lie, as Sharp has argued,[75] "not so much in the work-load of an agency's field offices as in the frequency with which they decide matters themselves and how important such matters are." But whatever the manner and scope of decentralization it is bound to enlarge the responsibilities of the ECAFE Secretariat. How it responds will depend not only on the quality of its staff, but also on its cohesion, teamwork, purposefulness, and leadership. In these respects there is undoubted room for improvement.

The Secretariat has been up against daunting and at times dispiriting circumstances. It is not easy, as already indicated, to recruit and retain able staff, though it is doubtful if the leadership has always seized promising recruiting opportunities as energetically as the situation demanded. Working and living conditions have greatly improved in Bangkok over the last decade; but it is still a physically debilitating place. The lack of strength in depth in the Secretariat means that very few specialists have sometimes to cope with immense tasks. The achievements of ECAFE would have been much less had its Secretariat not battled valiantly and, on the whole, successfully against these difficulties.

But when all these and other headaches have been duly noted, it may be fairly doubted whether the strength of its teamwork is commensurate with present and future challenges. It is not simply, for instance, that the engineer and the economist within its ranks, each with a different view of what is possible and important, do not always pull together. The ECAFE record and much else in underdeveloped countries show that both of them in general need to appreciate better the limitations of diagnosing and prescribing on the basis of most advanced Western techniques, whether of economic theory or scientific technology. But even a relatively homogeneous unit like the Research and Planning Division seems

74. ECOSOC Res. 856(XXXII), Aug. 4, 1961.
75. Sharp, *Field Administration,* p. 507.

to function more as separate cells, with surprisingly little significant contact between them, than as one coherent group. Again on such matters as field trips and consultant funds there is a tendency for division chiefs to think in terms of "fair shares" rather than priorities.

More surprising is the lack of real debate between the professional staff, not only about problems of diagnosis and prescription but also about the whole character, methods, and limitations of international economic cooperation. The senior staff is too prone to report all meetings and field trips successful and all studies well received. This aura of apparent complacency contrasts sharply with, for instance, the tradition of critical self-analysis Gunnar Myrdal established at ECE. It is almost as if, like the delegates, no one wished to risk hurting the heart, the status, or the pride of the club. The institutional setting in which the Secretariat functions is heavily influenced, however, by the Executive Secretary himself. ECAFE has so far had three Executive Secretaries, each of whom by force of circumstance as well as of character and background has interpreted his role differently.[76]

The first Executive Secretary, Lokanathan, who was more of a fighter than a diplomat, trod roughly on many toes within and outside the United Nations in his struggles to give ECAFE a standing and significance for Asian countries. Nor was he a good administrator. But if he did not have the virtues of an Indian Civil Service (ICS) background neither did he have its vices. Had he been a bureaucrat by upbringing, ECAFE might well have become simply a pliable appendage of Headquarters rather than an agency with a distinctive character and direction of its own. The faults and weaknesses of Lokanathan stemmed largely from his own sense of dedication. It is, however, a considerable tribute to both his imagination and courage that ECAFE has been mainly concerned since he left to steer the course he charted.

C. V. Narasimhan, Lokanathan's successor, was by contrast a most accomplished administrator whose dynamic energy, diplo-

76. The role of the Deputy Executive Secretary is something of a mystery. Its importance obviously depends greatly on the Executive Secretary. If, as has happened since Lokanathan, the Executive Secretary and his Deputy are both professional administrators, the Deputy may well become little more than a figurehead. Considering the workload of the Secretariat and the difficulty of getting additional posts, this senior and highly paid post might be used to better effect.

macy, and personality succeeded in breathing life and action into a number of stationary ideas and projects. He streamlined the ECAFE work program and won the confidence of some influential quarters that had distrusted his predecessor. More a salesman than an innovator, his efficient, personable leadership left a stamp on all he achieved. It was a misfortune for ECAFE when the Secretary-General transferred him to New York.

The present Executive Secretary, U Nyun, began with two clear advantages over his predecessors. He was already an experienced ECAFE man and came from a small country, Burma. As a devout Buddhist he is also, in a sense, more Asian than his predecessors. Although an ex-ICS man, he has neither the tremendous administrative drive nor the capacity to persuade by force of personality that his predecessor displayed. But his high moral sense and luminous sincerity may well be no less persuasive. He evidently believes the Executive Secretary is not a political figure and should concentrate his message on the senior officials, the element of continuity in government, who attend ECAFE meetings, rather than on the politicians in the capitals. This may, in fact, be a canny reading of where decisive policy-making power in Asia really resides, though whether government officials are noticeably susceptible to the ideals of internationalism is another matter. It is essential to maintain that ECAFE and its Executive Secretary are concerned only with nonpolitical matters; but it would be idle to live strictly by this conviction in practice. The fact that some major political hurdles had first to be surmounted before activities like the Mekong Project, Asian Highway, and trade consultations got under way would seem to underline the point.

But when all due recognition has been given to the role of the Secretariat, it still remains true that in terms of the broad currents of history which produce and are mirrored by international organizations, the power of an international secretariat is very limited. It takes initiatives only in default of governments taking them; the quality of the machinery and service at the disposal of governments is no substitute for the will to use it. No matter how persuasive and effective the Secretariat may be, the extent to which cooperation actually occurs will not exceed the limits of national interest generously interpreted. Unfortunately for ECAFE national economic self-interest in its region became heavily circumscribed by political inhibitions, suspicions, and animosities.

CHAPTER 16

The Politics of Cooperation

From the outset ECAFE could hardly avoid being a cockpit for the revolutionary forces and ideas that were remaking the political map of Asia. In the first place the creation of the Commission was in itself a political decision; it represented the first important admission of the United Nations that the world included Asia in its own right and not merely as the responsibility of a few colonial powers. Just as Europeans or Latin Americans possessed common feelings that transcended their differences, so after World War II a definite Asian outlook came into focus. This expressed itself in a detestation of colonialism, racialism, and foreign domination, a deeply felt consciousness of poverty and international inequality, and an ambition for economic advancement and more equal opportunity.

The tremors of this Asian nationalism were bound to shake the foundations of a regional economic organization whose membership at that time was so patently unrepresentative of Asian peoples and wishes. Its full impact was consequently felt on questions of membership. Although Asian delegates debated them as straightforward issues between the rights of self-determination and the perpetuation of colonial power and privilege, it was the political control of ECAFE that was really at stake. For their only alternative to gaining political control was to accept the low valuation the Western powers placed on the functions and future of ECAFE. In terms of voting strength they did not win this battle until 1951 when Indonesia became a full member. The enthusiasm of recently emancipated African nations to use the United Nations to force the pace of decolonization is very reminiscent of the immediate postwar temper of Asian nationalism. Indeed, what has been happening to the balance of voting power in the General Assembly was foreshadowed by what happened to it in ECAFE.

Within the United Nations family of organizations it was ECAFE which thus first experienced the full force of the postwar revolt against colonialism. The atmosphere of its early Commission sessions was emotional and touchy; there was an almost irresistible urge to pay off old scores. Asian delegates were sensitive to national pride and apt to take offense at slights real or apparent. The constitution of the Commission, its terms of reference and rules of procedure, were part of the political tradition of Western countries rather than of Asian. They had little experience of parliamentary government and even less of international conference techniques. Consequently they became easily irritated or confused when Western delegates invoked constitutional points to thwart their proposals.[1] Their lack of instructions only heightened the sense of frustration.

As already indicated, Asian delegates and Executive Secretary Lokanathan hoped that ECAFE would be able to do for its region what the European Recovery Program (ERP) was doing for Western Europe. It seems unlikely, however, that newly independent Asian governments had given any serious thought at that time to the question of foreign aid. All of them were deeply absorbed in establishing the authority of the state over their territory. They had still to define their national economic objectives. Having just thrown out foreign domination through the front door they were naturally sensitive to letting it in through the back in the form of strings attached to foreign aid. Nevertheless, there was no denying that in varying degrees all had suffered grievously from the war and all were desperately poor. If Western Europe, a much richer area, was given substantial external assistance, they felt that Asians had a strong moral case for receiving parallel treatment. How precisely this should be arranged Asian delegates did

1. "The representatives of under-developed countries were so keen to accelerate economic development," the Indian delegate, K. B. Lall, remarked to the Industry and Trade Committee as late as 1956, "that they did not attach so much importance to matters of form and procedure as did certain other delegates, who had spoken words of caution." Doc. E/CN.11/I&T/124, June 18, 1956, para. 59.

not make clear; but at least they were prepared to use ECAFE for the purpose. The United States completely rejected, however, any notion of extending the Marshall Plan concept to Asia or of channeling financial assistance through ECAFE. The expectations Asian governments had entertained of the Commission were rudely disappointed. In the process they lost and have never fully recovered the belief that more could be obtained from the West by acting together rather than singly. The overwhelmingly bilateral character of the aid subsequently given by the West underlined this harsh lesson. The cause of regional cooperation had suffered its first major setback.

The Soviet Union was, in fact, the only outside power to favor ECAFE's elaborating an aid program for Asia.[2] It might be argued that Soviet membership gave the West sufficient reason for not channeling aid through ECAFE. But the West proposed no alternative channel. In retrospect it would seem that a great opportunity had been missed of fostering an attachment among Asian countries to the idea of regional cooperation before their political alignments became hopelessly divided by Cold War politics. But that was not how the situation and prospect of Asia looked to the United States when the Marshall Plan was launched.

To the United States, South-east Asia immediately after the war was a responsibility of the colonial powers, not an area of paramount United States interest. Its foreign aid operations were, therefore, confined to North-east Asia, including China and the Philippines. When the Marshall Plan began in 1948 some Congressional pressure was put on the United States administration to extend its principles and aims to Asia.[3] The administration insisted, however, that first priority must be given to Western Europe; it was here that Communist expansion had first to be halted. In any case, the administration argued, even if the funds were available, the basis for a massive aid program did not exist in Asia; Asia simply did not have the institutions, traditions, or established administrative and economic structures which made the Marshall Plan so effective. In Asia the problem was not just a severe dollar shortage but long-term economic development. That was a horse of a very different color and much more needed

2. For Soviet statement to the Commission, see Doc. E/CN.11/11, June 17, 1947.
3. Wolf, *Foreign Aid: Theory and Practice in Southern Asia.*

to be known about its capabilities before it could be backed with impunity.

The first step in formulating a United States policy of assistance for economic development was the Point Four Program President Truman announced in 1949 for "making the benefits of scientific advances and industrial progress available for the improvement and growth of underdeveloped areas." [4] But what decisively changed the whole character and scope of United States aid policy to Asia was the victory of communism in China. Following the findings of various survey missions sent to the region in 1950 a series of bilateral aid programs was launched the following year. The Commonwealth responded to the needs of Asia by establishing the Colombo Plan. Although its inauguration in 1950 adopted the phraseology and methods of ERP, which doubtless had a certain psychological appeal both in Asia and the United States, it became, in fact, little more than a loose and flexible clearing arrangement for bilaterally negotiated aid programs.[5] Nor, as it turned out, did the creation of EPTA the previous year help to foster an attachment to the idea of regional cooperation through ECAFE.

In the field of aid and trade the West held all the strong cards. Understandably, most Asian countries came to demand the most direct contact with the source of assistance. Bilateral negotiations had the further advantage of giving some of them more opportunity to emphasize the political and military dangers necessitating additional aid. When political bribery enters into the distribution of aid, political blackmail becomes its natural counterpart. Thus, although colonial rule was rapidly liquidated in Asia, the matrix of enforced bilateralism established by colonial power has actually been sustained by foreign aid. Japanese reparations and trade with the Communist bloc countries had much the same effect. By these means powerful disincentives to intraregional trade

4. William Adams Brown, Jr. and Redvers Opie, *American Foreign Assistance* (Washington, Brookings, 1953).

5. The early initiatives which led to the Colombo Plan, especially from the Australian side, appeared to envisage an OEEC-type organization which would receive and dispense large sums of aid. If this was in fact the main idea, substantial US backing was obviously necessary to make it feasible. Consequently, when the US indicated that its aid would be bilateral, the Colombo Plan had to become something rather different. The whole story needs thorough investigation.

became built into the ECAFE region's total pattern of trade. Even such preferential trade arrangements as exist in the region largely favor trade with outside countries.[6] As already indicated the mutual economic ties of Asian countries in general have actually grown weaker since the war.[7] In the face of these strong bilateral currents, ECAFE has found it a slow, uphill struggle to make regional cooperation seem both relevant and significant for its Asian members.

But even this task the Western powers appeared determined to frustrate. Their early negativism was most vigorously exemplified in British policy toward the Commission. Of all the outside powers Britain was best fitted to play a leadership role in ECAFE. France and the Netherlands forfeited Asian respect by attempting forcibly to reimpose their colonial rule in Indo-China and Indonesia. The United States had known China and tutored the Philippines; but it had yet to learn how to deal with other Asians. The Soviet Union offered them a mixture of moral support and anti-Western propaganda with a dogmatic persistence they found increasingly more irritating than encouraging. Britain, on the other hand, had a vast experience to draw upon. It could put together a delegation with a personal knowledge of a far larger part of the region than any other country could command. All this ability and knowledge was not, however, used for noble purposes within ECAFE. True, Britain was among the first to assign a liaison officer to ECAFE. On occasion the cautious empiricism of the British provided a useful antidote to some of the more fanciful notions bandied about in earlier ECAFE meetings. Will it work? What will it achieve? How much will it cost in staff, money, and meetings? These were important questions Asian delegates rarely asked. The chief British delegate from 1947 to 1951, P. J. Stent, an able ex-ICS official, frequently asked them. He was also helpful on awkward points of procedure and drafting. Yet he became in the eyes of a number of Asians, especially in those of the Secretariat, the very embodiment of perfidious Albion. This was an

6. Ceylon, India, Malaya, Pakistan, Singapore, Sarawak, North Borneo, and Brunei participate in the British Commonwealth preferential system; Cambodia, Laos, and South Viet-Nam in the French Community's preferential system; while the Philippines has a preferential quota agreement with the United States.

7. See pp. 297–98.

exaggeration. Although blunt, overbearing, and patronizing at times, he was actually a good deal more sympathetic to Asian aspirations and ECAFE than his official instructions.[8]

From the beginning an influential section of the British Foreign Office was highly skeptical of the value of regional commissions as such. It saw, for instance, no material British stake in the proceedings of ECAFE except in so far as they affected trade. For the rest, the Commission spelled trouble and expense and the risk of courting Asian resentment through the necessity to counter Soviet propaganda. The Foreign Office attached no importance to, if it ever understood, the significance of ECAFE for it hoped the Commission would die of inanition or be abolished in the 1951 ECOSOC review, as soon as Asians realized that ECAFE was not going to be a channel of external aid. Thou shalt not kill—unless the Asian Commonwealth members agree—but should not strive officiously to keep alive, fairly summarizes the British brief at the time the Colombo Plan was launched. Britain hoped the Colombo Plan, especially if the United States joined, would replace ECAFE as the chief international agency for economic development in the region. When ECAFE was not, in fact, abolished, Britain adopted an attitude of bored indifference to its activities, which was reflected in the decision to save the expense of being represented at technical meetings by properly qualified experts and to rely instead on the staff of local embassies and high commissions.[9] Although the tone became sweeter, judged by its positive content British policy toward ECAFE showed no perceptible change until about 1957.

The United States, while affecting an air of sympathetic aloofness during this early period, was no less negative. United States delegations, like their British ally, were also instructed to keep ECAFE's activities confined to research and studies. There was no offer of practical assistance, no inspiring message. Asian delegates had to listen instead to sermons on the virtues of self-help, private

8. E.g., this same chief British delegate drafted and personally agreed with Part IV of the *ECAFE Annual Report to ECOSOC* for 1951 in which the Commission favorably appraises its own achievements. Doc. E/CN.11/306, Apr. 16, 1951.

9. Even at the 1951 ECAFE Trade Promotion Conference in Singapore, the British delegation was headed only by a relatively junior Board of Trade official. The Singapore press did not fail to compare this level of representation with the high-powered Soviet delegation. See *The Straits Times,* Oct. 23, 1951.

enterprise, the classical theory of comparative economic advantage, and other immutable economic laws. Needless to say, this kind of preaching was not well received. It nevertheless took the United States a long time to propound less dogmatic economic prescriptions.[10]

France and the Netherlands often spoke more in tune with Asian sentiment but both were gravely compromised by their actions in Indo-China and Indonesia. With most Asian delegates they cut little ice.[11] It was what the United States and British delegates said that really mattered. In any case, on virtually all crucial votes, France and the Netherlands sided with Britain and the United States. So did Australia and New Zealand. It is hard to understand what this coalition of outside powers hoped to gain by consistently voting down Asian wishes. Sooner or later this fact was bound to get back to the parliaments and press of Asian countries and there redound to the disadvantage of the West. They could not prevent, much less influence, Asian economic development in this way. Apparently, they failed to grasp that economic problems cannot be solved by majority decisions. It took the Lahore Agreement of 1951 [12] to make them recognize and accept this simple point. The significance of this political landmark must not, however, be exaggerated. The Lahore Agreement, it is true, has never had to be invoked; it was the spirit of the Agreement that counted. Had Asian countries maintained the solidarity of outlook it enshrined, the progress of regional cooperation might well have been greater. But in fact, they became hopelessly divided on most policy issues and thereby helped to strengthen the influence of the West in ECAFE. And for most of the 1950s that influence was not markedly positive or encouraging as regards the development of ECAFE's functions.

The evolution of United States policy toward ECAFE has to be seen in the context of its approach to all three regional economic

10. E.g., in 1956 the US was still reminding Asians that "interference with the natural laws of supply and demand were of short-term benefit; and decisions and actions taken to remedy the imbalance (in their overseas trading accounts) must be based upon the true demands of the market place." Doc. E/CN.11/Trade/6, Nov. 25, 1957.

11. Though note again the respect accorded the first permanent French delegate to ECAFE. See p. 314.

12. See p. 51.

commissions. Two important convictions informed that approach. First, the United Nations represented a hierarchy of responsibility in which the regional commissions were completely subordinated to ECOSOC and their secretariats to Headquarters. They were not legally autonomous bodies like the specialized agencies. To set forth general propositions and secure for them a steadily increasing weight of government authority in their passage from the regional commissions to the General Assembly was the proper mode of international action. Any tendency toward regional autonomy or the acceptance of the notion that the commissions and their secretariats were primarily responsible to the member governments of the regions must be firmly resisted. Similarly, the regional secretariats, the United States insisted, must observe the political and administrative decisions of Headquarters; they should not even deal with one another without Headquarters clearance.

But practical economic cooperation does not and could not take place according to this rather formal view of the functioning of the United Nations. In any case, it overlooked the important point that the regional commissions and their subsidiary bodies are empowered to make recommendations direct to their member governments. It could hardly have been otherwise when those bodies were designed partly to assist governments to find solutions to urgent practical problems. Even the legal adviser to the Department of State failed at times to interpret properly the relationship between ECOSOC and its regional commissions. This United States constitutional thesis was politically convenient, however, in so far as the lobbying power of the United States in ECOSOC and at Headquarters was more formidable than in the regions.

Second, United States officials clung to the global thinking that went into the United Nations Charter long after the political renaissance of underdeveloped countries showed that historical forces were on the side of greater regional initiatives and groupings. In the important field of international trade cooperation, for instance, United States officials have long been wedded to GATT. Throughout much of the 1950s there seem, indeed, to have been no strong champions of the regional commissions within the State Department. The Department's influential ECOSOC Bureau was naturally anxious to make the Council important. That made it wary of allowing too much autonomy to the regional commissions:

their activities must not get out of hand and above all, they must not assume operational responsibilities. Hence the feeling in the State Department that stronger political and administrative discipline, especially financial control, must be exercised over them by Headquarters.[13]

United States policy toward the regional commissions must also be understood in relation to the political atmosphere of Washington, particularly during the early years of the Eisenhower Administration when the baleful influence of McCarthyism seemed all-pervasive. At a time when it was far from easy to persuade Congress to vote the appropriation needed for the United States contribution to the United Nations, it seemed to United States officials that all sorts of harebrained, ambitious, or politically suspect notions were emanating from the regional commissions and making their task more difficult. Thus ECAFE's special coverage of economic development in mainland China [14] made a deplorable impression on the State Department. Likewise the use made of the Commission by the World Federation of Trade Unions (WFTU) for spreading what United States citizens could only regard as tendentious propaganda.[15] The newspapers congressmen read were quick to print such news. Economic planning and trade promotion talks were other highly suspect notions. In addition a number of United States officials thought Dr. Lokanathan was anti-United States and too pro-Indian. Some even suspected him of left-wing tendencies though, in fact, he had been a fairly conservative economist all his life. It is not irrelevant in this connection to remember the marked deterioration of relations between India and the United States at the time John Foster Dulles took charge of the State Department. During the 1956 Commission session at Bangalore, for instance, Indian journalists noted that the Soviet delegates approvingly quoted Nehru in nearly all their statements but United States delegates rarely did so.

This background accounts for the continuing negative or foot-dragging position of the United States within ECAFE during much

13. As early as 1951, when ECOSOC confirmed the Commissions' permanent status, the US favored bringing them under more effective control of the Council.

14. See pp. 89–90.

15. See p. 32.

of its first decade. It frequently sent well-qualified experts to technical meetings and its delegates usually studied the documents thoroughly and took the proceedings, reports, and resolutions seriously. That cannot be said of all delegations. United States delegates gradually learned not to annoy the Asians by hitting the Soviet Union harder than Russian delegates had hit the United States. It is also fair to say that while silly, careless, or undiplomatic statements from other governments went unremarked, those of the United States would be searched for hidden meanings. But too often this careful attention to details made such support as was forthcoming look grudging and qualified, whereas on proposals it disliked the United States came down hard. At other times it would reserve its position on the financial implications of proposals whose financial implications were barely perceptible. The total image presented was that of a dutiful policeman concerned only with maintaining law and order.

The low point in United States relations with the regional commissions was probably reached around 1955. By this time, it should be said, ECE and ECLA and their Executive Secretaries seemed more out of favor than ECAFE and its Executive Secretary. At any rate the Administration felt obliged to protest to Secretary-General Hammarskjold personally about their activities and apparent independence from Headquarters control. The Secretary-General did not, however, accept the validity of its complaints although both he and de Seynes believed firmly in centralized Headquarters control over subordinate bodies.

A more positive United States approach may be dated from 1956 when what began in the Administration as an inquiry into the staff composition of the regional commissions turned into a general appraisal of United States policy toward them. From this emerged a deliberate decision to be more constructive and try to make ECAFE more useful.[16] In 1956 an able United States official was assigned as full-time liaison officer to ECAFE. Its second Executive Secretary, Narasimhan, who was appointed that same year,

16. It may well have been a relevant part of US rethinking that looking over the Asian scene at this point, it was plain that neither SEATO nor the Colombo Plan could be made effective instruments of regional cooperation. The Simla Conference the previous year showed that Asian countries did not wish to establish any new organizations. Nor were the chances of bringing them together under US auspices any brighter. The hope for regional cooperation lay with ECAFE.

quickly won United States confidence, not least because of his efforts to streamline the Commission's work program. But the strong financial backing the United States gave to the Mekong Project in 1958 was perhaps the most conspicuous sign of its change of heart over ECAFE. It still maintains a rigid position on all matters relating to Communist China. But on other economic questions, it became noticeably less dogmatic. For instance, although the United States reluctantly accepted the idea of a conference of Asian planners,[17] its delegates seemed better able to discuss the subject of economic planning without giving the impression that sacred United States taboos were being violated. Again, it neither openly encouraged nor resisted at first the recently mounting pressure for a greater decentralization of United Nations economic and social activities; but by 1961 it had become a cosponsor of an ECOSOC resolution on the subject.[18]

Britain closely supported the United States position regarding the regional commissions in general and ECAFE in particular. Perhaps its delegates showed more feel for tone and timing if only because it has always been a special British concern to avoid public altercations among Commonwealth members. But it never differed from the United States on major policy issues. Another special British concern is that ECAFE should not detract from the prestige of the Colombo Plan, and perhaps this gave it an additional reason for agreeing with the United States that the Commission should not assume operational responsibilities.

Some time around 1956 or 1957, as a result of an interdepartmental appraisal initiated by the Foreign Office, British policy toward ECAFE also veered in a more constructive direction. More properly qualified experts were subsequently sent to represent Britain at technical meetings. It took the British government a long time to realize that some aspects of ECAFE's technical work, particularly on standardization problems, can have important commercial implications. In recent years the British delegation to the Commission session has been led by a government minister

17. See p. 109.

18. See p. 337. It should also be recorded that the chief of the State Department's ECOSOC Bureau, Walter Kotschnig, who had typified US insistence on firm ECOSOC control over the regional commissions, acted as *rapporteur* for the appraisal "Five-Year Perspective 1960–1964," on the findings of which the Council based its first important resolution on the theme of decentralization. See p. 336.

instead of a high commissioner or ambassador from the region. British officials appear to have cooperated well with Narasimhan, whose judgment and efficiency they evidently respected. His administrative background and long association with the Colombo Plan while an Indian government official doubtless helped to inspire their confidence. Even on so sensitive an issue as ocean freight rates the British position became less rigid.[19] Again, although Britain did not encourage intraregional trade talks, which it feared might give Japan a commercial advantage, the more telling fact was that it did not oppose them. Its contribution to the Mekong Project has been less than that of either France or the United States, but it was also a more disinterested contribution.

The role of both France and the Netherlands in ECAFE has been far less significant than that of the United States or Britain. Both to some extent have used ECAFE to fashion a new relationship with the region, including a commercial stake, following the loss of their Asian colonies. In this connection the active interest of France in the Mekong Project has already been noted.[20] The Dutch have played no comparable part in any major ECAFE activity and their representation has been generally undistinguished, though their helpful participation in the Working Party on Economic Development and Planning deserves mentioning. Australia and New Zealand have more or less kept closely in step with United States and British policy except in the field of international trade where they have usually supported Asian complaints against the unfair workings of market forces or the commercial policies pursued by industrial nations. It is also apparent that both countries are conscious of the need to offset their exclusively white immigration opportunities by positive good neighbor policies toward South-east Asia.

Not surprisingly, the character and evolution of Soviet strategy in ECAFE has been both very different and more complex than that of the Western powers. Inexperienced in parliamentary practice and seemingly tied by rigid instructions, Russian delegates in the early years of ECAFE, as in the UN as a whole, were frequently incorrect on points of procedure and uncompromising on matters

19. See p. 259.
20. See pp. 189, 200.

of substance. Where their instructions appeared to be inadequate, they made no contribution at all. If a resolution did not fit their specifications exactly, they abstained rather than compromise. Unlike United States and British delegates they did not bother to lobby and line up votes beforehand on important issues but demanded instead a roll call vote, thereby committing countries to the record. Their sharp interventions undoubtedly exacerbated the atmosphere of meetings already polluted by political controversy and procedural wranglings.

Yet on a number of important policy issues the Soviet Union was far more in tune with Asian sentiment than the West. It was, as already mentioned, the only outside power to favor ECAFE elaborating recommendations regarding the external aid requirements of its region. It repeatedly advocated the industrialization of Asian countries through the development of heavy industry as the only sure safeguard of their independence. It also suggested the wholesale mechanization of the region's agriculture, liberation of its trade from dependence on foreign monopolies, and reliance on government loans instead of private investment. Finally, it supported the creation of committees on trade, labor, and industry within ECAFE.

Much of the Soviet Union's position in this early period was rooted in its own experience and traditions and cannot simply be dismissed as political expediency. Had it been combined with more discriminating attacks on the Western position, its standing and influence in ECAFE would almost certainly have been greater. But the rules of the Cold War and its own inflexibility caused it to preach its own economic orthodoxy and anti-Western propaganda to an extreme Asian delegates eventually found exasperating. For instance, Russian delegates persistently accused Britain and the United States of using technical assistance as a cloak for colonial exploitation.[21] In an effort presumably to drive a wedge between Asia and the West, their anti-Western attacks implied that Asian countries were still dominated by the colonial powers. Asian delegates hotly refuted the charge. At the 1953 Commission session, the Indian Minister of Commerce severely rebuked the Soviet delegation for constantly harping on this theme. Asian countries, he roundly declared, were not unaware of the things

21. See Doc. E/CN.11/306, Mar. 7, 1951.

the Soviet Union thought important and it insulted their intelligence to suggest that they could not look after their own interest. He did not blame the United States for acting out of enlightened self-interest in helping underdeveloped countries.[22] When, the following session, the Soviet Union once more asserted that the technical assistance from the West was motivated by political and military considerations, the Pakistan delegate "wondered whether the USSR representatives understood that in raising this point at every session, they were offending those countries for which they professed solicitude." [23] By this stage the Soviet Union's stock in ECAFE must be judged to have slumped badly.

The Soviet Union's preaching gained headlines in the local press but made little headway with Asian delegates for the good and sufficient reason that it offered them no tangible assistance. As the Soviet Union was in a poor position for some years after the war to compete with the Western powers in this respect [24] it could only disparage the assistance they offered. When Russian delegates did come forward with offers of trade, credits, and technical assistance, their political propaganda was considerably attenuated.[25] It is probably this fact as much as the death of Stalin that accounts for a change in Russian strategy within ECAFE after 1953. In addition, the Soviet Union may have realized that by greatly offending the national pride of newly independent Asian nations, its repeated attacks on continuing Western imperialism had gone too far. At any rate it became more discriminating and moderate in its judgments. From a refusal to acknowledge that any Asian country outside the Communist bloc had made economic progress, it began to single out and extol the achievements of Burma, India, and Indonesia. Afghanistan and Ceylon were later added to the list of those to be commended. The progress of this favored group of politically nonaligned countries was con-

22. Doc. E/CN.11/363, Apr. 15, 1953.

23. Doc. E/CN.11/389, Mar. 25, 1954.

24. "However attractive a policy of foreign economic aid might have looked to Soviet political strategists before 1953, it would certainly have pressed hard on an economy ill-prepared for additional burdens." Joseph Berliner, *Soviet Economic Aid* (New York, Praeger, 1958).

25. Including their challenges on the question of Chinese representation. See p. 32. The first broad indication of the Soviet Union's interest in trade with the ECAFE region was actually given at the first ECAFE Trade Promotion Conference in 1951.

trasted with the persistent economic difficulties of those such as Pakistan and Thailand, which had been drawn into military alliances with the West.

While blaming the ECAFE region's trading difficulties on the trade embargo the United States had initiated against Communist China, the Soviet Union declared its readiness to conclude long-term bilateral agreements that provided a stable market at stable prices. It was also willing to consider payment in national currencies, installment terms, and requests for technical assistance. As regards this last point, a Soviet contribution to EPTA, albeit in nonconvertible rubles, was announced to the Commission in 1954. The Soviet message was plain. If the Asians wanted to industrialize they could obtain all they needed from the Soviet Union. If they wanted to expand trade, that could best be done with the Communist bloc and above all by abolishing the embargo on trade with Communist China and bringing it into ECAFE. India welcomed the Soviet Union's change of attitude, "however slow and halting," and hoped its propositions would be made more concrete and substantial.[26]

Until 1953 the Soviet Union had not troubled to send delegates from Moscow to ECAFE technical meetings. In that year, however, a technically strong Russian delegation participated in the Subcommittee on Electric Power and took a keen interest in the proceedings. Since then it has generally sent well-qualified experts to most meetings and has not used these forums for purely political purposes. On the tenth anniversary of the Commission in 1957 the Soviet Union joined in the chorus of tributes to its usefulness. There is no reason to suppose that its appreciation was not genuine.[27]

The constant political clashes within ECAFE between the Soviet

26. Both India and Pakistan were skeptical of the possibility of any appreciable expansion of the insignificant trade between Asia and the Soviet Union. For Indian statement to 1953 session of the Industry and Trade Committee, see Doc. E/CN.11/I&T/78, July 9, 1953, and for Pakistan statement to its 1954 session, see Doc. E/CN.11/I&T/101, May 13, 1954.

27. For a larger treatment of the Soviet Union's role in ECAFE, see Alvin Z. Rubinstein, "Soviet Policy in ECAFE: A Case Study of Soviet Behavior in International Economic Organization," *International Organization, 12,* No. 4 (1958). This article is largely devoted to proving that the Soviet Union has sought in ECAFE to advance its political objectives in southern Asia. As international organizations are instruments of national diplomacy, this is not in itself a surprising discovery.

Union and the West contributed to that exhaustion of Asian impatience which led to the Lahore Agreement. But continuing outside political interference in the region generally had the further consequence of inducing Asians to seek to create machinery for political and economic cooperation in which they would not be overwhelmed by the voices of non-Asian countries. As early as 1947 an Asian Relations Conference at New Delhi resolved to establish an Asian Relations Organization.[28] One of its principal tasks was to organize another such conference in China; but the developing civil war there made this impossible. In 1949 an emergency conference of mainly Asian and Middle Eastern countries met in New Delhi again, at the invitation of India, to consider the crisis in Indonesia. "Is it not natural," Nehru asked the delegates, "that the free countries of Asia should begin to think of some more permanent arrangement than this Conference for effective mutual consultation and concerted effort in the pursuit of common aims . . . ?" [29] The Conference accordingly recommended that "participating governments should consult among themselves in order to explore ways and means of establishing suitable machinery having regard to the areas concerned for promoting consultation and co-operation within the framework of the UN." [30] But again nothing came of the idea. In April and May 1954, on the initiative of the Prime Minister of Ceylon, the Prime Ministers of Burma, India, Indonesia, and Pakistan gathered in Colombo to discuss common economic and political interests. In the absence of an agreed agenda, the proceedings were inevitably dominated by a preoccupation with the hydrogen bomb explosions, hostilities in Indo-China, and the intensified clash between Communist and anti-Communist groups in South-east Asia which this conflict portended.[31] Burma was anxious to discuss economic cooperation and joint planning; but the Prime Ministers decided to pursue instead an Indonesian proposal that they should sponsor a big African-Asian conference. The membership, organization, and aims of the proposed conference were agreed on by the Colombo Powers—as this group of

28. See p. 19.
29. Nehru, *Independence and After*.
30. *The Times* (London), Jan. 24, 1949.
31. Ibid. Apr. 29–30, and May 1, 1954.

sponsoring countries came to be labeled—at a further meeting in December 1954.[32] It was to meet at Bandung in April 1955.

The Bandung Conference, at which sixteen Asian and thirteen African countries were represented, took up on an even larger scale the threads of the earlier conferences of 1947 and 1949.[33] Among other declarations, it voiced strong sentiment in favor of economic and technical cooperation among Asian countries. This included the stabilization of primary product prices, the promotion of intraregional trade and shipping, joint industrial ventures, and regional training and research institutes. But while the Africans favored establishing new machinery for economic cooperation—ECA did not then exist—the Asians, with the exception of Indonesia, did not. The Conference recommended instead that fuller use be made of existing international organizations. ECAFE thus emerged unscathed from Bandung.

On the plane of economic cooperation, Bandung traversed much the same ground as that covered by Dr. Lokanathan's Aide Mémoire and the discussion of it at the Tokyo session of ECAFE a few weeks previously.[34] The participation for the first time of African delegates meant, however, that its discussions had of necessity to be more or less confined to general principles. The Bandung Conference was no doubt of great symbolic importance, but from the standpoint of economic cooperation it achieved little of practical value. An opportunity to realize some of its objectives arose at the Simla Conference the following month and was not grasped.[35] In 1959 the Prime Minister of Ceylon, S. W. R. D. Bandaranaike, convened a meeting of the Colombo Powers at an official level to prepare an economic conference to further the decisions of Bandung. With his assassination in September 1959, however, the initiative died with him.

The unity of feeling displayed at these various conferences did not, therefore, penetrate below the level of general principles to the plane of practical cooperation. The pan-Asian sentiment they kindled was largely compounded of anti-European sentiment in

32. Ibid., Dec. 30, 1954.

33. For a useful account of its proceedings see George McT. Kahin, *The Asian-African Conference* (Ithaca, Cornell University Press, 1956).

34. See pp. 292–93.

35. See pp. 295–96.

particular or anti-Western sentiment in general. The strength of such resentment varied from one Asian country to another according to the impact of colonial rule and the manner of its passing. It was shared even by those which became closely linked with the West in political and military alliances. But it did not in itself constitute a sufficient basis for regional economic cooperation. What most inhibited practical action on this level was the distrust bred of different Asian attitudes to the Cold War in general and Communist China in particular.

Already in 1950 the President of the Philippines was calling for the Asian equivalent of the North Atlantic Treaty Organization (NATO). It was imperative, he declared, "that the free countries of Southeast Asia, with the active support of the United States, should consider at the earliest possible moment the conclusion of a parallel safeguard for Asia." He agreed that it "was and still is necessary for Asian countries to consult and to cooperate with one another in order to hasten their emergence as independent countries. But the great danger that confronts us at the moment is the tide of totalitarian subversion and conquest which threatens to engulf the very freedom we have won and others expect to win." [36] One strand in this thought led to SEATO; and another, much later, to the Association of South East Asia (ASA). Other Asian countries followed the path of India and adopted a policy of political neutrality or nonalignment toward the Cold War. Their protest at the failure of the Western powers to consult and share with them sufficiently in decisions affecting Asia culminated in the Bandung Conference.[37] By that time, however, outside interference in the shape of a Communist bloc and a pro-Western bloc had sharpened the lines of political division in the region. This source of mistrust was strong enough to prevent any new machinery for economic cooperation from being established at a policy-making level. But neither were Asian countries prepared to use ECAFE for this purpose. In the circumstances its function remained largely technical assistance.

It would be unrealistic to assume, therefore, that without the membership of the outside powers, regional cooperation through

36. Quoted in Cornelio Balmaceda, "Communism in Asia," address delivered at Harvard University, June 9, 1951.

37. Kahin, *The Asian-African Conference.*

ECAFE would have made more substantial progress. All the same their presence often tended to blur and confuse the emergence of a clear Asian viewpoint. Without them there would at least have been less scope for adopting unhelpful positions or making provocative statements because it was known that these would be supported by some outside patron. In this respect South Korea, South Viet-Nam, and Taiwan contributed on occasion more than their fair share to exacerbating political controversy within the Commission. It was also evident at times that an outside power was deliberately using an Asian ally to express its own viewpoint.

Cold War issues were not the only source of political distrust within ECAFE. Pakistan's membership in SEATO, for instance, aggravated its poor relations with India, but was not the principal cause of bad feeling between them. That must be traced back to the circumstances out of which a Pakistan state was born. This bad feeling was a particularly tragic situation for ECAFE as Pakistan has been consistently suspicious of or opposed to any proposal initiated or strongly supported by India. When faced with the choice, it preferred global action to regional action and bilateral negotiations to multilateral operations because, whatever the additional advantages to Pakistan, this would at least minimize Indian influence. The fact that ECAFE's first two Executive Secretaries and many of its staff were Indian heightened its suspicions that India dominated the organization. Pakistan has accordingly taken a very limited view of the purpose of regional cooperation. It has been against using ECAFE at a policy-making level or giving it any important role in United Nations technical assistance operations. India has certainly given ECAFE over the years a great deal of positive support as well as staff. Indian delegates were prominent with suggestions during the 1950s because they had a more mature outlook than other governments and a greater experience of the problems of economic development planning. If, nevertheless, an unfortunate impression got around that ECAFE was some kind of Indian conspiracy, it was perhaps because they often introduced Lokanathan's proposals as well.

India was well fitted to represent the aspirations of the new Asia. Its achievement of independence was the first major breach in the walls of colonial domination. Through the Indian National Congress, its government from the outset was given firm purpose and direction. Its civil service was unrivaled in the region. In Nehru it had a leader who could express with rare honesty, lucidity, and insight what most Asian intellectuals—the revolutionary host in Asia—felt and thought. India may not have deliberately claimed the leadership of Asia but Nehru, as one of his biographers has remarked,[38] was acutely conscious of a special position that made India pre-eminently fitted to play this role. "India's pivotal position between Western Asia, South-East Asia and the Far East," Nehru declared in 1949, "made it the crossroads of that part of the world. India is the central point of the Asian picture. . . . India's role of leadership may not be so welcome to others although it may satisfy our vanity. But it is something we cannot escape. We cannot escape the various responsibilities that arise out of our geography and history." [39]

Be that as it may, it is clear that in the strongly competitive situations fashioned by the Cold War, this poor and almost powerless country gained immense international prestige. After a long period of colonial rule, this was bound to flatter the national ego of its intellectual elite. But this naturally did not make them widely popular in the region. A common complaint heard even in countries that are also politically nonaligned is that the Indian ruling class is patronizing, overbearing,[40] and filled with self-delusion about its own achievements in relation to Indian realities. It should also be remembered that the overseas migration and settlement of Indians during the colonial period left situations that inevitably irritated relations between India and its neighbors once colonial rule disappeared. The Indian community in Burma and the Indian Tamils of Ceylon are good instances in point. Burmese nationalism, for instance, was anti-Indian as well as anti-British. It might also be added that nationalist feelings throughout South-east Asia have been similarly intensified by the presence and activities there of large numbers of Chinese.[41]

38. Michael Brecher, *Nehru; A Political Biography* (London, Oxford University Press, 1959), p. 593.

39. Ibid.

40. According to Kahin, *The Asian-African Conference,* Indonesian and Ceylonese delegates at the Bandung Conference were antagonized by what they regarded as the overbearing and patronizing attitude of Nehru and V. K. Krishna Menon.

41. Nicholas Mansergh states that a recurrent feature of the Asian Relations Conference of 1947 was the distrust delegates from Burma, Ceylon, Indonesia, and

Differences in size and economic strength among Asian countries are a further contributing cause of political mistrust. This element combined with memories of its prewar Co-Prosperity Sphere policy largely accounts for the suspicions smaller Asian countries still entertain about Japan. The Indian government is similarly conscious of having a "Big Brother" image among these smaller states. The writer learned in New Delhi that for this reason Indian delegates to ECAFE meetings are instructed to be restrained and not too positive on proposals that interest them so as not to arouse the suspicions of smaller states. The level of its representation at many meetings could certainly have been better in recent years. Even at the Commission session held at New Delhi in 1961, the Indian delegation took very much a back seat in the proceedings. It was almost as if India had decided to be neutral toward ECAFE as well.

Apart, then, from profound differences in their political alignments and the special differences between Pakistan and India, there have been other irritating causes which have made frank friendship between Asian countries so difficult. Even the Colombo Powers skated around the real obstacles to setting up new machinery for political and economic cooperation. But that they existed was plainly advertised when Burma and Ceylon declined to accept the Indian invitation to the Simla Conference in 1955.[42]

In the course of its struggle for regional cooperation, ECAFE has slowly managed to cultivate among its Asian members a sense of common economic interest that transcends their political differences. The inauguration of the Mekong Project was in this sense a great political triumph, though whether it can withstand the onslaughts of Cold War politics is still an open question. ECAFE also finally succeeded in persuading its Asian members to set about, through the Asian Highway project, to systematically improve their land communications with one another. Again, whatever may be the practical results of the intraregional trade consultations it sponsored, ECAFE has at least emancipated Asian thinking from an almost exclusive preoccupation with the prob-

---

Malaya expressed about Indian and Chinese penetration of South-east Asia. "The Asian Conference," *International Affairs* (London), 23 (July 1947).

42. See p. 295.

lems of interregional trade. But real as these achievements are they do not yet amount to a significant degree of regional cooperation. The stirrings in this direction that have manifested themselves outside ECAFE are still primarily motivated and delineated by political considerations. Thus ASA consists of countries that are indisputably pro-Western in their political alignment. For this reason Indonesia, which might seem to be a "natural" member of such a grouping, has so far declined to join for fear this would compromise its political neutrality.[43] Nevertheless, the economic compulsions to come together may well outgrow the political inhibitions that divide Asian countries.

The experience of ECAFE suggests that if Asians are to move in the direction of devising and implementing joint policies in the fields of trade, industry, and economic planning, they should come together without the outside powers. For this purpose the Consultative Group of Experts that the Executive Secretary convened toward the end of 1961 [44] proposed the creation of an Organization for Asian Economic Cooperation. It should be designed to formulate and execute agreed programs of action and have the authority to make its decisions effective, though provision would have to be made for exceptional difficulties and circumstances. It should have a council of ministers as its policy-making organ and an executive committee of officials to prepare and supervise the execution of detailed measures of cooperation in specific fields. One of its principal tasks, for instance, would be to try to implement the conclusions reached by various ECAFE bodies. The proposed organization would be serviced and assisted by the ECAFE Secretariat and have its headquarters in Bangkok.

It remains to be seen whether this United Nations initiative will at last bring Asian governments together to work out practical policies for realizing the advantages of regional economic cooperation. One of the essential conclusions of this broad survey of ECAFE experience is that Asia cannot afford to contract out of the movement toward closer regional economic groupings in the world community. International organization cannot alter

43. Perhaps Indonesian suspicions of ASA were deepened by the fact that the proposal emanated from and was negotiated by the foreign ministries and not the economic ministries of Malaya, the Philippines, and Thailand.

44. See p. 303.

the distribution of economic power; nor can it guarantee the interests of the weak against the policies of the strong. But it can mobilize and maximize the collective strength of the weak and institutionalize their will to do so. Every step taken by Asian states toward their great solidarity is thus a step toward an improvement in their bargaining power with the economically strong countries. This, in turn, is a necessary condition of any significant reduction in the economic inequalities between rich and poor countries.

APPENDICES

APPENDIX I

Terms of Reference of ECAFE

The Economic and Social Council

Having considered General Assembly resolution 46 (I) of 11 December 1946, in which the General Assembly "recommends that, in order to give effective aid to the countries devastated by war, the Economic and Social Council, at its next session, give prompt and favourable consideration to the establishment of . . . an Economic Commission for Asia and the Far East," and

Having noted the report of the Working Group for Asia and the Far East of the Temporary Sub-Commission on Economic Reconstruction of Devastated Areas,

Establishes an Economic Commission for Asia and the Far East with terms of reference as follows:

1. The Economic Commission for Asia and the Far East, acting within the framework of the policies of the United Nations and subject to the general supervision of the Council, shall, provided that the Commission takes no action in respect to any country without the agreement of the Government of that country:

(*a*) Initiate and participate in measures for facilitating concerted action for the economic reconstruction and development of Asia and the Far East, for raising the level of economic activity in Asia and the Far East and for maintaining and strengthening the economic relations of these areas both among themselves and with other countries of the world;

(*b*) Make or sponsor such investigations and studies of economic and technological problems and developments within territories of Asia and the Far East as the Commission deems appropriate;

(*c*) Undertake or sponsor the collection, evaluation and dissemination of such economic, technological and statistical information as the Commission deems appropriate;

(*d*) Perform such advisory services, within the available resources of its secretariat, as the countries of the region may desire, provided that such services do not overlap with those rendered by the specialized agencies or the United Nations Technical Assistance Administration;

(*e*) Assist the Economic and Social Council, at its request, in discharging its functions within the region in connexion with any economic problems, including problems in the field of technical assistance;

(*f*) In carrying out the above functions deal as appropriate with the social aspects of economic development and the interrelationship of the economic and social factors.

2. The territories of Asia and the Far East referred to in paragraph 1 shall include Afghanistan, Brunei, Burma, Cambodia, Ceylon, China, the Federation of Malaya, Hong Kong, India, Indonesia, Iran, Japan, Korea, Laos, Mongolia, Nepal, North Borneo, Pakistan, the Philippines, Sarawak, Singapore, Thailand and Viet-Nam.

3. The members of the Commission shall consist of Afghanistan, Australia, Burma, Cambodia, Ceylon, China, the Federation of Malaya, France, India, Indonesia, Iran, Japan, Korea, Laos, the Mongolian People's Republic, Nepal, the Netherlands, New-Zealand, Pakistan, the Philippines, Thailand, the Union of Soviet Socialist Republics, the United Kingdom of Great Britain and Northern Ireland, the United States of America and Viet-Nam, provided that any State in the area which may hereafter become a Member of the United Nations shall be thereupon admitted as a member of the Commission.

4. The associate members shall include Brunei, Hong Kong, North Borneo and Sarawak, and Singapore.

5. Any territory, part or group of territories within the geographical scope of the Commission as defined in paragraph 2 may, on presentation of its application to the Commission by the member responsible for the international relations of such territory, part or group of territories, be admitted by the Commission as an associate member of the Commission. If it has become responsible for its own international relations, such territory, part or group of territories, may be admitted as an associate member of the Commission on itself presenting its application to the Commission.

6. Representatives of associate members shall be entitled to participate without vote in all meetings of the Commission, whether sitting as Commission or as Committee of the Whole.

7. Representatives of associate members shall be eligible to be appointed as members of any committee, or other subordinate body, which may be set up by the Commission and shall be eligible to vote and hold office in such body.

8. The Commission is empowered to make recommendations on any matters within its competence directly to the Governments of members or associate members concerned, Governments admitted in consultative capacity, and the specialized agencies concerned. The Commission shall submit for the Council's prior consideration any of its proposals of activities that would have important effects on the economy of the world as a whole.

9. The Commission shall invite any Member of the United Nations not a member of the Commission to participate in a consultative capacity in its consideration of any matter of particular concern to that non-member.

10. The Commission shall invite representatives of specialized agencies and may invite representatives of any intergovernmental organizations to participate in a consultative capacity in its consideration of any matter of particular concern to that agency or organization following the practice of the Economic and Social Council.

11. The Commission shall make arrangements for consultation with non-governmental organizations which have been granted consultative status by the Economic and Social Council, in accordance with the principles approved by the Council for this purpose and contained in Council resolution 288 B (X), parts I and II.

12. The Commission shall take measures to ensure that the necessary liaison is maintained with other organs of the United Nations and with the specialized agencies. The Commission shall establish appropriate liaison and co-operation with other regional economic commissions in accordance with the resolutions and directives of the Economic and Social Council and the General Assembly.

13. The Commission may, after discussion with any specialized agency functioning in the same general field, and with the approval of the Council, establish such subsidiary bodies as it deems appropriate, for facilitating the carrying out of its responsibilities.

14. The Commission shall adopt its own rules of procedure, including the method of selecting its chairman.

15. The Commission shall submit to the Council a full report on its activities and plans, including those of any subsidiary bodies, once a year.

16. The administrative budget of the Commission shall be financed from the funds of the United Nations.

17. The Secretary-General of the United Nations shall appoint the staff of the Commission, which shall form part of the Secretariat of the United Nations.

18. The headquarters of the Commission shall be located at the seat of the office of the United Nations in Asia and the Far East. Until such time as the site of the office of the United Nations in Asia and the Far East shall be determined, the working site of the Commission shall remain in Bangkok.

19. The Council shall, from time to time, make special reviews of the work of the Commission.

APPENDIX II

Rules of Procedure of ECAFE

Chapter I—Sessions

RULE 1

The following principles shall apply as regards date and place for the sessions of the Commission:

(*a*) The Commission shall at each session recommend the date and place for its next session subject to the approval of the Council and in consultation with the Secretary-General. Sessions of the Commission shall also be held within forty-five days of the communication to the Executive Secretary of a request to that effect by the Economic and Social Council, and, in that case, the Secretary-General shall establish the place of such sessions in consultation with the Chairman of the Commission;

(*b*) In special cases the date and place of the session may be altered by the Secretary-General in consultation with the Chairman of the Commission and the Council's Interim Committee on Programme of Conferences. At the request of the majority of the members of the Commission, the Secretary-General, in consultation with the Chairman of the Commission and the Council's Interim Committee on Programme of Conferences, may also alter the date and place of the session;

(*c*) Sessions shall ordinarily be held at the office of the United Nations in Asia and the Far East. The Commission may recommend holding a particular session elsewhere.

RULE 2

The Executive Secretary shall, at least forty-two days before the commencement of a session, distribute a notice of the opening date of the session, together with three copies of the provisional agenda and of the basic documents relating to each item appearing on the provisional agenda. Distribution shall be similar to that under rule 48.

RULE 3

The Commission shall invite any Member of the United Nations not a member of the Commission to participate in a consultative capacity in its consideration of any matter of particular concern to that Member.

Chapter II—Agenda

RULE 4

The provisional agenda for each session shall be drawn up by the Executive Secretary in consultation with the Chairman.

RULE 5

The provisional agenda for any session shall include:

(*a*) Items arising from previous sessions of the Commission;
(*b*) Items proposed by the Economic and Social Council;
(*c*) Items proposed by any member or associate member of the Commission;
(*d*) Items proposed by a specialized agency in accordance with the agreements of relationship concluded between the United Nations and such agencies;
(*e*) Items proposed by non-governmental organizations in Category A, subject to the provisions of rule 6; and
(*f*) Any other items which the Chairman or the Executive Secretary sees fit to include.

RULE 6

Non-governmental organizations in category A may propose items on matters within their competence for the provisional agenda of the Commission, subject to the following conditions:

(*a*) An organization which intends to propose such an item shall inform the Executive Secretary at least sixty-three days before the commencement of the session, and before formally proposing an item shall give due consideration to any comments he may make;
(*b*) The proposal shall be formally submitted with the relevant

basic documentation not less than forty-nine days before the commencement of the session.

RULE 7

The first item upon the provisional agenda for each session shall be the adoption of the agenda.

RULE 8

The Commission may amend the agenda at any time.

Chapter III—Representation and Credentials

RULE 9

Each member shall be represented on the Commission by an accredited representative.

RULE 10

A representative may be accompanied to the sessions of the Commission by alternate representatives and advisers and, when absent, he may be replaced by an alternate representative.

RULE 11

The credentials of each representative appointed to the Commission, together with a designation of alternate representatives, shall be submitted to the Executive Secretary without delay.

RULE 12

The Chairman and the two Vice-Chairmen shall examine the credentials and report upon them to the Commission.

Chapter IV—Officers

RULE 13

The Commission shall, at its first meeting of each year, elect from among its representatives a Chairman and two Vice-Chairmen, designated as First and Second Vice-Chairmen, who shall hold office until their successors are elected. They shall be eligible for re-election.

RULE 14

If the Chairman is absent from a meeting, or any part thereof, the Vice-Chairman designated by the Chairman shall preside.

RULE 15

If the Chairman ceases to represent a member of the Commission, or is so incapacitated that he can no longer hold office, the First Vice-Chairman shall become Chairman for the unexpired portion of the term. If the First Vice-Chairman also ceases to represent a member of the Commission, or is so incapacitated that he can no longer hold office, the Second Vice-Chairman shall become Chairman for the unexpired portion of the term.

RULE 16

The Vice-Chairman acting as Chairman shall have the same powers and duties as the Chairman.

RULE 17

The Chairman, or the Vice-Chairman acting as Chairman, shall participate in the meetings of the Commission as such, and not as the representative of the member by whom he was accredited. The Commission shall admit an alternate representative to represent that member in the meetings of the Commission and to exercise its right to vote.

Chapter V—Secretariat

RULE 18

The Executive Secretary shall act in that capacity at all meetings of the Commission and of its sub-commissions, other subsidiary bodies and committees. He may appoint another member of the staff to take his place at any meeting.

RULE 19

The Executive Secretary or his representative may at any meeting make either oral or written statements concerning any question under consideration.

RULE 20

The Executive Secretary shall direct the staff provided by the Secretary-General and required by the Commission, its sub-commissions, and any other subsidiary bodies and committees.

RULE 21

The Executive Secretary shall be responsible for the necessary arrangements being made for meetings.

RULE 22

The Executive Secretary in carrying out his functions shall act on behalf of the Secretary-General.

RULE 23

Before new proposals which involve expenditure from United Nations funds are approved by the Commission, the Executive Secretary shall prepare and circulate to members an estimate of that part of the cost involved in the proposals which could not be met out of the resources available to the secretariat. It shall be the duty of the Chairman to draw the attention of members to this estimate, and invite discussion on it before the proposals are approved.

Chapter VI—Conduct of Business

RULE 24

A majority of the members of the Commission shall constitute a quorum.

RULE 25

In addition to exercising the powers conferred upon him elsewhere by these rules, the Chairman shall declare the opening and closing of each meeting of the Commission, shall direct the discussion, ensure the observance of these rules, and shall accord the right to speak, put questions to the vote and announce decisions. The Chairman may also call a speaker to order if his remarks are not relevant to the subject under discussion.

RULE 26

During the discussion of any matter, a representative may raise a point of order. In this case, the Chairman shall immediately state his ruling. If it is challenged, the Chairman shall forthwith submit his ruling to the Commission for decision, and it shall stand unless overruled.

RULE 27

During the discussion of any matter, a representative may move the adjournment of the debate. Any such motion shall have priority. In addition to the proposer of the motion, one representative shall be allowed to speak in favour of, and one representative against, the motion.

RULE 28

A representative may at any time move the closure of the debate whether or not any other representative has signified his wish to speak. Not more than two representatives may be granted permission to speak against the closure.

RULE 29

The Chairman shall take the sense of the Commission on a motion for closure. If the Commission is in favour of the closure, the Chairman shall declare the debate closed.

RULE 30

The Commission may limit the time allowed to each speaker.

RULE 31

Draft resolutions, and substantive amendments or motions, shall be introduced in writing and handed to the Executive Secretary, who shall circulate copies to the representative at least twenty-four hours before they are discussed and voted upon, unless the Commission decides otherwise.

RULE 32

Upon the request of any member, any motion and amendment thereto made by any speaker shall be given to the Chairman in writing and shall be read by him before any further speaker is called upon and also immediately before a vote is taken on such motion or amendment. The Chairman may direct that any motion or amendment be circulated to the members present before a vote is taken.

This rule shall not apply to formal motions such as one for closure or adjournment.

RULE 33

Principal motions and resolutions shall be put to the vote in the order of their submission unless the Commission decides otherwise.

RULE 34

When an amendment revises, adds to or deletes from a proposal, the amendment shall be put to the vote first, and, if it is adopted, the amended proposal shall then be put to the vote.

RULE 35

If two or more amendments are moved to a proposal, the Commission shall vote first on the amendment furthest removed in substance from the original proposal; then, if necessary, on the amendment next furthest removed; and so on, until all the amendments have been put to the vote.

RULE 36

The Commission may, at the request of a representative, decide to put a motion or resolution to the vote in parts. If this is done, the text resulting from the series of votes shall be put to the vote as a whole.

Chapter VII—Voting

RULE 37

Each member of the Commission shall have one vote.

RULE 38

Decisions of the Commission shall be made by a majority of the members present and voting.

RULE 39

The Commission shall take no action in respect of any country without the agreement of the Government of that country.

RULE 40

The Commission shall normally vote by show of hands. If any representative requests a roll-call, a roll-call shall be taken in the English alphabetical order of the names of the members.

RULE 41

All elections shall be decided by secret ballot.

RULE 42

If a vote is equally divided upon matters other than elections, a second vote shall be taken at the next meeting. If this vote also results in equality, the proposal shall be regarded as rejected.

RULE 43

After the voting has commenced, no representative shall interrupt voting except on a point of order in connexion with the actual conduct of the voting. Brief statements by members consisting solely of explanations of their votes may be permitted by the Chairman, if he deems it necessary, before the voting has commenced or after the voting has been completed.

Chapter VIII—Languages

RULE 44

English and French shall be the working languages of the Commission.

RULE 45

Speeches made in one of the working languages shall be interpreted into the other working language.

Chapter IX—Records

RULE 46

Summary records of the meetings of the Commission shall be kept by the secretariat. They shall be sent as soon as possible to the representatives of members and to the representatives of any other government agency or organization which participated in the meeting concerned. Such representatives shall inform the secretariat not later than seventy-two hours after the circulation of any summary of any changes they wish to have made. Any disagreement concerning such changes shall be referred to the Chairman, whose decision shall be final.

RULE 47

The corrected version of the summary records of public meetings shall be distributed as soon as possible in accordance with the usual practice of the United Nations. This shall include distribution to non-governmental organizations in category A and to the appropriate non-governmental organizations in category B and on the Register, and on appropriate occasions to consultative members.

RULE 48

The corrected version of the summary records of private meetings shall be distributed as soon as possible to the members of the Commission, to any consultative member participating in the meeting concerned, and to the specialized agencies. They shall be distributed to all the Members of the United Nations if and when the Commission so decides.

RULE 49

As soon as possible, the text of all reports, resolutions, recommendations and other formal decisions made by the Commission, its sub-commissions or other subsidiary bodies and its committees shall be communicated to the members of the Commission, to the consultative members concerned, to all other Members of the United Nations, to the specialized agencies, and to the non-governmental organizations in category A and to the appropriate non-governmental organizations in category B and on the Register.

Chapter X—Publicity of Meetings

RULE 50

The meetings of Commission shall ordinarily be held in public. The Commission may decide that a particular meeting or meetings shall be held in private.

Chapter XI—Relations with Non-Governmental Organizations

RULE 51

Non-governmental organizations in categories A and B and on the Register may designate authorized representatives to sit as observers at public meetings of the Commission.

RULE 52

Written statements relevant to the work of the Commission or its subsidiary bodies may be submitted by organizations in categories A and B on subjects for which these organizations have a special competence. Such statements shall be circulated by the Executive Secretary to the members and associate members of the Commission except those statements which have become obsolete—e.g., those dealing with matters already disposed of.

RULE 53

The following conditions shall be observed regarding the submission and circulation of such written statements:

(*a*) The written statement shall be submitted in one of the official languages;
(*b*) It shall be submitted in sufficient time for appropriate con-

sultation to take place between the Executive Secretary and the organization before circulation;

(*c*) The organization shall give due consideration to any comments which the Executive Secretary may make in the course of such consultation before transmitting the statement in final form;

(*d*) A written statement submitted by an organization in category A or B will be circulated in full if it does not exceed 2,000 words. Where a statement is in excess of 2,000 words, the organization shall submit a summary, which will be circulated, or shall supply sufficient copies of the full text in the two working languages for distribution. A statement will also be circulated in full, however, upon the specific request of the Commission or of one of its subsidiary bodies;

(*e*) The Executive Secretary may invite organizations on the Register to submit written statements. The provisions of paragraphs (*a*), (*c*) and (*d*) above shall apply to such statements;

(*f*) A written statement or summary, as the case may be, will be circulated by the Executive Secretary in the working languages and, upon the request of a member or associate member of the Commission, in either of the official languages.

RULE 54

(*a*) The Commission and its subsidiary bodies may consult with organizations in category A or B either directly or through a committee or committees established for the purpose. In all cases, such consultations may be arranged on the invitation of the Commission or the subsidiary body or on the request of the organization;

(*b*) On the recommendation of the Executive Secretary and at the request of the Commission or one of its subsidiary bodies, organizations on the Register may also be heard by the Commission or its subsidiary bodies.

RULE 55

The Commission may recommend that an organization which has special competence in a particular field should undertake specific studies or investigations or prepare specific papers for the Commission. The limitations of rule 52(*d*) shall not apply in this case.

Chapter XII—Sub-Commissions, Other Subsidiary Bodies and Committees

RULE 56

After discussion with any specialized agency functioning in the same field, and with the approval of the Economic and Social Council, the Commission may establish such continually acting sub-commissions or other subsidiary bodies as it deems necessary for the performance of its functions and shall define the powers and composition of each of them. Such autonomy as may be necessary for the effective discharge of the technical responsibilities laid upon them may be delegated to them.

RULE 57

The Commission may establish such committees and sub-committees as it deems necessary to assist it in carrying out its tasks.

RULE 58

Sub-commissions or other subsidiary bodies and committees, sub-committees and working parties shall adopt their own rules of procedure unless otherwise decided by the Commission.

Chapter XIII—Reports

RULE 59

The Commission shall, once a year, submit to the Economic and Social Council a full report on its activities and plans, including those of any subsidiary bodies.

Chapter XIV—Amendments and Suspensions

RULE 60

Any of these rules of procedures may be amended or suspended by the Commission provided that the proposed amendments or suspensions do not attempt to set aside the terms of reference laid down by the Economic and Social Council.

APPENDIX III

DATA ON ECAFE BUDGET 1952–60
(in U.S. Dollars)

					Official Secretariat Travel		*Consultants*			
Year	*Total expenditures (actual)*	*Salaries and wages*	*Common staff* [1] *costs*	*Common services* [2]	*Budget*	*Actual expenditures*	*Budget*	*Actual expenditures*	*Costs of Commission session*	*Costs of all meetings of subsidiary bodies*
1952	1,011,077	662,287	170,332	68,550	47,000	37,832	30,280	28,923	—	—
1953	1,129,892	753,037	211,327	58,889	40,000	34,759	32,800	24,420	26,546	6,110
1954	1,081,553	725,418	201,423	43,155	40,740	33,482	37,830	23,843	25,809	13,625
1955	1,149,746	784,178	204,935	56,272	38,800	35,765	34,000	21,413	30,979	5,560
1956	1,201,657	810,940	208,916	46,530	39,000	35,890	30,600	28,298	19,046	9,261
1957	1,439,840	956,262	303,163	73,542	45,000	39,932	40,000	27,893	—	9,235
1958	1,718,763	1,111,629	379,571	66,056	42,000	38,146	48,000 [3]	20,728	12,103	13,454
1959	1,848,868	1,161,154	393,533	82,823	43,800	39,972	49,500 [3]	26,384	28,926	11,297
1960	1,809,202	1,181,142	408,539	90,625	48,400	39,635	53,500 [3]	27,857	—	11,487
	12,390,598	8,146,047	2,481,739	586,442	384,740	335,413	356,510	229,759	143,409	80,029

[1] Common staff costs include staff allowances for dependents and educational grants; contributions to the joint staff pension fund and medical insurance schemes; compensation payments; travel and removal expenditures on appointment, transfer, and separation; and small amounts on staff training and welfare.

[2] Common services include communications, rental of premises, contractual services for maintenance of premises, stationeries and office supplies, operation and maintenance of transport, freight, cartage and express, and miscellaneous supplies and services.

[3] Including temporary assistance.

It will be noticed that the expenditure on consultants and official Secretariat travel has consistently fallen below the appropriations for this purpose. The underspending on consultants may be due to the fact that unfilled posts in the Secretariat have enabled some consultant costs to be charged to salaries and wages. As regards the underspending on official Secretariat travel, however, it would appear that the Secretariat has simply not been doing as much travel as it is able or thinks necessary. A relatively large number of vacant posts may again have contributed to this situation. But general underspending must be a matter of concern to those wishing to strengthen ECAFE's resources.

Bibliography

The principal sources of publicly available information on ECAFE, its constitution, powers, practices, problems, activities, decisions, and achievements are the documentation prepared for its annual Commission sessions, the proceedings of the Commission, its annual report to ECOSOC, the annual Economic Survey, and the quarterly *Economic Bulletin for Asia and the Far East.* Interesting over-all appraisals of the functions and achievements of ECAFE can be found in the three ECAFE Annual Reports to ECOSOC, United Nations Documents E/CN.11/306, 1951, E/CN.11/430, 1956, and E/CN.11/506, 1959. The summary records of its Committees on Industry and Natural Resources, Inland Transport and Communications, and Trade are also publicly available. No summary records are kept for the proceedings of lesser subsidiary bodies or of the Committee for Coordination of Investigations of the Lower Mekong.

Of the very small amount of interpretative literature on ECAFE the following are especially useful:

LOKANATHAN, P. S., "ECAFE—The Economic Parliament of Asia," *Indian Yearbook of International Affairs,* 2 (1953).

PURCELL, VICTOR, "The Economic Commission for Asia and the Far East," *International Affairs,* 24 (April 1948).

SCHAAF, C. HART, "The United Nations Economic Commission for Asia and the Far East," *International Organization,* 7, No. 4 (1953).

It is not proposed here to repeat all the footnote references cited in the study. For the purpose of ready reference, however, there follows a select list of the printed articles, surveys, and reports of ECAFE grouped according to the main fields of activity. In the case of articles from the *Economic Bulletin,* the year of publication is given in parentheses; the titles of reports are followed by United Nations Sales Numbers.

Economic Development and Planning

Fields of Economic Development Handicapped by Lack of Trained Personnel in Certain Countries of Asia and the Far East, UN Sales No.:51.II.F.6.

Foreign Investment Laws and Regulations of the Countries of Asia and the Far East, 1951.II.F.1.

Mobilization of Domestic Capital in Certain Countries of Asia and the Far East, 1951.II.F.3.

Mobilization of Domestic Capital, Report and Documents of the Second Working Party of Experts, 1953.II.F.4.

Programming Techniques for Economic Development with special reference to Asia and the Far East, 60.II.F.3.

Formulating Industrial Development Programmes with special reference to Asia and the Far East, 61.II.F.7.

Articles in the Economic Bulletin

"The Economic Reclassification of Government Budgets and Accounts," *1*, No. 3 (1951).

"Problems of National Income Estimation in ECAFE Countries," *2*, No. 1 (1951).

"Inflation and the Mobilization of Domestic Capital in Underdeveloped Countries in Asia," *2*, No. 3 (1951).

"Some Financial Aspects of Development Programmes in Asian Countries," *3*, Nos. 1–2 (1952).

"Taxation and Economic Development in Asian Countries," *4*, No. 1 (1953).

"Deficit Financing for Economic Development with special reference to ECAFE Countries," *5*, No. 3 (1954).

"Economic Development and Planning: Problems and Techniques," *6*, No. 3 (1955).

"Economic Concepts of Budget Deficits," *7*, No. 1 (1956).

"Economic Development and Planning: Policies and Means of Implementation," *7*, No. 3 (1956).

"Laws and Regulations Affecting Foreign Investment in Asia and the Far East," *8*, No. 1 (1957).

"Economic Development and Planning: The Agricultural Sector," *8*, No. 3 (1957).

"Taxation and Development of Agriculture in Underdeveloped Countries with special reference to Asia and the Far East," *9*, No. 1 (1958).

"Economic Development and Planning: Industrialisation," *9*, No. 3 (1958).

"Economic Development and Planning: Social Aspects," *10,* No. 3 (1959).
"Savings in Economic Growth of Post-war Japan," *11,* No. 2 (1960).
"Economic Development and Planning: Transport," *11,* No. 3 (1960).
"Economic Development and Planning: Conference of Asian Economic Planners," *12,* No. 3 (1961).

TRADE

Trade Between Asia and Europe, UN Sales No.: 1953.II.F.3.

Articles in the Economic Bulletin

"Devaluation, Price Movements and Changes in External Trade in ECAFE Countries," *1,* No. 2 (1950).
"Scope for Multilateral Compensation Payments of ECAFE Countries," *5,* No. 1 (1954).
"Gains from Trade in ECAFE Countries, July 1950 to June 1953," ibid.
"The Application of Multiple Exchange Rates in selected Asian Countries," *5,* No. 3 (1954).
"A Statistical Note on Changes in the Terms of Trade and their Effects on National Income and Trade Balance in the ECAFE Region," *8,* No. 1 (1957).
"Regional Trade Co-operation: An Exploratory Study with special reference to Asia and the Far East," *13,* No. 1 (1961).

FLOOD CONTROL AND WATER RESOURCES DEVELOPMENT

Flood Damage and Flood Control Activities in Asia and the Far East, UN Sales No.: 1951.II.F.2.
Methods and Problems of Flood Control in Asia and the Far East, 1951.II.F.5.
Proceedings of the Regional Technical Conference on Flood Control in Asia and the Far East, 1953.II.F.1.
River Training and River Bank Protection, 1953.II.F.6.
The Sediment Problem, 1953.II.F.7.
Proceedings of the Regional Technical Conference on Water Resources Development in Asia and the Far East, 1956.II.F.3. and 1959.II.F.2.
Standards for Methods and Records of Hydrologic Measurements, 1954.II.F.3.
Glossary of Hydrologic Terms Used in Asia and the Far East, 1956. II.F.7.

Development of Water Resources in the Lower Mekong Basin, 1957.II.F.8.

A Case Study of the Damodar Valley Corporation and its Project, 60.II.F.7.

Hydrologic Networks and Methods, 60.II.F.2.

Earthmoving by Manual Labour and Machines, 61.II.F.4.

Multiple-Purpose River Basin Development:

Part I. *Manual of River Basin Planning,* 1955.II.F.1.

Part IIA. *Water Resources Development in Ceylon, China:Taiwan, Japan and the Philippines,* 1956.II.F.2.

Part IIB. *Water Resources Development in Burma, India and Pakistan,* 1956.II.F.8.

Part IIC. *Water Resources Development in British Borneo, Federation of Malaya, Indonesia and Thailand,* 1959.II.F.5.

Part IID. *Water Resources Development in Afghanistan, Iran, Republic of Korea and Nepal,* 61.II.F.8.

Minerals

Coal and Iron Resources of Asia and the Far East, UN Sales No.: 1952.II.F.1.

Regional Conference on Mineral Resources Development, 53.II.F.5.

Lignite Resources of Asia and the Far East, their Exploration, Exploitation and Utilization, 1957.II.F.3.

Survey of Mining Legislation, with special reference to Asia and the Far East, 1957.II.F.5.

Proceedings of the Symposium on the Development of Petroleum Resources of Asia and the Far East, 1958, 59.II.F.3.

Copper, Lead and Zinc Ore Resources in Asia and the Far East, 60.II.F.8.

Proceedings of the United Nations Seminar on Aerial Survey Methods and Equipment, 60.II.F.5.

Mining Developments in Asia and the Far East, 1953–1954, 1954.II.F.2; for *1954–1955,* 1956.II.F.4; for *1956,* 1957.II.F.4; for *1957,* 59.II.F.4; for *1958,* 60.II.F.4; for *1959,* 61.II.F.3.

Electric Power

Rural Electrification, UN Sales No.: 1954.II.F.1.

Electric Power in Asia and the Far East, 1951–1955, 1957.II.F.6.

Article in Economic Bulletin

"On Electric Power Production and Development in ECAFE Countries," *2*, No. 2 (1951).

INDUSTRIAL ORGANIZATION

Articles in Economic Bulletin

"Industrial Organisation in the Public Sector in ECAFE Region," *2*, No. 3 (1951).
"Some Commercial and Economic Aspects of Public Enterprise in Certain Asian Countries," *5*, No. 1 (1954).
"Modernisation of Small Industries in Asia," *11*, No. 1 (1960).

INLAND TRANSPORT

Comparative Study of Various Types of Marine Engines, 1955, UN Sales No.:55.II.F.2.
Locomotive Boiler Water Treatment, 1956.II.F.6.
Convention Regarding the Measurement and Registration of Vessels Employed in Inland Navigation, 1957.II.F.9.
Uniform System of Buoys and Shore Marks for Inland Waterways in Asia and the Far East, 1957.II.F.7.
Report of the Seminar on Engineering and Traffic Aspects of Highway Safety, 58.II.F.3.

AGRICULTURE

Marketing of Major Edible Oils (Liquid) and Oil-Seeds in the ECAFE Region, UN Sales No.:1956.II.F.5.
Credit Problems of Small Farmers in Asia and the Far East, 1957.II.F.2.
Agricultural Economic Research in Asia and the Far East, 58.II.F.4.
Food and Agricultural Price Policies in Asia and the Far East, 58.II.F.2.

SOCIAL PROBLEMS AND POPULATION

Survey of Housing and Building Materials in Asia and the Far East, UN Sales No.:1956.II.F.9.
Study on Building Costs in Asia and the Far East, 61.II.F.9.
Community Development and Economic Development:
Part I. *A Study of the Contribution of Rural Community Development Programmes to National Economic Development in Asia and the Far East,* 60.II.F.6.

Part IIA. *A Case Study of the Ghoshi Community Development Block, Uttar Pradesh, India,* 60.II.F.6.

Part IIB. *A Study of Farmers' Associations in Taiwan,* 60.II.F.6.

Articles in Economic Bulletin

"Aspects of Urbanization in ECAFE Countries," *4,* No 1 (1953).

"Acceleration of Population Growth in ECAFE Countries since the Second World War," *6,* No. 1 (1955).

"Population and Food Supplies in Asia and the Far East," *7,* No. 1 (1956).

"Population Trends and Related Problems of Economic Development in the ECAFE Region," *10,* No. 1 (1959).

Index